Shipboard Management

Shipboard Management supports students undertaking qualification at all stages of maritime training, enhancing and developing knowledge and understanding of the key issues in the Merchant Shipping (Training and Certification) Regulations 1997, as subsequently amended by the 2015 Regulations and other legislation.

Informed by real-world experience of commercial shipboard operations, *Shipboard Management* offers an essential study guide addressing the issues which are most frequently confronted in the context of ship management. It is designed to foster the ability to analyse and apply the dynamics of the legal and operational structures in which the shipboard management team must engage in merchant vessel operations. Students will progress through increasingly difficult levels of learning activity in order to develop problem-solving abilities. The text focuses on the application of skills and techniques that are fundamental to commercial shipping and that meet the demands of the Merchant Shipping (Standards of Training, Certification and Watchkeeping) Regulations.

This will be essential reading for all students and candidates on MCA-accredited Deck training courses, and for seafarers wishing to apply for Certificates of Equivalent Competency. It is also a key reference for professionals in ship-owning and management companies, and for maritime lawyers.

Simon Daniels is a consultant marine lawyer and will be known to many maritime professionals for managing the law and business parts of the Merchant Vessel Operations programme at Warsash Maritime Academy.

Designed cover image: danr13/Getty Images

First published 2024
by Routledge
4 Park Square, Milton Park, Abingdon, Oxon OX14 4RN

and by Routledge
605 Third Avenue, New York, NY 10158

Routledge is an imprint of the Taylor & Francis Group, an informa business

British Library Cataloguing-in-Publication Data
A catalogue record for this book is available from the British Library

Library of Congress Cataloging-in-Publication Data
Names: Daniels, Simon, author.
Title: Shipboard management / Simon Daniels.
Description: Abingdon, Oxon [UK]; New York, NY: Routledge, 2024. | Includes bibliographical references and index. | Contents: Introduction: learning the law – Sources of law – Conventions overview – The International Convention for the Safety of Life at Sea-SOLAS – Survey Requirements – Seaworthiness and risk management – Risk management in polar operations – The International Convention on Standards of Training, Certification and Watchkeeping for Seafarers 1978, its regulations and its amendments-STCW – The International Convention for the Prevention of Pollution from Ships-MARPOL – MARPOL - issues o-overview – The MLC-the application of the convention – The management of seafarers – The master's responsibility – The master and shipboard management – Routines and emergencies – The master and the owner – Leadership and shipboard management – Port state control – Pilotage – Piracy and stowaways – The role of evidence in criminal proceedings – Essentials of contract law – Contract formation – Contract-What can possibly go wrong? – Agency – Charterparties – The Bill of Lading – Liability in negligence – Marine insurance – Salvage.
Identifiers: LCCN 2023047705 (print) | LCCN 2023047706 (ebook) | ISBN 9781032422459 (hardback) | ISBN 9781032422435 (paperback) | ISBN 9781003361916 (ebook)
Subjects: LCSH: Maritime law. | Shipping–Management. | Ships–Safety regulations. | Bills of lading. | Freight and freightage. | Marine pollution–Law and legislation. | Marine insurance–Law and legislation.
Classification: LCC K1150 .D36 2024 (print) | LCC K1150 (ebook) | DDC 343.09/6–dc23/eng/20231016
LC record available at https://lccn.loc.gov/2023047705
LC ebook record available at https://lccn.loc.gov/2023047706

ISBN: 978-1-032-42245-9 (hbk)
ISBN: 978-1-032-42243-5 (pbk)
ISBN: 978-1-003-36191-6 (ebk)

DOI: 10.4324/9781003361916

Typeset in Times New Roman
by Deanta Global Publishing Services, Chennai, India

Shipboard Management

Simon Daniels

Routledge
Taylor & Francis Group
LONDON AND NEW YORK

Contents

Table of Cases

A

Action Navigation Inc v Bottigliere Di Navigazione SPA (The Kitsa) [2005] 1 Ll R 432
Adler v Dickson [1954] 3 WLR 696
Aldworth v Stewart (1866) 176 ER 865
Alize 1954 and another v Allianz Elementar Versicherungs AG and others [2021] UKSC 51 On appeal from: [2020] EWCA Civ 293
Argonaftis, The [1989] 2 Ll R 487
Astra, the [2013] EWHC 865
Attorney General of Belize v Belize Telecom Ltd [2009] UKPC 10
Austin v Commissioner of Police of the Metropolis [2009] UKHL 5

B

Barber Blue Sea v Trailer Marine Transport Corporation, US District Court Florida 1989
Barnard v Adams (1850) 51 US 270
Bowater Steamship Company Ltd, Petitioner, v Earl Patterson, Etc et al, The, US Supreme Court 1962/206/371 US860/83 S Ct 116/9 L Ed 2d 98 /6-25-1962

C

Canada (Attorney General) v McNally Construction Inc. (C.A.), 2002 f CC 633
Caparo Industries plc v Dickman [1990] 2 AC 605
Carlill v Carbolic Smoke Ball Company [1892] EWCA Civ 1
Club Cruise Entertainment v Department of Transport [2008] EWHC 2794 QBD
Compania Naviera Maropan S/A v Bowater's Pulp and Paper Mills Limited (The Stork): CA 1954 [1955] 2 QB 68, [1954] 2 Lloyds Rep 397, [1955] 2 All ER 241; [1955] 2 WLR 998
Compania Vascongada v Churchill [1906] 1 KB 237
Currie v Misa (1875) Ll R 10 Ex 153

D

Dairy Containers Ltd v Tasman Orient Line CV (The Tasman Discoverer) [2004] 2 Ll R 647
Didymi Corporation v Atlantic Lines And Navigation Company Inc (The Didymi) [1988] 2 Ll R 108
Dolphin Maritime & Aviation Services Ltd v Sveriges Angfartygs Assurans Forening (The Swedish Club) [2009] EWHC 716 (Comm)
Donoghue (or McAlister) v Stevenson [1932] All ER Rep 1; [1932] AC 562*Dowell and Others v General Steam Navigation Company* (1855) 5 El & Bl 195

E

El Amira, The, and the El Minia [1982] 2 Ll R 28
Equitable Life Assurance Society v Hyman [2002] 1 AC 408
Esso Petroleum Company Ltd v Hall Russell & Company Ltd [1989] 1 Ll R 8
Evergreen Marine (UK) Limited (Appellant) v Nautical Challenge Ltd (Respondent) [2021] UKSC 6
Alize 1954 and another (Appellants) v Allianz Elementar Versicherungs AG and others (Respondents) [2021] UKSC 51

F

Folger Coffee v Olivebank 201 F.3d 632 (5th Cir. 2000)
Foo Fatt Chuen v Jacobsen Cheong Weng Hin & Others [2012]

G

G W Grace & Co Ltd v General Steam Navigation Co Ltd [1950] 2 KB 383, [1950] 1 All ER 201, 83 Ll R 297
Gandara v Bennett and others, Appeal judgment, ILDC 2135 (US 2008), 528 F 3d 823 (11th Cir 2008), 22nd May 2008, United States; Court of Appeals (11th Circuit) [11th Cir]
Giant Shipping Ltd as Owners of MT Posidon v Tauber Oil Company New York Society of Maritime Arbitrators 8 April 2002
Glencore International v Alpina Insurance Co. Ltd [2003] EWHC 2792
Golden Strait Corporation v Nippon Yusen Kubishka Kaisha (the Golden Victory) [2007] UKHL 12, [2007] 2 AC 353; [2007] 2 Ll R 164
Grand China Logistics Holding (Group) Co Ltd v Spar Shipping AS [2016] EWCA Civ 982

H

Hadley v Baxendale (1854) 9 Exch 341
Henry Ewbank, The, 11 F. Cas. 1166, 1170 (D. Mass. 1833) (No. 6376)

Herculito Maritime Limited & others v Gunvor International BV & Others [2021] EWCA Civ 1828
Heron II, The [1969] 1 AC 350
Heskel v Continental Express [1950] 83 Ll L Rep 438; *Rasnoimport v Guthrie & Co Ltd* [1966] 1 Ll R 1
Hong Kong Fir Shipping v Kawasaki Kisen Kaisha [1962] 2 QB 26
Hook v Cunard Steam Ship Co [1953] 1 All ER 1021

I

Ireland v Livingston (1872) LR 5 395

K

K Line Pte Limited v Priminds Shipping (HK) Co Limited (The Eternal Bliss) [2021] EWCA Civ 1712
Kingdom of the Netherlands v Russian Federation, ITLOS/PV.13/C22/1/Rev.1, November 2013
Kleinwort Benson Ltd v Malaysian Mining Corporation [1989] 1 WLR 379
Knight Frank LLP v Aston Du Haney: CA (Civ Div): 12 April 2011
Koompahtoo Local Aboriginal Land Council v Sanpine Pty Ltd [2007] HCA 71

L

Laing v Union Marine Insurance Co (1895) 1 Com Cas 11
Lansat Shipping Co Ltd v Glencore Grain BV, The Paragon [2009] EWHC 551
Leeds Shipping Company Ltd v Societe Francaise Bunge, (The Eastern City) [1958] 2 Ll R 127
Lima, The (1837) 166 ER 434
Lister v Hesley Hall Ltd [2001] UKHL 22
Lister v Romford Ice and Cold Storage Co Ltd [1956] AC 555

M

Mangouras v Spain (12050/04)
Marc Rich & Co AG and Others v Bishop Rock Marine Co Ltd and Others [1995] 3 All ER 307; [1995] UKHL 4; [1996] 1 AC 211; [1995] CLC 934; [1995] 2 LLR 299; [1996] ECC 120; [1995] 3 WLR 227; [1995] 2 Lloyd's Rep 299
Maredelanto Compania Naviera SA v Bergbau-Handel GmbH (The Mihalis Angelos) [1970] 3 All ER 125
Masefield AG v Amlin Corporate Member Ltd [2010] EWHC 280
McFadden v Blue Star Line [1905] 1 KB 697
Mediterranean Salvage & Towage Ltd v Seamar Trading & Commerce Inc (The Reborn) [2009] EWCA Civ 531

Merchants Marine Insurance Co. v North of England P and I Association (1926) 26 Ll. L. R. 201
Moel Tryvan v Andrew Weir [1910] 2KB 844
More OG Romsdal Fylkesbatar AS v The Demised Charterers of the Ship Jotunheim [2005] 1 Ll R 181
Mott Macdonald Ltd v Trant Engineering Ltd [2021] EWHC 754

N

Nautica Marine Ltd v Trafigura Trading LLC(The Leonidas) [2020] EWHC 1986 (Comm)
Noble Chartering Inc v Priminds Shipping Hong Kong Co Ltd [2021] EWCA Civ 87; [2021] 2 Ll R 36

O

Ocean Prefect Shipping Limited v Dampskibsselskabet Norden AS (Ocean Prefect) [2019] EWHC 3368 (Comm)
Oceangas (Gibraltar) Ltd v Port Of London Authority (The Cavendish) [1993] 2 Ll R 292
Olley v Marlborough Court Ltd [1949] 1 KB 532
Owners of Cargo ex SS Ardennes v Owners of SS Ardennes [1951] 1 KB 55
Owners of the cargo lately laden on board the ship David Agmashenebeli v Owners of the David Agmashenebeli [2002] 2 All ER (Comm) 806; [2003] 1 Ll R92
Owners of cargo lately laden on board the ship or vessel 'Starsin' and others v Owners and/or demise charterers of the ship or vessel 'Starsin'; Homburg Houtimport BV v Agrosin Private Ltd HL [2003] UKHL 12 [2003] 2 WLR 711, [2004] 1 AC 715, [2003] 1 CLC 921, 2003 AMC 913, [2003] 1 Lloyd's Rep 571, [2003] 1 All ER (Comm) 625, [2003] 2 All ER 785, [2003] 1 LLR 571

P

Port Line v Ben Line [1958] 2 QB 146
Poussard v Spiers (1875) LR 1; QBD 410
Pyrene Co v Scindia Navigation Co [1954] 2 QB 402

Q

Quadra Commodities S.A. v XL Insurance Company SE and Others [2022] EWHC 431 (Comm)

R

R v Aziz [1996] 1 AC 41, HL
R v Deller [1952] 36 Cr App Rep 184

R v Goodwin [2005] EWCA Crim 3184; [2006] 1 W.L.R. 546
R v Hunt [1987] AC 352
R v Kylsant and Another (1931) 48 TLR 62
R v P & O European Ferries (Dover) Ltd [1991] 93 Cr App R 72
R v Prince (1875) LR 2 CCR 154
R v Sillars, 2018 ONCJ 816
Raymundo Cerrato Solano V Gulf King 55, Inc; Gulf King Services, Inc; Gulf King 55 In Rem (2000) 212 F3d 902 (United States Court Of Appeals, 5th Circuit)
River Gurara, The [1998] QB 610
RMS Titanic, Incorporated, (Appellant) v The Wrecked And Abandoned Vessel ... believed to be the RMS Titanic, in rem, Appeal from the United States District Court for the Eastern District of Virginia, at Norfolk (2006)
Rowbotham & Sons v General Steam Navigation Company Ltd, the Heron [1934] 49 Ll R 78
Royal Caribbean Cruises Ltd v Rawlings [2022] 1 Ll R 643

S

Salomon v A Salomon & Co Ltd [1897] AC 22
Scott Hoyle v Julia Mary Rogers and Nicola Lucinda Rogers and Secretary of State for Transport (1st Intervener) and International Air Transport Association (2nd Intervener) [2014] 3 WLR 148, [2014] CP Rep 30, [2014] EWCA Civ 257, [2014] 3 All ER 550
Seadrill Ghana Operations Limited v Tullow Ghana Limited [2018] EWHC 1640 (Comm)
Shiloh Spinners Limited v Harding [1973] AC 69
S*lebent Shipping Company Ltd v Associated Transport Line LLC, the Star B* Award of the Society of Maritime Arbitrators of New York 19 November 2003
SK Shipping Europe Plc v (among others) (3) Capital VLCC 3 Corp and (5) Capital Maritime and Trading Corp [2020] EWHC 3448
S L Oldendorff & Co GmbH v Trade Export S A [1974] AC 479
Shell International Petroleum Company Ltd v Gibbs (The Salem) [1982] EWCA Civ J0212-3
Smit Salvage BV & Others v Luster Maritime SA & Another (The Ever Given) [2023] EWHC 697 (Admlty)
Spaight v Tedcastle (1880) 6 AC 217
Spector v Norwegian Cruise Line Ltd, 545 US 119 (2005)
Splitt Chartering ApS & Others v Saga Shipholding Norway AS & Others [2021] (EWCA CIV 1880)
Standard Chartered Bank v Dorchester LNG (2) Limited (The Erin Schulte) [2014] EWCA Civ 1382
Steven P Passarello and Others v Rowena T Grumbine and Others, No 1399 WDA 2010; 2011 PA Super 199
*Stewart v Dutra Construction Company (*03-814) 543 U.S. 481 (2005) 343 F.3d 10
Stilk v Myrik [1809] EWHC KB J58; (1809) 170 ER 1168; KB

Suisse Atlantique v Rotterdamsche Kolen Centrale [1967] 1 AC 361
Sweet v Parsley [1970] AC 132

T

Target Holdings Ltd v Redfems [1995] UKHL 10; [1996] AC 421
Tasman Orient Line CV v New Zealand China Clays Ltd and Others [2010] 2 Ll R 13
Taylor v Caldwell (1863) 3 B & S 826; 122 ER 309; [1863] EWHC QB J1
Torepo, The [2002] EWHC 1481 (Admlty), [2002] 2 Ll R 535
Transfield Shipping Inc v Mercator Shipping Inc, the Achilleas [2008] UKHL 48
Tweddle v Atkinson (1861)1 B & S 393; 121 ER 762

U

United States of America v Wolfgang Schröder [2007] United States District Court, Alabama Southern District

W

W M Morrison Supermarkets Plc v Various Claimants [2018] EWCA Civ 2339
Wilforce Llc v Ratu Shipping Co SA [2022] EWHC 1190
Williams v Roffey Bros & Nicholls (Contractors) Ltd [1991] 1 QB 1
Wills v Amber [1954] 1 Lloyd's Rep 253
Winterbottom v Wright (1842) 10 M& W 109; 152 All ER 402
Woolmington v DPP [1935] AC 462
Worrow v General Steam Navigation Company Ltd [1950] 84 Ll R 576

Y

Yam Seng PTE Ltd v International Trade Corporation Ltd [2013] EWHC 111 (QB)

Statutory Provisions

International Law

Athens Convention 1974
European Convention on Human Rights 1950
Hague Rules 1924
Hague-Visby Rules 1968
Hamburg Rules 1978
International Code for Ships Operating in Polar Waters 2017 (the Polar Code) – see SOLAS, STCW
International Convention on Civil Liability for Bunker Oil Pollution Damage 2001
International Convention on Civil Liability for Oil Pollution Damage 1992
International Convention for the Control and Management of Ships' Ballast Water and Sediments 2004 (BWM)
International Convention on Load Lines 1966
International Convention for the Prevention of Pollution from Ships 1973–1978 as amended (MARPOL)
International Convention for the Safety of Life at Sea 1974 as amended (SOLAS)
International Convention on Standards of Training, Certification and Watchkeeping for Seafarers 1978 as amended (STCW)
International Maritime Dangerous Goods Code 1965 (IMDG) – see SOLAS, MARPOL
International Safety Management Code 1998 (ISM) – see SOLAS
International Ship and Port Facility Security Code 2004 (ISPS) – see SOLAS
Maritime Labour Convention 2006 as amended (MLC)
Nairobi International Convention on the Removal of Wrecks 2007
Port Marine Safety Code 2000
Rotterdam Rules (adopted 2008)
Salvage Convention 1989
United Nations Charter 1945
United Nations Convention against Illicit Traffic in Narcotic Drugs etc 1988
United Nations Convention on the Law of the Sea (UNCLOS) 1982
United Nations Maritime Code 1994
York-Antwerp Rules 1890

UK Law

Statutes

Bills of Lading Act 1855
Carriage of Goods by Sea Act 1971
Carriage of Goods by Sea Act 1992
Civil Evidence Act 1968
Contracts (Rights of Third Parties) Act 1999
Corporate Insolvency and Governance Act 2020
Corporate Manslaughter and Corporate Homicide Act 2007
Criminal Justice Act 1967
Criminal Law Act 1967
Courts Act 1971 (as amended)
Employment Rights Act 1996
Equality Act 2010
European Communities Act 1972
European Union (Withdrawal) Act 2018
Firearms Act 1968
Firearms Control Act 2000
Health and Safety at Work etc. Act 1974
Human Rights Act 1988
Insurance Act 2015
Marine Insurance Act 1906
Merchant Shipping Act 1995
Merchant Shipping and Maritime Security Act 1997
Misrepresentation Act 1967
Pilotage Act 1987
Protection From Harassment Act 1997
Sale of Goods Act 1979
Sexual Offences Act 2003
Supreme Court Act 1981
Territorial Waters Jurisdiction Act 1878
Theft Act 1968
Unfair Contract terms Act 1977

UK Statutory Instruments

Hours of Work and Entitlement to Leave Application of the Merchant Shipping (Maritime Labour Convention) (Hours of Work) Regulations 2018
Merchant Shipping (Accident Reporting and Investigation) Regulations 2012
Merchant Shipping (Alcohol) (Prescribed Limits Amendment) Regulations 2015
Merchant Shipping (Maritime Labour Convention) (Survey and Certification) Regulations 2013
Merchant Shipping (Musters Training and Decision Support Systems) Regulations 1999

Merchant Shipping (Official Log Book) Regulations 1981
Merchant Shipping (Pilot Ladders and Hoists) Regulations 1987
Merchant Shipping (Polar Code) (Safety) Regulations 2021
Merchant Shipping (Safety of Navigation) Regulations 2002
Merchant Shipping (Safety of Navigation) Regulations 2020
Merchant Shipping (Safety of Navigation) (Amendment) Regulations 2011
Merchant Shipping (Standards of Training, Certification and Watchkeeping) Regulations 2015
Merchant Shipping (Standards of Training, Certification and Watchkeeping) Regulations 2022
Merchant Shipping (Training and Certification) Regulations 1997
Merchant Shipping (Vessel Traffic Monitoring and Reporting Requirements) Regulations 2004
Merchant Shipping and Fishing Vessels (Health and Safety at Work) Regulations 1997
Merchant Shipping and Maritime Security Act 1997

1 Introduction: Learning the Law

This book is intended to be a critical resource, primarily to support students undertaking qualification at all stages of maritime training, enhancing and developing their knowledge and understanding of the key issues in the Merchant Shipping (Training and Certification) Regulations 1997, as subsequently amended by the 2015 Regulations and other legislation. At the time of going to press, the UK Government has proposed new Regulations in the draft Merchant Shipping (Standards of Training, Certification and Watchkeeping) Regulations 2022, which are intended to implement amendments to the STCW Convention into UK law.

The education and training for seafaring competence is designed to serve the demand for maritime skills which are best learned by college phases that deliver basic knowledge and sea phases which put that knowledge into practice and make sense of it within the concept of safe marine operations. Seafarers at all levels are taking their skills in marine operations learned in theory and apply them in the workplace. Ultimately, however, marine operations can only work within the structure of the law, providing the basis for the legally enforceable rules and regulations that govern the maritime industry, and forms the foundation upon which shipboard management must work.

But this book goes much further than that; it is your guide, mentor and friend, with the goal of enabling seafarers to take responsibility for the lifelong learning process in merchant shipping operations, which is the foundation for building confidence to manage the process of problem-solving, and goes far beyond the Training Regulations, meeting the demand of the seafarer in the twenty-first century.

It has been written with the experience of many years of legal practice and academic leadership in marine operations and offers an essential study guide addressing the issues which are most frequently confronted in shipboard management.

Notice that it is not a text book which devises a system that delivers a solution; that is your job. It is designed to foster your ability to analyse and apply the dynamics of the legal and operational structures in which the shipboard management team must work together. Nobody would ever say that the law is easy, but it is a fact of life that it touches every aspect of marine operations; with knowledge and understanding, you have a sporting chance of getting out of a problem as fast as you got into it.

DOI: 10.4324/9781003361916-1

International marine operations cannot work within the bubble of one country's system; the complex, global nature of the industry, maritime law is international in its scope and we shall get an insight into how the system works for operations wherever in the world the ship may be.

You will learn how to:

- Locate and organise relevant legal information from a wide range of secondary sources;
- Evaluate legal information and its use in the investigation of practical maritime law issues;
- Deploy legal research and scholarly skills at a basic level, with some guidance, using established legal research methods and procedures;
- Communicate information, legal concepts and ideas effectively, referencing sources accurately;
- Plan and carry out work independently with some support/guidance and exercise some responsibility for the achievement of group tasks.

The essential tools to deliver this learning give you:

- An understanding of the issues which are most frequently confronted in the context of ship management;
- The ability to analyse and apply the dynamics of the legal structure which defines the relationship between the parties with whom the Master and the shipboard management team engage in merchant vessel operations;
- Key skills in problem solving that are fundamental to commercial shipping.

At its basic level – to get through the examinations process – this book will give you the skills to persuade the assessor that you have achieved the learning outcomes demanded by the syllabus of Flag States that must meet the common standards in global marine operations. It just so happens that the UK syllabus presents a very fair standard in the international law of the sea, defining those common standards. But your future employability is key to the wider mission of this book. The syllabus will ensure your competence, but it will not automatically give you a job. So, the priorities of employers worldwide are also met in this work, in particular meeting their demands for:

- Self-reliance and the readiness to accept responsibility;
- People skills – teamwork, communication skills and contributing to discussions;
- General employment skills – not just analysing problems but solving problems;
- Practical skills – taking the specialist knowledge of shipboard operations from the classroom to the workplace.

Since the first draft of this book was contemplated, a great deal of feedback has been gathered from students in maritime training, as well as experienced seafarers, in order to achieve something which truly meets their demands. That means giving them the insight to map out their long-term career paths, taking them from purely shipboard operations to a wider career ashore. The aim of this book has therefore been enhanced to enable the reader to respond to varied employment opportunities, both afloat and ashore, building upon their nautical knowledge and experience, and providing a sound understanding of the principles of marine operations management. The objective is to enhance employability throughout the commercial maritime industry, enabling the reader to achieve excellence in shipboard management, while seizing the opportunities presented by new career horizons.

You might even be thinking of that now, which is no bad thing. You need to be frank with yourself, because this can be the start of a vital turning point in your life, and you need to get it right. Sometimes that moment can be well ahead in your career, as you are managing all the risks demanded of a Master or Chief Mate; it may, equally, be at the beginning. You might even develop an appetite for the law; specialist legal practices always need members in their team who have experience at sea, and a maritime qualification can assist in the route to the Solicitors Qualifying Examination.

Any introduction needs to establish the starting point of the book. In this case, the starting point asks the question, what is the purpose of the law? At its heart, the law provides a framework which is designed to resolve disputes between people or between individuals and the State. In the civil context, laws provide a system in which individuals can bring their disputes before an impartial fact-finder, a Judge or Arbitrator – and a solution is determined according to the law. In criminal cases, the Court assesses the evidence which it hears both from the Prosecutor and from the Defendant, and reaches a determination as to whether the law has been broken beyond reasonable doubt.

A starting point must have some defined consequence; in this case the consequence is the management of risk, which lies at the heart of maritime business. There is a fact of life about shipping, that Risk and Reward are very subjective. Their perception – even definition – will vary from business to business – and from individual to individual. The reason for this is that the values gauged in Risk and Reward depend upon the individual or business, and each has different dynamics with their own opportunities and tensions. For the businessperson, risk management is the absolute key to the justification of involvement in marine operations, with the objective to reduce to an acceptable level the different risks related to the tasks which have to be managed within that firm.

In the twenty first century, the investor's risk analysis depends considerably upon the technical specification of the vessel, to minimise the danger of loss or damage. In this way it defines the nature of merchant shipping, and can be well-illustrated by the attention which is being devoted today, to the construction and development of the latest generation of ice-strengthened crude carriers and dry bulk ships capable of navigating in the High Arctic. These ships exploit the opportunities presented by global warming, which have combined to make the extraction and transport of crude oil and minerals not just possible but economically feasible. In order to meet that investment demand, seafarers must have the greatest knowledge and understanding of the navigation of such vessels, and the Laws and Regulations within which they must operate. The safety of life and the marine environment will depend upon it, and a casualty that causes loss or damage will inevitably lead to shareholder flight. If the Owners go bankrupt, their seafarers have no job left; while their criminal conviction will leave them in some far-flung prison, where human rights get lost in translation.

It is not just a matter of learning Laws and Regulations, but of understanding the importance of meeting the obligations which arise out of them. In an age in which it is too easy to rely upon technology and ignore the human element underpinning seafaring, the personal consequences on the seafarer have no limits. Captain Arthur Raymer delivered a speech at the Missions to Seamen Conference, in which he concluded:

> *The acid test of the sea lies in a man's work ... The age-old perils still persist – they seem to be nullified by radio, navigational aids, international organisations and every kind of mechanical ingenuity. They have certainly transformed much of the sea life but if vigilance and care are relaxed, if the man-made scientific aids fail, the old sea demons of storm, rock, shoal, ice and fire lie in wait to pounce. The loss of many well-found ships gives the lie to the theory that science has taken danger out of the modern sailor's life.*

Captain Raymer delivered that speech in 1931; so nothing much has changed.

So the seafarer has a duty to take the standard of care, reasonably expected of such a professional in their position, to guard against acts or omissions which might cause loss or damage to persons or the marine environment and the breach of such duty of care which results in damage will give rise to a claim in the law of negligence, at the very least, or a criminal prosecution – or even both.

The MCA is a global leader in maritime regulation, but its guidance falls short of legal professional training. This book may illuminate some of the complexities of law which underpin the business of risk management, but before continuing, we need to understand some technicalities which must be mastered in learning the law – and demonstrating that you have mastered it. Here are just two of the most important technicalities, which you will need to understand.

The Mystical World of Case Citations

The chapter on sources of law introduces the reader to the different processes in criminal and civil law. In both types, legal rules and principles are settled by Court Judgments, which create precedents that must be understood. The law has developed a form of shorthand, called a case citation, to show where the cases can be found. There are many different law reports, but their citation has a common interpretation. Let us take the example of the criminal prosecution of P & O Ferries arising out of the *Herald of Free Enterprise* disaster:

R v P & O European Ferries (Dover) Ltd [1991] 93 Cr App R 72
R: This was a criminal prosecution, brought by the State, which is referred to in litigation under the title Regina (or, since the accession of Charles III, Rex). In civil proceedings, the first party named will be the Plaintiff (since 1999 re-titled the Claimant). If the report is of an appeal, the first party named will be the Appellant.

P & O European Ferries (Dover) Ltd: The full title identifying the Defendant.
[1991]: Year in which the case was reported (not necessarily the year it was judged).
93: The volume of the Law Report for that year.
Cr App R: Abbreviation of the Criminal Appeal Reports, the Law Report containing the case.
72: The page on which the headnote starts, commencing the report.

Bibliographies and Referencing

What is a Bibliography?
The Bibliography is a list of all the sources which you consulted or researched when managing your assignment.

What is its purpose?
Its purpose is to enable the assessor to satisfy themselves that the sources researched are valid and add value to the work. It will also clarify the depth of research and the student's intellectual reflection, for the Bibliography will identify all the sources consulted, whether or not they were relied upon – that is part of the task management exercise.

And most importantly …
It acknowledges your sources of information, protecting you against the serious charge of plagiarism (the passing off of others' ideas as your own).

What goes into it?
Textbooks, law reports, articles from journals, interviews, internet sites – the list is limited largely by your reflection upon the task.

There are three features to remember:

- Always give credit where credit is due by citing your sources in your text;
- Give sufficient detail in your final reference list for your reader to easily trace your sources;
- Be consistent with your layout, punctuation and typography.

How do I show references in my text are from another work?

- Short quote – enclose in quotation marks within your sentence;
- Long quote – start on a new line, use single spacing and indent;
- Paraphrase – put another person's ideas into your own words.

How do I cite a reference?
There are several forms of referencing, but the following example is universally understood:

Daniels, S, 2022, *Responsibility and Accountability in Maritime Law*, Informa Law from Routledge, Abingdon

Daniels, S: The author and first initial.

2022: The year of the last edition.

Responsibility and Accountability in Maritime Law: the title.

Informa Law from Routledge: the publisher.

Abingdon: the place of publication.

2 Sources of Law

During the course of commercial activities involving ships, many legal questions will arise which, if unresolved, may grow into problems that need a solution before they incur liability for the shipowner and seafarer. Such issues will be managed by the parties and their advisers as part of their day-to-day business, without any wish to get involved in litigation, but the laws which define the systems in the Flag State must be applied wherever the ship may be in the world, while the Port State laws must be applied in their sovereign jurisdiction. The relationship between international law and domestic law is the foundation upon which maritime law must stand and, in this chapter, we are introduced to maritime law and management with a foundation of legal theory and how that is put into practice. We shall see where it all starts, with Sources of Law, and the structure of the Sovereign State, which we must then place in the context of international shipping, with the international law of the sea.

The Starting Point

Ultimately, the domestic court in any jurisdiction must act within the limits defined by its constitution and its laws. Those are the cornerstones of a State, and cannot be lawfully overridden by another State; hence, it is called State Sovereignty.

There is nothing particularly complicated about defining a State: it is a community of people – conveniently described as a Society – which is controlled by the State's management power having a monopoly of legitimate force over them. In a democracy the force of law is defined and limited according to the normative ethics of that Society, upon which no external power should trespass.

Legal structure was given in international terms by the United Nations Charter, adopted in 1945, which is based on the sovereign equality of all Members[1] and enshrines the tenet that States have supreme authority within their territory to exercise unfettered legal jurisdiction, safe from interference from any intervention from other States to impose their will by law or force within their territory. Naturally, State Sovereignty has been guarded jealously with the evolution of the body of law which regulates the relationship between States; this extends not just to the acts of

1 Art. 2 (1) UN Charter (States, Sovereign Equality).

DOI: 10.4324/9781003361916-2

States themselves but also the subjects of those States, with or without their State's authority. Key to that relationship is the fact that the High Contracting Parties have signed what amounts to a contract between them. A State which fails to implement the law in its domestic statute book will therefore be exposed to liability to the other States Parties by failing to carry out its duty and implement it.

The Master has always been subject to the law of the Flag State. The Master, in law, is the ultimate authority for the vessel over which they have sole command and they are responsible to the Flag State for compliance with all its laws, for the Master's authority and accountability are derived primarily from the laws of the Flag State.

This starting point underlines the Master's responsibility, which goes beyond the routine observance of maritime regulations, for the Master is the Flag State's representative, and will be required to meet the Flag State's standards on both civil and criminal laws. In a 2022 civil case brought by a passenger alleging a breach of their civil rights by the Master,[2] a passenger was accused of sexual assault and was duly detained on board a cruise ship, *Explorer of the Seas*, registered under the flag of the Bahamas (which followed the laws of the jurisdiction in which the case was heard). The assault was alleged to have taken place while the vessel was in international waters in the course of a ten-day voyage in the Pacific.

The Master has no powers to try and sentence an individual – that is reserved for the Courts – but they have an overriding duty to maintain order and discipline, which was the basis in this case for the Master ordering that the passenger be confined to a conference room and then to a guest cabin for five days until the ship returned to Sydney. The passenger subsequently brought civil proceedings seeking damages for wrongful detention and false imprisonment.

The Court of Appeal of New South Wales acknowledged the Master's power or authority to detain, but the Master must make that decision on a reasonable cause to believe that the relevant detention or confinement was necessary for the preservation of order and discipline, or for the safety of the vessel or persons or property on board. The Court was satisfied that the Master had acted justifiably and with good reason.[3]

Clearly this addresses the starting point, that the applicable law is that of the Flag State. But how can States manage their affairs and relations with each other, in order to produce a system of maritime control?

The International Law of the Sea

The State is primarily obliged to meet its treaty obligations with other signatories; in context this takes us to the United Nations Convention on the Law of the Sea[4] (UNCLOS), which defines the critical issues of sovereignty and the associated

2 *Royal Caribbean Cruises Ltd v Rawlings* [2022] 1 Ll R 643.

3 This case was distinguished from that of *Hook v Cunard Steam Ship Co* [1953] 1 All ER 1021 in which the Master detained the Claimant in order to avoid bad publicity for the Owners. See below, on the Management of Seafarers.

4 United Nations Convention on the Law of the Sea, signed in 1982, replacing four 1958 treaties. UNCLOS came into force in 1994. As of January 2015, 166 countries have signed the Convention.

jurisdiction over ships of whatever flag. The convention preserves the sovereign jurisdiction of Flag States over their ships wherever they are in the world, limiting the Coastal State's sovereign jurisdiction subject to the right of ships of all States to … *innocent passage through the territorial sea.*[5]

This underlines the overarching principle that the ship is, in law, very much a piece of sovereign territory of the State in which she is registered, and will be controlled and regulated by that State's laws, of whatever sort, wherever she may be in the world. Article 87 enshrines the ancient doctrine of the freedom of the high seas outside the territorial sea[6] as follows:

> *The high seas are open to all States, whether coastal or land-locked. Freedom of the high seas is exercised under the conditions laid down by this Convention and by other rules of international law. It comprises, inter alia ... freedom of navigation ... freedom of overflight.*

Article 2, however, assures the Coastal State its sovereign jurisdiction, to the exclusion of other States', from its land territory to an adjacent belt of sea, described in Article 3 as the territorial sea *up to a limit not exceeding 12 nautical miles, measured from baselines.*

Article 2 further assures a State its *sovereignty to the air space over the territorial sea as well as to its bed and subsoil.*

So, what of some conflict between Flag State and Coastal State in terms of criminal jurisdiction? UNCLOS clearly must determine the applicable regulation in a Coastal State's sovereign jurisdiction:[7]

> 1 *The criminal jurisdiction of the coastal State should not be exercised on board a foreign ship passing through the territorial sea to arrest any person or to conduct any investigation in connection with any crime committed on board the ship during its passage, save only in the following cases:*
> (a) *if the consequences of the crime extend to the coastal State;*
> (b) *if the crime is of a kind to disturb the peace of the country or the good order of the territorial sea;*
> (c) *if the assistance of the local authorities has been requested by the master of the ship or by a diplomatic agent or consular officer of the flag State; or*
> (d) *if such measures are necessary for the suppression of illicit traffic in narcotic drugs or psychotropic substances.*

5 Article 17.
6 And the exclusive economic zone, over which the coastal State does not enjoy sovereign jurisdiction save for the protection of resources.
7 Article 27.

As a result, the very fact that the Master assented to the process of certification by the authority of the Flag State makes out an unassailable argument that they have voluntarily subjected themselves to all the laws of the Flag State and, necessarily, the applicable laws of a Port State in whose sovereign jurisdiction they have voluntarily entered.

How Is International Law Made?

There are, basically, three stages in the birth of new International Law:

1 Participating States meet at a Convention and negotiate a Draft Instrument. These States will be the High Contracting Parties;
2 The Draft Instrument is adopted by the Representative Governments of those States;
3 The States then ratify or endorse the text of the engrossed Convention.

Enforcement

Even though the State has adopted and ratified a Convention, it must still be implemented in their legal system, in order that its provisions can be enforced. This means passing some domestic law which enforces the terms of the Convention within its jurisdiction, whether that jurisdiction is the State's geographical land or whether it is a ship to which that State has allocated its flag, and wherever in the world that ship may be. In practice, that means that domestic law must be brought into force which would lead to consequences in law if the people managed by the State fail to observe that law.

How Is Domestic Law Made? The UK Perspective

The principle of State sovereignty defines the supreme authority within that territory, which is managed by laws in which no other State has any legitimate right to interfere, either in the making or in the administration of those laws.

The management of international marine operations clearly demands a global application of laws by which sovereign States agree to be bound, but the way in which the State manages its laws and governance is a matter entirely beyond the control of another State. The only solution open to another State is to identify grounds for arguing that the defaulting State has failed to meet the Convention to which it has signed.

It is as well to illustrate the process of how laws are made, by a very broad introduction to English Statute Law. The process is broadly thus:

1. A Bill proposing a maritime Statute can be introduced in either the House of Commons or the House of Lords; most commonly it is first laid before the Commons;

2. First reading: usually a formality, the short title of the Bill is read out and is followed by an order for the Bill to be printed;
3. Second reading: the big opportunity for MPs to debate the main principles from the floor of the House. Passed by a simple majority;
4. Committee stage: where detailed examination of the Bill takes place – line by line (sometimes comma by comma);
5. Report stage: the amended Bill can be debated, and further amendments proposed;
6. Third reading: usually takes place immediately after report stage as the next item of business on the same day. Debate is usually short, with a vote at the end;
7. It then proceeds to the Second House, the House of Lords, and follows much the same pattern;
8. First reading: the long title (indicating the content of the Bill) is read out;
9. Second reading: the first opportunity for the Lords to debate the key principles and main purpose of the Bill and to flag up any concerns or specific areas where they think amendments are needed;
10. Committee stage: where detailed examination of the Bill takes place – line by line again;
11. Report stage gives all members of the Lords a further opportunity to examine and make amendments to the Bill;
12. Unlike the House of Commons, amendments can be made at third reading in the House of Lords, provided the issue has not been fully considered and voted on during either committee or report stage;
13. When the Bill has passed through third reading in both Houses it is returned to the first House for the second House's amendments to be considered;
14. Both Houses must agree on the exact wording of the Bill;
15. In exceptional cases, when the two Houses do not reach agreement, the Bill falls. If certain conditions are met, the Commons can use the Parliament Acts to pass the Bill, without the consent of the Lords, in the following session;
16. Finally, when a Bill has completed all its parliamentary stages in both Houses, it must have Royal Assent, the Monarch's agreement, before it becomes a Statute, although constitutionally this is a formality.

This process appears draconian but reflects the absolute requirement to take the greatest care with the law that follows, because once it is on the Statute Books, the Act is there forever, unless it is amended or repealed by a subsequent Act. For example, the Statute of Marlborough 1267 is still in force; in 2015 the Law Commission published a draft Bill repealing several anachronistic sections; but it concluded that *the repeal of these provisions will not affect Chapters 1 and 23 of the Statute of Marlborough. These appear to have continuing value.*[8]

8 The Law Commission, 2015, Statute Law Repeals: Twentieth Report. Draft Statute Law (Repeals) Bill, London.

For this reason, a mechanism must be found to resolve the problem arising when some technical piece of legislation must be passed, and must be subject to frequent updates, which is frequently encountered with maritime standards. In this case, the substantive Act which we have observed though its stages, can confer powers on Ministers, in our case usually the Secretary of State for Transport, to make more detailed orders, rules or regulations. The Act must contain the broad framework, but statutory instruments are used to provide the necessary detail that would be too complex to include in the Act itself. In short, if Parliament tells the Secretary of State to jump, the Secretary of State's only question is, how high?

Having established the law by Statute, the function of the judicial system is to interpret what Parliament intended. This may be necessary where the legislation includes words that have more than one meaning, or words whose meaning changes depending on their context. What the Judges cannot do, is to change the Will of Parliament. This is why the nineteenth century case of *Regina v Dudley and Stephens*[9] keeps appearing in litigation when it comes to cases of necessity and assisted suicide, but Parliament has repeatedly declined to change the law, and so the old Common Law must still be followed.

Sovereignty and Maritime Conventions

The Flag State will depend on the Master no matter where the ship is, for the State will depend on one person as their representative, to manage the State's responsibility to other States and protect their sovereign territory, the ship herself. The Master's responsibility as the representative of the Flag State will undoubtedly demand priority for meeting Port State laws, which inevitably underlines the requirement for just one person to be held accountable in the event of the breach of those laws. It is for the Master to show that their conduct in the risk management process was that reasonably to be expected of someone in that position, as held in *Grace v General Steam*:

> *the Master should not be deprived of his remedy merely because, in ignorance of the danger, he entered a port which well-informed men might erroneously have pronounced to be safe; nor is he to be given damages if he sustains injury in conditions which fall short of the danger-point merely because well-informed men might have erroneously pronounced his entry to be foolhardy.*[10]

In short, the Flag State has accredited the Master to be their representative on their bit of sovereign jurisdiction, which is the ship. Theirs, in law, is the ultimate authority for that ship and they are responsible to the Flag State for compliance

9 Addressed more fully below.

10 *G W Grace & Co Ltd v General Steam Navigation Co Ltd* [1950] 2 KB 383, [1950] 1 All ER 201, 83 Ll R 297.

with its maritime regulations. There are particularly good reasons for the Flag State's unfettered management control of the Master:

- The State maintains order, so their appointed Master gives up absolute freedom only to the Flag State authority;
- The State must itself maintain management control to meet its obligations under UNCLOS towards others, whether in International Waters or the Territorial Seas of other States.

But then, the State clothes the Master with absolute discretion; in the UK this is set out in the Merchant Shipping (Safety of Navigation) (Amendment) Regulations 2011,[11] which does nothing more than implement the provisions in the International Convention for the Safety of Life at Sea (SOLAS), Chapter V Regulation 34–1:

> *The owner, the charterer, the company operating the ship ... or any other person shall not prevent or restrict the master of the ship from taking or executing any decision which, in the master's professional judgement, is necessary for safety of life at sea and protection of the marine environment.*

This puts beyond the reach of any misunderstanding that nobody, be they owner, manager or even Port State controller, can overrule the Master's professional judgment in the discharge of their responsibilities as the Flag State's representative. Of course, the Master will still be accountable if they are in breach of the law of the Port State while in their territorial sea – their sovereign jurisdiction. The core issue is that the Master must answer, not just for how they meet their responsibility for the safety of life at sea and the protection of the marine environment, but also for how they observe the plethora of all the laws of the State in which they find themselves. They will have no immunity against the criminal law of the Port State.

UNCLOS clarifies this beyond doubt; Article II provides that the sovereignty of a Coastal State extends to an adjacent belt of sea, described as the territorial sea, which *shall extend to a limit not exceeding 12 nautical miles, measured from baselines determined in accordance with this Convention.* Clearly, therefore, if it passes legislation clearly defining the Master's obligations to the Port state, then the Master must comply within the State's territorial sea. A good example under UK legislation is section 98 Merchant Shipping Act 1995:

> *If a ship which is in a port in the United Kingdom or is a United Kingdom ship and is in any other port, is dangerously unsafe, then ... the master and the owner of the ship shall each be guilty of an offence.*

The difficulty emerges in two circumstances:

- Where the extent of the territorial sea is unclear or disputed;
- Where the statute implementing the provision is unclear.

11 2011 No 2978.

The mischief arises out of management control by the Port State of its own litigation process. The State is primarily obliged to meet its treaty obligations with other signatories; in context this takes us to the United Nations Convention on the Law of the Sea[12] (UNCLOS), which defines the critical issues of sovereignty and the associated jurisdiction over ships of whatever flag. The convention preserves the sovereign jurisdiction of Flag States over their ships wherever they are in the world, limiting the Coastal State's sovereign jurisdiction subject to the right of ships of all States to … *innocent passage through the territorial sea.*[13]

This underlines the overarching principle that the ship is, in law, very much a piece of sovereign territory of the State in which she is registered and will be controlled and regulated by that Sate's laws, of whatever sort, wherever she may be in the world. The State, in turn, is obliged to implement the minimum standard defined in the Convention concerned; it can implement a higher standard, but not a lower one. Of course, how it interprets that standard can be open to dispute.

It is imperative to understand the foundation of UNCLOS and Sovereign Jurisdiction limits, in particular reconciling Articles 2 and 3 with Flag State rights in Article 17, in understanding the key issues of the enforcement of laws within a Sovereign Jurisdiction. The critical feature of UNCLOS Article 3 defines the right of every State to establish its sovereign jurisdiction up to the 12-mile limit of the territorial sea. The question arises, then, of just how Port State jurisdiction can apply concurrently with, or take precedence over, Flag State jurisdiction of ships in territorial waters. In the 2005 United States case of *Spector v Norwegian Cruise Line*,[14] the United States Supreme Court considered whether domestic American legislation, in this case the Americans with Disabilities Act 1990, applied to foreign-flag cruise ships in American territorial waters, by application of the Clear Statement Rule. But if a State simply ignores the Convention which it has adopted, what is to be done?

12 United Nations Convention on the Law of the Sea, signed in 1982, replacing four 1958 treaties. UNCLOS came into force in 1994. As of 2020, 168 countries have ratified the Convention, while an additional 14 UN member states have signed, but not ratified.

13 Article 17.

14 *Spector v Norwegian Cruise Line Ltd*, 545 US 119 (2005).

3 Conventions Overview

What Are the Key Maritime Conventions in Marine Operations Management?

- International Convention for the Safety of Life at Sea 1974 (SOLAS);
- International Convention for the Prevention of Pollution from Ships 1973–1978 (MARPOL);
- International Convention on Standards of Training, Certification and Watchkeeping for Seafarers 1978 (STCW);
- International Convention for the Control and Management of;
- Ships' Ballast Water and Sediments 2004 (BWM);
- Maritime Labour Convention 2006 (MLC).

What Other Conventions Are Relevant to Maritime Operations?

- Athens Convention 1974 (compulsory insurance);
- International Convention on Civil Liability for Oil Pollution Damage 1992 (bulk cargo pollution);
- International Convention on Civil Liability for Bunker Oil Pollution Damage 2001 (bunker pollution);
- Nairobi International Convention on the Removal of Wrecks 2007.

The Enforcement of Conventions in Domestic Law

The relationship between international law and domestic law is the foundation upon which maritime law must stand. The essential feature is defined around the High Contracting Parties having signed what amounts to a contract between them. A State which fails to implement the law in its domestic statute book will therefore be exposed to liability to the other States by failing to carry out its duty and implement it. It is a matter between them, and they cannot blame the Master. The Convention can only be enforced between those States Parties whose democratic organs have embodied the Convention in domestic law. Therefore, legal individuals (people, incorporated companies) do not acquire any rights under a Convention itself and cannot be liable for breaches of a Convention, unless the State's constitution legislates for that, as we shall see.

DOI: 10.4324/9781003361916-3

The general principle is that the Contracting States will enforce the provisions of the Convention by implementing the appropriate domestic legislation as far as their own ships are concerned and set the penalties for infringements, where these are applicable. A vital feature is that the State can implement in its law a higher standard than that set out in the Convention, or the same standard; they cannot, however, implement a lower standard than that set out in the Convention. (How this is interpreted is sometimes a matter of bitter dispute between States Parties, as evidenced in the annals of the STCW Convention with its bewildering number of amendments.) Consequently, once the domestic law is in force, the prime responsibility for compliance with that law lies with the owner, who is responsible for the ship to whom the Flag State has allocated is flag. In this respect, the Port State will be the oft-quoted 'safety net' monitoring compliance; but the Port State will carry this out under the laws of its sovereign jurisdiction, if the vessel is in its territorial sea, in accordance with UNCLOS. Life is not easy, though and the experience encountered with SOLAS, for example, showed that the Port State would enforce the standards in its own laws, even if they were higher than those of the Flag State, thus detaining a ship which had met the minimum standards in SOLAS. It was not until the system of Memoranda of Understanding was in place, that tensions were resolved.

The Master will be accountable as the owner's representative but will also owe personal responsibility for those laws which the Flag State make them accountable, wherever the ship may be, as well as the Port State if within their territorial sea. The prime responsibility for compliance with the requirements laid down in international maritime conventions lies with the shipowner, which must observe the laws of the Flag State; but responsibility for ensuring such compliance remains with the Flag State. The Port State will be the 'safety net' monitoring compliance for the Convention minimum standards, and will carry this out under its sovereign jurisdiction – as long as the vessel is in its territorial sea.

The transnational nature of a Convention means that it cannot be enforced against the Master or the owner. Of course, the very tools of enforcement are absent: there are no transnational law enforcement officers who would have the power to make use of them anyway. The enforcement mechanism in the UN Charter generally reserves powers to the Security Council to determine the existence of any threat to the peace, breach of the peace or act of aggression and may impose mandatory sanctions if the dispute cannot be resolved. As the world has witnessed in recent years, however, the Security Council demands unanimity in voting, and just one member can defeat a resolution. If the resolution passes successfully, however, the sanction will be on a State level, such as trading or diplomatic; and rarely does it sanction the use of armed force to maintain or restore international peace and security. The enforcement tools of international law thus cannot be implemented against individual legal entities.

But that is not the exclusive case, for a State may endorse a Treaty with the power to enforce it against individual bodies within its jurisdiction, if it stipulates in its own constitutional laws that it has such power. Which brings us to the essential case of *Bowater v Patterson.*

The Case of the *Gladys Bowater*[1]

The Claimant, the Bowater Steamship Company Limited, was a UK-registered company which owned the *Gladys Bowater*, a fine, UK-registered ship that, in July 1959, found herself the innocent party in a dispute that escalated into a row over international Conventions. Her owners were part of the Bowater group of companies that did not have an outstanding industrial dispute with the American-based International Woodworkers of America (IWA), which instituted a secondary picket at the vessel's discharge at Buffalo, New York, where the unloading was to be carried out by longshoremen who did not belong to the IWA but, before unloading commenced, a lone IWA picket appeared and the longshoremen refused to break the picket for another three days, when an injunction was served on the picket, who had to comply with the order granted by the US District Court, and the longshoremen proceeded to unload the ship. The injunction had to be answered at the return hearing, and defended proceedings ensured, which ended up in the Supreme Court in 1962. Among Bowater's five key points, it argued that the industrial action targeting the *Gladys Bowater* was unlawful, because Bowater were entitled to the protection under a 145-year-old commercial treaty to regulate Maritime Commerce between the United States and Great Britain, which had been signed and ratified by both States Parties in 1815, conferring rights and obligations which guaranteed *liberty freely and securely to come with their ships and cargoes to all such places.* The treaty explicitly conferred the defined rights and obligations not only upon the two States Parties but also upon the inhabitants of the two countries. In this case the Court held that the United States had to fulfil its treaty obligation of protecting the guaranteed freedoms in two ways: firstly, by not violating its treaty obligations and, secondly, by empowering the Courts to take whatever steps would be necessary to protect and maintain the rights and obligations of individuals, in this case to grant injunctive relief to prevent the Defendants from acting contrary to the treaty.

This has been upheld more recently in the United States as a general principle that, if a Convention is self-executing in the USA, it has the force of domestic law without the need for implementing legislation by Congress and, in 2008, the decision was followed in *Gandara v Bennett*.[2]

The effect of this has a bearing close to the heart of Europe today, because private persons (individuals and companies) may be the direct addressees of European Regulations which have direct effect in Member States when the Regulation in question is applied to them within the sovereign jurisdiction of the State in question. This is nothing new; indeed, it was the defining feature in the *Van Gend en Loos* case, which was decided in 1963. With the UK's withdrawal from the European Union, its consequence is that a person (such as the Master or the owner) can still enforce the rights of which they are beneficiaries or obey the Regulations

1 *The Bowater Steamship Company Ltd, Petitioner, v Earl Patterson, Etc.* et al., US Supreme Court 1962/206/371 US860/83 S Ct 116/9 L Ed 2d 98 /6-25-1962.

2 *Gandara v Bennett and others*, Appeal judgment, ILDC 2135 (US 2008), 528 F 3d 823 (11th Cir 2008), 22nd May 2008, United States; Court of Appeals (11th Circuit) [11th Cir].

by which they are bound within the Member State's jurisdiction, even if that State has not itself complied with the Regulation. The essential components are that the Regulation must confer those rights and it must be self-executing in Member States.

So how does a State rationalise its international obligations with its domestic law? The English Legal System embraced and enforced the terms of the European Convention on Human Rights by the Human Rights Act 1998, which happily codified a number of ethical duties, including Article 7 (No Punishment Without Law) – although this was not the first codification of the right under English law (that belonged to Magna Carta), so that, taken as a whole, an argument may be made for applying the English criminal process (as opposed to constituent laws) transnationally in order to determine the criminal liability of the Master.

This, however, would defy a major ethical issue: in 1918 President Woodrow Wilson of the United States addressed a joint session of Congress in which he declared the inalienable right of people to choose freely the politics by which they are governed, and to follow the social development as they choose. It necessarily follows they must be free to shape their own culture, which means making their own laws and, if it so happens, be free to make their own mistakes.

In consequence, it would offend the most basic ethical values of the transnational forum to argue for a solution which conflicts with the rights of sovereign States to determine their own judicial process; that is, the system which tries the Accused for liability under their chosen system. Indeed, there are irreconcilable differences between the adversarial system, led by English law, and the inquisitorial system of most European Continental States who would support their system with the compelling authority of Cicero and, later, Imperial Rome. The task of determining which is the preferred system is hardly one which ethically can be imposed upon a sovereign State against its will. This was undoubtedly the guiding principle which led the International Maritime Organization to tread carefully when drafting its Guidelines on Fair Treatment of Seafarers, which emphatically were not intended to come into conflict with the laws of any sovereign jurisdiction nor with transnational regulation of the seafarer's human rights, but rather to provide guidance which underpinned the seafarer's rights to fair treatment at all times.

By the same inalienable freedom of choice, there is nothing to stop a sovereign State from exercising the equal freedom of picking and choosing which legal principles and processes it admires in other jurisdictions. While English criminal law involves patterns and processes which are dependent upon the adversarial system, principles of English civil law have been embraced globally, perhaps the most notable example being the re-statement of liability in negligence held obiter in a case in which the villain of the piece was a dead snail lurking in a bottle of ginger beer.[3] Paradoxically, the two galaxies of criminal and civil law clash where they meet this very case, which gave birth to the concept of criminal negligence, and fundamental to the golden thread running through this work that the emergent criminalisation

3 *Donoghue (or McAlister) v Stevenson* [1932] All ER Rep 1; [1932] AC 562.

phenomenon, at the centre of the primary research question, is fatally flawed by its reliance upon criminal negligence in finding a conviction against the Master that conveniently suits the normative ethics of Port and Coastal States.

The Case of the *Arctic Sunrise*

The case arose when several crew members of the Dutch-flagged *Arctic Sunrise* attempted to board an oil rig owned by the Russian-owned natural gas company Gazprom, on 18 September 2013. The crew members that boarded the platform were detained by the Russian coastguard. The *Arctic Sunrise*, which was operated by Greenpeace International, proceeded to leave the security zone around the platform. It was subsequently boarded and seized by Russian forces. The crew were arrested and detained, and later charged with the somewhat obscure offence of *Piracy of an organised group*. Both the vessel and crew remained in detention, and the Russian authorities compounded their problems by boarding the vessel again on 28 September to carry out an investigation, without the consent of the Flag State.

On 4 October 2013, the Netherlands instituted Annex VII arbitration proceedings against Russia and, on 23 October, submitted a request for provisional measures to the International Tribunal of the Law of the Sea (ITLOS), pending the constitution of the Annex VII proceedings, in accordance with Article 290 of UNCLOS. A public hearing on the request for provisional measures will be held at ITLOS on 6 November. Article 292 sets out the procedure to be followed when a State detaining a foreign-flagged vessel has not complied with the prompt release provisions of the Convention. It requires the prompt release of vessels detained upon the posting of reasonable bond or other security provided for in two cases, namely: (a) regarding ships arrested to ensure compliance with the laws of the coastal State regarding living resources of the exclusive economic zone (Article 73(2)); and (b) vessels detained for violation of laws relating to the protection of the marine environment (Articles 220(6) and 226(1)(b)).

Russia did not defend its position very persuasively to the Flag State claim that the incident fell within the regime of the exclusive economic zone, which is governed by Article 73(1) of UNCLOS permitting the boarding, inspection and arrest of vessels by the coastal State in the exercise of its sovereign rights to explore, exploit, conserve and manage the living resources in the exclusive economic zone. Russia did not plead that the actions of the *Arctic Sunrise* had breached national laws regarding the living resources of the exclusive economic zone; but, according to a Russian diplomatic note of 18 September, the vessel was seized in view of the danger posed to the platform, the possible risk of environmental damage and the refusal of the vessel to comply with the coastguard's instructions. In a tortuous argument justifying the allegation of piracy, Russia referred to the regime of the exclusive economic zone, the continental shelf and the 1958 Convention on the High Seas (regarding suspected piracy) in diplomatic notes to the Netherlands.

Dealing with the circumstance that the Gazprom structure was an oil rig not a ship, Article 56 provides that, within the exclusive economic zone, the coastal

State has exclusive jurisdiction over artificial structures and installations *including jurisdiction with regard to customs, fiscal, health, safety and immigration laws and regulations*. A reasonable safety zones around such structures may be established, to ensure the safety both of navigation and of the structures themselves, and Russia had established a security zone around the Prirazlomnaya platform, in which navigation was prohibited; but the *Arctic Sunrise* was boarded and detained after it had left the security zone. The Netherlands claimed that the actions of Russia, in boarding, arresting and detaining the *Arctic Sunrise* in the Russian exclusive economic zone, constituted a breach of obligations owed to the Netherlands as Flag State regarding freedom of navigation and the right to exercise jurisdiction over the *Arctic Sunrise*. The Netherlands concluded that UNCLOS does not provide any legal basis for the exercise of enforcement jurisdiction by Russia over the *Arctic Sunrise* in the circumstances.

On the same day that the request for provisional measures was submitted to ITLOS, Russia released a statement noting that it did not accept the arbitration proceedings initiated by the Netherlands, and that it did not intend to participate in the request for provisional measures. The statement referred to the declaration made by Russia upon ratification of UNCLOS in 1997, in which Russia stated that it did not accept the compulsory dispute settlement procedures of section 2 of Part XV *concerning law-enforcement activities in regard to the exercise of sovereign rights or jurisdiction*; as such, therefore, Russia denied that the Tribunal had any jurisdiction over Russia, seeking to exclude all disputes regarding the exercise of sovereign rights or jurisdiction under UNCLOS from compulsory dispute resolution and not just those disputes related to marine scientific research or the living resources of the exclusive economic zone. In this case, rather than seeking to defend its position on jurisdiction before the arbitration tribunal, Russia averred that it would not engage with the proceedings on any level.

Whatever arguments were proposed by Russia in cherry-picking its obligations, under Article 290, ITLOS has jurisdiction to grant provisional measures in the case if it considers that the Annex VII tribunal to be constituted would have prima facie jurisdiction, and that the urgency of the situation so requires. In considering the request for provisional measures, ITLOS very fairly examined the Russian declaration made upon ratification of UNCLOS and considered whether an Annex VII Tribunal would have jurisdiction to hear the dispute, regardless of the Russian position towards the proceedings.[4] In its Order of 22 November 2013, the Tribunal ordered the Russian Federation to release immediately the *Arctic Sunrise* and all persons who have been detained, and on 14 August 2015 the Permanent Court of Arbitration found that the Russian Federation had breached its obligations owed by it to the Netherlands as Flag State and ordered compensation to be assessed.[5] Characteristically, Russia still refused to recognise the ruling, even though it was

4 The 'Arctic Sunrise' Case (Kingdom of the Netherlands v. Russian Federation), ITLOS/PV.13/C22/1/Rev.1, November 2013.

5 https://pcacases.com/web/sendAttach/1438.

a Convention signatory. Russia and the Netherlands eventually reached a financial settlement in 2019.

The moral of the story raises issues about the trust which may be placed in certain States, which continues to create tensions between Flag and Port States, and will be discussed further.

4 International Convention for the Safety of Life at Sea – SOLAS

On 28 May 1912, a committee of the United States Senate published the report of its investigation into the loss of the White Star Line's RMS *Titanic*, which famously foundered just 15 days earlier, with the loss of 1,517 passengers and crew. Its findings were coloured by over-dramatic language that undoubtedly satisfied the domestic demand to find someone to blame, expressing indignation for the loss of American lives in preference to objectivity, but highlighted some key causes of the collision and loss of life:

- The ship was not equipped with enough lifeboats. There may have been a sufficient number in accordance with the rules of the British Board of Trade, but it is a conceded fact that the great loss of life occurred because there was an insufficient number to meet the necessities of the case and rescue the passengers and crew;
- The ship did not carry searchlights. *If a proper searchlight had been upon this vessel, in my judgment, the accident could have been avoided*;
- The failure to supply the proper officers with binoculars … *unquestionably an act of negligence*;
- Proper attention was not paid to the wireless messages. *This appears to me to have been an inexcusable act of negligence*;
- Speed was not reduced in a dangerous ice zone. *The disaster was attributable to the want of due care upon the part of the company and of those in charge of the ship.*

The British inquiry took very much longer to complete, but was unquestionably more technical rather than dramatic, and reflected a more professional approach to its task. It was this approach which guided the future of casualty reporting, to investigate marine accidents, to learn lessons and make recommendations to help prevent future accidents of a similar nature. This, indeed, underlines the policy objectives today of the work of the Marine Accident Investigation Branch, which was founded in 1989 following the *Herald of Free Enterprise* disaster.

Nevertheless, there was broad consensus between the two reports on a number of key matters; in addition to its findings of the key causes, the American report recommended that navigation in sea lanes should be carefully defined and water-tight subdivision introduced to limit sinking. No matter how they drew their conclusions

DOI: 10.4324/9781003361916-4

on causes and recommendations, however, their findings would carry no weight in international maritime law, because there was no international maritime law, although the principles of State sovereignty could not be denied. Clearly there had to be some international measure which all participating States would be committed to adopt. As a result, the first international conference on the safety of life at sea was held in London at the invitation of the British Government, and the text of this, the first SOLAS Convention, was signed on the 20 January 1914. It was due to enter into force in July 1915, but never saw the light of day due to the First World War. Paradoxically, the war expedited improvements in naval architecture for stability and the safety of life, before a second Convention was adopted in 1929 and entered into force in 1933. The current version was adopted in 1974 and entered into force in 1980, but amendments follow to keep pace with current knowledge about seaworthiness, and the 2009 amendments to SOLAS and associated codes came into force in January 2020. Chapters of SOLAS are subdivided into regulations, which are individually identified in updates and amendments, although the guidance published on the amendments are not simple to follow and demand concentration.

The Chapters of SOLAS

The principal objective of SOLAS is to define the minimum standards for the construction, equipment and operation of ships, which are compatible with their safety. Flag States are responsible for ensuring that ships under their flag comply with the minimum requirements, and it is they who have the task of inspecting vessels, for the purpose of issuing certificates as proof of compliance with the Flag State standard, reflecting nothing less than the SOLAS minimum requirements. That being said, Port State Control acts as the 'safety net' which monitors compliance during the currency of a certificate.

SOLAS Chapter I – General Provisions

Chapter I sets out regulations for Flag States to meet the minimum standards concerning the survey of ships and the evidence of surveys in the form of issuing certificates signifying that the ship meets the requirements of the Convention. The Chapter also includes provisions for monitoring by Port States, the 'safety net' for compliance.

Chapter II-1 Construction: Subdivision and Stability

The subdivision of passenger ships into watertight compartments must be such that after assumed damage to the ship's hull the vessel will remain afloat and stable. Requirements for watertight integrity and bilge pumping arrangements for passenger ships are also laid down as well as stability requirements for both passenger and cargo ships.

The loss of the *Costa Concordia* in 2012 resulted in a review of Chapter II-1 under the 2020 amendments, resulting in a set of amendments to SOLAS Chapter

II-1 relating to subdivision and stability, with the aim of simplifying the Convention requirements with just one new Regulation 4 with sub-paragraphs relating to application, alternative methodologies, degree of subdivision and the effectiveness of the subdivision was introduced. Important amendments also require the stability information to be provided to the Master.

Chapter II-2 – Fire protection, Fire Detection and Fire Extinction

This provides the minimum standards for fire safety provision for all ships and specific measures for passenger ships, cargo ships and tankers.

Chapter III – Life-Saving Appliances and Arrangements

This chapter is intended to set out the minimum standards to ensure that ships are equipped with fully rely on the survival craft and life-saving apparatus such as life jackets.

The requirements for life-saving appliances and arrangements, including requirements for life boats, rescue boats and life jackets, was amended in 2020, making mandatory the requirements for maintenance, thorough examination, operational testing, overhaul and repair of lifeboats and rescue boats, launching appliances and release gear. The aim is to prevent accidents with survival craft and provides for a uniform, safe and documented standard related to the servicing of these appliances, as well as the authorisation, qualification and certification requirements to ensure that a reliable service is provided.

Lessons learned from casualties such as the *Costa Concordia* have resulted in amendments to SOLAS require passenger ships carrying more than 36 passengers to be built with evacuation analysis early in the design process come into force. The analysis should be used to identify and eliminate, as far as practicable, congestion which may develop during an abandonment due to normal movement of passengers and crew along escape routes, including the possibility that crew may need to move along these routes in a direction opposite to the movement of passengers. In addition, the analysis should be used to demonstrate that escape arrangements are sufficiently flexible to provide for the possibility that certain escape routes, assembly stations, embarkation stations or survival craft may not be available as a result of a casualty.

Chapter IV – Radiocommunications

The need for this provision was emphasised in the original SOLAS Convention, as a result of the *Titanic* disaster. The record of radio messages has survived, and speaks eloquently of the need for some regulation. At 00.15 the Master gave the wireless operators the co-ordinates for a distress call, and just two ships responded at once, the *Frankfurt*, nearly 170 miles away, and the *Olympic*, nearly 500 miles away. Within minutes, however, the call was being answered by the Cunard liner *Carpathia*, who replied *Putting about and heading for you.* She was the nearest ship to respond, being 58 nautical miles away. Controversially, the Leyland liner *Californian*, never responded at all.

Chapter IV now incorporates the Global Maritime Distress and Safety System (GMDSS). All passenger ships and all cargo ships of 300 gross tonnage and more on international voyages are required to carry equipment designed to improve the chances of rescue following an accident, including satellite emergency position indicating radio beacons (EPIRBs) and search and rescue transponders (SARTs) for the location of the ship or survival craft.

UK legislation was amended by the Merchant Shipping (Radiocommunications) (Amendment) Regulations 2021, which give effect to the SOLAS 2022 amendments, and are set out in MSN 1903.

It should also be noted that the GMDSS book is a statutory log, which means that it does not require corroborative evidence to prove the contents. SOLAS requires it to be kept in the responsibility of the ship's security officer, so woe betide them if the book contains unreliable entries.

Chapter V – Safety of Navigation

This is one of the most important provisions for marine operations. It sets out provisions for marine operations to apply in general to all ships on all voyages, for the purpose of improving safety of navigation, and to reduce the risk of accidents occurring at sea.

The latest version of Chapter V was implemented by the Merchant Shipping (Safety of Navigation) Regulations 2020, and further guidance is found in MGN 610.

Regulation 34 of Chapter V – addresses safe navigation and avoidance of dangerous situations.

1 Prior to proceeding to sea, the master shall ensure that the intended voyage has been planned using the appropriate nautical charts and nautical publications for the area concerned, taking into account the guidelines and recommendations developed by the Organization.

2 The voyage plan shall identify a route which:
- Takes into account any relevant ships' routeing systems;
- Ensures sufficient sea room for the safe passage of the ship throughout the voyage;
- Anticipates all known navigational hazards and adverse weather conditions;
- Takes into account the marine environmental protection measures that apply, and avoids as far as possible actions and activities which could cause damage to the environment.

3 The owner, the charterer, or the company, as defined in Regulation IX/1, operating the ship or any other person, shall not prevent or restrict the master of the ship from taking or executing any decision which, in the master's professional judgement, is necessary for safe navigation and protection of the marine environment.

This perpetuates the vital provision in maritime law of the Master's Absolute Discretion.

The MCA is particularly concerned to ensure that Chapter V is well-understood, which will be discussed in greater detail later in this book, but broadly includes:

- Planning and conducting Safe Navigation;
- Establishing Safe Navigational Watchkeeping Arrangements and Procedures;
- Compass skills;
- Manoeuvring the Ship.

Chapter VI – Carriage of Cargoes

The Chapter covers all types of cargo (except liquids and gases in bulk) *which, owing to their particular hazards to ships or persons on board, may require special precautions* and define requirements for stowage and securing of cargo or cargo units, such as containers.

SOLAS was amended with effect from July 2016, requiring as a condition of loading, that a packed container must have a verified gross mass ('VGM') which is presented to the Master. It applies to all exports, including tank containers, flat rack containers, bulk containers and containers on a chassis or trailer, although a container on a chassis or trailer on a ro-ro ship engaged on short international voyages is exempt. The responsibility for providing and communicating the VGM is on the shipper, or cargo owner, and as it is a requirement of an international Convention, the Master will have the right to reject the cargo if the VGM is missing.

However, the cargo is stowed and secured, it must effectively be done to prevent, as far as is practicable, throughout the voyage, damage or hazard to the ship and the persons on board and loss of cargo overboard. Containers shall not be loaded to more than the maximum gross weight indicated on the Safety Approval Plate under the International Convention for Safe Containers (CSC). Although the emphasis is on container ships, appropriate precautions should also be taken during loading and transport on ro-ro ships, especially with regard to the securing arrangements on board such ships, taking care to ensure the strength of the securing points and lashings.

Chapter VII – Carriage of Dangerous Goods

Naturally, the Convention takes particular care to make provision for dangerous cargoes, and a cautionary tale is well worth reporting.

On 29 July 1957, Strick Line accepted hand-over of their new break bulk liner *Seistan*, designed and built for the London service to Gulf ports. Meeting the British Board of Trade requirements, she was compliant with the Fire Appliance Rules 1952 and her Safety Equipment Certificate was valid until July 1959, in accordance with the normal regulations then in force. She had loaded a mixed general cargo in London, bound for Khorramshahr. Among the cargoes loaded were two cases of Toe Puff, described in the Dangerous Cargoes list as: *Several layers of fabric impregnated with cellulose nitrate solvent, rosin* [a solid form of resin] *and dye. Liable to spontaneous combustion. To be packed in hermetically sealed tins and packed in wooden cases and to be stowed away from inflammable cargo and not in the same hold as explosives*. This cargo was loaded in Number 5 hold, which also contained 156 tonnes of commercial explosives, Geophex and gelatine, together with cases of safety fuses and detonators. Given the advice contained in the Dangerous Cargoes list, this demonstrated a breach of the duty of care bordering on recklessness.

On 17 February 1958, as the vessel was entering the Arabian Gulf, via the Mediterranean and Red Sea, smoke was seen issuing from a deck ventilator in the vicinity of No. 5 hold. The hold was immediately filled with steam to smother any flames, an operation which continued 05.30 the next morning, when she anchored about two miles east of the South Sitra Beacon off Bahrein, to discharge the explosives and mitigate the risk. About half the explosive cargo was discharged into a barge alongside and the steam smothering resumed, as the vessel was moved closer to port, even though the fire had not been extinguished. With nightfall on 19 February a glow was observed in the vicinity of Number 5 hold, and at 21.35 a massive explosion destroyed the vessel, shattering the stern and wrapping the after part of the main deck forward over the superstructure. What was left of the ship caught fire and sank by the stern in 40 feet of water. Of the ship's company of 53, the Master, Captain Chappel, seven British officers and all but 18 of the Indian hands were killed, along with four men on a tug which lay alongside.

Chapter VII covers all types of cargo (except liquids and gases in bulk) *which, owing to their particular hazards to ships or persons on board, may require special precautions*. The regulations include requirements for stowage and securing of cargo or cargo units (such as containers) and are subdivided into three parts:

Part A applies to the carriage of dangerous goods in the packaged form under seven regulations, while Part A-1 deals with carriage of dangerous goods in solid form in bulk. Regulation 1, 2 and 3 explain how it is applied and clarifies the terminology which is used in the chapter along with the requirements to carry dangerous goods in the packaged form.

The dangerous cargoes are classified by categories for the stowage of the cargo, with the aim of limiting the risk of error and take preventive action to minimise the risk of damage. As a result failure to check the labels or documentation, or failure to follow the emergency procedure, could lead to serious claims of negligence or even criminal accountability.

Part B of this chapter explains the details about construction and equipment for carrying dangerous liquid chemical in bulk, with clarity, again, on the terminology which is used in the chapter and how it is applied to chemical tankers which carry such cargoes.

Part C sets out detailed requirements for construction and equipment for carrying liquified gas in bulk as cargo. Again, clarity is given to the terminology and the regulations explain how they are applied to gas tankers which carry such cargoes.

The lessons of the *Seistan* are clear indeed.

Chapter IX – Management for the Safe Operation of Ships

The Chapter makes mandatory the International Safety Management (ISM) Code, which requires a safety management system to be established by the shipowner or any company who has assumed responsibility for the ship (the 'Company').

The ISM Code in its current form was adopted by the IMO in 1993 in the wake of the *Herald of Free Enterprise* disaster, in which Mr Justice Sheen concluded in his report that *All concerned in management, from the members of the Board of Directors down to the junior superintendents, were guilty of fault in that all must be regarded as sharing responsibility for the failure of management. From top to bottom the body corporate was infected with the disease of sloppiness.*

The provisions of ISM will be discussed fully later in this book.

Chapter X – Safety Measures for High-Speed Craft

The Chapter makes mandatory the International Code of Safety for High-Speed Craft (HSC Code), consisting of three regulations which address the safety requirements of fast craft, be they monohulls, catamarans, hydrofoils or hovercraft. The need for such regulation arises out of the human element which suffers from awareness issues with distance and closing speeds, giving way to the risk of collision. As early as 2002, the MAIB noted in a casualty report on a collision between the high-speed craft *Diamant* and the ro-ro passenger ferry *Northern Merchant* the dangers of travelling at high speed, in areas of high traffic density and restricted visibility.[1] When compared with conventional merchant ships, accidents with high-speed craft reveal quite different issues related to bridge personnel and operations, and reliance on navigational equipment and procedures can give rise to casualties which the HSC Code is designed to avoid.

Chapter XI – Maritime Safety and Security

This chapter is divided into two sections:

Chapter XI-1 – Special Measures to Enhance Maritime Safety

The Chapter clarifies requirements relating to authorisation of recognised organisations (responsible for carrying out surveys and inspections on Administrations' behalf); enhanced surveys; ship identification number scheme; and port State control on operational requirements.

Chapter XI-2 – Special Measures to Enhance Maritime Security

Prior to entering a port, or whilst in a port, within the territory of a Contracting Government, a ship shall comply with the requirements for the security level set by

1 Report on the investigation of the collision between Diamant/Northern Merchant, MAIB, April 2003.

that Contracting Government, if that security level is higher than the security level set by the Administration for that ship.

Regulation XI-2/3 of the chapter enshrines the International Ship and Port Facilities Security Code (ISPS Code). Part A of the Code is mandatory and part B contains guidance as to how best to comply with the mandatory requirements. Regulation XI-2/8 confirms the role of the Master in exercising his professional judgement over decisions necessary to maintain the security of the ship. It says he shall not be constrained by the Company, the charterer or any other person in this respect.

Regulation XI-2/5 requires all ships to be provided with a ship security alert system. Regulation XI-2/6 covers requirements for port facilities, providing among other things for Contracting Governments to ensure that port facility security assessments are carried out and that port facility security plans are developed, implemented and reviewed in accordance with the ISPS Code. Other regulations in this chapter cover the provision of information to IMO, the control of ships in port (including measures such as the delay, detention, restriction of operations including movement within the port, or expulsion of a ship from port), and the specific responsibility of Companies.

Regulation XI-2/8 confirms the role of the Master in exercising his professional judgement over decisions necessary to maintain the security of the ship. It says he shall not be constrained by the Company, the charterer or any other person in this respect.

Chapter XII – Additional Safety Measures for Bulk Carriers

The Chapter includes structural requirements for bulk carriers over 150 metres in length. It explains some basic issues about the damage stability requirements for bulk carriers, which forms a foundation to explaining aspects of naval architecture such as structural strength and other structural requirements for bulk carriers. Given this knowledge, it then deals with the surveys and maintenance requirements, with further information on compliance.

For the highly technical specialist, it is relevant to draw in a project conducted by the International Association of Classification Societies, (IACS), which critically analysed the structural design rules required to be complied by solid bulk carriers and oil tankers.

Chapter XIII – Verification of Compliance

This chapter makes mandatory the IMO Member State Audit Scheme Compliance, which entered into force in January 1916, requiring submission to undergo periodic audits by the approved organization following the audit standard to verify compliance with and implementation of the present Convention.

Chapter XIV – Safety Measures for Ships Operating in Polar Waters

The chapter has made mandatory[2] the Introduction and part I-A of the International Code for Ships Operating in Polar Waters (the Polar Code). Amendments are made by the Maritime Safety Committee (MSC) from time to time by Resolutions as an alternative to the Draconian requirements to amend a Convention; so, for example, in 2021, Resolution msc.494(104) amended the performance standards for shipborne voyage data recorders (VDRs) (Resolution msc.333(90).

The Polar Code was drafted to apply across a raft of maritime conventions, but the IMO gave it the force of mandatory law when it adopted SOLAS chapter XIV under the title Safety measures for ships operating in polar waters. In addition to the safety of life at sea, environmental issues have been given special attention since case of the *Exxon Valdez*. It is, after all, the risk of environmental disaster that consumes the normative ethics of the people in the Coastal State – but they are the ones who, ultimately, drive the laws which criminalise the Master.

2 From 1 January 2017.

5 Survey Requirements

All ships must be surveyed and verified by officers of the Flag State Administrations or their recognised organisations – in the UK this will involve a Flag State inspection by a surveyor from the MCA, or by a surveyor of Lloyd's Register acting as the MCA's agent. In this respect, SOLAS is not the only Convention to be applied, but also SOLAS, MARPOL, BWM and MLC, among others. The principal ship certificates issued under provisions of the SOLAS Convention comprise:

- Passenger ship safety certificate (PSSC);
- Cargo ship safety construction certificate (SCC);
- Cargo ship safety equipment certificate (SEC);
- Cargo ship safety radio certificate (SRC);
- Cargo ship safety certificate (CSSC);
- Minimum safe manning document (SMD).

The plethora of surveys and certificates involved in this process has been simplified by the Harmonised System of Survey and Certification, which seeks to standardise the period of validity and the intervals between surveys for the nine main convention certificates to a maximum period of validly for all certificates except a passenger ship safety certificate to five years. The streamlined format of the HSSC is designed to benefit the industry in terms of flexibility of survey schedule, reduced numbers of surveyors, survey time and paperwork, all therefore reducing costs.[1]

The survey requirements to be followed will be those contained in the enabling legislation, passed under domestic law which implements the standard adopted by the UK Government; it may be the Convention standard, or a higher standard. Survey and Certification of UK Ships are set out in MSN 1848. So, for example, we find certification requirements contained in the Merchant Shipping (Survey and Certification) Regulations 2015.

In looking at the process for passenger ships, it is useful to bear in mind the definition under SOLAS Regulation I/2 as a ship that carries more than 12 passengers. Therefore, a ship carrying fewer than 13 passengers on a voyage may operate and be certificated for that voyage as a cargo ship. A passenger is a person other than:

1 See MSN 1751.

DOI: 10.4324/9781003361916-5

- The Master or member of the crew or other person employed or engaged in any capacity on board a ship on the business of that ship;
- A child under one year of age (SOLAS Reg I/2).

Having dealt with that, we can turn to the survey of passenger ships, which is addressed under Regulation 6 of the 2015 Regulations:

(1) *... a United Kingdom passenger ship shall be subject to the [following] inspections and surveys.*
(2) *Those inspections are an annual inspection of the ship's bottom, of which two inspections within any five year period are to take place out of the water at intervals not exceeding 36 months.*
(3) *Those surveys are –*
   (a) *before the ship is put in service, a passenger ship initial survey, and*
   (b) *before the end of every period of 12 months following the issue of the ship's Passenger Ship Safety Certificate, a passenger ship renewal survey.*

To extend an example to cargo ships, surveys of cargo ship safety equipment are dealt with under Regulation 7:

A United Kingdom cargo ship of 500 gross tons or more engaged on international voyages shall be subject to the following surveys of its life-saving appliances and other equipment –

(a) *before the ship is put in service, a cargo ship safety equipment initial survey;*
(b) *at the intervals specified in Merchant Shipping Notice MSN 1751 a cargo ship safety equipment renewal survey;*
(c) *within three months before or after the second or third anniversary date of a Cargo Ship Safety Equipment Certificate, a cargo ship safety equipment periodical survey;*
(d) *within three months before or after each anniversary date of the ship's Cargo Ship Safety Equipment Certificate, other than where a periodical survey is required to be carried out within that period, an annual survey.*

Surveys of cargo ship radio installations are addressed under Regulation 8:
A United Kingdom cargo ship of 300 gross tons or more engaged on international voyages shall be subject to the following surveys of its radio installations:

(a) *before the ship is put in service, a cargo ship radio installations initial survey;*
(b) *at the intervals specified in Merchant Shipping Notice MSN 1751 a cargo ship radio installations renewal survey;*
(c) *within three months before or after each anniversary date of the ship's Cargo Ship Safety Radio Certificate, a cargo ship radio installations periodical survey.*

Surveys of cargo ship structure, machinery and equipment fall under Regulation 9:

(1) *A United Kingdom cargo ship of 500 gross tons or more shall be subject to the following surveys of its structure, machinery and equipment, other than equipment to which regulations 7 and 8 apply:*
   (a) *before the ship is put in service, an initial survey;*
   (b) *at the intervals specified in Merchant Shipping Notice MSN 1751 a cargo ship structure renewal survey;*
   (c) *within three months before or after the second or third anniversary date of a Cargo Ship Safety Construction Certificate, a cargo ship structure etc intermediate survey;*
   (d) *within three months before or after each anniversary date of the ship's Cargo Ship Safety Construction Certificate, other than where a cargo ship structure etc renewal or intermediate survey is required to be carried out within that period, a cargo ship structure etc annual survey; and*
   (e) *subject to paragraph (2), two inspections of the ship's bottom to take place out of the water within any five year period, and at intervals not exceeding 36 months.*

(2) *For the purpose of paragraph (1)(e), where a cargo ship structure etc renewal survey takes place within three months after the end of the five year period of validity of a Convention Certificate, and that certificate has been extended in accordance with regulation 17(3) or (4), the period of extension of the certificate shall be deemed to be within the five year period.*

When a survey to meet the requirements set out in these Regulations has been satisfactorily completed in respect of a ship engaged on international voyages, the Certifying Authority shall issue:

(a) *in the case of a passenger ship, a Passenger Ship Safety Certificate, unless the ship is only engaged on short international voyages when a short international voyage Passenger Ship Safety Certificate shall be issued;*
(b) *in the case of a cargo ship of 300 gross tons or more, a Cargo Ship Safety Radio Certificate; and*
(c) *in the case of a cargo ship of 500 gross tons or more –*
   (i) *a Cargo Ship Safety Equipment Certificate or, as the case may be, a Cargo Ship Safety Construction Certificate; or*
   (ii) *after an initial or renewal survey in accordance with regulations 7 to 9 a Cargo Ship Safety Certificate.*

The Master and the Owner share responsibility for compliance, as defined under Regulation 10:

(1) *The owner and master of every ship to which this regulation applies shall ensure that –*

(a) *the ship and its equipment is maintained so as to ensure that the ship in all respects remains fit to proceed to sea without danger to the ship or persons on board;*

(b) *after any survey of the ship required by these Regulations has been completed, no change shall be made in the structural arrangements, machinery, equipment and other items covered by the survey, without the approval of the Certifying Authority, except by direct replacement; and*

(c) *whenever an accident occurs to a ship or a defect is discovered, either of which affects the safety of the ship or the efficiency or completeness of its life-saving appliances or other equipment –*

(i) *it is reported at the earliest opportunity to the Certifying Authority, or a proper officer, and*

(ii) *if a United Kingdom ship is in such a case in a port outside the United Kingdom it is also reported to the appropriate authorities of the country in which the port is situated.*

(2) *If a report is made under paragraph (1)(c)(i), the Certifying Authority or proper officer shall determine whether a survey is necessary, and if so, require one to be carried out.*

(3) *If the survey referred to in paragraph (2) shows that repairs are required, or if any important repairs or renewals are otherwise made to the ship or its equipment, a further survey shall be carried out on the completion of those repairs or renewals.*

If a ship fails a survey, then Regulation 12 is quite categoric:

(1) *Where a surveyor determines that the condition of a ship to which this regulation applies does not correspond substantially with the particulars on one or more of the certificates referred to in these Regulations or is such that the ship is not fit to proceed to sea without danger to the ship or persons on board, the surveyor shall advise the owner or master of the corrective action which in the surveyor's opinion is required, and shall notify the Certifying Authority.*

The consequence is that the ship will be detained. The statutory power to detain a ship is set out in section 95 Merchant Ship Act 1995:

Where a ship which is:

(a) *in a port in the United Kingdom, or*

(b) *at sea in United Kingdom waters, appears to a relevant inspector to be a dangerously unsafe ship, the ship may be detained.*

(2) *... the power of detention conferred by subsection (1) above is exercisable in relation to foreign ships as well as United Kingdom ships.*

Disobedience by the Master can have serious criminal consequences. Under section 98 Merchant Shipping Act 1995:

(1) *If a ship which:*
 (a) *is in a port in the United Kingdom, or*
 (b) *is a United Kingdom ship and is in any other port, is dangerously unsafe, then, subject to subsections (4) and (5) below, the master and the owner of the ship shall each be guilty of an offence.*

Life, however, sometimes does not go according to plan. In May 2006, a somewhat ageing cruise ship, the *van Gogh*, had been due to carry out a series of three short cruises from Harwich to various Norwegian ports. On the first two cruises, the gastrointestinal norovirus broke out among both passengers and crew. On the morning of 28 May, the vessel arrived back in Harwich, having completed the second cruise, when an intensive process of cleaning and sanitation of the ship was ordered and immediately implemented. In this way, everything possible was done to ensure that the third cruise would be virus-free.

Captain Rudge, surveyor for the MCA, would not be persuaded that any process would clear the risk in time, and without further health evidence, issued a detention notice in the terms of his powers and detained the ship until further notice on the grounds that the ship was dangerously unsafe under section 95. The trouble was, that he did not have such a power in respect of a risk to health, and there was no evidence that there was a risk to life as the Act envisaged; but Regulation 28 of the Merchant Shipping and Fishing Vessels (Health and Safety at Work) Regulations 1997 did. After leaving the ship on the evening of 28 May, he continued to consider the detention and at home that evening prepared a second Detention Notice, but this was not taken on board the ship or sent to anyone at that time. Compounding the confusion, Captain Rudge returned to the vessel two days later, on 30 May, and handed the Master a copy of the second notice and also the leaflet *Arbitration on Detention of Merchant Ships and Fishing Vessels* and its associated leaflet *Notice of Reference*, which he should have served at the time when he delivered the first notice. However, following his re-inspection of the ship and a review of the situation on board, he was satisfied that the detention could be lifted, and issued a Notice of Release to the Master and the ship's superintendent later that day, before he left the ship. Meanwhile, the Claimants suffered financial loss and damage for the cancelled cruise.

The Claimants could have followed the procedure under section 96 of the 1995 which provides:

> *Any question as to whether any of the matters specified in relation to a ship in a detention notice in pursuance of section 95(3)(b) in connection with any opinion formed by the relevant inspector constituted a valid basis for that opinion shall, if the master or owner of the ship so requires by a notice given to the relevant inspector within 21 days from the service of the detention notice, be referred to a single arbitrator appointed by agreement between the parties for that question to be decided by him.*

Unfortunately, they failed to follow this procedure, even after service of the notice, so they had to consider some other sort of redress and so sued the Department for Transport instead, on the grounds that they were vicariously liable for Captain Rudge's act of conversion in depriving them of their property, resulting in loss and damage.

At the Trial, Flaux J had to wrestle, no doubt, with some very practical issues surrounding the need to justify the use of detention powers of Port State Control in this case. Rudge had no lawful justification for issuing the notice that he did under the 1995 Act and then seeking to rectify the problem retrospectively, after the damage had been done. What saved him, was that whatever this was, it was not a civil tort of conversion, which was the ground in which the Claimants had sought compensation. A conversion occurs when a person without authority or permission intentionally takes the personal property of another or deprives another of possession of personal property, and treats the property as his own; in this case he did not physically take possession of the ship, and he did not purport to deal with the ship in a way that denied the Claimants' title to her.[2]

Moreover, the whole purpose for the arbitration provision is to vest powers in an arbitrator to make an award for loss occasioned by the surveyor's acts or omissions, because the Claimants would not have any other recourse. It was most unfortunate that the arbitration provision was not invoked; but fortunate for Port State Control that their vicarious liability was not tested in Open Court.

2 *Club Cruise Entertainment v Department of Transport* [2008] EWHC 2794 QBD (the *van Gogh*).

6 Seaworthiness and Risk Management

For better or for worse, the evolution of the law of seaworthiness owes its existence to the importance of maritime commerce to Britain's prosperity, from its burgeoning in the eighteenth century when the confidence of merchant venturers needed underpinning – and to a great extent it is still the influence of commercial risk which guides the law today.

The Marine Insurance Act 1906 has contributed heavily to the success of maritime trade, so it gives us a good starting point to define the nature of seaworthiness today. Section 39 does this, admittedly obliquely, in defining a warranty for seaworthiness:

(1) *In a voyage policy there is an implied warranty that at the commencement of the voyage the ship shall be seaworthy for the purpose of the particular adventure insured.*
(2) *Where the policy attaches while the ship is in port, there is also an implied warranty that she shall, at the commencement of the risk, be reasonably fit to encounter the ordinary perils of the port.*
(3) *Where the policy relates to a voyage which is performed in different stages, during which the ship requires different kinds of or further preparation or equipment, there is an implied warranty that at the commencement of each stage the ship is seaworthy in respect of such preparation or equipment for the purposes of that stage.*
(4) *A ship is deemed to be seaworthy when she is reasonably fit in all respects to encounter the ordinary perils of the seas of the adventure insured.*

Given the imperative of commercial risk in the carriage of goods, it is unsurprising that further guidance on seaworthiness is given in the statutory limitation rules defining and limiting rights and obligations for the carriage of goods by sea. Article III (1) of the Hague-Visby Rules have been incorporated into the Carriage of Goods by Sea Act 1971, stating:

The carrier shall be bound before at the beginning of the voyage to exercise due diligence to:

a. *Make the ship seaworthy;*

DOI: 10.4324/9781003361916-6

b. *Properly man, equip and supply the ship;*
c. *Make the holds, refrigerating and cool chambers, and all other parts of the ship in which goods are carried, fit and safe for their reception, carriage and preservation.*

It is up to the Merchant Shipping Act 1995 to carry the concept of seaworthiness further into the realms of safety, in terms of empowering the MCA to inspect and, if necessary, detain a ship which they find to be dangerously unsafe, as we have seen, under section 95. How the phrase *dangerously unsafe* is to be interpreted, is provided in section 94, which states that a ship is dangerously unsafe if she is unfit to go to sea without serious danger to human life, by reason of:

(a) *the condition, or the unsuitability for its purpose, of–*
  (i) *the ship or its machinery or equipment, or*
  (ii) *any part of the ship or its machinery or equipment;*
(b) *undermanning;*
(c) *overloading or unsafe or improper loading;*
(d) *any other matter relevant to the safety of the ship ...*

One of the foundation cases in determining the meaning of seaworthiness remains *McFadden v Blue Star Line*.[1] Channell J now famously stated:

> *A vessel must have that degree of fitness which an ordinary careful and prudent owner would require his vessel to have at the commencement of her voyage having regard to all the probable circumstances of it ... Would a prudent owner have required that it (i.e., the defect) should be made good before sending his ship to sea, had he known of it? If he would, the ship was not seaworthy ...*

This provides a valid commentary that can be applied to the definition of seaworthiness, which demands that the vessel is not just structurally fit within the meaning of SOLAS to meet the demands of the voyage contemplated, but also that the duty of seaworthiness extends to include:

- A crew which is competent to man the ship and corresponding with the safe manning certificate;
- Up to date chart systems and passage planning that is efficient and managed;
- Sufficient bunkers for the voyage;
- Stowage meeting the stability requirements of the ship;
- Efficient technical systems on board;

1 *McFadden v Blue Star Line* [1905] 1 KB 697.

- All documents required by Flag State and Port State laws law up to the satisfactory completion of the voyage and discharge of cargo and passengers (including SMS and ISPS certificates).

The Case of the *CMA CGM Libra*

Statutory definitions apart, the standard owed by the Master (and the Owner) varies according to factors such as the nature of the voyage, the cargo type and the likely dangers that might be encountered during the passage. It is all about managing the risk to a level that meets the threshold defined as the standard of duty reasonably to be expected in those circumstances, given the knowledge available at that time. In the case of the *CMA CGM Libra*, Lord Hamblen was faced with a judgment on how the statutory limitation rules distinguished between a vessel's quality of seaworthiness or navigability and the crew's act of navigating. As he put it: *It is said that there is a distinction between seaworthiness, which concerns the attributes and equipment of the vessel, and the navigation and management of the vessel, which concerns how the crew operates the vessel using those attributes and equipment.* He concluded:

> *The carrier's obligation under the Hague Rules is not subject to a category-based distinction between a vessel's quality of seaworthiness or navigability and the crew's act of navigating. The crew's failure to navigate the ship safely is capable of constituting a lack of due diligence by the carrier. It makes no difference that the delegated task of making the vessel seaworthy involves navigation.*[2]

The Court of Appeal outlined the factual context in the grounding of the *CMA CGM LIBRA* on leaving the port of Xiamen, China, on a voyage to Hong Kong. The Admiralty Judge in the lower Court, Teare J, found that the vessel's defective passage plan was causative of the grounding and that this involved a breach of the carrier's seaworthiness obligation under Article III Rule 1 of the Hague Rules. The case proceeded to the Supreme Court, where the appellant shipowners contended that the decisions of the courts below were wrong, that the vessel was not unseaworthy and/or due diligence was exercised, and that any negligence in passage planning was a navigational fault which is exempted under Article IV Rule 2(a) of the Hague Rules.

The Court applied the prudent owner test in *McFadden v Blue Star Line* in what he described as *the usual or conventional test on unseaworthiness* established in that case, and found that, in this case, the prudent owner would have required the defective passage plan to be made good before the vessel put to sea, and that it was inconceivable that the prudent owner would have acted otherwise.

2 *Alize 1954 and another v Allianz Elementar Versicherungs AG and others* [2021] UKSC 51 On appeal from: [2020] EWCA Civ 293.

Article IV of the Rules offers the Owner the nautical fault defence if the Claimant's damage results from an act of the Master, or the servants of the owner, in the navigation or management of the ship. In this case, they did not follow the IMO Guidelines for Voyage Planning and ignored the presence of numerous depths less than those charted outside the fairway to be noted on the chart in the passage planning. Then, with the voyage underway, they left the passage which they had planned and navigated outside the fairway to save some time, entering an area of uncharted wrecks and isolated shoals, when she grounded.

With the vessel underway, the second breach may have availed the owners of the nautical fault defence, but the Court found that the second breach arose out of the first, as neither the passage plan nor the chart contained the necessary warning. The Court accordingly concluded that the grounding was caused by the actionable fault of the owners, who were thus liable as a result of unseaworthiness as defined by Article III of the Rules.

It is noteworthy that the downstream consequences for the Master may go far beyond the realms of due diligence. The Merchant Shipping (Safety of Navigation) Regulations 2020 create criminal offences for breach of Chapter V (Safety of Navigation) of SOLAS. As a result, Regulation 9 of the 2020 Regulations create offences out of a range of breaches of Chapter V, including 9 2 (e) regulation (safe navigation and avoidance of dangerous situations), and upon conviction the Defendant may be liable to a fine, or, upon indictment, to a term of imprisonment.

This would have been a very relevant issue indeed had the 2020 Regulations applied to the Master in the *Tasman Pioneer*.

The Case of the *Tasman Pioneer*

On the evening of 1 May 2001, the container ship *Tasman Pioneer* left Yokohama, bound for Pusan in South Korea, with a passage plan to steer west along Japan's Pacific coast and then via the Japan Inland Sea across the Korea Strait. By the following day, however, the Master, Captain Hernandez, was concerned that she was running late.

There was evidence that he had been put under a certain amount of pressure from the Owners, Tasman Orient Line (the Defendant Carrier) and its management company, Technomar, to maintain his original schedule; of course, it had to be carried out in accordance with the Master's responsibility for safety and, as a commercial factor, it was not unreasonable. The Master was also concerned to arrive at Kanmon Strait at a favourable point of the tide because of the significant current in that area.

As a result, the Master took the commercial decision to shorten the voyage time by some 40 minutes and thus amend his original passage plan by taking the channel between the island of Biro Shima and the promontory of Kashiwa Shima, the south-western extremity of the island of Shikoku. At this stage, the Master's decision to alter course certainly took a navigational decision which departed from the passage plan, opening his accountability in respect of SLOAS Chapter V Regulation 34, but had done so in good faith – he was endeavouring to save time and keep to schedule, in accordance with his contractual obligations to meet the ship managers' legitimate demands.

Having altered course, he entered the channel at 02.50 on 3 May – but then, disastrously, the ship lost all images on her starboard radar. He apparently realised that he was now in a precarious position and made a command response to abort the passage through the channel. This manoeuvre was not successful, though, and the ship struck bottom off Biro Shima with such force that her speed was immediately slowed from 15 knots to some 6 or 7 knots. Shortly afterwards the ship took a list to port and water was discovered in the forward ballast tanks and in the forward cargo holds 1 and 2.

It was apparent to the Master that he was now exposed to profoundly serious personal consequences for his actions, amounting potentially to criminal negligence in Japanese territorial waters for which he would very likely be arrested. His fears would have been very rational: in 1970 Japan became the first nation in the world to provide criminal sanctions for acts of pollution that endanger human health, and it would have been a topic of discussion in shipboard circles that Japan's environmental crime laws provide a solid statutory foundation for the prosecution of a variety of crimes related to different acts of pollution, in particular maritime pollution arising out of a ship's foundering. Moreover, Japan's penal code notoriously extended imprisonment to Defendants who had been convicted of professional negligence in road traffic cases and, no doubt, the Japanese authorities would seek to apply this in a maritime context.

The Master ordered the pumps activated but, given his fears for his personal position he did not alert the Japanese Coastguard, as he was obliged to do, or seek other assistance, in particular a salvage tug. The ship then sailed at close to full speed for a further 2 hours, some 22 nautical miles, to get as far away from Japanese sovereign jurisdiction as possible, before anchoring in a sheltered bay. It was only then that the Master contacted the ship managers in Greece, without, however, specifying the cause of damage or its full extent. The managers then arranged for the Coastguard to be advised of the incident and for salvors to be engaged under a Lloyd's Open Form salvage contract. But by now the Master had compounded his criminal accountability for dishonesty, in making up a false story that the ship had hit an unidentified submerged object, and coaching the crew in how they should lie to the investigators – which could only have been motivated by his implementing a plan designed to absolve himself from responsibility or blame for the grounding and lend a veneer of plausibility to his falsehood.

By the time when the salvage team arrived some 14 hours later, the ship was down by the head so severely that the main deck at the forward holds was already under water and the salvage operation commenced with the removal of containers stowed on deck, badly damaged themselves, before the trim could be corrected sufficiently to allow the vessel to be beached, which was done on 10 May, enabling the cargo to be unloaded and temporary repairs to be carried out to the hull. Eight days later she was refloated and towed to Onomichi dockyard for repairs.

She was declared to be a total loss, however and was broken up in September 2001.

The Claimant cargo owners had no interest in the criminal prosecution of the Master because that would not have recovered any damages for the loss of their cargo, and the Master would not have owned sufficient assets against which they could have enforced Judgment for any meaningful sum. They therefore sought to recover damages from the carrier.[3]

It was their case that the Defendant Carrier was liable for the damage to their Claimant cargo owners caused by the negligent navigation of the Master and, in particular, they identified the Master's misconduct post-grounding on that he:

- Failed to notify the Japanese Coastguard;
- Delayed notifying ship management;
- Continued at full speed;
- Ordered crew to alter the ship's charts and lie to investigators.

It was their case that the Master owed them a duty to take reasonable care to avoid actions that might cause them loss; that on the evidence of his conduct post-grounding he had broken that duty of care and that, had he acted properly, salvors would have arrived earlier and on deck cargo would probably have been saved.

The Hague-Visby Rules had been incorporated into the Bill of Lading, Article IV of which defines the carrier's Nautical Fault Defence, in that neither the carrier nor the ship shall be responsible for loss or damage arising or resulting from act, neglect or default of the master … in the navigation or in the management of the ship.

Given that the Claimant cargo owners pleaded all the criteria required to establish negligence, and the Carrier's vicarious liability for their Master's conduct, it was necessary for the Defendant Carrier to argue their case for the Nautical Fault Defence, on the basis that Carriers are responsible for loss or damage caused by matters within their direct control, such as the seaworthiness and manning of the ship at the commencement of the voyage; but they are not responsible for loss or damage due to other causes, including acts or omissions of the Master or crew during the voyage, which are outside their direct control; indeed, they could not override the Master's professional judgment in the navigation of the ship under SOLAS Chapter V.

The Court's evaluation of the evidence about the Master's good faith was not comforting. His initial explanation of the casualty had been that the ship had hit an unidentified floating object and the Court heard that he then schooled the crew to adopt this explanation in the inquiry conducted by the Japanese Coastguard, during which the truth eventually emerged. Mr Justice Williams took the view that his initial decision to use the passage east of Biro Shima and his subsequent attempt to abort the transit, were navigational decisions which he had, indeed, taken in good

3 *Tasman Orient Line CV v New Zealand China Clays Ltd and Others* [2010] 2 Ll R 13.

faith – he was endeavouring to save time and keep to schedule, in accordance with his contractual obligations to meet the ship managers' legitimate demands. Where he abandoned his good intentions lay in his actions after the grounding, held the Judge; in particular, his failure to promptly notify the Coastguard and his managers of the casualty and the ship's position and condition; more seriously still, for its implications of dishonesty, in his fabrication of the story that the ship had hit an unidentified submerged object, which could not have been motivated by his paramount duty to the safety of the ship, crew and cargo. The whole sum of his conduct, the Judge held, *was intended to allow him to misrepresent and lie about the true circumstances of the casualty so as to absolve himself from blame and in particular to hide his reckless decision to transit the inside channel of Biro Shima Island in order to take a short cut route.*[4]

For all its blatancy in terms of gross negligence, the uncomfortable theme clearly establishes the priority given by the Master to his obligation towards the commercial success of the voyage. Where there is a risk to his own exposure to prosecution, the Master must rapidly make a risk–benefit analysis – will the risk to his personal position outweigh the commercial pressure, or vice versa?

The issue penetrates deeper still into the owner's consciousness with the issue of corporate manslaughter. With the evolution of the crime of criminal negligence, the Master may well be arraigned on an indictment with the downstream consequence of incriminating the owner in a very serious crime indeed. It is hardly surprising, therefore, that modern maritime management practice identifies a priority in putting clear water between them and the Master when it comes to corporate accountability, which will be discussed in the next section.

The *Tasman Pioneer* case leaves a great many questions of unfinished business in the Master's role in commercial risk, which clearly remains a defining feature of their relationship with the owner. In other circumstances, the owner might wish to distance themselves from the Master.

The Master has risks and responsibilities not just as the owner's representative, however, but also as the representative of the Flag State whose laws they must uphold. The Master's shipboard management function must first identify the risk in its context, which requires an identification of potential risks, and then mapping out the scope of risk management, to lay the foundation for the question: is it an acceptable risk? We need to consider the objectives of stakeholders: the safety of life and the ship, Port State interests including the environment and, of course, those who have some interest or risk in the outcome of the marine adventure. Central to the management function, therefore, is the Assessment of the risk, for failure to assess it could precipitate all the elements in a case of criminal accountability.

4 Ibid., p. 19.

7 Risk Management in Polar Operations

Any Coastal State in ice-covered areas have the right under Article 234 of UNCLOS to adopt and enforce non-discriminatory laws and regulations for the prevention, reduction and control of marine pollution from vessels in ice-covered areas within the limits of the exclusive economic zone beyond their territorial jurisdiction, for the safety of navigation and where marine pollution could cause major harm to or irreversible disturbance to the pristine environment of the boreal wilderness. In fact, this article was actually adopted as a result of pressure by the Canadian government.[1] Naturally, Canada appreciates that environmental interests are not the only ones at stake; Canadian business has real opportunities, as well.

For all the claims and counterclaims, the geo-political complexion of the region prima facie puts it in the territory of Canada. The Northwest Passage runs across the top of Canada through the Arctic Ocean, between Pond Inlet, on Baffin Island, in the east and Herschel Island in the west. It was the diminutive Royal Canadian Mounted Police ship *St Roch* that pioneered the route. The RCMP serves as both the police and government representatives in the Arctic. Their duties include enforcing Canadian laws and regulations; selling hunting licences; collecting customs duties and taxes; delivering the mail; registering vital statistics; making government allowance, pension and welfare payments; delivering supplies to isolated RCMP outposts; transporting the sick and injured to hospital; and transporting Inuit children to and from residential schools.

With the possibilities presented by global warming, the Canadian government is experiencing new challenges to its claims of sovereignty to territories as far as the North Pole which, of course, would include the Northwest Passage. Canada's claim roused a number of national governments, particularly Russia and Denmark (by reason of Greenland) as well as the United States. Canada's perspective is that they have full sovereignty encompassing the islands/waterways and thereby will assert complete control over all activity in that specific region, in accordance with the general principles defined in UNCLOS, based on the rules concerning determination of baselines in the archipelagic context defined in Part IV. The Canadian government has continually stated that it does support international shipping through the Northwest Passage, as long as Canadian domestic laws, rather

1 Sale R and E Potatov, 2010, The Scramble For The Arctic, Frances Lincoln, London.

DOI: 10.4324/9781003361916-7

than international law, are followed. In July 2007, Prime Minister Stephen Harper reinforced the Canadian position by announcing the construction of up to eight Polar Class 5 Arctic Offshore Patrol Ships and the establishment of a deep-water port in the far North. They would have an insurmountable task to compete with the Arctic policy of President Putin's Russia, however, and the glaring risk of unassailable Russian domination in the region is rendered in sharp focus by the growth of its Arctic warship fleet. In 2020, he approved Russia's *Basic Principles of Russian Federation State Policy in the Arctic to 2035*,[2] defining their Arctic interests, goals and mechanisms of implementation for a generation. The principles preserve the Arctic as a region of peace that remains one of Russia's main national interests in the region, but they are underpinned by Russia's current investment in armed icebreakers for its military forces, and its developing fleet of nuclear icebreakers is currently unassailable.

That being said, in 2022 Russia's Head of Marine Operations Headquarters of the Northern Sea Route to fulfil all of the escort duties in the future. Nevertheless, by 2030, Russia aims to operate at least 13 icebreakers on the route, including 9 nuclear vessels. By that time the official NSR development plan forecasts that 150 million tonnes of cargo will flow along the route, a 5-fold increase over the 30 million or so tonnes in 2022. But such plans were made before the downstream consequences of the invasion of Ukraine, which prompted the West to impose sanctions on Russian oil and for European countries to reduce their reliance on Russian energy to near-, if not net-zero. As a result, future cargo flows of oil and gas will likely be directed to the East as Russia searches for new markets. Moreover, grim predictions of collateral risks from the war saw dramatic downturns in the composition of traffic using the Northern Sea Route. While in previous years around one-third of vessels travelling along the NSR were non-Russian, in 2022 only a handful of foreign ships ventured onto the route. Even China's giant operator, COSCO, which for the past decade had sent up to 15 vessels onto the route each summer, did not dispatch a single ship during the year. By comparison, traffic through Canada's Northwest Passage saw a record-level of transits with 17 ice-strengthened commercial ships pass through.

South of the disputed Arctic waters, the challenges of navigation through winter ice remain despite the increase in global warming. The noted ship *Gladys Bowater* that we encountered earlier in this book was one of a fleet of six, all but identical motorships that were intended to carry raw materials between Bowater's sources in Scandinavia and North America, and deep into the St Lawrence Seaway, indeed the *Gladys Bowater* was the first UK flag ship to transit the seaway on her maiden voyage in 1959. They were all built to the high specification of Lloyds 100 A1 *strengthened for ice class 3*, with sophisticated navigation equipment and steering technology on board. There was no compulsion for such measures but, for all the engineering progress and effects of global warming, even in the twenty-first

2 Basic Principles 2035.

century, the geography remains as hazardous as ever, as evidenced in The United States Coast Pilot:[3]

> *Each season has its own weather problems, each waterway its own peculiarities ... The ice threat is compounded by fierce winter storms which bring a variety of wind, wave, and weather problems on an average of every 4 days. A combination of strong winds, rough seas, and cold temperatures can result in superstructure icing, in which sea spray and sometimes precipitation can freeze to a ship's superstructure. This adds tremendous weight and creates dangerous instability ... Fog can form in any season, but it is most likely in spring and early summer, particularly over open waters. Along the shore, fog is also common in autumn. Occasionally, steam fog will develop during the winter.*

The high seas are open to all States, as expressly provided under Article 87 of UNCLOS, which creates nothing new, but serves to perpetuate this ancient international law and, as Lord Bingham emphasises,[4] the State must comply with its obligations under international law as a fundamental pillar of the rule of law by which it judges and will be judged by others.

The structural demands of safety and stability in polar waters has now been clothed with the force of law in SOLAS Chapter XIV,[5] which since 2017 has made mandatory, the Introduction and part I-A of the International Code for Ships Operating in Polar Waters (the Polar Code). Amendments are made by the Maritime Safety Committee (MSC) from time to time by resolutions as an alternative to the draconian requirements to amend a Convention; so, for example, in 2021, Resolution msc.494(104) amended the performance standards for shipborne voyage data recorders (VDRs) (Resolution msc.333(90). In turn, it is obligatory for States signing up to SOLAS to implement the provisions in their domestic law, by the Flag State, or Port or Coastal State. The Merchant Shipping (Polar Code) (Safety) Regulations 2021 implement the safety requirements of the Polar Code into UK domestic shipping legislation.

The Polar Code applies to ships which operate in polar waters including both those in Antarctica (south of 60°S) and those within the Arctic as specified in SOLAS Chapter XIV and includes mandatory measures covering safety (Part I-A) and pollution prevention (Part II-A), with recommended provisions for both parts.

Operational assessment is a critical part of voyage planning and the attendant risk management in polar waters. In order to establish procedures or operational

3 United States Coast Pilot 6, 38th Edition, 2008, The Office of Coast Survey (OCS), an Office of the National Ocean Service (NOS), National Oceanic and Atmospheric Administration (NOAA) Narragansett, RI.

4 Bingham, T, 2007, The Rule of Law, CLJ 67.

5 Safety measures for ships operating in polar waters.

limitations, an assessment of the ship and its equipment shall be carried out, taking into consideration the following:

1 The anticipated range of operating and environmental conditions, such as:
   - Operation in low air temperature;
   - Operation in ice;
   - Operation in high latitude;
   - Potential for abandonment onto ice or land.
2 Ten categories of hazards are listed in Section 3 of the Introduction to the Code, such as ice which may affect hull structure, stability characteristics, machinery systems, navigation, the outdoor working environment, maintenance and emergency preparedness tasks and malfunction of safety equipment and systems;
3 Any additional hazards, if identified.

With this in mind, ships voyaging in polar waters must carry equipment capable of clearing melted ice, freezing rain, snow, mist, spray and condensation from the windows on the bridge. All lifeboats must be partially or completely enclosed. There must be adequate thermal protection for all persons on board; on passenger ships, an immersion suit or thermal protective aid for each person must be available. Special ice equipment for ice removal, such as electrical and pneumatic devices, and tools such as axes or wooden clubs must be on board the vessel. Extinguishing equipment, operable in cold temperatures, must be protected from ice. These extinguishers must be suitable for persons wearing bulky and cumbersome cold weather gear.

There are three categories of ship which can operate in polar waters, based on whether they are equipped for operation in medium first-year ice, thin first-year ice or less severe ice conditions. Sufficient stability in intact condition when subject to ice accretion on the hull is paramount and stability calculations must take into account the icing allowance. Ships intended to operate in low air temperatures must be constructed with materials suitable for operation in such temperatures. In ice-strengthened vessels, the structure of the ship must be able to resist both global and local structural loads.

Part 1 of the Code contains provisions for safety measures, arranged in specific chapters:

- General;
- Polar water operational manual;
- Ship structure;
- Subdivision and stability;
- Watertight and weathertight integrity;
- Machinery installations;
- Fire safety/protection;
- Life-saving appliances and arrangements;

- Safety of navigation;
- Communication;
- Voyage planning;
- Manning and training.

The provisions for pollution protection arranged in Part II are set out in the following chapters:

- Prevention of pollution by oil;
- Control of pollution by noxious liquid substances in bulk;
- Prevention of pollution by harmful substances carried by sea in packaged form;
- Prevention of pollution by sewage from ships;
- Prevention of pollution by garbage from ships.

The levels of training required for deck officers working on ships that operate in polar waters consist of Basic Training and Advanced Training. In Basic Training, all Masters, chief mates and officers in charge of a navigational watch on ships operating in polar waters must hold a certificate of proficiency (CoP) in Basic Training for Ships Operating in Polar Waters in accordance with STCW Convention Regulation V/4 Para 1 of the STCW Convention. To be issued with a CoP for Basic Training, a deck officer must complete an MCA-approved basic training programme for ships operating in polar waters. The requirement for Advanced Training requires that the Master or chief mate on ships operating in polar waters must hold a Certificate of Proficiency in Advanced Training for Ships Operating in Polar Waters in accordance with STCW Convention Regulation V/4 Para 3. Naturally the requirements for an Advanced Certificate are more demanding. To be issued with a CoP for Advanced Training for Ships Operating in Polar Waters an officer must comply with the following:

- They have met the requirements for certification in basic training for ships operating in polar waters;
- They must have completed two months approved seagoing service in the deck department at either operational or management level polar waters or equivalent;
- They must have completed an MCA approved Advanced Training Programme for Ships operating in Polar Waters.

Given the environmental risks inherent in crude oil pollution, the scale of the disaster presented by the unit size of crude tankers feeds the human need to find somebody to blame, and when the damage is exacerbated by the very remoteness and pristine natural beauty of the environment, the phenomenon of human psychology demands criminal accountability. Professor E Scott Geller[6] has drawn

6 Geller, E, 2011, Psychological Science and Safety: Large-Scale Success at Preventing Occupational Injuries and Fatalities, Current Directions in Psychological Science, Washington DC 20: 109–114.

conclusions from the standpoint of psychology that there is hardly ever a single person to blame for such a disaster, but the human reaction is to demand that the alleged offender be punished by the criminal law, and a single person is already accountable in the person of the Master. How they discharge their accountability is a matter for them.

In March 1989 the *Exxon Valdez* ran aground in Prince William Sound on the Alaskan coast. Roger Howard[7] estimated that, within 5 hours, at least 11 million gallons of crude oil had spilled into the sea, covering some 11,000 square miles of ocean that contaminated 1,200 miles of coastline. Eighty per cent of the cargo stayed on board the vessel, though; ironically, thanks largely to the vessel's Master, Captain Hazelwood, whom the US Coast Guard praised for exemplary handling of the stricken ship, which helped to prevent more cargo spilling into the sea and possibly saving human life as well.[8] Nevertheless, he was prosecuted by the State of Alaska on an indictment which included felonies of criminal mischief, operating the *Exxon Valdez* while intoxicated, and reckless endangerment, as well as a misdemeanour, or less serious charge, of negligently discharging oil. The Jury Trial lasted 2 months, resulting in his acquittal on all the charges except the misdemeanour, when he was sentenced to 1,000 hours of community service, which consisted of picking up rubbish along Alaskan roadside verges, and a compensation order of $50,000.[9] No other individual faced criminal charges, certainly nobody from Exxon, who promptly blamed their Master.[10]

The Master navigating through the High Arctic will be very conscious of four obligations:

- Their obligation to the Flag State as Master;
- Their obligation to observe the Port or Coastal State's rights in the region, however uncertain the geographical boundaries may be;
- Their obligation to the shipowner as Agent as well as Employee;
- Their obligation to protect their own interests, given the industry's conceptualisation of their criminalisation.

The shipowner will be keenly aware of their obligations to the Flag State and to the various Port or Coastal States whose laws they will have to observe. China's faltering economic performance in the wake of the Covid pandemic demanded radical plans to reassert itself and crude traders forecast an aggressive comeback.

7 Howard, R, 2009, The Arctic Gold Rush, Continuum, NY, p. 130. He observes that some pressure groups put the estimate much higher.

8 Behar, R, 1989, Joe Hazelwood's Bad Trip on the *Exxon Valdez*, Time Magazine, NY.

9 Mauer, M, 2010, Criminal Charges were levied after *Exxon Valdez* Spill, Anchorage Daily News, a subsidiary of the McClatchy Company, Sacramento, CA.

10 Exxon subsequently embarked on a spirited defence to criminal litigation in which it was originally fined $150 million, the largest fine ever imposed for an environmental crime; but the Court later reduced this to $25 million in recognition of Exxon's cooperation in cleaning up the spill and paying certain private claims.

As a result, in January 2023 global demand for crude tankers was expected to increase by 10 per cent and product tankers by 12 per cent, while newbuilding supply would only expand by 4 per cent and 2 per cent, respectively, meaning that the world tanker fleet would be hard-pressed to meet the demand.[11] When the *Stena Arctica* was completed in 2005, she was the world's largest tanker in her ice class. Capable of lifting 117,100 tonnes of crude, the Owners were taking no chances, with a heavily reinforced hull that is wide-bodied and shallow, so that she can minimise risk when navigating through hazardous waters, and a propulsion system massively over-specified than that for normal tankers, helping her to get out of trouble as fast as she got into it. She is still in service, and that is not unusual; about a quarter of the world's tanker fleet was over 20 years old in 2023.

The regulatory demands are high, as the international community demands in the modern era of environmental awareness. The revised structural requirements in SOLAS reflect those demands, forcing upward trends in shipbuilding costs that must be balanced somewhere if the Owners' shareholders are going to make the dividends that make their investment risks worthwhile. But the opportunities for profit will be seized, and the seafarer will be at the sharp end if things go wrong.

In May 2023 Russia announced the decision to manage year-round operations in the Northern Sea Route of the High Arctic, which were scheduled to start in 2024. The CEO of Rosatom, which operates the country's nuclear icebreaker fleet, said that the initiative would be made in partnership with the Russian gas company Novatek. The six-day blockage of the Suez Canal in 2021 caused by the grounding of the *Ever Given*, led to daily damages of around US$10 billion to global trade, and led to an increase in oil and liquefied natural gas prices which horrified traders worldwide. Nobody would want such a threat to disrupt maritime trade again, and the Russians are in an excellent position to exploit that, wasting no time in drawing the world's attention to the Northern Sea Route. There is little doubt that the development opportunity of the Northern Sea Route has closely involved China, which has become an increasingly close ally of Russia since the start of the Ukraine war. Although not a member of the Arctic Council, China has shown great interest in the Northern Sea Route, which offers an effective solution to reduce its dependence on the Strait of Malacca, a narrow stretch of water which, if blocked, could hinder 90 per cent of China's trade and 80 per cent of its crude oil imports.

The casualties of the summer of 2010 have been conveniently forgotten, when two Russian-flag tankers owned by the Murmansk Shipping Company, *Indiga* and *Varzuga*, were sailing through the partly ice-covered Northern Sea Route accompanied by the two nuclear powered icebreakers, *Rossia* and *Taimyr*, when the *Varzuga* crashed into the stern of the *Indiga*. The Russian Port State authorities declined to give the exact position, but reported that they collided in difficult

11 www.tradewindsnews.com/tankers.

ice conditions, exacerbated by poor visibility. The authorities further reported that *Indiga* suffered some hull damage but she was not rendered unseaworthy, and no spill was reported.[12] And that was in the summer. Given the average age of the world's tanker fleet, risk management in the High Arctic demands very high professional skills in its seafarers.

12 Source: Barents Observer.

8 The International Convention on Standards of Training, Certification and Watchkeeping for Seafarers 1978, Its Regulations and Its Amendments – STCW

The Convention

The 1978 STCW Convention was the first to establish a basic consensus which determined minimum international standards for training, certification and watchkeeping for seafarers. It was bred from 40 years of declining standards, which originated in the post-war world in which newly independent states were establishing cheap ship registers as a way of gaining economic emancipation, resulting in a reduction in taxation and crew costs that were far lower than British companies could afford within the national laws, and the costs associated with UK crews were making them uncompetitive with rival owners.

The downstream consequence was a global deterioration of standards of training, certification and watchkeeping, as national governments permitted far cheaper and therefore more attractive ship management costs; and far from acknowledging the standards in other countries, they made determined efforts to undercut them. As a result, standards and procedures varied widely, and the stigma of being called a Flag of Convenience hardly troubled them at all.

By the 1970s, industrial action had all but extinguished the British merchant fleet, and the world was becoming dependent on cheap crews and standards, which was endangering the safety of life at sea. The early factors can be summarised:

- A lack of precision in standards of training; for example, in the minimum of sea-time and specific knowledge without defining the skill and competency that were required;
- The number of crew manning a ship was being eroded, largely thanks to the economies of scale and technological advances;
- Ships were benefitting from faster turn-around times in port;
- More frequent crew changes were following the faster turn-arounds, and the mix of different language, education and training backgrounds resulting from multinational manning were presenting noticeable difficulties;
- Challenges of rapid changes in the maritime economy had to be met, in which global trading in commodities made it difficult for traditional operations to predict freight rates;
- Expertise, particularly in traditional shipboard management duties and responsibilities, was struggling to meet the demands of this new generation;

DOI: 10.4324/9781003361916-8

- Fleet expansion was developing as a result of the new patterns in marine operations, in which traditional companies were merging or disappearing altogether, and the fleets under new Flags of Convenience were growing rapidly to meet the demand of the global economy.

The new STCW Convention reflected an international consensus on minimum standards relating to training, certification and watchkeeping for seafarers, which continues to evolve today. The 1995 amendments represented a major revision of the Convention, in response to the emerging need to bring the Convention up to date and to respond to critics who pointed out the many vague phrases which permitted States to take advantage of loopholes; the IMO itself acknowledged the weakness of the phrase *to the satisfaction of the Administration*, which resulted in different interpretations being made.

The 1995 amendments entered into force on 1 February 1997. One of the major features of the revision was the division of the technical annex into regulations, divided into Chapters as before, and a new STCW Code, to which many technical regulations were transferred. Part A of the Code is mandatory while Part B is recommended. Dividing the regulations in this way was said to make administration easier and simplify the task of revising and updating them simpler, so that the IMO can make changes to Codes without a full round of the process to amend the Convention. The unequal commitment by Flags of Convenience towards minimum standards demanded a review of how the IMO could respond to compliance and implementation, for implementation is down to the Flag State, while Port State control also acts to ensure compliance within its territorial seas, leading to tensions between States.

Amendments adopted at a Diplomatic Conference in Manila, Philippines, in June 2010, made important changes aimed at bringing the Convention and Code up to date with developments since they were adopted in 1978 and revised in 1995. The main changes included:

- Improved measures to prevent fraudulent practices associated with certificates of competency and strengthen the evaluation process (monitoring of parties' compliance with the convention);
- Revised requirements on hours of work and rest and new requirements for the prevention of drug and alcohol abuse, as well as updated standards relating to medical fitness standards for seafarers;
- New certification requirements for able seafarers;
- New requirements relating to training in modern technology such as electronic chart display and information systems (ECDIS);
- New requirements for training in marine environment awareness and training in leadership and teamwork;
- New training and certification requirements for electro-technical officers;
- Updating of competence requirements for personnel serving on board all types of tankers, including new requirements for personnel serving on liquefied gas tankers;

- New requirements for security training, plus provisions to ensure that seafarers are properly trained to cope if their ship comes under attack by pirates;
- Introduction of modern training methodology including distance learning and web-based learning;
- New training guidance for personnel serving on board ships operating in polar waters;
- New training guidance for personnel operating dynamic positioning systems.

STCW Convention Chapters

Chapter I: General Provisions

Regulation I/2 deals with the content of the certificate and endorsement form. All certificates must include a translation into English if that is not the official language of the issuing country.

The revised Regulation I/4 includes enhanced procedures concerning the exercise of Port State to allow intervention in the case of deficiencies deemed to pose a danger to persons, property or the environment. This can take place if certificates are not in order or if the ship is involved in a collision or grounding, if there is an illegal discharge of substances resulting in pollution, or if the ship is manoeuvred in an erratic or unsafe manner.

The revised Regulation I/7 provides that States Parties to the Convention are required to provide detailed information to the IMO concerning administrative measures taken to ensure compliance with the Convention, education and training courses, certification procedures and other factors relevant to implementation. The information is reviewed by panels of competent persons, nominated by Parties to the Convention, who report on their findings to the IMO Secretary-General, who, in turn, reports to the Maritime Safety Committee (MSC) on the Parties which fully comply. The MSC then produces a list (the so-called White List) of *Confirmed Parties* in compliance with the Convention. The MSC has a great deal of influence in revising terms in maritime Conventions, and demand a healthy respect.

Chapter II: Master and Deck Department

The Chapter establishes basic principles in maintaining a safe navigational watch, containing mandatory minimum requirements for certification of officers in charge of a navigational watch on ships of 500 gross tonnage or more. It addresses matters including watch arrangements, fitness for duty, navigation, navigational equipment, navigational duties and responsibilities, the duties of the look-out, navigation with a pilot on board and protection of the marine environment.

Officers in charge of a navigational watch include Masters and Chief Mates and Officer of the Watch (OOW's); as well as deck ratings forming part of a navigational watch. The regulations also include basic principles to be observed in keeping watch in port and mandatory minimum requirements for a watch in port on ships carrying hazardous cargo.

The Chapter was revised and updated in 2010. The provisions state that every candidate for certification shall:

- Be required to demonstrate the competence to undertake, at the operational level, the tasks, duties and responsibilities listed in the Regulations;
- At least hold the appropriate certificate for performing VHF radiocommunications in accordance with the requirements of the Radio Regulations;
- If designated to have primary responsibility for radiocommunications during distress incidents, hold the appropriate certificate issued or recognised under the provisions of the Radio Regulations.

In addition to certification as evidence of reaching the minimum standard, an approved programme of onboard training is also required with obligations that:

- During the required period of seagoing service, the candidate receives systematic practical training and experience in the tasks, duties and responsibilities of an officer in charge of a navigational watch;
- It is closely supervised and monitored by qualified officers aboard the ships in which the approved seagoing service is performed;
- It is adequately documented in a training record book or similar document.

Chapter VIII deals with certain key aspects of watchkeeping. MGN 315 presents comprehensive guidance on the range of issues:

- General application for Masters and officers in charge of a navigational watch;
- Fitness for duty;
- Performing the navigational watch;
- Watchkeeping arrangements, handing over the watch and taking over the watch;
- Maintaining a safe look-out and relationship with the look-out;
- Restricted visibility, safe speed, stopping distance and vessel at anchor;
- Certification.

The MCA emphasises the critical point that the Officer of the Watch is the Master's representative and is primarily responsible at all times for the safe navigation of the vessel and for complying with the International Regulations for Preventing Collisions At Sea, known as the ColRegs. The Officer of the Watch must ensure that at all times an efficient look-out is maintained and that ColRegs are complied with. Further emphasis is placed on the need at all times:

- To proceed at a safe speed;
- To ensure that vessel's engines are at the disposal of the Officer of the Watch and there should be no hesitation in using them in case of need;
- To know the handling characteristics of the vessel, including the stopping distance, and should appreciate that other vessels may have different handling characteristics;

- To maintain safe navigation during their entire watch with particular concerns for avoiding collision and stranding;
- To be aware of the serious effects of operational or accidental pollution of the marine environment and shall take all possible precautions to prevent such pollution;
- To have a bridge team avoiding the risk that the Officer of the Watch acts as sole look-out during periods of darkness or restricted visibility.

Much of this chapter responds to the findings in marine accident reports, which conclude that a large number of casualties are attributed to fatigue. Hours of work and rest are defined not only by STCW and laid down by the ILO Convention on Seafarers' Hours of Work and the Manning of Ships, 1996 but also by their Maritime Labour Convention. Any relaxation of the requirements by the Master can only be made to meet overriding operational conditions while the vessel is at sea, permitting only work which cannot be delayed for safety, security or environmental reasons or which could not reasonably have been anticipated at the commencement of the voyage.

The human element in marine operations demands that everybody involved in ship operations, whether shipboard or shoreside, is alert to the factors which can contribute to fatigue, and provisions made to prevent fatigue should ensure that excessive or unreasonable working hours are not undertaken, although the material factors vary from ship to ship and crew to crew.

In addition, drug and alcohol abuse render the seafarer unfit to perform watchkeeping duties that involve attention to safety, prevention of pollution and security. Seafarers found to be under the influence of drugs or alcohol should not be permitted to perform watchkeeping duties or duties that involve designated safety, prevention of pollution and security duties, until they are no longer impaired in their ability to perform those duties.

Readers should be aware that other chapters of STCW cover:

- Engine department;
- Radiocommunication and radio personnel;
- Special training requirements for personnel on certain types of ships;
- Emergency, occupational safety, medical care and survival functions;
- Alternative certification.

The STCW Code

The regulations contained in the Convention are supported by sections in the STCW Code. Generally speaking, the Convention contains basic requirements which are then enlarged upon and explained in the Code, which consists of two parts:

- Part A is mandatory. The minimum standards of competence required for seagoing personnel are given in detail in a series of tables.

- Part B contains recommended guidance which is intended to help Parties implement the Convention. The measures suggested are not mandatory and the examples given are only intended to illustrate how certain Convention requirements may be complied with. However, the recommendations in general represent an approach that has been harmonised by discussions within IMO and consultation with other international organisations.

As a very brief guide, the practice guidance on safe manning covers areas including:

- Maintaining safe navigational, port, engineering and radio watches, as well as general surveillance of the ship;
- Mooring and unmooring the ship safely;
- Managing the safety functions of the ship when employed in a stationary or near-stationary mode at sea;
- Performing operations, as appropriate, for the prevention of damage to the marine environment;
- Maintaining the safety arrangements and the cleanliness of all accessible spaces to minimise the risk of fire;
- Providing for medical care on board ship;
- Ensuring safe carriage of cargo during transit;
- Inspecting and maintaining the structural integrity of the ship;
- Operating in accordance with the approved ship's security plan and the ability to operate:
  - All watertight closing arrangements and maintain them in effective condition, and deploy a competent damage control party;
  - All onboard fire-fighting and emergency equipment and life-saving appliances, carry out such maintenance of this equipment as needs to be done at sea, and muster and disembark all persons on board;
  - The main propulsion and auxiliary machinery including pollution prevention equipment and maintain them in a safe condition to enable the ship to overcome the foreseeable perils of the voyage.

An Evolving Process of Proposals

MSN 1868 (Amendment 1) defines and explains the safe manning requirements contained in the Merchant Shipping (Standards of Training, Certification and Watchkeeping) Regulations 2015 – however, in May 2022 the Government published proposals for new Merchant Shipping (Standards of Training, Certification and Watchkeeping) Regulations 2022, to implement the amendments to STCW into UK law. It was a process in which the Government sought the opinions of maritime industries, as a result of which a consultation on the proposed changes was completed in the summer of 2021, with a view to amending the 2015 Regulations. Although the substance of the proposals has not changed since the consultation took place, the legislative approach is now to replace the 2015 Regulations with a new set of regulations.

In particular, they relate to those seafarers on ships using gases or other low-flashpoint fuels and on passenger ships, as well as provisions aimed at improving the employability of UK seafarers by encapsulating developments in marine technology to make the sector a cleaner, safer and more efficient place to work. The proposed 2022 Regulations were published in accordance with the enhanced scrutiny procedure required by Schedule 8 to the European Union (Withdrawal) Act 2018. The procedure was triggered because the proposed 2022 Regulations revoke subordinate legislation made under section 2(2) of the European Communities Act 1972.

Meanwhile, amendments to the Convention and Code relating to seafarers on ships operating in polar waters are implemented in the Merchant Shipping (Polar Code) (Safety) Regulations 2021.

The Regulations summarise very clearly the Master's duties for maintaining watchkeeping arrangements at sea and while the ship is alongside. Part 4 is particularly valuable, setting out issues of safe manning and watchkeeping arrangements. Summarising Regulation 56:

- The Master must ensure that the watchkeeping arrangements for the ship are at all times adequate for maintaining safe navigational, engineering and radio watches, taking into account the prevailing circumstances and conditions; in accordance with Chapter VIII and the STCW Code;
- In addition, the Master must give directions to the Officers of the Watch in accordance with the Code's principles to be observed in keeping a navigational watch); and any requirements specified in MSN 1868 (Amendment 1b).

Regulation 57 defines the provisions when the ship is safely moored, or safely at anchor under normal circumstances in port, when the Master must arrange for an appropriate and effective watch to be maintained for the purposes of safety. Arrangements in port for ships carrying hazardous cargo (which may be flammable, toxic, health-threatening or polluting to the marine environment) demand a separate section, in Regulation 58, obliging the Master to ensure that a safe deck watch and safe engineering watch are maintained by the ready availability on board of a duly qualified officer or officers and, where appropriate, ratings in support of a team function.

Part 5 of the Regulations imposes responsibilities on companies, Masters and others; in particular, under Regulation 61:

- A company must ensure that a seafarer assigned to any of its ships, other than a hovercraft, holds an appropriate certificate in respect of any function that person performs on that ship;
- A seafarer on any of its ships has had training specified in Part 2 (training and certification: ships) or Part 3 (training and certification: hovercraft) in respect of any function that person performs on that ship;
- Documentation and data relevant to a seafarer employed on its ships are maintained and readily available for inspection and include, without being limited

to, documentation and data on their experience, training, medical fitness and competency in assigned duties.

On-board training is addressed in this Regulation, which obliges the company to provide written instructions to the Master setting out the policies and the procedures to be followed to ensure that all officers and ratings who are newly employed on board the ship are given a reasonable opportunity to become familiar with the shipboard equipment, operating procedures and other arrangements needed for the proper performance of their duties, before being assigned to those duties.

STCW and the Human Element

Perhaps the most important feature of STCW is defined within the meaning of the Human Element, with the aim to enhance maritime safety, security and the quality of the marine environment by addressing human element issues to improve performance.

The human element is a conveniently broad phrase which covers the entire spectrum of human responses to demands placed on seagoing crews, shore-based management, regulatory bodies, recognised organisations, shipyards, legislators and other relevant parties, all of whom need to cooperate to address human element issues effectively. Two features highlighted as the cause of marine casualties have repeatedly been observed:

- Fatigue;
- Complacency.

These two features thus present the biggest pressures on the ability to maintain performance within safety limits. In reality they are unlikely to be eliminated, but can be reduced to a level of acceptable risk from human error.

It is ultimately a matter of shipboard risk management, which, in recent times, owed much to the loss of the *Herald of Free Enterprise*. Her foundering at Zeebrugge in 1986 resulted in the worst UK peace-time maritime disaster since the *Titanic* in 1912. Just as the *Titanic* resulted in the SOLAS Convention, so the *Herald* case resulted in a new generation in safety management, precipitating the International Safety Management Code.

The human element is an important element in the IMO's overarching principles, with a strategic plan which provides that the issues that define the human element will inform the review, development and implementation of new and existing requirements, including skills, education and training, and human capabilities, limitations and needs of seafarers. Great reliance is placed on information communicated by STCW Parties, so the part played by the Master in reporting to the Owners issued defined in the Master's obligations in ISM Code 5.1 cannot be understated, in particular the responsibility with regard to implementing the safety policy of the Company and periodically reviewing the SMS and reporting its deficiencies to the shore-based. This information will be communicated, ultimately to the IMO which will be considered in comprehensive reviews of STCW, not the least covering the imperatives of analysing the implementation issues of STCW with a view to possibly initiating a comprehensive review of the Convention in the near future, and addressing the human element-related work emanating from the IMO's work on Maritime Autonomous Surface Ships.

In terms of Flag State concerns, the MCA commits substantial work through the Human Element Team, producing guidance on seafarer wellbeing and human performance, and analysis of the human element in maritime incidents. It also produces a review of Human Element, Leadership and Management Training (HELM). This is a mandatory course for Masters and Officers aimed at building the skills and competencies to manage and lead crew on board. The MCA also collaborates with the Health and Safety Executive, the UK Government's national regulator for workplace health and safety.

9 International Convention for the Prevention of Pollution from Ships – MARPOL

The Story of MARPOL

The *Torrey Canyon* was a Suezmax size oil tanker with a deadweight capacity of 120,000 tons of crude oil. She was built in the United States in 1959 with a deadweight capacity of 66,000 tons but was jumboised by Sasebo Heavy Industries in Japan. Sailing under the Liberian flag, there was no evidence that she had any hull or machinery defects.

On 18 March 1967, *Torrey Canyon* was under way from Kuwait to the terminal at Milford Haven, UK, loaded close to capacity with 119,328 tons of crude oil on a charter fixed with BP Trading Limited. At about 08.50, she ran aground on the Seven Stones reef, between the Isles of Scilly and Land's End in Cornwall. Over the next 12 days, the entire cargo spilled into the sea. It was the most serious crude pollution event in the world at that time and, within two months, the IMO's Legal Committee held an extraordinary meeting proposing changes in ship design and operation, and subsequently developed a comprehensive framework for compensating victims of pollution incidents and established the International oil Pollution Compensation Funds (IOPC Funds).

Most relevantly, a Conference in 1973 adopted the International Convention for the Prevention of Pollution from Ships, the first MARPOL. Political agendas hindered passage of the proposals, in which it was submitted that, while accidental pollution was spectacular, intentional pollution in the process of marine operations was still the bigger threat. By 1976, MARPOL had only received three ratifications – Jordan, Kenya and Tunisia – representing less than one per cent of the world's merchant shipping fleet.

The downstream consequences of the 1973 Yom Kippur War precipitated a major recession in marine operations, with an impact on safety and environmental protection, until a series of tanker accidents led to a new IMO Conference which, confronted with the facts, adopted measures affecting tanker design and operation. The changes were incorporated into both the Protocol of 1978 relating to the 1974 Convention on the Safety of Life at Sea (1978 SOLAS Protocol) and the Protocol of 1978 relating to the 1973 International Convention for the Prevention of Pollution from Ships. This was adopted in 1978, which explains why today's Convention is referred to as MARPOL 73/78, eventually coming into force in 1983.

DOI: 10.4324/9781003361916-9

MARPOL is managed by the Marine Environment Protection Committee (MEPC) and today covers all aspects of marine pollution from ships. It is arranged in sections entitled annexes.

Scope and Extent

Annex I addresses the prevention of pollution by oil, defining the permissible limits of deliberate discharges from tankers. The revised Annex I came into in force in 2007:

- The total quantity of oil which a tanker may discharge in any ballast voyage whilst under way must not exceed 1/15,000 of the total cargo carrying capacity of the vessel;
- The rate at which oil may be discharged must not exceed 60 litres per mile travelled by the ship;
- No discharge of any oil whatsoever must be made from the cargo spaces of a tanker within 50 miles of the nearest land.

Annex II details the discharge criteria and measures for the control of pollution by noxious liquid substances carried in bulk. The revised Annex II also came into force in 2007. There is an overlap with SOLAS, for the carriage of chemicals in bulk is covered by regulations in SOLAS Chapter VII – Carriage of dangerous goods, and MARPOL Annex II – Regulations for the Control of Pollution by Noxious Liquid Substances in Bulk.

Both Conventions require chemical tankers built after 1 July 1986 to comply with the International Bulk Chemical Code (IBC Code), which sets out the international standards for the safe carriage, in bulk by sea, of dangerous chemicals and noxious liquid substances. The Code prescribes the design and a construction standard of ships involved in the transport of bulk liquid chemicals and identifies the equipment to be carried to minimise the risks to the ship, its crew and to the environment, with regard to the nature of the products carried.

The IBC Code sets out a list chemicals and their hazards, and identifies both the ship type required to carry that product and the environmental hazard rating. In the unlikely event that any chemical tanker still operating was built before 1 July 1986, they should only comply with the IBC Code's predecessor, the Code for the Construction and Equipment of Ships Carrying Dangerous Chemicals in Bulk (BCH Code). This follows a legal rule (confusingly called a convention) that laws should not be made to have retrospective effect, an old English concept that, in theory at least, is respected globally.

Current MARPOL provisions in Annex II define the discharge criteria and measures for the control of chemical pollution. Some 250 substances were evaluated and included in the list appended to the Convention; the discharge of their residues is allowed only to reception facilities until certain concentrations and conditions (which vary with the category of substances) are complied with.

MARPOL sets out the particular substances in five categories in Annex II:

- Category X: Noxious liquid substances that, if discharged into the sea from tank cleaning or deballasting operations, are deemed to present a major hazard to either marine resources or human health and therefore justify the prohibition of the discharge into the marine environment.
- Category Y: Noxious liquid substances that, if discharged into the sea from tank cleaning or deballasting operations, are deemed to present a hazard to either marine resources or human health or cause harm to amenities or other legitimate uses of the sea and therefore justify a limitation on the quality and quantity of the discharge into the marine environment.
- Category Z: Noxious liquid substances that, if discharged into the sea from tank cleaning or deballasting operations, are deemed to present a minor hazard to either marine resources or human health and so justify less stringent restrictions on the quality and quantity of the discharge into the marine environment.
- Other substances: substances which present no harm to marine resources, human health, amenities or other legitimate uses of the sea, such as apple juice, clay slurry, coal slurry, dextrose solution, glucose solution, kaolin slurry, molasses and water.

Where the provisions permit the discharge into the sea of residues of substances in Category X, Y or Z or of those provisionally assessed as such or ballast water, tank washings or other mixtures containing such substances, the following discharge standards will apply:

- The ship must be proceeding en route at a speed of at least seven knots in the case of self-propelled ships or at least four knots in the case of non-self-propelled ships;
- The discharge must be made below the waterline through the underwater discharge outlet(s) not exceeding the maximum rate for which the outlet(s) is (are) designed;
- The discharge must be made at least 12 nautical miles from the nearest land in water of not less than 25 m depth.

There are exceptions which relax the rules in the following circumstances:

- It is necessary to secure the safety of a ship or save life at sea;
- It results from damage to a ship or its equipment, provided that all reasonable precautions have been taken after the occurrence of the damage or discovery of the discharge to prevent or minimise the discharge, and except if the owner or the Master acted either with intent to cause damage, or recklessly and with knowledge that damage would probably result;
- It is approved by the Flag State, when being used for the purpose of combatting specific pollution incidents in order to minimise the damage from pollution. Any such discharge will be subject to the approval of any coastal state government in whose jurisdiction the discharge is expected to occur.

Annex III is designed to prevent pollution by harmful substances in packaged form. Chemicals which are carried in packaged form, in solid form or in bulk are regulated by Part A of SOLAS Chapter VII – Carriage of dangerous goods, which includes provisions for the classification, packing, marking, labelling and placarding, documentation and stowage of dangerous goods.

MARPOL Annex III also sets out regulations for the prevention of pollution by harmful substances in packaged form and includes general requirements for the issuing of detailed standards on packing, marking, labelling, documentation, stowage, quantity limitations, exceptions and notifications for preventing pollution by harmful substances.

For the purpose of Annex III, *harmful substances* are those identified as *marine pollutants* in the International Maritime Dangerous Goods Code, (IMDG). Both SOLAS and MARPOL refer to IMDG, which was developed by IMO as a uniform international code for the transport of dangerous goods by sea.

Annex IV addresses the prevention of pollution by sewage from ships. It contains a set of regulations regarding the discharge of sewage into the sea from ships, including regulations regarding the ships' equipment and systems for the control of sewage discharge, the provision of port reception facilities for sewage, and requirements for survey and certification.

It is generally considered that on the high seas, the oceans are capable of assimilating and dealing with raw sewage through natural bacterial action. Strictly, under Annex IV, the discharge of sewage into the sea is prohibited, except when the ship has in operation an approved sewage treatment plant or when the ship is discharging comminuted and disinfected sewage using an approved system at a distance of more than three nautical miles from the nearest land. Sewage which is not comminuted or disinfected may be discharged at a distance of more than 12 nautical miles from the nearest land when the ship is en route and proceeding at not less than 4 knots, and the rate of discharge of untreated sewage shall be approved by the Port State Administration, which, in turn, is required to ensure the provision of adequate reception facilities at ports and terminals for the reception of sewage, without causing delay to ships.

The Annex entered into force in 2003 and was revised in the following year, before entering into force in 2005. The revised Annex applies to ships, engaged in international voyages, of 400 gross tons and above or which are certified to carry more than 15 persons. The Annex requires ships to be equipped with either an approved sewage treatment plant or an approved sewage comminuting and disinfecting system or a sewage holding tank.

The MEPC is responsible for managing the revision process of the Convention and, in 2013, an amendment introduced, inter alia, a definition for Special Areas as well as relevant requirements for the discharge of sewage from passenger ships in Special Areas and for port reception facilities. The discharge of sewage from passenger ships within a Special Area is generally prohibited under the new regulations, except when the ship has in operation an approved sewage treatment plant which has been certified by the Port State Administration. The sewage treatment plant installed on a passenger ship intending to discharge sewage effluent in Special Areas should additionally meet the nitrogen and phosphorus removal standard when tested for its Certificate of Type Approval by the Administration.

Readers should research online to identify current seas designated Special Areas. So, for example, the discharge requirements for the Baltic Sea Special Area took effect in 2019 for new passenger ships, and in June 2021 for existing passenger ships except for those en route directly to or from a port located outside the Special Area and to or from a port located within defined coordinates within the Special Area, but that do not make any other port calls within the Special Area; but from June 2023 that exception was removed. At least clarity has been established.

Annex V: is designed to eliminate pollution by garbage discharged into the sea from ships. Unless expressly provided otherwise, Annex V applies to all ships, which means all ships of any type whatsoever operating in the marine environment, from merchant ships to fixed or floating platforms to non-commercial ships like pleasure crafts and yachts. Article V was designed to be optional, but more than 150 Countries have signed up to it.

MARPOL Annex V generally prohibits the discharge of all garbage into the sea, except as provided otherwise in regulations related to food waste, cargo residues, cleaning agents and additives, and animal carcasses. Save the exceptions, garbage includes all kinds of food, domestic and operational waste, all plastics, cargo residues, incinerator ashes, cooking oil, fishing gear, and animal carcasses generated during the normal operation of the ship and liable to be disposed of continuously or periodically.

Garbage does not include fresh fish and parts thereof generated as a result of fishing activities undertaken during the voyage, or as a result of aquaculture activities.

Naturally, the effectiveness of MARPOL's discharge requirements depends largely upon the availability of adequate port reception facilities, especially within Special Areas. As a result, the Convention obliges Port State administrations to ensure the provision of adequate reception facilities at ports and terminals for the reception of garbage without causing undue delay to ships, and according to the needs of the ships using them. It is worth pointing out that MARPOL extends exceptional authority to Port State Control inspectors, permitting them to enter a foreign-flagged ship at a port or an offshore terminal of its State, in the case of Article V *where there are clear grounds for believing that the master or crew are not familiar with essential shipboard procedures relating to the prevention of pollution by garbage.*

In addition to Special Areas, Chapter 3 of MARPOL Annex V makes use of the environment-related provisions of the Polar Code mandatory, and requires that ships trading the Polar Regions must comply with strict environmental provisions specific to the harsh conditions in Polar waters – the Arctic waters and the Antarctic area.

Under Regulation 10.2, all ships of 100 gross tonnage and above, every ship certified to carry 15 persons or more, and every fixed or floating platform must carry a garbage management plan on board, which includes written procedures for minimising, collecting, storing, processing and disposing of garbage, including the use of the equipment on board. It must designate the person responsible for the plan and be written in the working language of the crew. The following section requires all ships of 400 gross tonnage and above and every ship which is certified to carry 15 persons or more engaged in voyages to ports and offshore terminals under the jurisdiction of another Party to the Convention and every fixed or floating platform to provide a Garbage Record Book and to record all disposal and incineration operations. The date, time, position of the ship, description of the garbage and the estimated amount incinerated or discharged must be logged and signed. The Garbage Record Book must be kept for a period of two years after the date of the last entry. This regulation does not in itself impose stricter requirements – but it makes it easier to check that the regulations on garbage are being adhered to as it means ship personnel must keep track of the garbage and what happens to it. It could also prove an advantage to a ship when local officials are checking the origin of discharged garbage – if ship personnel can adequately account for all their garbage, they are unlikely to be wrongly penalised for discharging garbage when they have not done so. Appendix 2 of MARPOL Annex V provides a standard form for a Garbage Record Book.

Annex VI has received the closest attention because of its relevance to global warning. It was introduced in 1997 and contains regulations for the Prevention of Air Pollution from Ships. The critical purpose was to minimise airborne emissions from ships (sulphur oxides, nitrogen oxides, Ozone-depleting substances, volatile organic compounds emitted as gases in shipboard incineration) and their contribution to local and global air pollution and environmental problems. Annex VI entered into force in 2005 and was revisions in 2008, came into force in 2010, giving time for shipowners to comply.

The MEPC's plan is the progressive reduction globally in emissions of the offending gases, and the introduction of emission control areas (ECAs) to reduce emissions of those air pollutants further in designated sea areas. Proposals for total bans were subject to a feasibility review, but the sulphur limit of 0.5 per cent became effective in 2020. Once again the reader is urged to check the flow of announcements, not the least being the MEPC's session in July 2023 revising the IMO's greenhouse gas reduction targets for the maritime sector, outlining *a basket of technical and economic measures to be developed to set global shipping on an ambitious path towards phasing out greenhouse gas emissions.*[1]

In addition, Annex VI prohibits deliberate emissions of ozone depleting substances, which include halons and chlorofluorocarbons (CFCs). New installations containing ozone-depleting substances are prohibited on all ships. No new ships may be constructed with installations containing hydro-chlorofluorocarbons (HCFCs), which were phased out in 2020.

New mandatory measures to cut the carbon intensity of international shipping have been under constant review, and amid the Covid restrictions in 2021, the MEPC met remotely to adopt amendments to Annex VI that combine technical and operational approaches to improve the energy efficiency of ships, as well as establishing a new foundation for progressive measures to reduce greenhouse gases. The new measures will require all ships to calculate their own Energy Efficiency

1 The IMO's own words.

Existing Ship Index following technical means to improve their energy efficiency and to establish their annual operational carbon intensity indicator and rating, which links greenhouse gas emissions to the amount of cargo carried over distance travelled. Ships will get a rating of their energy efficiency, from A – the best – to E, the acceptable level being C. A ship rated D for three consecutive years, or E, is required to submit a corrective action plan, to show how the required index (C or above) would be achieved. These amendments are expected to deliver the first ratings in 2024.

The hazards of global warming have been understood by nearly all authorities as being exacerbated by man-made pollution, and the effects were observed alarmingly around the world with every consecutive summer since 2022, forcing naval architects to satisfy a new demand in marine operations. As long ago as 2013, marine engine builder Rolls Royce was engrossed in a venture to develop a twenty-first century version of the Chine Clipper ship, in order to persuade a new age of maritime investors to take a leap into the subjective world of risk and reward which balances the profitability of merchant ship design in the ever-growing world of environmental regulation. The B9 ship project, in which Rolls Royce was a partner, owed its rationale to the inevitable demand upon shipowners to operate within the IMO's regulations and, with such an impetus, it joined a feverish race in merchant ship design that somehow goes back to the future. The result was an ultra-modern dry cargo vessel's hull, with a remarkable sail-plan of square sails on three masts that undeniably resembles the sail plan of the clipper ships, brought into the twenty-first century by technology that dispenses with rigging and all the associated crewing costs and health and safety risks, with operating systems managed directly from the bridge; but, somewhat mirroring the era of the early steamships, augmented by marine engines – in this case, fuelled by environmentally sensitive biomethane gas. Initial analysis following towing tank tests suggested an estimated fuel consumption for the wind-assisted vessel of 46 per cent to 55 per cent less than an equivalent conventional ship on the same route. Just as the tea clippers could recover their construction costs from their tea cargo profits in 5 years, so, it was estimated that Rolls Royce's ship design would pay off the investment costs within 5 years of what the project team claim to be a trading life of 30 years: 1½ times that currently of a new dry bulk carrier. The trouble is that the new project had to attract investment of $22 million within 2 years, or the cost of research and development could not be justified to the investors who must take the risk. Nothing changes very much.

10 MARPOL – Issues of Accountability

MARPOL makes a strict liability offence of a pollution event in the Coastal State's waters and, by the same token, gives the Master a due diligence defence, which need only be proved on the civil burden of the balance of probabilities that they could not reasonably have done more in the discharge of their Flag State duties. Even if that were established, UNCLOS provides for monetary penalties only for a pollution offence except in the case of a wilful and serious act of pollution in the territorial sea – again, hardly an issue to conducting when the Master is exercising their Flag State duties. But tensions between Flag States and Port States have arisen due to the conflicting agendas which define their social priorities, and the seafarer gets caught between them. No better example can be found than that of the case of the Master and Mate of the *Hebei Spirit*.

The Case of the *Hebei Spirit*

In a very competent summary of Korean Environmental Law, Hong Sik Cho clarified the historical background which explains the rationale of South Korea's law on environmental protection and its enforcement. He observed that the enactment of the country's first national environmental law, the Pollution Prevention Act, took place in 1963, the year in which Korea's initial five-year economic plan was initiated by then President Park Chung Hee. Korea's phenomenal rate of economic growth was accelerating by more than eight per cent every year, which was more than double that enjoyed by most others. Hong Sik Cho observed that Korean people thought everything had to be done 'faster and faster'; but it was achieved at a terrible cost, for the downstream consequence of this massive industrialisation expansion resulted in a rapid and worrying deterioration of the country's natural environment, which, in later years, was dubbed a 'poison prosperity' which led to a reassessment of the need for environmental protection in the national consciousness. Hong Sik Cho may have surprised even himself when he discovered that political activists who had devoted themselves to the democracy movement in the 1970s and 1980s became environmental activists themselves, when the state of their environment became so seriously apparent.[1] As a result, a structured

1 Hong Sik Cho; Environmental Law, Vol. 29, 1999.

DOI: 10.4324/9781003361916-10

movement of Non-Governmental Organisations, or NGO's, developed to champion environmental causes, in a trend which has won the support of the body of the Korean people, because they have awoken to the environmental catastrophe which they had nearly brought upon themselves with their industrial expansion. The effect which such concerns have upon the normative ethics of coast state society provides a compelling rationale for criminalisation – if not justification.

It is against this background that the case of the *Hebei Spirit* followed. At about 07.30 on 7 December 2007, near South Korea's Port of Daesan, a crane barge owned by Samsung Heavy Industries, that had been involved in a towage operation in which a tug had lost control after the line parted in heavy seas, collided with the *Hebei Spirit*, carrying 260,000 tonnes of crude oil. Although no casualties were reported, the collision punctured 3 of the 5 tanks aboard the *Hebei Spirit* and resulted in the leaking of some 10,800 tonnes of crude.

The spill occurred near one of South Korea's most beautiful and popular beaches, contaminating one of Asia's largest wetland areas. It was disastrous for wildlife because these areas were relied upon by migratory birds as well as resident wildfowl and marine life. As a national maritime park, with a host of fish farms, the region provided the living for hundreds of Korean families. Now these resources were annihilated, under the glare of the world's media, which compounded the humiliation of the people and their government.

The South Korean government declared a state of disaster in the region, with a clean-up cost estimated at US$330 million, involving 30 aircraft and 327 vessels. News cameras carried highly emotive pictures of hundreds of thousands of volunteers and celebrities including popular Korean actress Park Jin Hee helping to clean up the beaches in the campaign. According to the South Chungcheong provincial government, 33 days after the casualty, the number of volunteers topped the 1,000,000 mark. The government called an emergency meeting of ministers involved and Prime Minister Han Duck-Soo called for a major campaign to minimise damage, while, with just ten days to go before the presidential elections, the candidates in this comparatively young democracy hastened to the area in order to show sympathy for those who had lost their livelihoods. The political consequences of inaction would rapidly manifest themselves at the ballot box. Sympathy was not enough: the Will of the People demanded the accountability of an Accused, and the Master was that person.

South Korean criminal procedure shares features both of the adversarial and inquisitorial systems, having been founded on a merger of American and German criminal procedures. It was not until February 2008 that a limited system of jury trials was adopted for criminal cases and environmental cases, and all questions of law and fact are determined by judges.

On reflection, it was, perhaps, unsurprising that normative ethics of South Korean society demanded that the State should react with criminal prosecutions against those whom it believes to be accountable. Naturally, the evidence must first be examined in order to establish the facts of the case which, no doubt, would establish a solid foundation upon which to prosecute the Accused. But the trial of the Master of the *Hebei Spirit*, Captain Jasprit Chawla, an Indian national, pre-dated the casualty report dramatically. In a press statement released by the Prosecutor's Office in January 2008 after the indictments had been signed, it was announced that the decision had been taken to prosecute Captain Chawla as well as his first officer of the *Hebei Spirit* and the skippers of the barge and two tug boats that towed it, all for failure to exercise due caution:

> *Captain Chawla (of Hebei Spirit) overlooked the possibility of collision and carelessly assumed that the tug boat fleet would safely pass by a distance of about 280 metres (918 ft).*

The South Korean criminal legal system distinguishes between serious offences and less serious offences, and crimes of a violent nature are distinguished from property-related crimes. There was no element of dishonesty in the case against Captain Chawla, mitigating the seriousness of the case against him even further. In the event, the Trial Judgment, in June 2008, cleared Captain Chawla and his chief mate of all charges, although the skippers of the tugs were jailed for marine pollution offences – one of whom was also convicted of a serious offence of dishonesty, for falsifying navigation records.

Then, within a week, the State Prosecutors lodged an appeal, which would require a re-hearing of the case against Captain Chawla and his chief mate. It was now abundantly clear that the State's Central Maritime Safety Tribunal would have to deliver its final adjudication well in advance of the appeal hearing. As it happened, it took just under a year for that to happen.[2] Responsible Examiner Jong Eui Kim concluded that the collision was caused when the crane barge ensemble lost its towing ability in bad weather, yet still continued to navigate without taking any safety measures, such as warning the other vessels nearby or performing emergency anchoring. Despite the fact that the *Hebei Spirit* was anchored in an area frequented by navigating vessels, it was found that her command management was negligent in performing its duty and was idle in handling the situation, whereby it failed to take early and active preventative measures. In addition, it was averred, the fact that the tanker's main engine was not operable amounted to negligence in engine readiness, in a situation where there was a risk of collision, resulting in the failure to take preventative measures. The examiner concluded that the cause of South Korea's worst-ever pollution event was the crane's jib puncturing the cargo tanks of the *Hebei Spirit*, resulting in the cargo spilling into the sea. The report followed with a conclusion that the pollution event had been exacerbated due to *inappropriate emergency measures taken by Hebei Spirit after the collision occurred, which increased the speed at which the oil spilt.*

However argued, flawlessly or otherwise, the Tribunal's adjudication was finally signed on 4 December 2008 – just 6 days short of the date set for the appeal

2 Central Maritime Safety Tribunal, Decision Junghaeshim No. 2008-26, Marine pollution caused by the collision of "Samsung No. 1" (barge), towed by tugboats "Samsung T-5" and "Samho T-3," and M/V "Hebei Spirit" (oil tanker), Notice of Decision on 4 December 2008.

hearing, on 10 December, when the Court reversed the decision of the lower Court and convicted Captain Chawla, who was sentenced to 18 months' imprisonment, not for the physical spill, but on 2 charges alleging property-related offences of criminal damage – damage to his own ship, that is. As regards his actual misconduct, the Court held that Captain Chawla's criminal accountability rested on a number of key mistakes, although only limited fault attached to his acts or omissions before the crane barge actually hit the vessel. Before the collision, he should have gone full astern to drag anchor to prevent the collision with the drifting crane barge. Then after the collision he should not have pumped inert gas into the cargo holds, which had the effect of increasing the spillage when the explosive risk was low. Additionally, he should have shifted ballast in order to create a sufficient list to take the cargo away from the hole in the damaged hull, which would have prevented the oil spill.

The global maritime industry was outraged, but was powerless to intervene; the process was entirely subject to the sovereign right of South Korea, to determine its own judicial process; that is, the system which tries the Accused for liability under the chosen system of the State's constitution. No matter how the international community responded to the decision, the South Korean process met the demands of its society; it is very pertinent that Agence France-Presse reported that about a hundred residents of the area affected by the spill clapped outside court after the judges issued their Judgment. One said laconically,

> *We are satisfied with the verdict.*[3]

The Defendants promptly appealed but, in April 2009, the Supreme Court dismissed the appeals in relation to the charges of pollution, although it accepted the appeal in relation to the somewhat bizarre charge of the wilful destruction of the *Hebei Spirit*, for which they had received prison sentences. This decision upholding the pollution convictions was reached in the teeth of a storm of protest worldwide from supporters of the 'Hebei Two' and has not been forgotten by the maritime world. Its real value now, however, is to illustrate the difficulty encountered in a globalised society, which perceives that a decision, however inviolate in the law of the relevant jurisdiction, nevertheless offends the normative ethics of that globalised society – and the most vulnerable individual in that society is the one who is most exposed to the hazards of the domestic jurisdiction of a Port State: the Master.

Conclusions and Cautionary Tales

It may be argued that the decision of the Korean Supreme Court presented a miscarriage of Justice. In fact it may not be justice, but it is the law, and it is this

3 See AFP newswire report, Court jails tanker officers over S Korea's worst oil spill, 10 December 2008; www.afp/article/ALeqM5i762frrt2NK0zY7cuE7p6WxxRJiw.

tension between justice and fairness which has brought the topic of criminalisation to the top of the maritime agenda. The position in law underlines the tension between Port and Coastal States on one side and Flag States on the other, focusing on the interpretation by Coastal States of their sovereign authority to enforce their society's approach to the characteristics of a moral wrong and how that must interface with their international obligations to Convention partners such as Flag States. The Court in any democracy, after all, is bound by the constitutional parameters of its powers, which have been accorded to it by the State, that is, by its own People in a democratic system. If the State loses confidence in the international process to serve the People in that democratic system, then, in their conviction, domestic law, rather than their international obligations, should prevail, rather than the other way around. It is as a result of this logical argument that international consensus on pollution control in territorial waters has been eroded. The downstream consequence results in the phenomenon of criminalisation, creating offences which lead to the prosecution of offenders that previously were not considered crimes by act or omission, but which have been made crimes by Society notwithstanding the human rights of the offender.

Public concern for global warming has perpetuated the concern for emissions, which has driven the MEPC towards ever stricter regulation, which has been implemented in Port State jurisdictions, as Captain Evans Hoyt discovered in Marseille in 2018. Captain Hoyt was Master of the cruise ship *Azura*; in November 2018 he pleaded Guilty to burning bunker fuel containing 1.68 per cent sulphur – above the European limit of 1.5 per cent as it then was, relating to passenger ships. Captain Hoyt was prosecuted, along with the owners, after a spot check. Mitigation was difficult because Captain Hoyt knew that the fuel was illegal, but the Defence case at the Trial argued that European environment rules unfairly distinguished between cruise ship limits and those for cargo vessels, which is higher, revealing an unfair discrimination in the law.

The maximum penalty was one year in prison and a €200,000 fine. In the event, the Court fined him €100,000, but specified that Carnival, the parent company of the owners, should pay €80,000 of the sum.

11 The International Convention for the Control and Management of Ships' Ballast Water and Sediments – BWM

Invasive species are groups of living organisms that are not native to the marine area which they have colonised, with the consequence that they can compete with native organisms for limited resources predate them and causing extinctions of native flora and fauna, and the native species have no defence because evolution has not equipped them to combat the invaders. As a result, non-native colonisation has been identified as one of the top five major threats to the ecosystem.

One of the most efficient methods of migration for invasive marine species is through ballast water. An example of dangerously successful colonisation can be found in the case of the green crab; originating in Europe, it found its way into ballast water, which was discharged at the end of the voyage and, consequently, has been identified in Southern Australia, South America, South Africa and coastlines in the United States. It has few predators, aggressively hunts and eats its prey, destroys seagrass, and outcompetes local species for food and habitat. Efforts to eradicate such invasive species in the water column have proved all but impossible; thus, the key is to control their migration in ballast water exchange.

The International Convention for the Control and Management of Ships' Ballast Water and Sediments was adopted in 2004 but did not enter into force until 2017. It supports the provisions of UNCLOS regarding the prevention, reduction and control of pollution of the marine environment, and the rationale in UNCLOS Article 196:

> *States shall take all measures necessary to prevent, reduce and control pollution of the marine environment resulting from the use of technologies under their jurisdiction or control, or the intentional or accidental introduction of species, alien or new, to a particular part of the marine environment, which may cause significant and harmful changes thereto.*

There is a strict audit trail, as the Ballast Water Management Convention requires all ships to implement a Ballast Water and Sediments Management Plan, and officers and crew are under a duty to familiarise themselves with their duties to implement and maintain the plan. All ships must carry a ballast water record book, and the inevitable evidence of an international ballast water management certificate; they are also required to carry out ballast water management procedures to a given standard. Parties to the Convention are given the option to take additional measures

DOI: 10.4324/9781003361916-11

which are subject to criteria set out in the Convention and to guidelines produced by the MEPC. In addition to the work of the MEPC, Scientific and Technical Research and Monitoring calls for Parties individually or jointly to promote and facilitate scientific and technical research on ballast water management; and monitor the effects of ballast water management in waters under their jurisdiction.

It is important to note that, just with other Conventions, parties may take more stringent measures with respect to the prevention, reduction or elimination of the transfer of harmful aquatic organisms and pathogens through the control and management of ships' ballast water and sediments, consistent with international law – that is their sovereign right. It is the ship's responsibility to ensure that they observe the Regulations of the Flag State into whose jurisdiction they are sailing.

The Convention applies to all vessels that operate in the waters of more than one Party to the Convention – in other words, ships on international voyages. It applies to all vessels, regardless of size or tonnage, to which a Convention State has allocated its flag. There are obvious exceptions, such as ships with permanent ballast water in sealed tanks and not subject to discharge, while the usual Convention exceptions apply to warships, naval auxiliary or ships owned or operated by a State and used only on Government non-commercial service.

There are exceptions to the obligation to meet the ballast water management standards, which do not apply to:

- The uptake and discharge of ballast water necessary for ensuring the safety of the ship in emergency situations;
- The accidental discharge or ingress of ballast water as a result of damage to the ship or its equipment;
- The uptake or discharge of ballast water for the purpose of avoiding or minimising pollution incidents from the ship;
- The uptake and subsequent discharge on the high seas of the same ballast water;
- The discharge of ballast water from a ship at the same location where the whole of the ballast water originated, provided no mixing of unmanaged ballast water from other areas has occurred. If mixing occurs, the ballast water is subject to management in accordance with the Convention.

Port States must ensure that ports and terminals where cleaning or repair of ballast tanks occurs, have adequate reception facilities for the reception of sediments.

Article 7 of the Convention sets out provisions for Survey and Certification. Ships are required to be surveyed and certified and may be inspected by Port State Control officers who can verify that the ship has a valid certificate; they can inspect the Ballast Water Record Book, and, or in the alternative, take samples of the ballast water. If there are concerns, then a detailed inspection may be carried out and the Port State shall take such steps as will ensure that the ship shall not discharge ballast water until she can do so without presenting a threat of harm to the environment, human health, property or resources. That being said, Article 12 is devoted to avoiding undue delay to ships, providing that all possible efforts shall be made to avoid a ship being unduly detained or delayed.

The Ballast Water Management Plan must be in an approved format (Regulation B-1) which must be kept on board and duly maintained. The plan is specific to each ship and includes a detailed description of the actions to be taken to implement the Ballast Water Management requirements and supplemental Ballast Water Management practices.

Ships must have a Ballast Water Record Book (Regulation B-2) to record when ballast water is taken on board; circulated or treated for Ballast Water Management purposes; and discharged into the sea. It should also record when Ballast Water is discharged to a reception facility and accidental or other exceptional discharges of Ballast Water.

Ballast Water Exchange is set out in detail in Regulation B-4. All ships using ballast water exchange should, whenever possible, conduct ballast water exchange at least 200 nautical miles from the nearest land and in water at least 200 metres in depth, taking into account Guidelines developed by IMO. In cases where the ship is unable to meet these terms, the exchange should be as far from the nearest land as possible, and in all cases at least 50 nautical miles from the nearest land and in water at least 200 metres in depth. When these requirements cannot be met areas may be designated where ships can conduct ballast water exchange. All ships shall remove and dispose of sediments from spaces designated to carry ballast water in accordance with the provisions of the ships' ballast water management plan.

There is a ballast water exchange standard and a separate ballast water performance standard. Ballast water exchange could be used to meet either of two performance standards:

- Ballast Water Exchange Standard – Ships performing Ballast Water exchange shall do so with an efficiency of 95 per cent volumetric exchange of Ballast Water. For ships exchanging ballast water by the pumping-through method, pumping through three times the volume of each ballast water tank shall be considered to meet the standard described. Pumping through less than three times the volume may be accepted provided the ship can demonstrate that at least 95 per cent volumetric exchange is met;
- Ballast Water Performance Standard – Ships conducting ballast water management shall discharge less than 10 viable organisms per cubic metre greater than or equal to 50 micrometres in minimum dimension and less than 10 viable organisms per millilitre less than 50 micrometres in minimum dimension and greater than or equal to 10 micrometres in minimum dimension; and discharge of the indicator microbes shall not exceed the specified concentrations.

Ultimately, the Convention requirements are all about risk assessment. The fundamentals are based on scientific analysis of the problem, and then applied to mediate a solution which both the risk society of a Port State and the commercial demands central to the Flag State can live with. The result is a risk management model that both sides can live with.

Risk management is nothing more than the activity which co-ordinates recognition of risk, risk assessment, developing strategies to manage it and mitigation of risk using managerial resources. The objective is to reduce different risks related to a pre-selected domain to the level accepted by society through statutory authority. We shall be looking at risk management is its broader context in another chapter but, within the meaning of risk in ballast water management, the science driving the Convention is defined in two parts:

- Species-specific studies, in which the assessment is defined by an analysis of particular units or groups of harmful species;
- Environmental risk assessment, applied to voyages where the ballast is loaded and then discharged in bioregions which share few or no natural organic characteristics, giving rise to very different biodiversities, that can be seriously damaged by cross-contamination.

It is a fact of life that risk in this context would be hard to eliminate completely, but risk management seldom seeks to achieve this; instead, the science assumes that society accepts that acceptable risk scenarios exist, which can be identified by risk assessment, to which can be applied risk mitigation strategies, which burdens the shipowner with a cost that is achievable within their vessel operation cost. The Convention, therefore, is designed to achieve a solution which is not necessarily ideal for the Port or the Flag State, but is something which both can live with. If a Port State's risk society demands more protection, that would have to be achieved in higher standards in their domestic Regulations.

12 The Maritime Labour Convention – MLC – Overview

The Maritime Labour Convention, 2006 was not established and monitored by the IMO, but by the International Labour Organisation (ILO). The broad picture described by the ILO placed the MLC as the 'fourth pillar' of maritime regulation covering international shipping, alongside the Convention for the Safety of Life at Sea (SOLAS), the Convention for the Prevention of Pollution from Ships (MARPOL), the Convention for the Training, Certification and Watchkeeping of Seafarers (STCW). Since then, of course, a fifth pillar has been established with the Convention for the Control and Management of Ships' Ballast Water and Sediments (BWM).

It was designed to create a single, coherent instrument setting out the minimum international standard and drawing together more than 65 international labour standards related to seafarers adopted over the last century. Its function is to protect seafarers' employment and social rights on board a ship – indeed, anywhere while the seafarer's employment agreement subsists.

The Articles set out the broad principles and responsibilities, while the Regulations set out the basic requirements. The Code contains the details for the implementation of the Regulations. It comprises Part A (mandatory Standards) and Part B (non-mandatory Guidelines). The content areas are covered in five Titles:

- Title 1. Minimum requirements for seafarers to work on a ship:
    a) No person below the minimum age shall be employed or engaged or work on a ship;
    b) The minimum age at the time of the initial entry into force of this Convention is 16 years;
    c) A higher minimum age shall be required in the circumstances set out in the Code.

- Title 2. Conditions of employment:
    a) The terms and conditions for employment of a seafarer shall be set out or referred to in a clear written legally enforceable agreement and shall be consistent with the standards set out in the Code;
    b) Seafarers' employment agreements shall be agreed to by the seafarer under conditions which ensure that the seafarer has an opportunity to

DOI: 10.4324/9781003361916-12

review and seek advice on the terms and conditions in the agreement and freely accepts them before signing;

c) To the extent compatible with the Member's national law and practice, seafarers' employment agreements shall be understood to incorporate any applicable collective bargaining agreements.

- Title 3. Accommodation, recreational facilities, food and catering:
  a) Each Member shall ensure that ships that fly its flag provide and maintain decent accommodations and recreational facilities for seafarers working or living on board, or both, consistent with promoting the seafarers' health and wellbeing;
  b) The requirements in the Code implementing this Regulation which relate to ship construction and equipment apply only to ships constructed on or after the date when this Convention comes into force for the Member concerned;
  c) Unless expressly provided otherwise, any requirement under an amendment to the Code relating to the provision of seafarer accommodation and recreational facilities shall apply only to ships constructed on or after the amendment takes effect for the Member concerned.

- Title 4. Health protection, medical care, welfare and social security protection:
  a) Each Member shall ensure that all seafarers on ships that fly its flag are covered by adequate measures for the protection of their health and that they have access to prompt and adequate medical care whilst working on board;
  b) The protection and care under paragraph 1 of this Regulation shall, in principle, be provided at no cost to the seafarers;
  c) Each Member shall ensure that seafarers on board ships in its territory who are in need of immediate medical care are given access to the Member's medical facilities on shore;
  d) The requirements for on-board health protection and medical care set out in the Code include standards for measures aimed at providing seafarers with health protection and medical care as comparable as possible to that which is generally available to workers ashore.

- Title 5. Compliance and enforcement:
  a) The Regulations in this Title specify each Member's responsibility to fully implement and enforce the principles and rights set out in the Articles of this Convention as well as the particular obligations provided for under its Titles 1, 2, 3 and 4;
  b) Paragraphs 3 and 4 of Article VI, which permit the implementation of Part A of the Code through substantially equivalent provisions, do not apply to Part A of the Code in this Title;
  c) In accordance with paragraph 2 of Article VI, each Member shall implement its responsibilities under the Regulations in the manner set out in the

corresponding Standards of Part A of the Code, giving due consideration to the corresponding Guidelines in Part B of the Code;

d) The provisions of this Title shall be implemented bearing in mind that seafarers and shipowners, like all other persons, are equal before the law and are entitled to the equal protection of the law and shall not be subject to discrimination in their access to courts, tribunals or other dispute resolution mechanisms. The provisions of this Title do not determine legal jurisdiction or a legal venue.

In fairness, a considerable amount of the Convention's concerns had been addressed in long-standing UK laws, such as the right to a safe and secure workplace that complies with safety standards, the right to decent working and living conditions on board ship, and the right to health protection, medical care, welfare measures and other forms of social protection. Examples of sections in the Merchant Shipping Act 1995 include:

- 30 Payment of seamen's wages;
- 38 Right, or loss of right, to wages in certain circumstances;
- 42 Obligation of shipowners as to seaworthiness;
- 43 Crew accommodation;
- 44 Complaints about provisions or water;
- 45 Expenses of medical and other treatment during voyage;
- 73 Relief and return of seamen, etc.

Notwithstanding that, British companies had adopted practices earlier still, predating Regulations by decades. The General Steam Navigation Company demanded very high standards in their Masters and expected all employees to use their initiative, but also provided the sea staff with exceptional welfare and conditions on board ship; indeed, their vessel *Kingfisher* was delivered in 1944, the first to be built in which each rating had his own cabin, and set a Company trend, and General Steam was so far ahead of its time, that not until the twenty-first century did the International Labour Organisation bring the global shipping industry into such thinking with the MLC.

The dovetailing between Convention obligations and existing domestic laws is achieved through the concept of substantial equivalence. Aimed at ensuring flexibility in the implementation of maritime instruments, the concept is defined in Article VI(3) of the MLC, which provides that a ratifying State may, unless expressly provided otherwise in the Convention, implement the rights and principles of the Convention in a manner different from that set out in mandatory standards if it satisfies itself that the relevant legislation or other implementing measure is conducive to fulfil the achievement of the general object and purpose of the provisions of those standards and gives effect to those provisions.

It will be noted that the State's obligation is to *satisfy itself* that its existing legislation *is conducive* to meeting the general object and purpose of the Convention standards; this may cause tension between States implementing and monitoring the standards, raising issues as to whether obligations have been met in good faith. Substantial equivalence had already been acknowledged in Article 2(a) of the Merchant Shipping (Minimum Standards) Convention, 1976, to reflect the idea that deviations from the terms of the Convention could be admitted as long as the general level of protection remained the same. In 1990 the International Labour Office expressed its position that:

> *The test for substantial equivalence may be, first, whether the State has demonstrated its respect for or acceptance of the main general goal of the Convention and enacted laws or regulations which conduce to its realisation; and if so, secondly, whether the effect of such laws or regulations is to ensure that in al material respects the subordinate goals of the Convention are achieved.*[1]

The position of the UK on substantial equivalence was clarified in guidance contained in December 2020.[2] It defined two kinds of substantial equivalence under UK Regulations:

- Those embedded in Regulations, as an alternative means for UK ships to comply with the provisions of the MLC, which are available to all ships subject to any limitations of restrictions specified in the Regulations;
- Ship-specific substantial equivalences – generally relating to crew accommodation.

MGN 472 adopts am approach through a broad consultation between the shipowners' and the seafarers' representatives; effectively, this means that in all cases any individual application meets the approval of the UK Chamber of Shipping, Nautilus and the National Union of Rail, Maritime and Transport Workers (RMT). Other organisations may be consulted if a more specialised sector of the industry is involved.

Defining Issues

1 *The Seafarer*

As an international instrument defining seafarers' rights, the fundamental questions arises as to who a seafarer is. The MLC states that any person, including the

1 Committee of Experts on the Application of Conventions and Recommendations, 1990, General Survey of the Reports on the Merchant Shipping (minimum Standards) Convention (no. 147) and the Merchant Shipping (improvement of Standards) Recommendation (no. 155), 1976, International Labour Office.

2 MGN 472 Amendment 3. Maritime Labour Convention, 2006; Guidance on the procedure for applying for a Substantial Equivalence.

Master, who is employed or engaged or works in any capacity on board a ship on the business of the ship but does not include a person who –

- Is training in a sail training vessel;
- Is onboard a sail training vessel other than for training but is not engaged in or responsible for the navigation of the vessels; and has no emergency safety responsibilities on the vessel.

The MCA's interpretation of a seafarer was set out in MGN 471[3] and identified certain differences in interpretation:

- The Master's own conditions of employment should be protected by the MLC, the same as any other person working on board the ship; but the MCA observed that the Master is the owner's representative and the owner has primary responsibility for ensuring seafarers' rights under the Convention. The distinction between Master and crew is highlighted in the Merchant Shipping (Maritime Labour Convention) (Hours of Work) Regulations 2018, by which the Master will commit an offence under Regulation 25, which may lead to prosecution, for failure to observe hours of rest;
- The definition of a seafarer may vary according to the type of ship concerned;
- The MCA emphasises the relevance of adding the words *whose normal place of work is on a ship* which ensures that surveyors, pilots and visiting technical consultants are not caught by the definition. It also offers a somewhat obscure example of a passenger who happens to answer some business e-mails while on holiday on board, but cannot claim to be a seafarer.

That being said, the term 'seafarers' includes persons such as shopkeepers, resident entertainers and hairdressers who are employed by a franchise company to work on board. It may also include self-employed persons who work on board the ship on the business of the ship, but does not apply to those persons whose work is not part of the routine business of the ship and whose principal place of work is ashore, for example, marine professionals such as harbour pilots, inspectors or superintendents; scientists researchers, divers, specialist offshore technicians. Importantly, the term does not include those who are working on a seagoing ship on an occasional and short-term basis, for example, fitters, guest lecturers and entertainers, repair technicians, surveyors or port workers. If the individuals perform other duties on board the vessel including drills they are considered to be seafarers.

For special purpose ships, the MCA will, on application from the shipowner, consider issuing a statement stating that Special Personnel on board a UK ship are not considered as seafarers and therefore are not subject to the MLC.[4]

3 MGN 471 Amendment 1 Maritime Labour Convention, 2006 definitions.
4 MGN 674 Application of the special purpose ships code.

The issue of whether a cadet is a seafarer, was addressed by the MCA,[5] which sets out guidance that cadets and other trainees fall within the definition of seafarers because they are engaged and therefore require a seafarer's employment agreement (SEA) under the MLC.

But certain of the provisions relating to SEAs are not easily applied to the engagement of cadets and other trainees on board ship. In particular, most trainees will have a training agreement with their training provider or sponsor, rather than an employment agreement with a shipowner, which may cover both the cadet's shipboard experience and their time at a training establishment. Some trainee seafarers are not paid wages, but receive instead a training bursary, creating issues of interpretation in terms of employment law.

Where a training provider places cadets on a ship, there may be no formal agreement between the cadet and the shipowner. Indeed the cadet may be engaged on several different ships, with different shipowners, during their period of training. MGN 485 sets out the conditions under which a training agreement will be accepted as an SEA subject to UK provisions which meet the requirements of substantial equivalence to the MLC.

Notwithstanding that, the training agreement will be recognised as substantially equivalent to an SEA but must include information about frequency and method of payment, including information about any charges made for transfer of funds, and exchange rates if applicable. It is permissible for the amount paid when the seafarer is at sea, and the amount paid when the seafarer is at college (when their living expenses will be greater), to be different, provided that this is made clear in the agreement. If they are required to conduct work, account for their hours of work and are eligible for protection under the Employment Rights Act 1996, they will be seafarers.

The safety and security issues demanded in modern shipping is not new, but the provisions of armed guards must be addressed by the MLC. Whether an armed guard is a seafarer will depend on Flag State Rules and Regulations; but the Master will remain accountable for the consequences of all acts on board their ship. Whether they can discharge that burden will depend on the evidence.

2 *The Ship*

The UK has interpreted this as all ships ordinarily engaged in commercial activities to mean all vessels that are not employed for personal pleasure. But, confusingly, such vessels may apply voluntarily for a Maritime Labour Certificate, which will be necessary for commercial activities. The Merchant Shipping (Maritime Labour Convention) (Survey and Certification) Regulations 2013 apply to all United Kingdom ships on international voyages, subject to exceptions:

5 MGN 485Maritime Labour Convention, 2006: Seafarer Employment Agreements – Application to Trainees

- Pleasure vessels;
- Fishing vessels;
- Ships of traditional build;
- Warships or naval auxiliaries;
- Vessels which are not ordinarily engaged in commercial activities;
- Vessels which operate only within 60 miles of a safe haven, and do not operate to or from, or call at, a port in a country other than the United Kingdom, and in this sub-paragraph 'safe haven' means a harbour or shelter of any kind which affords safe entry and protection from the weather.

But the key question remains, as to what is a ship?

Under the MLC, the term 'ship' means a ship other than one which navigates exclusively in territorial waters, thus covering all ships ordinarily engaged in commercial activities – but there are exceptions.

The definition of a ship under English law has long suffered from ambiguity and conflicting meanings. One might argue that we have not moved on very far since Lord Scrutton observed in 1926:

> *One might possibly take the position of the gentleman who dealt with the elephant by saying that he could not define an elephant but he knew what it was when he saw one.*[6]

Beware of Conflicts with other jurisdictions, because there is no single definition under English law, so it is necessary to explore the range of authorities that might assist in offering some consensus.

There is no common definition of a ship in English statutes. Thus:

- The Marine Insurance Act 1906 Schedule 1 r 15 provides that the term 'ship' includes the hull, materials and outfit, stores and provisions for the officers and crew, and, in the case of vessels engaged in a special trade, the ordinary fittings requisite for the trade, and also, in the case of a steamship, the machinery, boilers, and coals and engine stores, if owned by the assured;
- In the Carriage of Goods By Sea Act 1971 Article 1 in the Schedule follows the Hague Rules as amended by the Brussels protocol 1968 to define a 'ship' as *any vessel used for the carriage of goods by sea*;
- Section 24 Supreme Court Act 1981 states that a 'ship' includes any description of vessel used in navigation;
- The Pilotage Act 1987 follows the meaning of 'Ship' as defined in the Harbours Act 1964:
- *'ship,' where used as a noun, includes every description of vessel used in navigation, seaplanes on the surface of the water.*

6 *Merchants Marine Insurance Co. v North of England P and I Association* (1926) 26 Ll. L. R. 201, at 203

The UN Maritime Code 1994 has been somewhat clearer and, as a body of international guidance, might carry more persuasive influence between jurisdictions:

> *'ship,' with the exception of the warship, is any waterborne craft intended for seagoing navigation, exceeding 12 m in length and a gross tonnage of 15 tons, or authorized to carry more than 12 passengers.*

But in the interpretation of some common understanding, some insuperable conflicts have arisen.

The case of *R v Goodwin*[7] involved an appeal against conviction by the accused, Mark Goodwin, who was charged following a collision between the jet ski which he was riding with another jet ski, whose rider was injured, and indicted on a single count of Conduct endangering ships, structures or individuals, contrary to Section 58(2)(a) Merchant Shipping Act 1995, which states that if a person, while on board his ship or in its immediate vicinity, does any act which causes or is likely to cause the death of or serious injury to any person, he shall be guilty of an offence.

In delivering Judgment, Lord Phillips CJ said that the relevant provisions, as the title 'Merchant Shipping' suggested, were primarily aimed at shipping as a trade or business, not at pleasure craft such as jet skis:

> *While it may be possible to extend the meaning of ship to vessels which are not employed in trade or business or which are smaller than those which would normally be so employed, if this is taken too far the reduction can become absurd.*[8]

This decision raised great controversy and other jurisdictions have held quite differently. In the 2002 Canadian case of *Attorney-General v McNally Construction,*[9] the issue arose as to whether a range of trade agreements applied to the procurement by a Government department of a jet-propelled patrol boat for use in the coastal waters of the Maritime provinces. In the Appeal hearing in Ottawa in 2002, the Court considered decisions from wider jurisdictions, including the United States, and in particular the

2005 case of *Stewart v Dutra Construction Company.*[10] This involved a claim under the Jones Act, but unfortunately the Jones Act did not define the term 'Vessel,' so the Judges drew on a range of authorities to conclude in a unanimous decision that a 'vessel' included any watercraft capable of transportation.

Notwithstanding confusion under English law, further substance followed with the decision in the Canadian case of *Sillars.*[11] The Defendant had been charged

7 *R v Goodwin* [2005] EWCA Crim 3184; [2006] 1 W.L.R. 546.
8 Para 32.
9 *Canada (Attorney General) v. McNally Construction Inc. (C.A.)*, 2002 f CC 633.
10 *Stewart v Dutra Construction Company (03-814) 543 U.S. 481* (2005) 343 F.3d 10.
11 *R v Sillars*, 2018 ONCJ 816.

with impaired operation of a vessel causing death, operating a vessel with over 80 mg of alcohol in 100 mg of blood, dangerous operation of a vessel and criminal negligence causing death. The Defendant had been paddling a canoe at the time, so the Court had to rule whether this constituted a vessel. Section 214 of the Canadian Criminal Code defined a vessel as *a machine designed to derive support in the atmosphere primarily from reactions against the earth's surface of air expelled from the machine.* Drawing assistance both from Canadian and United States jurisdictions, the Court took notice of the fact that the United States federal offence of 'boating under the influence' pertained to all boats, ranging from canoes to the largest ships. It concluded that a canoe was a vessel.

Such well-articulated conclusions offer a solution which can be applied in the international context to define a 'Vessel' having the minimum characteristics as those contained in *Sillars*; but there has to be some clarification as to whether the words 'Ship' or 'Vessel' are to be used to mean the same thing, supporting the definition in Title 47 of the US Code that *The term 'ship' or 'vessel' includes every description of watercraft or other artificial contrivance, except aircraft, used or capable of being used as a means of transportation on water, whether or not it is actually afloat.*

The definition produced grave concern in criminal law, however, because of the loophole which thereby enabled a Defendant abusing powered watercraft to evade Guilt in a criminal offence. It was not until the Merchant Shipping (Watercraft) Order 2023 that legislation closed the gap by applying the dangerous use provisions of the Merchant Shipping Act 1995 to powered watercraft; thus Article 3 states that watercraft means any type of craft which:

(a) *is capable of moving under its own mechanical power,*
(b) *is used, navigated or situated wholly or partly in or on water, and*
(c) *is capable of being used to carry one or more persons.*

Subsection 2 then preserves the English Courts' fondness for distancing such objects from merchant vessels by stating that it does not include a ship or fishing vessel.

Further confusion arises under English law in conflict with the ILO. In UK Revenue legislation, the definition of a ship was addressed for the purpose of seafarer deduction Regulations; acknowledging that the word 'ship' is not defined in tax law, 'offshore installations' used in the offshore oil and gas industry are specifically identified and are not regarded as ships for the purposes of the deduction. Examples of offshore installations, include the following:[12]

- Fixed production platforms;
- Floating production platforms;
- Floating storage units;

12 HS205 Seafarers' Earnings Deduction (2020). Updated 6 April 2022.

- Floating production storage and offloading vessels;
- Mobile offshore drilling units (drillships, semi-submersibles and jack-ups);
- Flotels;
- Any vessel engaged in exploitation of mineral resources by means of a well whilst standing or stationed in any waters, is an offshore installation.

By this definition, therefore, a drillship or survey vessel taking samples would not be a 'ship.' But this creates potential absurdities that shipowners and mariners must understand. As early as the 1970s, *Wimpey Sealab* had the benefit of a leap in technology which provided a 'stay-still' solution, delivering a computerised dynamic positioning system while she surveyed coal deposits off the north coast of England. She then traded the North Sea for the comparatively calm climate of the English Channel – and the tense business of carrying out her survey work amidst one of the world's busiest sea-lanes, sometimes in fog as supertankers, gas carriers and busy passenger ferries passed by, when the wash from their movement often made it difficult for the ship's dynamic positioning equipment to meet the exacting demands of keeping exactly on-station, and even a modest movement could buckle or break the long, thin drill that stretched down to the sea-bed. In order to do her job, under conditions in which conventional mooring was impossible, she was steered with the help of satellite navigation and her position was maintained by a digital computer into which was fed information such as wind speed and direction, and her heading controlled by computer, with sophisticated satellite technology, while the Master still retained command of the ship. The skills demanded in navigation and wider shipboard management functions are obvious and relevant to the competency of the seafarers; precisely the same skills are demanded of shipboard teams in such vessels today, yet the UK Revenue law defies the definition of a seafarer in the context of the MLC.

Finally, the UN Maritime Code 1994 has been somewhat clearer and, as a body of international guidance, might carry more persuasive influence between jurisdictions:

> *'ship,' with the exception of the warship, is any waterborne craft intended for seagoing navigation, exceeding 12 m in length and a gross tonnage of 15 tons, or authorized to carry more than 12 passengers.*

3 *The Owner*

Notwithstanding complexities of definition, the question of ownership responsibility must be addressed. In English law, the Merchant Shipping Act 1995 mainly defines the owner or bareboat charterer as employer, but can be every agent managing loading, preparing and sending the ship to sea when it comes to seaworthiness for the seaman's safety throughout the voyage. A 2021 case on a separate matter had an effect on the definition of responsibility. In the case of the *Stema Barge II*[13]

13 *Splitt Chartering APS v Saga Shipholding Norway AS (the Stema Barge II)* [2021] EWCA CIV 1880.

the Court of Appeal considered the meaning of 'operator' within the context of its application to the Limitation Convention 1976. It clarified the point that, while there may be more than one owner, charterer, manager or operator, only those who are involved in the management and control of the vessel will be held accountable (in this context enabling them to limit their liability under the Limitation Convention 1976. Those who merely provide assistance to a vessel will be unable to limit their liability and, by extension of the analogy, would fall outside the definition of responsibility in English law.

Under the MLC, the Shipowner includes the manager, agent or bareboat charterer, who has agreed to take over the duties and responsibilities imposed on Shipowners regardless of whether any other organisation or persons fulfil certain of the duties or responsibilities on behalf of the Shipowner. In this case, it is important to declare the use of a regulated private recruitment service. Overlaps and distinctions with English law must be understood.

MLC amendments 2022

This overview addresses the foundations and detail of the Convention, but amendments adopted by the IMO in May 2022 make important changes to the 2006 draft.[14] The full reference can be found in the footnote but some of the key changes are summarised here.

Amendments to the Convention and its standards responded to particular issues in the following:

- Regulation 1.4 – Recruitment and placement. The purpose of the Code is to ensure that seafarers have access to an efficient and well-regulated seafarer recruitment and placement system.

The amendment requires each Member (Flag State) to establish a system of protection, by way of insurance or an equivalent appropriate measure, to compensate seafarers for monetary loss that they may incur as a result of the failure of a recruitment and placement service or the relevant shipowner under the seafarers' employment agreement to meet its obligations to them, and ensure that seafarers are informed, prior to or in the process of engagement, of their rights under that system.

- Regulation 2.5 – Mandatory Repatriation Requirements for Seafarers to Ensure that Seafarers are Able to Return Home.

The amendment provides that Members shall facilitate the prompt repatriation of seafarers, including when they are deemed abandoned where, in violation of the requirements of this Convention or the terms of the seafarers' employment

14 www.ilo.org/wcmsp5/STCMLC/Part II/2022.

agreement, the shipowner fails to cover the cost of the seafarer's repatriation, or has left the seafarer without the necessary maintenance and support, or has otherwise unilaterally severed their ties with the seafarer including failure to pay contractual wages for a period of at least two months. It requires that Port States, Flag States and labour-supplying States shall cooperate to ensure that seafarers engaged on a ship to replace seafarers who have been abandoned in their territory, or on a ship flying their flag, shall be accorded their rights and entitlements under this Convention.

- Regulation 3.1 – Accommodation and recreational facilities.

Appropriate seafarers' recreational facilities, amenities and services, including social connectivity, as adapted to meet the special needs of seafarers who must live and work on ships, shall be provided on board for the benefit of all seafarers, taking into account Regulation 4.3 and the associated Code provisions on health and safety protection and accident prevention.

As to recreational facilities, mail and ship visit arrangements, reasonable access to ship-to-shore telephone communications, where available, with any charges for the use of these services being reasonable in amount. So far as is reasonably practicable, shipowners should also provide seafarers on board their ships with Internet access, with charges, if any, being reasonable in amount.

As to runs ashore, Members should, so far as is reasonably practicable, provide seafarers on board ships in their ports and at their associated anchorages with Internet access, with charges, if any, being reasonable in amount.

- Regulation 3.2 – Food and catering.
  - (a) food and drinking water supplies, having regard to the number of seafarers on board, their religious requirements and cultural practices as they pertain to food, and the duration and nature of the voyage, shall be suitable in respect of quantity, nutritional value, quality and variety, and shall be provided free of charge during the period of engagement;
  - (b) the organization and equipment of the catering department shall be such as to permit the provision to the seafarers of adequate, varied, balanced and nutritious meals prepared and served in hygienic condition.

- Regulation 4.1 – Medical care on board ship and ashore.

This Regulation is aimed mainly at Port and Flag States and address access to medical care for seafarers working on board ships. Amendments include new paragraphs:

- Each Member shall ensure prompt disembarkation of seafarers in need of immediate medical care from ships in its territory and access to medical facilities ashore for the provision of appropriate treatment.

- Where a seafarer has died during a ship's voyage, the Member in whose territory the death has occurred or, where the death has occurred on the high seas, into whose territorial waters the ship next enters, shall facilitate the repatriation of the body or ashes by the shipowner, in accordance with the wishes of the seafarer or their next of kin, as appropriate.

Medical care ashore is addressed with new paragraphs:

- Each Member should ensure that seafarers are not prevented from disembarking for public health reasons, and that they are able to replenish ships' stores, fuel, water, food and supplies.
- Seafarers should be considered to be in need of immediate medical care in cases of, but not limited to:
  - (a) any serious injury or disease;
  - (b) any injury or disease which might lead to temporary or permanent disability;
  - (c) any communicable disease which poses a risk of transmission to other members of the crew;
  - (d) any injury involving broken bones, severe bleeding, broken or inflamed teeth or severe burns;
  - (e) severe pain which cannot be managed on board ship, taking account of the operational pattern of the ship, the availability of suitable analgesics and the health impacts of taking these for an extended period;
  - (f) suicide risk;
  - (g) a tele-medical advisory service recommending treatment ashore.
- In this respect, amendments to Regulation 4.3 are relevant, addressing Health and safety protection and accident prevention:
- (b) reasonable precautions to prevent occupational accidents, injuries and diseases on board ship, including through the provision of all necessary appropriately sized personal protective equipment and measures to reduce and prevent the risk of exposure to harmful levels of ambient factors and chemicals, as well as the risk of injury or disease that may arise from the use of equipment and machinery on board ships.
- In relation to fatal accidents, each Member shall ensure that:
- All deaths of seafarers employed, engaged or working on board ships that fly its flag are adequately investigated and recorded, and reported on an annual basis to the Director-General of the International Labour Office to be published in a global register;
- The fatality data to be reported under subparagraph (a) of paragraph 5 of Standard A4.3 should be in the format, and using the classification, as specified by the International Labour Office.
- The fatality data should include, but not be limited to, information on the type (classification) of death, ship type and gross tonnage, location of fatality (at sea, in port, at anchorage), and seafarer's sex, age, occupational position and department.

13 The MLC – The Application of the Convention

The MCA follows the ILO Guidelines on Flag State Inspections, but incorporating the MLC amendments 2014. In summary, each ship, regardless of whether she is required to have a Maritime Labour Certificate or not, will be surveyed or inspected twice in every five years, with the intermediate survey or inspection being carried out between the second and third years, following the normal pattern of international Convention certificates. To achieve cost-efficiency and minimise inconvenience, MLC surveys should be carried out at the same time as International Safety Management (ISM) Code audits of individual ship Safety Management Certificates (SMC).

The survey must be carried out by the Flag State; thus, in the UK inspections will be performed by the MCA or its designated Recognised Organisation (RO), generally Lloyd's Register. It is important to understand that the RO merely acts as the Flag State's agent, having no executive powers of its own.

Survey and Certification

MSN 1848 (Amendment 2) deals with the Survey and Certification of UK Ships. Vessels of 500 gross tonnes and over operating internationally or in a foreign port require a Maritime Labour Certificate. The Certificate is valid for five years, subject to an intermediate inspection between the second and third year, after which the certificate may be endorsed.

The Regulations do not apply to pleasure vessels, fishing vessels, ships of traditional build, warships or naval auxiliaries and ships not ordinarily engaged in commercial activities. Problems arise with superyachts, for which there is no compulsory application under the MLC and, therefore no 'seafarers' for whom provision under the five titles must be made, because the MLC categorically does not apply to 'pleasure vessels.' But if a yacht is not MLC compliant because it was exempt and subsequently gets, for example chartered and therefore must comply, the compliance procedure would be essential. A seafarer in such circumstances would no longer be 'exempt,' all seafarers would then have to have an SEA and the domestic legislation in the Flag State would have to be applied. Hence voluntary compliance would be a wise precaution.

DOI: 10.4324/9781003361916-13

The Survey & Certification regime is structured in three parts:

- Initial survey: before the first issue of a Maritime Labour Certificate to the ship;
- Renewal survey: at five yearly intervals following the initial survey, for issue of a new Maritime Labour Certificate;
- Intermediate survey: between the second and third years of validity of the Maritime Labour Certificate to ensure that the ship continues to comply with the UK Maritime Labour Convention standards.

Ships which fall outside the mandatory provisions may still apply for a voluntary survey, enabling the owner to seek the issue of a certificate; for example, a coaster engaged solely in UK waters may be chartered on a voyage to a non-UK port, or a yacht may be chartered.

The survey (which results in a Certificate) or inspection (which does not) must cover the following working and living conditions under the MLC:

- Minimum age (16) (but no under 18s may work as a seafarer at night);
- Medical certification;
- Qualification of seafarers (Training and Certification Regulations);
- Seafarers' employment agreements;
- Use of any licensed or certified or regulated private recruitment and placement service;
- Hours of rest;
- Manning levels for the ship;
- Accommodation;
- On-board recreational facilities;
- Food and catering;
- Health and safety and accident prevention;
- On board medical care;
- On-board complaint procedures;
- Payment of wages;
- Financial security for repatriation;
- Financial security relating to shipowners' liability.

If the ship requires a certificate, or the shipowner has requested one, on completion of a successful survey, a Maritime Labour Certificate will be issued. It will be invalidated, however, in the following circumstances and can only be reissued following another survey:

- If a satisfactory intermediate survey is not carried out within the specified period;
- If the certificate is not endorsed following an intermediate survey;
- If the ship transfers to another flag;
- If the shipowner named on the Certificate ceases to be the shipowner;

- If substantial changes are made or damage sustained to the ship's accommodation and recreational facilities for seafarers or its food and catering facilities.

In addition, the MCA may suspend the validity of a Maritime Labour Certificate if an improvement notice has been issued[1] and has not been complied with within the specified period or if there is clear evidence that the ship does not comply with the relevant requirements. More seriously still, the MCA may also cancel a certificate it there is reason to believe it was issued based on incorrect information.

The DMLC

The Certificate must have a Declaration of Maritime Labour Compliance (DMLC) attached. The DMLC contains the evidence needed for Port State inspections that the vessel had met all the Flag State requirements at the time when the certificate was issued. It consists of two parts:

- Part I is completed by the attending surveyor, identifying the topics for survey, and setting out by reference relevant UK standards concerning the MLC. It will also refer to any relevant ship-type specific requirements under national legislation and record any provisions of substantial equivalence or exemptions applicable to the ship and, therefore, the contents may vary slightly from ship to ship.
- Part II is to be completed by the shipowner and approved by the attending surveyor when the initial survey is completed. It also sets out owner's procedures for ongoing compliance with the MLC.

For the obvious reason of Port State inspections, the following documents must be carried on board and made available on request to seafarers, flag state inspectors, authorised officers in port states and shipowners' and seafarers' representatives:

- The current valid Maritime Labour Certificate;
- The DMLC, which must be posted in a conspicuous place where it is available to seafarers;
- A copy of the Convention and its amendments.

The Seafarer's Employment Agreement (SEA)

The Application of Title 2 of the MLC deserves closer attention, for it sets out the conditions which define the conditions of the seafarer's employment, providing the framework which the Master will apply to the management of the seafarer's employment. It forms the contractual basis of the seafarer's employment, setting out the terms defining the seafarer's rights and obligations, but the management function will be addressed in the next chapter

1 Improvement notices are defined under section 261 of the Merchant Shipping Act.

The SEA is described with guidance from the MCA in MGN 477. Every seafarer working on a ship on an international voyage must have a written agreement with the shipowner, which complies with the MLC minimum requirements and will be approved by the MCA, forming part of the certification process. The adjective 'minimum' is important; the SEA may contain more than the minimum, but cannot contain less. A model format is attached as Annex 2 to MGN4 77.

The normal rules of contract apply, so there must be two parties, the seafarer and the shipowner as employer; if the seafarer is not directly employed by the shipowner but is employed by a third party, such as a crewing agency, the employer must still be a party to the SEA, in order to achieve privity of contract and, therefore, responsibility.

The SEA must include a statement by the seafarer and the shipowner confirming –

(a) That the shipowner has provided a sufficient opportunity for the seafarer to review and take advice on the terms and conditions of the agreement;
(b) That the shipowner has explained the rights and responsibilities of the seafarer under the agreement;
(c) That the seafarer enters into the agreement freely.

The SEA will be constituted in several parts, depending on the relationship between the seafarer and the shipowner.

Part 1: All Agreements.

The SEA must contain all the following terms:

1. The full name, birthplace and date of birth (or age at the time of entering into the agreement) of the seafarer;
2. The name and address of the shipowner;
3. The place where the agreement is entered into;
4. The date on which the agreement is entered into;
5. The capacity in which the seafarer is to be employed or engaged;
6. If the agreement has been made for a definite period, the termination date;
7. If the agreement has been made for an indefinite period, the period of notice of termination required and the circumstances in which such notice may be given;
8. If the agreement has been made for a voyage, the destination port and the period following arrival after which the agreement terminates;
9. The health and social security protection benefits to be provided to the seafarer by the shipowner;
10. The maximum duration of service periods on board following which the seafarer is entitled to repatriation (which must not exceed a period of 12 months minus the number of days annual leave to which the seafarer is entitled);
11. The seafarer's entitlement to repatriation (including the mode of transport and destination of repatriation) and the circumstances in which the seafarer is required to meet or reimburse the shipowner for the costs of repatriation;

12. The maximum sum which the shipowner will pay to the seafarer in respect of compensation for any loss of personal property arising from the loss or foundering of the ship.

Part 2: where the seafarer is an employee of the shipowner, the following provisions will be included:

1. The wages (either the amount or the formula to be used in determining them);
2. The manner in which wages must be paid, including payment dates (the first of which must be no more than one month after the date on which the agreement is entered into, with all subsequent dates being no more than one month apart) and the circumstances (if any) in which wages may or must be paid in a different currency;
3. The hours of work;
4. The paid annual leave (either the amount or the formula to be used in determining it);
5. Any pension benefits to be provided to the seafarer by the shipowner, including any entitlement to participate in a pension scheme;
6. The grievance and disciplinary procedures;
7. Details of any collective bargaining agreement which is incorporated (in whole or in part) into the agreement or is otherwise relevant to it.

Part 3: where the seafarer is not an employee, Part 2 will not apply but the following will be included:

1. The remuneration (either the amount or the formula to be used in determining it);
2. The manner in which the remuneration must be paid, including payment dates (the first of which must be no more than one month after the date on which the agreement is entered into, with all subsequent dates being no more than one month apart) and the circumstances (if any) in which the remuneration may or must be paid in a different currency.

The Convention demands that the SEA must be accompanied by the following documents:

- As soon as is practicable after entering a seafarer employment agreement, the shipowner must provide to the seafarer the agreement signed by the seafarer and by or on behalf of the shipowner;
- The shipowner must ensure that a copy of the seafarer employment agreement for each seafarer on a ship is held on board, and must allow each seafarer to see the copy of their seafarer employment agreement on request;

- As soon as is practicable after a seafarer employment agreement is terminated, the shipowner must provide to the seafarer a record of their employment under that agreement, which must contain:
    1. Name, port of registry, gross or register tonnage and official number of ship;
    2. Description of voyage;
    3. Capacity in which seafarer is employed;
    4. Date on which employment started;
    5. Date of discharge.
- The record must not contain provision as to the quality of the seafarer's work; and must not contain provision as to the seafarer's wages.

It is as well to repeat the point that the MLC only applies to international voyages; in the case of coastal voyages the provisions of the Merchant Shipping Act 1995 apply, in which Section 25 applies as it ever did to UK ships:

> *an agreement in writing shall be made between each person employed as a seaman in a United Kingdom ship and the persons employing him and shall be signed both by him and by or on behalf of them.*
>
> *The agreements made under this section with the several persons employed in a ship shall be contained in one document (in this Part referred to as a crew agreement) except that in such cases as the Secretary of State may approve –*
>
> (a) *the agreements to be made under this section with the persons employed in a ship may be contained in more than one crew agreement; and*
> (b) *one crew agreement may relate to more than one ship.*

The provisions in the crew agreement have been approved in a general format by the MCA, but the shipowner can apply for the approval of their own terms, or, indeed, for exemptions. In any circumstance, the crew agreement must be carried on board the ship throughout the voyage and, by Subsection 8:

> *If a ship goes to sea or attempts to go to sea in contravention of the requirements of this section the master or the person employing the crew shall be liable on summary conviction to a fine not exceeding level 4 on the standard scale and the ship, if in the United Kingdom, may be detained.*

Whether an SEA or a Section 25 crew agreement, the UK's employment laws apply; a breach of contract by either party therefore will give rise to a prima facie claim in civil law. The Employment Rights Act 1996 was designed to protect employees from unfair dismissal, and Section 199 disapply a number of sections to merchant seamen; but Part X of the 1996 Act still applies, and section 94(1) states *An employee has the right not to be unfairly dismissed by his employer*. Section 95 defines the circumstances in which an employee is dismissed in law:

> *An employee is dismissed by his employer if (a) the contract under which he is employed is terminated by the employer (whether with or without notice), (b) he is employed under a limited-term contract and that contract terminates by virtue of the limiting event without being renewed under the same contract, or (c) the employee terminates the contract under which he is employed (with or without notice) in circumstances in which he is entitled to terminate it without notice by reason of the employer's conduct.*

To conclude, therefore, it matters not how the seafarer is employed, their civil rights in unfair dismissal remain under English law.

14 The Management of Seafarers

Discipline and Dismissal

The Master has always held powers of managing the employment of seafarers. The Maritime Labour Convention has diluted such powers, following the position in UK employment law that, in all cases within its influence, the ultimate power of dismissal rests with the employer, leaving the Master with the power simply to dismiss them from the ship. That being said, the Master has a relationship with the employer that makes them their employee, representative and agent, so if the employer delegates its power to the Master to terminate the seafarer's employment, the Master will do so, but the employer will still remain liable under the Seafarer's Employment Agreement and, indeed, the English laws of unfair dismissal under Part X of the Employment Rights Act 1996.

There is a golden rule in shipboard management, that the Master has the overriding duty to maintain order and discipline; but that may not always be easy. The Master will exercise their powers in obedience to the employer's instructions, and in accordance with any associated Standing Orders, but it must be borne in mind that the Master is also representative of the Flag State and must obey and implement Flag State laws. There are occasions when the interests of the owners and the Flag State may clash, but the laws of the Flag State must always take priority. Today, that will frequently arise with the human rights of the seafarer, who is entitled to the protection afforded by the Human Rights Act 1998; in fact, English law afforded individuals human rights long before then.

The Master's Overriding Duty

The duty to maintain order and discipline demands that the Master tread a fine line between their obligations to the employer and the demand as Flag State representative to maintain its rights and laws. This should not be confused with the Master's authority and responsibility under the International Safety Management Code (ISM), which states under 5.1:

The Company should clearly define and document the master's responsibility with regard to:

1. Implementing the safety and environmental-protection policy of the Company;
2. Motivating the crew in the observation of that policy;

DOI: 10.4324/9781003361916-14

3. Issuing appropriate orders and instructions in a clear and simple manner;
4. Verifying that specified requirements are observed;
5. Periodically reviewing the SMS and reporting its deficiencies to the shore-based management.

The only two things the Master has to maintain order and discipline on board a ship are:

- Their skill in leadership;
- The Seafarer's Employment Agreement.

The Master's overriding duty actually has a closer association with the Master's absolute discretion, that ancient power that has been enshrined in SOLAS Chapter V Regulation 34-1. The maintenance of order and discipline has a critical effect on the safe operation of the ship, and today's position is merely an evolution of the Master's authority from an almost unbroken line of sources, when a seafarer could claim as justification for his actions an order from the Master *whose bidding the company were not to gainsay*.[1] The twentieth century world embraced a new order of ethics in human rights, though, which had an immense influence on the Master's powers, conferred by the Common and Statute Laws of the Flag State, which preserved the Master's absolute discretion but introduced the protection of seafarers' human rights in the exercise of that discretion.

The Case of *Hook v Cunard*[2]

As a clear illustration, this case reported in 1953 can surely have few equals in its field. Mr Hook had originally joined the Cunard Steam Ship Company in 1909 in the 'hotel' department, catering for the needs of the Company's passengers on Transatlantic voyages, and during his career he had earned an unblemished character. Accordingly, when the express liner RMS *Queen Elizabeth* sailed from Southampton for New York on 24 June 1950, Hook was employed on board as a steward in the First-Class passenger lounge. Among the passengers was Dr Greenberg, his wife and two children, including ten-year-old Linda. On the evening after the ship sailed, the Master, Captain Cove, instructed the Staff Captain to investigate a complaint by Dr Greenberg concerning an allegation by Linda that an indecent assault had been committed against her in the lounge that evening. She identified Hook, and Dr Greenberg was about to strike him when the Staff Captain intervened and told the Chief Steward that Hook was to work in the pantry for the rest of the voyage, away from the passengers. That was not good enough for Dr Greenberg, though, who demanded that Hook be put under lock and key and that, if he were not, he would inform the parents of other children among the passengers

1 Foster,W. 1908, English Factories in India 1646–50, The Clarendon Press, Oxford.
2 *Hook v Cunard Steamship Co* [1953] 1 All ER 1021.

of the facts. He also threatened that, on arrival in New York, he would have Hook arrested and prosecuted, with all the publicity that could be mustered against the Company.

Mr Hook denied the accusation; indeed, there was no evidence in corroboration of Linda's story and a statement signed by Dr Greenberg purporting to be her account of the incident was inconsistent with the account which she gave in the presence of the Staff Captain. But the Master ordered the steward to be kept under restraint in the isolation hospital for the remainder of the voyage and until the First-Class passengers had disembarked at New York.

On 6 July, after the *Queen Elizabeth* docked at Southampton, Mr Hook was discharged under the crew agreement and, on 7 November, was dismissed under his permanent contract. Of his claims for compensation for false imprisonment, breach of contract and wrongful dismissal, the Company paid into Court the full sums in respect of the second and third claims, but defended the claim of false imprisonment, which thus was the defining issue in the case.

False imprisonment is a common law tort under English law, which involves the unlawful confinement of an individual against their will by another individual in such a manner as to violate the confined individual's right to be free from restraint of movement – what today comes within the meaning of an individual's human rights as well as defining a particular tort.[3] The use of physical force presents compelling evidence, but force is not essential. Captain Cove argued manfully that he confined the Plaintiff in compliance with his duty to maintain order and discipline, ensuring no harm came to his ship or her passengers, preserving order among the ship's company and, indeed, protecting the steward from the threatening attitude of Dr Greenberg. To this extent, therefore, Hook's confinement was lawful, the Defence argued. Slade, J, cited *Aldworth v Stewart*,[4] in which Baron Channell, summing up to the jury, had sought to clarify the defining features which characterise the Master's authority. A hasty or intemperate blow, said Channell, could not be justified; in effect, the Master would be committing the criminal offence of an assault, for none of the State's laws are suspended just because that bit of its sovereignty is floating and not fixed on dry land. It was, and remains, necessity which clothes the Master with the authority of the Flag State, to carry out his overriding duty, to maintain order and discipline over the crew – even, in certain circumstances, over the passengers too. But this authority is limited to that necessity and must remain confined to his overriding duty; even in carrying out that duty, the Master must respect and maintain all the laws of the Flag State, and a claim of false imprisonment is as enforceable on board a ship as it is on dry land, under English law.

The Judge further drew on the case of *The Lima*,[5] in which the Court had held obiter how Parliament and the Courts which interpret Parliament's Will have

3 Most recently addressed in *Austin v Commissioner of Police of the Metropolis* [2009] UKHL 5 which concerned the police practice of 'kettling' in managing crowd control.

4 *Aldworth v Stewart* (1866) 176 ER 865.

5 *The Lima* (1837) 166 ER 434.

always valued highly that class of person categorised as the British mariner and, accordingly, have rushed to encourage and protect them in their careers. That being said, the Judge cautioned, the Master must be able to repose confidence in his authority so that he can discharge his overriding duty to maintain order and discipline on the ship, which is essential to the safety of navigation and, in the immortal culture of Victorian society, *the great commercial interests of the country*.[6] [7]

In finding Judgment for the Claimant, Slade J identified the key features in Mr Hook's case with those clearly forming the foundations in *Aldworth* and *The Lima*, and held that he was satisfied that the Defendants did not order his detention because they believed that it was necessary for any purposes of maintaining order and discipline, but they did it to placate Dr Greenberg, and, by placating Dr Greenberg, to avoid what the Master had described as 'unwelcome publicity.'

The general principle has been revisited more recently in 2022 Australian case of *Rawlings*.[8] In that case the Court of Appeal of New South Wales affirmed the Master's power or authority to detain the individual (in this case, a passenger) if they had reasonable cause to believe, and did in fact believe, that the relevant detention or confinement was necessary for the preservation of order and discipline, or for the safety of the vessel or persons or property on board. The Court was satisfied that it was this which guided the Master's decision, and so the confinement was justified; the same would apply if the individual were a seafarer, of course.

Does the Master's overriding duty lead to absolute responsibility for the crew?

While the Master's overriding duty demands an oversight of crew management, it does not render them accountable for misconduct of the crew as some sort of absolute liability, so they will not be liable for the consequences, either, unless negligent mismanagement can be shown. The Union Castle Line had an enviably unblemished reputation in marine operations, no doubt thanks in large part to the excellence of their Masters; but in the declining years of the Cape Run an incident led to global news coverage of an audacious crime on the *Capetown Castle*. Working closely to meet the demands of the South African mail contract, schedules were tight and, on the homeward leg to Southampton in January 1965, gold bullion had to be loaded with the minimum delay and carried with the maximum security aboard the express liner. The procedure had been tied and tested, without a single security incident before. Loading of the bullion always took place at Durban in

6 Ibid.

7 As a matter of principle, nothing much has changed – the Merchant Shipping (Safety of Navigation) Regulations 2002 (amended by SI 2011 No 2978; see footnote page 41) uphold the Master's absolute discretion for the safe navigation of the ship, enabling him to hire and fire seafarers under the crew agreement. If the employer is not so satisfied that the seafarer's dismissal under their permanent contract could be defended from a claim under the Employment Rights Act 1996, they will simply transfer the seafarer to another ship in the fleet – and another crew agreement.

8 *Royal Caribbean Cruises Ltd v Rawlings* [2022] 1 Ll R 643.

the number three hold, which had a specially constructed strong room with capacity for six hundred boxes, each one containing two ingots, bound and sealed with wire. If the gold to be loaded exceeded the capacity of the strong room, the surplus was loaded into an adjacent locker fitted with extra locks. The loading procedures were strict, and Masters had perfected orders over the years with watchfulness over the operation supervised by the Chief Mate; on completion of loading, the Master locked the room securely and kept the key throughout the voyage. Even then, routine inspection procedures were carried out while the vessel was under way. As soon as the ship arrived in Southampton the discharge routine of the bullion commenced, again rapidly and amid tight security.

But when *Capetown Castle* arrived in Southampton at the end of this voyage, 10 boxes were unaccounted for, amounting to a loss of £100,000. The Master, Captain Holland, was responsible, of course, but he was able to demonstrate that the security provisions had been met with absolute diligence, so he had discharged his responsibility and no criminal suspicion was attached to him. The liner had to maintain her strict voyage schedule to meet the mail contract, so investigations continued while she proceeded on her next voyage south. The inspection of the ship was incredibly thorough, and no doubt the undercover officers enjoyed the voyage on the way. They found evidence that the thieves must have been members of the crew, who knew the ship intimately and had cut through the thin metal plate of a ventilation shaft which entered the locker; then they removed the ten boxes, sealed up the outside of the shaft with tape and painted it over. Then, under cover of darkness, they removed the bullion and hid it beneath a store of sand that was used for holystoning the decks. Two members of the crew subsequently were charged with the theft of the bullion and the Trial took place in Winchester in June 1965, but the jury failed to reach a verdict; on a retrial, however, they were found Guilty and sentenced to a term of imprisonment. Clearly, Captain Holland could not be responsible for everything which took place among the crew; he had exercised all due diligence. It is alarming that the principle was not observed in the case of Captain Laptalo of the *Coral Sea*, which we discuss in Chapter 15, for it has great importance to the principle of the Master's responsibility.

The Code of Conduct

Realistically, the Master is not alone in deciding matters of discipline. Although they can exercise their discretion as they see fit and, in the extreme, can dismiss the seafarer from the vessel, they can be guided by The Code of Conduct for the Merchant Navy.[9] The Code of Conduct was compiled jointly by the UK Chamber of Shipping, Nautilus International and the National Union of Rail, Maritime and Transport Workers, and was approved by the MCA on behalf of the Flag State. It sets out disciplinary rules and procedures which apply when seafarers are employed to work on board ship.

9 The latest edition was published in August 2013 and updated August 2020.

Key points raised in the Code of Conduct address the underlying issues in maintaining order and discipline:

- The discharge of duties: the seafarer is obliged diligently to perform their duties under the job description in their SEA to the best of their ability. This often requires onboard supervision and training, but at the very least they must be competent to act with the standards expected from their certificates of competency;
- Punctuality: seafarers are required to be punctual in every aspect of their life on board ships, from shore-leave to reporting for watch-keeping duties. The Code points out that a late return from shore-leave can lead to delay and a resultant loss of time and money. It also points out that delay in relieving outgoing watchkeepers can give rise to poor interpersonal relations; what it does not state, but it is relevant nevertheless, is that delay in coming on watch may give rise to fears that the offender has been taken ill or has been lost or injured, particularly in heavy weather;
- Drugs and alcohol: alcohol abuse has traditionally been a problem at sea, and can affect the efficient operation of the vessel, particularly in navigation and engineering functions. It is noteworthy that section 58 Merchant Shipping Act 1995 addresses conduct endangering the ship or safety of life, 58(3) stating that if the act or omission was deliberate or amounted to a breach or neglect of duty or that the seafarer was under the influence of drink or drugs at the time of the act or omission, they will be guilty of an offence. As a result, the seafarer would face dismissal under their SEA. Equally, The Merchant Shipping (Alcohol) (Prescribed Limits Amendment) Regulations 2015 update the Railways and Transport Safety Act 2003. Section 78(2) of the 2003 Act states that a seafarer commits an offence if their ability to carry out their duties is impaired because of drink or drugs. Section 79 states that, when a seafarer is not on duty, but in the event of an emergency would or might be required by the nature or terms of his engagement or employment to take action to protect the safety of passengers, they would be guilty of an offence. A seafarer in breach of the limits under the 2015 Regulations, therefore, would be liable to dismissal for the first offence. Additional criminal penalties for the possession and abuse of drugs would also be implemented, not just under Flag State laws but also under Port State laws, in accordance with the United Nations Convention against Illicit Traffic in Narcotic Drugs and Psychotropic Substances of 1988;
- Treatment of Ship's property and accommodation area: the SEA is likely to include a provision creating a disciplinary or dismissal matter of damage to the ship's property and accommodation, with compensation provisions for such damage. In addition, the seafarer may be in breach of Flag State laws on criminal damage, as well as section 58 of the 1995 Act;
- Smoking: smoking policy will be clarified by shipowners, but many will adopt a No-Smoking policy, particularly on tankers and ships carrying dangerous flammable cargo. Some owners permit a designated smoking room on board, but the Code makes the point that smoking in cabins should also be prohibited in order to limit the risk of accidental fire;

- Weapons: any kind of offensive weapons which can be fatal or inflict serious personal harm are not allowed on board ships, and the downstream consequences of a violation could lead to summary dismissal under the SEA, let alone breaching the ships security code under ISPS. Moreover, weapons in the possession of private security guards on board ships could lead to serious criminal penalties if they are illegal within Port State laws, even if not under Flag State laws;
- Behaviour towards Colleagues on board the ship: anti-social behaviour such as, for example, abusive language, racism, sexual harassment, aggressive attitude and offensive personal habits and bullying on board can lead to suspension or dismissal for the first offence, and can also lead to criminal prosecution;
- Security on board: seafarers are not allowed to bring any unauthorised persons on board ship, which, if violated, could lead to criminal penalties both under Flag State and Port State laws. The Ship Security Plan under ISPS provisions will define measures against unwanted access to the ship, which will be enforced by the ship security officer, who is under a duty to is implement it to the best possible extent in order to maintain its effectiveness;
- Unlawful activities: as a general guide, any offence involving dishonesty or violence, such as theft or assault, can lead to dismissal under the SEA for the first offence, and subsequent criminal prosecution. It is noteworthy that a person commits theft if they dishonestly appropriate (in other words, take) property belonging to another with the intention of permanently depriving the other of it. It is one of the most frequent crimes on board ship, and obliges the Master, as Flag State representative, to ensure the collection of evidence and delivery of that evidence to the Flag State, generally the police authority in the port of registry. Of course, the Master may delegate this function, but would be unwise to do so, as the Master would still have to give evidence at the Defendant's Trial, as Flag state representative.

Discipline: The Master's Options

The Master has powers of discipline in accordance with their position as the owner's representative and agent, when they will take steps to resolve issues with the authority of the SEA. In addition, however, the Master will also act as the Flag State representative in discharging their overriding duty to maintain order and discipline; in both circumstances that may involve removing the seafarer from the vessel. In terms of their employment, the company will do the rest; if the seafarer violated a Flag State law, that may involve their criminal prosecution, in which case the Master will deliver evidence to the police, who will do the rest, before the Crown Prosecution Service makes a decision under the Police and Criminal Evidence Act 1984. Naturally, the criminal prosecution will take precedence, but if a conviction follows, then the employer could rely on that in any claims for damages from the seafarer, arising out of their misconduct.

Although the Master will be able to rely on their discretion in dealing with the matter, they would be well-advised to follow procedures set out in the International Safety Management Code for the ship, the SMS, which will have been approved by the Flag State, and the Master's powers are clearly defined under ISM 5.1 and 5.2. Once again, the Merchant Navy Code of Conduct will assist, with procedures according to the seriousness of the breach, from informal warnings for the most minor breaches, through various grades of warnings, to dismissal from the ship.

From the notification of the alleged misconduct, however serious, it is vital that written evidence is taken, and any property which is the subject of that misconduct is preserved. The evidence must be particular, and limited to what the witness saw, heard, did or said. It must then be signed by the witness, and preserved for the company and/or the police.

The seafarer must be informed of the issues in the allegation against them and a date and time set for the Master to conduct their inquiry, giving sufficient time for the seafarer to prepare and to answer each allegation against them.

Whatever the Master's decision, it must be recorded in the Official Log Book, and countersigned by the seafarer. Of course, the seafarer may not be thrilled to countersign the entry, but they should be made aware that they are not admitting the truth of the allegation, but the fact that the procedure took place.

Instances of gross misconduct may be defined in the SEA but, in any event, they will always include:

- Offences of dishonesty;
- Offences of violence;
- Section 58 offences: Conduct endangering ships, structures or individuals (Merchant Shipping Act 1995);
- Drugs and alcohol offences;
- Disobedience of a lawful order.

A repetition following a final warning will be treated as gross misconduct and entitle the Master to dismiss the seafarer from the vessel. It is critical to understand that this does not terminate the seafarer's employment under the SEA; that will be the final decision of the employer.

Less serious offences may include:

- Minor acts of negligence, neglect of duty, disobedience and assault;
- Unsatisfactory work performance;
- Poor timekeeping;
- Stopping work before the authorised time;
- Offensive or disorderly behaviour.

Less serious misconduct may lead to sanctions addressed in the SEA and or the SMS, and include:

- An informal warning administered at an appropriate level;
- A formal warning by an Officer;
- A written warning by a senior Officer;
- A final written warning by a senior Officer or the Master.

The reader may well be acquainted with the procedure, which may determine the grade of the individual conducting the disciplinary process. It is emphasised, however, that this should be the Master in all but the most trivial cases, because, if the case were to end up in a Tribunal or a Court, it would be the Master who would be cross-examined. They, after all, are the Company's representative and they are the Flag State's representative charged with the rights and obligations contained in its law – including its employment law. As a result, it is they who are best-placed to understand the procedure; if it is established that the procedure was not followed, then the case against the seafarer would fail. And only the Master has the absolute discretion to take action for the safe navigation of the ship or the marine environment.

Whatever the decision, after the hearing the seafarer will be given written notification of the outcome of the hearing and the reasons for the decision, notification of how long any warning will remain current and a copy of the entry in the Official Log Book. The log book entry is essential for any offence, because a less serious one may be repeated and lead to eventual dismissal, hence the need for evidence.

The seafarer may be dismissed from the ship in some distant port; if so, from the moment they are ashore, they may have the right to notify the UK Consul if they are a British national (or the Master of any nationality if a UK ship), or the consul of their own State, in the event of a contentious dismissal of crew under their SEA. The Consul may assist them with practical help, and supply a list of local lawyers, but the Consul will not give them legal advice. The key areas are:

- Seafarers' wages and wages disputes;
- Relief and repatriation of seafarers left behind;
- Official Log Book and certified extracts;
- Health, provisions and water;
- Seafarers' documents;
- Administration of oaths for affidavits.

Procedures are defined for an account of the seafarer's wages to be given following dismissal, and for their repatriation. In the latter regard, the reader is reminded that the MLC was amended in 2022 with an important amendment concerning Repatriation. Regulation 2.5 addresses Mandatory Repatriation Requirements for Seafarers to Ensure that Seafarers Are Able to Return Home. The amendment provides that Members shall facilitate the prompt repatriation of seafarers, including when they are deemed abandoned where, in violation of the requirements of this Convention or the terms of the seafarers' employment agreement, the shipowner fails to cover the cost of the seafarer's repatriation, or has left the seafarer without the necessary maintenance and support, or has otherwise unilaterally severed their ties with the seafarer including failure to pay contractual wages for a period of at least two months. It requires that Port States, Flag States and labour-supplying States shall cooperate to ensure that seafarers engaged on a ship to replace seafarers who have been abandoned in their territory, or on a ship flying their flag, shall be accorded their rights and entitlements under the MLC.

Employment Rights for Unfair Dismissal

And now the saga really begins. The Employment Rights Act 1996 (ERA) is the primary legislation defining basic employee rights in the UK. It particularly establishes the law and procedure for unfair dismissal; hence the need for the Master to ensure that the evidence and the procedures are all well-documented. Section 111 of the ERA states:

(*1*) *A complaint may be presented to an industrial tribunal against an employer by any person that he was unfairly dismissed by the employer*
(2) *Subject to subsection (3), an industrial tribunal shall not consider a complaint under this section unless it is presented to the tribunal –*
  (a) *before the end of the period of three months beginning with the effective date of termination, or*
  (b) *within such further period as the tribunal considers reasonable in a case where it is satisfied that it was not reasonably practicable for the complaint to be presented before the end of that period of three months*
(3) *Where a dismissal is with notice, an industrial tribunal shall consider a complaint under this section if it is presented after the notice is given but before the effective date of termination.*

In order to establish a case of unfair dismissal, the Claimant seafarer must establish five critical factors:

- The Claimant had been an Employee in order to make a claim under the Act to the Employment Tribunal;
- The Claimant had at least one year's continuous employment with the employer;
- The Claimant was below 65 or below the normal retirement age at the time of dismissal;
- The Claimant must have been dismissed;
- The Dismissal must have been Unfair.

It must be remembered that, in addition to their contract of employment (the SEA), downstream consequences of the seafarer's negligence or misconduct may lead them to being disqualified from holding a certificate of competency (section 61 MSA 1995 for officers, section 62 for others) and prosecution for criminal offences. Moreover, whether the employer wins or loses in a tribunal, their reputation as employers may be prejudiced; as a result, it is not unheard of for a seafarer to be dismissed from the ship, but the employer will not take the step to terminate their SEA but put them on another ship; stories are even heard of seafarers serving around the fleet, and ending up with the same ship at a later date.

Competency and Fitness

These matters are the key issues in STCW as amended by the 2010 Manila Amendments. The STCW Code is in two parts and contains critical guidance:

- Part A contains mandatory standards regarding provisions of the annex to the 1978 STCW Convention, as amended, including standards of competence candidates must demonstrate for the issue and revalidation of certificates of competency;
- Part B contains recommended guidance on provisions of the 1978 STCW Convention, as amended.

That being said, Flag States must implement their standards of competency and fitness into domestic regulations, which may provide the standard set out in the Convention, or a higher standard. They are not permitted to set a lower standard; in reality, however, that may be hard to define.

The EU Directive 2008/106/EC on the minimum level of training of seafarers incorporates into EU law, the minimum standards of training, certification and watchkeeping for seafarers serving on board EU vessels whose Flag States have adopted STCW. The directive sets out the rules on training and the standards of competence to be met by seafarers who are candidates for the issue or revalidation of certificates that allow them to perform the functions for which the relevant certificate of competency or proficiency is issued. The categories of seafarer to which these rules relate are:

- Masters;
- Chief mates;
- Deck officers and engineer officers;
- Chief engineer officers and second engineer officers;
- Certain categories of ratings (i.e., those working in an engine room, those who form part of a watch or those serving on certain types of ship);
- Personnel responsible for radiocommunication.

For certain categories of vessel, such as tankers and ro-ro passenger ships, there are special rules and mandatory minimum requirements concerning the training and qualifications of seafarers. The directive also lays down rules on education and training in the management of emergency situations, fire-fighting and the supply of medical aid, as well as for crew members responsible for catering services.

The Flag State issues the certificates, but can also suspend or cancel them, depending on the record of the seafarer. Seafarers are required to prove, at regular intervals, that they still meet the standards for skills and professional competence, and there are also health certificates issued to seafarers who meet the national standards for physical fitness (particularly regarding eyesight and hearing), which are also renewed periodically.

The multinational nature of crews in modern shipping demands special rules to ensure that they have met the standards of the Flag State; hence, all seafarers who serve on board a UK flagged vessel but whose certificate of competency was granted by another State, must hold a valid Certificate of Equivalent Competency (CEC). These certificates are issued on a like-for-like basis against a valid Certification of Competency and are issued in line with STCW but the process is not necessarily automatic, and the seafarer may have to provide additional evidence of competency, knowledge of the English language and UK Legal and Administrative processes (UKLAP), by taking an examination.

Notwithstanding the fact that the seafarer's SEA will have been endorsed by the employer, the Master must still carry out a number of checks when the crew board the vessel. In addition to their SEA, a crucial document which must be carried at sea, the Master must also conduct the following by checking the original certificates that the seafarers bring on board:

- Check seafarers' discharge books to make sure that they have the qualifications and certificates of competency for their jobs;
- Check that all seafarers have the necessary medical certificates for the work in their routine job description;
- Check that the seafarers engaged all meet the minimum age requirements for the work that will be expected of them, with or without supervision;
- Ensure that the seafarers all have the necessary travel documents;
- Check that the seafarers all can speak the ship's common working language;
- Check that the crew list contains the minimum set out in the ship's safe manning document.

The process is somewhat simplified by EU legislation, which directs that Member States must meet the following requirements:

- Maintain registers of all certificates of competency and certificates of proficiency and endorsements for masters and officers and, where applicable, ratings which are issued, have expired or have been revalidated, suspended, cancelled or reported as lost or destroyed, as well as of dispensations issued;
- Make available information on the status of certificates of competency, endorsements and dispensations to other EU countries or other parties to the STCW convention, as well as companies which request verification of the authenticity and validity of certificates – as of 1 January 2017, the information required must be made available by electronic means;
- Draw up standards of medical fitness for seafarers and procedures for the issue of a medical certificate in accordance with the directive and with Section A-I/9 of the STCW code – those responsible for assessing the medical fitness of seafarers must be medical practitioners recognised by that EU country for the purpose of such medical examinations.

EU States must also establish the necessary processes and procedures to carry out an impartial investigation in cases of incompetence, acts or omissions that may pose a direct threat to the safety of human life, the safety of goods at sea or the marine environment. Penalties or disciplinary measures are to be provided for and applied where:

- A company or master has engaged a person not holding a certificate as required by this directive;
- A master has authorised a seafarer to carry out a function for which a certificate is required but they are not the holder of such a certificate, a certificate recognised by the EU countries or a valid dispensation;
- A person has fraudulently obtained an engagement to perform a function or to serve in a capacity for which a certificate is required;
- Monitoring and evaluation of training.

The continuing training of seafarers is critical, to keep up with standards that are often improved in response to a casualty, hence EU countries must ensure that:

- There is continuous monitoring of all training, assessment of issuing competency certificates and the definition of a system of quality standards detailing objectives and scope;
- Training and teaching objectives as well as the equivalence of training levels with the requirements of the STCW convention are defined;
- The quality of examinations, assessments and the quality and experience of assessors is monitored;
- Independent evaluations of knowledge, understanding, skills and competence acquisition and assessment activities are carried out at intervals of no more than five years;
- Rest periods for watchkeeping personnel.

The MAIB has long warned about two cardinal evils in marine casualties, and have made recommendations to prevent fatigue and complacency, as a result of which the maintenance of records to ensure compliance with legislation on hours of work is critical, and default can lead to a criminal offence.

Hours of Work

Hours of work and rest were prescribed in STCW and then in MLC, and famously were defined in subtly different ways.

- Hours of Work are defined as the period when seafarers are required to do work on the business of the ship. On-call time is not counted as *Hours of work* unless the seafarer is required to work during that time. A seafarer whose normal period of rest on board ship is disturbed by a call-out, should have compensatory rest;
- Hours of Rest is defined as the time outside hours of work, and does not include short breaks.

In order to achieve consistency, the STCW Code has been amended regarding hours of rest so it is now in line with the MLC.

It is as well at this stage to understand how a seafarer is defined. Under UK law a seafarer is any person, including the Master, who is employed or engaged or who works in any capacity on board a seagoing merchant ship, whose normal place of work is on a ship. A person whose normal place of work is ashore but who is working on a ship on a temporary or one-off basis for the duration of a voyage is excluded; they are still covered for statutory hours, and covered by the Working Time Regulations 19981.

MSN 1877 addresses the UK's current legislation *Hours of Work and Entitlement to Leave Application of the Merchant Shipping (Maritime Labour Convention) (Hours of Work) Regulations 2018.*

The Regulations apply to all seafarers, including Masters, employed, engaged or working in any capacity on board a seagoing merchant ship, and whose normal place of work is on a ship.

The Regulations define the hours of rest as follows:

- A minimum of 77 hours of rest in any 7-day period and 10 hours rest in any 24-hour period;
- A schedule of hours of rest to be posted up on board the ship;
- Records of hours of rest to be maintained for each seafarer;
- In addition, seafarers shall have two and a half days of paid annual leave per month of employment, and an additional eight days of paid leave per year in respect of public holidays;
- Seafarers retain the right to take a case regarding their entitlements to paid leave to an employment tribunal;
- The owner must grant shore leave to benefit seafarers' health and wellbeing, where compatible with their operational duties;
- Shipowners – and the Master – must provide for inspection and enforcement by the MCA.

There are authorised exceptions to the limits on Hours of Rest under the 2018 Regulations, which may be authorised by the MCA provided that they are the result of an agreement between employers and seafarers, have due regard to the general principles of health and safety of workers, and comply with certain limits. Those conditions apply to individual seafarers and define the limits as follows:

a) The ten hours daily rest are divided into (no more than) three periods;
b) One of the periods is at least six hours long, and neither of the others is less than one hour long;
c) Intervals between consecutive periods are no more than 14 hours;
d) The exceptions may not apply to more than two 24-hour periods in a 7-day period;
e) There are at least 70 hours rest in any 7-day period;
f) The exceptions authorised do not apply for a period of more than two consecutive weeks;

g) Where the exception applies in relation to two periods separated by an interval, the interval shall be at least twice the duration of the longest of the two periods.

There is provision for emergencies. MSN 1877 (M) Amendment 1 states:

> *The Regulations recognise that situations may arise in which a seafarer may be required by the master to work during scheduled hours of rest. These include emergencies which threaten the safety of the ship, persons on board or the cargo or where another ship or person in distress requires assistance. In these circumstances, hours of rest schedules may be suspended until the normal situation is restored. The master shall ensure that any affected seafarer is then given an adequate rest period to avoid fatigue.*

The MCA may even consider applications falling outside these limits in relation to seafarers working on ships which operate only within 60 miles of a safe haven in the UK on domestic voyages, but which are not engaged in the transport of cargo or passengers.

Notwithstanding that, it is the responsibility of all seafarers to ensure that they are properly rested when they begin duty on a ship and that they obtain adequate rest when not on duty.

MSN 1877 sets out the key details in hours of work and rest, but emphasises that it must be read in relationship with the 2018 Regulations. In particular, *failure to comply with those obligations may be a criminal offence under the Regulations.*

The Employment of Young Persons

The MLC defines the minimum age requirements, which be the subject of checks at Port State inspections. The minimum age for seafarers is 16, although this is 18 if the work involves any:

- Night work;
- Hazardous tasks such as lifting, hauling, mooring, towing.

Under UK law, there are general provisions provided under the Merchant Shipping and Fishing Vessels (Health and Safety at Work) (Employment of Young Persons) Regulations 1998, which state that appropriate measures should be taken to protect young persons at work from the risks to their health and safety which are a consequence of their lack of experience, or absence of awareness of existing or potential risks or the fact that young persons have not yet fully matured. In particular, Regulation 5(2) states:

> *No young person shall be permitted to begin work in a ship unless an assessment has first been made, either separately or as an addition to the*

assessment made under regulation 7 of the General Duties Regulations, of the risks to the health and safety of young persons which might arise during the normal course of their working time taking into account the inexperience, lack of awareness of risks and immaturity of young persons, and paying particular attention to –

- *The fitting out and layout of working areas;*
- *The nature, degree and duration of exposure to physical, biological and chemical agents;*
- *The form, range and use of work equipment and the way in which it is handled;*
- *The organisation of processes and activities;*
- *The extent of the health and safety training provided or to be provided to the young persons concerned;*
- *Risks from agents, processes and work listed in the Schedule to the 1998 Regulations.*

Rest periods for young persons are more generous than for other seafarers:

> *Where a young person is engaged as a worker on any ship, he shall be provided with –*
>
> - *A rest period of at least 12 consecutive hours in every 24-hour period;*
> - *A rest period of at least two days, which shall be consecutive if possible, in every week.*
>
> *Where a young person's daily working time is more than four and a half hours, he shall be provided with a rest break of at least 30 minutes which shall be consecutive if possible.*

The minimum weekly rest period may be interrupted in the case of activities involving periods of work that are split up over the day or of short duration; and may be reduced to a period which is not less than 36 hours where this is justified by technical or organisational reasons.

Seafarer Complaints

The Master's overriding duty to maintain order and discipline underlines their shipboard management function, to manage the crew effectively. That has historically required the Master to deal with complaints from seafarers in the first instance, in anticipation of preventing escalation, when a complaint can become a real problem that spreads through the crew.

The Master's management function demands twenty-first-century skills in dealing with people in an atmosphere in which an autocratic nature is not tolerated. It is, therefore, essential that the first step in resolving a complaint is through negotiation. It is as well to remember that at this stage it is still a problem, not a dispute; the objective of negotiation is to solve the problem before it becomes one. A problem becomes a dispute when negotiations break down and the critical function of communication is lost. So, the alternative must be available at the earliest possible opportunity, and it must remain available until its possibility of success has been exhausted.

The benefits of negotiation deliver maximum control for a minimum cost, while the respect for the Master both ashore and on board the ship will increase. If, however, the Master and the seafarer are unable to resolve the complaint, it will have to be taken to the next level, and the process will move ashore; if it cannot be resolved within the Company, then it may end up in a Tribunal.

Regulation 13 of the Merchant Shipping (Maritime Labour Convention) (Survey and Certification) Regulations 2013 implements 5.1.4 of the Maritime Labour Convention, 2006 on complaints for UK ships:

1 *The shipowner and the master of a ship to which this regulation applies must ensure that there is available to a seafarer on that ship a procedure to lodge a complaint alleging a breach of the requirements of the Maritime Labour Convention and for that complaint to be resolved fairly, effectively and expeditiously.*

2 *A procedure to lodge a complaint and have it resolved must*

   (a) *seek to resolve the complaint at the lowest level possible,*

   (b) *enable a seafarer to complain directly to the master of the ship and appropriate external authorities,*

   (c) *include the right of the seafarer to be accompanied or represented during any hearing which takes place under that procedure,*

   (d) *comply with the requirements of MSN 1849.*

The seafarer must be provided with information on the complaints procedure, as well as the name of an individual on board who can give impartial advice on a confidential basis, and otherwise assist them in following the complaints procedure. If the requirements in the MLC are not met on board, the seafarer may lodge with the MCA a complaint alleging a breach of the requirements of the Maritime Labour Convention, which could lead to serious consequences for the Master and the owner.

Guidelines to the MLC assist in dealing with on-board procedures. In the UK, the MCA has consulted with shipowners' and seafarers' organisations, developing a model for fair, expeditious and well-documented procedures. The MLC guidance particularly states:

> *Many complaints may relate specifically to those individuals to whom the complaint is to be made or even to the master of the ship. In all cases seafarers should also be able to complain directly to the master and to make a complaint externally; and in order to help avoid problems of victimisation of seafarers making complaints about matters under this Convention, the procedures should encourage the nomination of a person on board who can advise seafarers on the procedures available to them and, if requested by the complainant seafarer, also attend any meetings or hearings into the subject matter of the complaint.*

In the first instance, the complaint will be addressed to the head of the department of the seafarer lodging the complaint or to the seafarer's superior officer. Who should then attempt to resolve the matter within prescribed time limits appropriate to the seriousness of the issues involved. If it cannot be resolved to the satisfaction of the seafarer, they may refer it to the Master, who should handle the matter personally. That being said, in the case of a serious complaint which involves potential allegations of serious misconduct, the seafarer should not be precluded from referring the complaint direct to the Master; all such procedures will, however, be set out in the ship's SMS. If the complaint cannot be resolved on board, the matter should be referred ashore to the Company, which will manage the complaint from that point, ensuring that the complaint is addressed in a timely manner in consultation with the seafarer.

Notwithstanding that, if the seafarer has a compliant that involves an allegation of a breach of the seafarer's rights under the MLC, then they can refer it to an MCA surveyor who boards for a Port State inspection, who will record the time that it was received, the details of the ship in question and the nature of the complaint. The surveyor will then check to ensure that the complaint relates to some requirement of the MLC and, if so, an initial investigation will be carried out, in accordance with Port State inspection rules.

It can be well-imagined that the Master would be well-advised to apply their dispute management skills at the earliest stage. The secret of success lies in the Master's skill in resolving a solution, which may not be ideal for one party or the other but is something which everybody can live with. The Master will start by separating individuals from the problem itself, so that they can fight the problem, not each other. That being achieved, the Master will focus on the interests of the parties: in other words, seeking to understand what the seafarer's priorities are, and then explaining the priorities of the employer. By identifying the areas of agreement and clarifying the issues that divide them, they can find a common interest, which leads to a solution.

Sometimes, there is no clear-cut solution but, by working with the seafarer, the Master can, at least, clarify the issues that divide them and identify the matters on which they agree, which makes it easier to explore a solution that may not be ideal for the seafarer or the Master on behalf of the Company, but it is something that they can both live with.

This does not imply that the Master should not be assertive; their overriding duty to maintain order and discipline ultimately depends on assertiveness. The aim of assertiveness, though, is not to enforce an autocracy but to satisfy the needs and wants of both parties, on the basis that:

- Both parties have needs to be met;
- Both parties have something to contribute to the efficient operation of the ship.

The effect of assertiveness can result in the Master's increased confidence in themselves, leading to the taking of initiatives rather than simply reacting to events, which can have a snowball effect leading to greater confidence in others.

15 The Master's Responsibility

Who is the Master? The Merchant Shipping Act 1995 defines the Master as every person (except a pilot) having command or charge of a ship. The Master must be duly certificated by the Flag State to hold that position, and must hold a Certificate of Equivalent Competency if their Master's Certificate had been given by another flag. It is axiomatic that the absence of the Master would violate the ship's safe manning certificate, at the very least, with the effect that, without the Master, she will not be going anywhere.

This chapter is all about responsibility and accountability. We shall examine how the Master's responsibility for the safety of life at sea and the protection of the marine environment has developed into a risk management function that renders them accountable in the event of a casualty event. Ultimately, only one person can take management responsibility for that, which, of course, is the Master; there again, the chain of responsibility can be a complex one, and as the Judge observed in the *Herald* Inquiry, the disease of sloppiness can be found throughout the whole of the body corporate; it just so happens that the Master must take responsibility, because that is a key part of their job description.

The Master and the Flag State

The principle of State Sovereignty defines the supreme authority within that territory, which is managed by laws in which no other State has any legitimate right to interfere, either in the making or in the administration of those laws. Whether we like it or not, we cannot interfere in the administration of the law of another sovereign State, which has so often been the cause of tensions leading to the criminalisation of the Master. Article 2 (1) of the United Nations Charter is so brief that it defies any misconstruction:

> *The Organization is based on the principle of the sovereign equality of all its members.*

The Flag State will depend on the Master no matter where the ship is, for the State will depend on one person as their representative, to manage the State's responsibility to other States and protect their sovereign territory, the ship herself. The Master's responsibility as the representative of the Flag State will undoubtedly

DOI: 10.4324/9781003361916-15

demand priority for meeting Port State laws, which inevitably underlines the requirement for just one person to be held accountable in the event of the breach of those laws. This must include the Master's criminal accountability for breaches of Port State laws and the Master's role in the risk management process of operating the ship. There are particularly good reasons for the Flag State's unfettered management control of the Master:

- The State maintains order, so their appointed Master gives up absolute freedom only to the Flag State authority;
- The State must itself maintain management control to meet its obligations under UNCLOS towards others, whether in International Waters or the Territorial Seas of other States.

But then, the State clothes the Master with absolute discretion; in the UK this is set out in the Merchant Shipping (Safety of Navigation) (Amendment) Regulations 2011, which does nothing more than implement the provisions in SOLAS Chapter V Regulation 34-1, the provision which enshrines the Master's Absolute Discretion in international law:

> *The owner, the charterer, the company operating the ship as defined in regulation IX/1, or any other person shall not prevent or restrict the master of the ship from taking or executing any decision which, in the master's professional judgement, is necessary for safety of life at sea and protection of the marine environment.*

The effect is that nobody can override the professional judgment of the Master in their decisions, and we shall meet it repeatedly in this book. But they will be accountable for those decisions. They must answer, not just for how they meet their responsibility for the safety of life at sea and the protection of the marine environment, but also how they observe the plethora of all the laws of the State in which they find themselves; for they will have no immunity against the criminal law of the Port State.

Most notably, it is the safety of navigation which the Master must observe, no matter where the ship may be, and Elder Brethren of Trinity House have historically sat with the Judge as Nautical Assessors, in order to give their opinion on matters of navigation and seamanship. A historical case may be compared with a recent one, to illustrate the evolution of the law.

The Cases of the *Heron* and the *Wilforce*

It was already getting light on the morning of 5 August 1933, as a short sea tankship, the *Steersman*, was proceeding down the Firth of Forth, approaching Bass Rock, on a voyage from Grangemouth to Stockton and Goole, laden with a cargo of motor spirit and manned by a crew of 12 hands, all told. The fog was dense, with a light, variable wind of about one knot, on an ebb tide setting to the eastward. The

Steersman was steaming slow ahead and making about three knots. Although it was already daylight, she was exhibiting the regulation masthead light, side lights and a fixed stern light, all of which were burning brightly. Her whistle was being duly sounded for fog at regulation intervals and a good look-out was being kept on board.

In these circumstances, a signal of one long blast was heard from a vessel apparently broad on the starboard bow and at a considerable distance. The engine of the *Steersman* was thereupon immediately stopped and her whistle was sounded with a long blast in reply. Thereafter the engines of the *Steersman* were kept stopped and, after an interval during which signals of one long blast were exchanged on several occasions, a steamship approached on a bearing of about five to six points on the starboard bow. This was the *Heron*, one of the General Steam Navigation Company's five super-sisters of passenger-cargo ships built after the First World War. They were much prized, with the best Masters the Company had, noted for their strict discipline learned at sea in the war, and skills earned with Extra-Master's Tickets. What could possibly go wrong?

The engines of the *Steersman* were accordingly put full speed astern, her wheel was put hard-a-starboard, three short blasts were sounded on her whistle and shortly afterwards repeated. Witnesses on the *Steersman* subsequently gave evidence that the *Heron* continued to come on at speed. At about 05.30, swinging to starboard and sounding one short blast on her whistle, and with her port side abaft amidships *Heron* struck the stem of the *Steersman*, causing the tankship damage, which formed the basis of Rowbotham's claim against General Steam[1] in that, in breach of their duty of care to the *Steersman*, *Heron* failed to keep any or any proper look-out; she was proceeding at an excessive speed and, on hearing forward of their beam the whistle signal of the *Steersman*, failed to stop their engines and then to navigate with caution; she then improperly and at an improper time altered course to starboard and/or caused or allowed the head of the *Heron* to fall to starboard; she failed to ease, stop or reverse engines in due time or at all; and, in support of their claim under the Particulars of Negligence, failed to comply with Articles 16,27 and 29 of the Collision Regulations. As drafted Particulars of Claim, it would meet entirely the provisions of Part 16 of today's Civil Procedure Rules for claims in negligence.

The President of the Court, Sir Boyd Merriman, delivered a substantial Judgment in which he analysed the evidence meticulously. In his conclusions he found:

> *Of course, it is manifest on that statement of facts that there is no particular reason why these vessels should have met at all, and somehow or other one has to reconcile the evidence and the pleadings, the evidence of one side and the other, with the fact that they say at some point, which must be fixed as nearly as possible, they come into collision, and come into collision, again on the evidence of both sides, approximately at right-angles.*

1 *C Rowbotham & Sons v General Steam Navigation Company Ltd, the Heron* [1934] 49 Ll R 78.

The Judge drew a dramatic picture of the last minute that ticked away before the collision:

> *The Steersman says that she first saw the Heron approximately six points on the starboard bow ... The Heron says that she heard the Steersman approximately two points ... at any rate two to 2 ½ points on the port bow, and saw her first two points on the port bow, bearing to cross her bow at right angles ... I do think this, that in a desperate situation something of the sort happened and was executed with very considerable skill and presence of mind on the part of the Heron ... Always assuming that she had any right to be going at that speed at the time and that, going at that speed, it was a wise thing to attempt to pass across the bows of the Steersman, I think that the manoeuvre itself, as a manoeuvre, was executed with daring and skill, and I say that much on behalf of the Master of the Heron ... But, on the other hand, I am satisfied that she had no sort of right to be going at that speed, or anything like it; she ought not to have put herself or the other ship into the position in which it was even thinkable that such a manoeuvre should be made.*

The Judge, accordingly, held that *Heron* was alone to blame for the collision.

In the intervening years, the responsibility for navigational decisions has changed little – but the Master's professional judgment has evolved considerably, to the extent, even, of statutory provision in section 187 of the Merchant Shipping Act 1995:

1. *Where, by the fault of two or more ships, damage or loss is caused to one or more of those ships, to their cargoes or freight, or to any property on board, the liability to make good the damage or loss shall be in proportion to the degree in which each ship was in fault.*
2. *If, in any such case, having regard to all the circumstances, it is not possible to establish different degrees of fault, the liability shall be apportioned equally.*

A contrasting illustration can be found in the 2022 case of the *Wilforce*,[2] in which the lookout on board *Western Moscow* was also condemned by the Court for their poor performance. Their vessel was navigating within the southern part of a Precautionary Area and intent on joining the westbound traffic lane, but the Court held the lookout particularly blameworthy for the collision with the *Wilforce*. It was not all one-sided, though. The failure of *Wilforce* to reduce speed substantially at a critical moment was the result of *Wilforce*'s failure to comply with the local rule which required her to be in a state of *maximum manoeuvring readiness*. Her passage plan provided for her to proceed at 12 knots, making 50 revolutions, which was consistent with full ahead manoeuvring revolutions, but she was making 69, and her speed approaching the Precautionary Area was unsafe, as a result of which

2 *Wilforce Llc v Ratu Shipping Co SA* [2022] EWHC 1190 (Admlty).

she was unable to reduce speed substantially when the actions of *Western Moscow* created a risk of collision. This breach of Rule 6 of the Collision Regulations and of local Rule 8 was particularly blameworthy because *Wilforce* was approaching the Precautionary Area.

The Court therefore found that both vessels were blameworthy, the one to keep a good lookout and the other to proceed at a safe speed. The Court concluded that the actions of *Western Moscow*'s poor lookout was especially striking because she was turning to port onto a westerly heading in the southern half of the Precautionary Area towards a vessel proceeding easterly in the southern half of the Precautionary Area where eastbound vessels would be expected. By contrast *Wilforce* appreciated the risk of collision because she was keeping a good lookout, but she must accept a proportion of blame because of her failure to react with safe speed.

The Master, therefore, holds the ultimate authority for that vessel wherever she is in the world and they are responsible to the Flag State for compliance with all the maritime regulations that prevail; the Officer of the Watch is the Master's representative, and the lookout must ensure that Rule 5 of the Collision Regulations is observed and *maintain a proper lookout by sight and hearing as well as by all available means appropriate to the prevailing circumstances and conditions so as to make a full appraisal of the situation and of the risk of collision.* The whole ethos of shipboard responsibility can be found in a poem, which may sound hilarious, but it is strikingly appropriate:

> *Great fleas have little fleas upon their backs to bite 'em,*
> *And little fleas have lesser fleas, and so ad infinitum.*
> *And the great fleas themselves, in turn, have greater fleas to go on;*
> *While these again have greater still, and greater still, and so on.*[3]

The obligations owed between Convention States essentially hinge upon the nature of a ship as being a part of the sovereign territory of the Flag State; thus, the ship is entitled to the protection which any part of a State has from intervention or injury by another State. By the same token, the Flag State must be accountable for harm inflicted by the ship upon another State. In all respects, the Flag State must be able to manage the risks, which it does by delegating responsibility – and accountability – to the individual in whom it has reposed its confidence by the accreditation of Master.

In addition, as a sovereign part of the Flag State, the rights and obligations conferred by the laws of the Flag State must be managed within the vessel, which naturally falls to the task of the Master. As a result, the Master must accept accountability to the State which put them in that position of responsibility in the first place. Theirs, in law, is the ultimate authority for that vessel and they are responsible to the Flag State for compliance with its maritime regulations; but the Flag State must exercise authority over the Master, who is the one and only representative

3 De Morgan, Augustus, 1872, A Budget of Paradoxes.

of the Flag State The Master has the power to delegate responsibility for virtually all matters (save the overriding duty to maintain order and discipline) to subordinates, whose obligations arise in the course of their watch – it is at that time that the officer of the watch is the Master's representative. But accountability must be defined by laws. The latest version of Chapter V was implemented by the Merchant Shipping (Safety of Navigation) Regulations 2020:

> *5 (1) A ship to which these Regulations apply must comply with each requirement in Chapter V applicable to that ship and referred to in paragraph (2).*

Regulation 9 (1) of the 2020 Regulations provides that any contravention of Regulations covering plans, procedures, surveys and systems may amount to an offence by the owner and Master. This underlines the Master's responsibility to ensure that the shipboard operation meets their headline responsibilities, which include a raft of statutory provisions:

- Safe manning and STCW Requirements;
- Hours of Work and Rest;
- Crew Management within the Maritime Labour Convention;
- Official Log Book;
- GMDSS Log Book;
- Health and Safety, and medical care;
- Accident Reporting;
- Surveys and Audits;
- Stowaways and Refugees;
- Keeping and amending the Continuous Synopsis Record;
- On-board training.

Regulation 9(2) sets out violations of matters such as navigation records, distress obligations, safe navigation and avoidance of dangerous situations which may give rise to the prosecution of the Master alone. On summary conviction before Magistrates, a fine may be imposed, but upon conviction on indictment in the Crown Court, the consequence may lead to imprisonment for a term not exceeding two years, or a fine, or both.

As if SOLAS needed reinforcement, international law has addressed the Master's authority through the International Safety Management Code 2002; in Part 5, the Code requires the Owners' shore-based management system to support the Master's responsibility and authority with clearly defined and documented Standing Orders implementing the safety and environmental-protection policy, motivating the crew in the observation of that policy, issuing appropriate orders and instructions in a clear and simple manner, verifying that specified requirements are observed, and reviewing the safety management system and reporting its deficiencies to the shore-based management.

In addition, the ISM Code obliges the Company to ensure that the safety management system operating on board the ship contains a clear statement that the

Master has the overriding authority and the responsibility to make decisions with respect to safety and pollution prevention; all they may ask of the Company is its assistance as may be necessary. In terms of the structural integrity of the vessel, responsibility rests with the Master to ensure the following:

- The condition of the ship, including its structure, machinery and equipment, is maintained to regulation standards;
- No material change is made after a survey, except by direct replacement;
- Whenever an accident occurs or a defect is discovered it is reported at the earliest opportunity to the Flag State.

Overarching all these provisions, rests the Master's Flag State responsibility, that, while they retain absolute discretion, they remain accountable for their command decisions, and foremost in their mind will be their responsibility for the safety of life at sea. The duty to render assistance under international law is primarily regulated by Article 98 of UNCLOS, which provides that every Flag State shall require their Master *to render assistance to any person found at sea in danger of being lost*, and then *to proceed with all possible speed to the rescue of persons in distress, if informed of their need of assistance, in so far as such action may reasonably be expected of him*. The only proviso obliges the Master to act *without serious danger to the ship, the crew or the passengers*, according to their discretion in exercising their professional judgment.

On 4 August 2020, the Master of the *Maersk Etienne*, a Danish-flagged tanker, was instructed by the Maltese rescue co-ordination centre to attend to a small fishing vessel in distress off the coast of Tunisia in the Gulf of Gabes. The Master has a duty under SOLAS V Regulation 33-1, on receiving information from any source that persons are in distress at sea, to proceed with all speed to their assistance; so they did, and made a legitimate deviation, while they rescued 27 migrants including a pregnant woman and a child. The Master proceeded towards Malta, but the ship was denied entry into port and remained anchored outside the Port State's contiguous zone. Such Port State refusal flew in the face of international provision made in May 2004, by which the Search and Rescue Convention and SOLAS were amended to impose an obligation on States to cooperate and coordinate to ensure that ships' masters are allowed to disembark rescued persons to a place of safety. In order to fulfil this objective, both conventions impose obligations to ensure cooperation takes place so that mariners who had provided assistance are promptly relieved, and to ensure that Masters providing assistance are released from their obligations with a minimum of deviation from the ship's intended voyage. But the reality let the Master down badly; a 38-day standoff ensued with the three States involved, Denmark, Tunisia and Malta refusing to accept responsibility for the migrants. Conditions began to deteriorate quickly with food and water supplies diminishing, while tensions escalated on board leading some of the migrants to jump into the sea. On 11 September, the migrants were transferred to an NGO operated vessel and finally disembarked in Pozzallo two days later. The consequence on the Master and the pressures on the stakeholders in the marine adventure can be imagined; that being said, the Master's Flag State responsibility is defined by the very high standard which is expected of them in exercising their professional judgment; in this case the Master made the right call all the way through the case.

From this point, we must address the rights and responsibilities of the Port State in respect of the Master.

The Master and the Port State

Article 87 of UNCLOS enshrines the ancient doctrine of the freedom of the high seas outside the territorial sea[4] as follows:

> *The high seas are open to all States, whether coastal or land-locked. Freedom of the high seas is exercised under the conditions laid down by this Convention and by other rules of international law. It comprises, inter alia ... freedom of navigation; ... freedom of overflight;*

Article 2, however, assures the Coastal State its sovereign jurisdiction, to the exclusion of other States,' from its land territory to an adjacent belt of sea, described in Article 3 as the territorial sea *up to a limit not exceeding 12 nautical miles, measured from baselines.*

Article 2 further assures a State its *sovereignty to the air space over the territorial sea as well as to its bed and subsoil.*

So, what of some conflict between Flag State and Coastal State in terms of criminal jurisdiction? UNCLOS clearly must determine the applicable regulation in a Coastal State's sovereign jurisdiction:[5]

1 *The criminal jurisdiction of the coastal State should not be exercised on board a foreign ship passing through the territorial sea to arrest any person or to conduct any investigation in connection with any crime committed on board the ship during its passage, save only in the following cases:*
   (a) *if the consequences of the crime extend to the coastal State;*
   (b) *if the crime is of a kind to disturb the peace of the country or the good order of the territorial sea;*
   (c) *if the assistance of the local authorities has been requested by the master of the ship or by a diplomatic agent or consular officer of the flag State;*
   (d) *if such measures are necessary for the suppression of illicit traffic in narcotic drugs or psychotropic substances.*

As a result, the very fact that the Master assented to the process of certification by the authority of the Flag State makes out an unassailable argument that he has voluntarily subjected himself to all the laws of the Flag State and, necessarily, the

4 And the exclusive economic zone, over which the coastal State does not enjoy sovereign jurisdiction save for the protection of resources.

5 Article 27.

applicable laws of a Port State in whose sovereign jurisdiction he has voluntarily entered.

Certainly the highest priority is given to the safety of life at sea, and Port State laws are generally very clearly defined. Section 98 Merchant Shipping Act 1995 imposes criminal liability for a dangerously unsafe ship in UK jurisdiction:

> *If a ship which (of any Flag) is in a port in the United Kingdom, or is a United Kingdom ship and is in any other port, is dangerously unsafe, then, subject to subsections (4) and (5) below, the master and the owner of the ship shall each be guilty of an offence.*

Section 94 defines a ship as dangerously unsafe if in the opinion of the Port State she is *unfit to remain at sea without serious danger to human life, or unfit to go on a voyage without serious danger to human life.*

The Master will be held accountable if the grounds meet the provisions in Section 98(2) that the condition, or the unsuitability for its purpose, of the ship or its machinery or equipment, or any part of the ship or its machinery or equipment; or undermanning; or overloading or unsafe or improper loading; or the sweeping provision *any other matter relevant to the safety of the ship*. The section does not clarify whether the human life is on board the ship or elsewhere if the ship is not under command, that is, through some exceptional circumstance she is unable to manoeuvre and keep out of the way of another ship.

In this case, Section 98(4) offers a defence if they can prove that *at the time of the alleged offence arrangements had been made which were appropriate to ensure that before the ship went to sea it was made fit to do so without serious danger to human life by reason of the matters relevant to its safety which are specified in the charge*; or *it was reasonable for such arrangements not to have been made*. A solution presents itself, therefore, that the Master should satisfy themselves with evidence that the hardware and software comprising the autonomous system was safe and reliable at the commencement of the voyage. Of course, it does not exclude the risk of accountability but it may reduce it to a satisfactory level that takes it out of the meaning of the Act.

The old maxim that ignorance of the law is no defence, should always be at the back of the Master's mind when they enter a Port State's territorial sea. Whether Port State justice maps onto that of the Flag State is irrelevant; the Port State will prevail. Of the many examples, we can analyse that of Captain Schröder, to illustrate the reality that, what the Master faces, may not be justice, but it is the law, and it is as well that the seafarer appreciates that.

> *Every captain, engineer, pilot or other person employed on any steamboat or vessel, by whose misconduct, negligence, or inattention to his duties on such vessel the life of any person is destroyed, and every owner, charterer, inspector or other public officer, through whose fraud, neglect, connivance, misconduct, or violation of law the life of any person is destroyed, shall be fined under this title or imprisoned not more than ten years or both.*[6]

6 18 USC Section 11153.

On 1 March 2006, Captain Wolfgang Schröder was in command of the container-ship *Zim Mexico III*, entering the Port of Mobile, Alabama. There were no special hazards or issue brought to mariners' attention and, the following day, having completed cargo operations, she was under way for departure.

To transit the channel out of the port, the vessel needed to swing 180 degrees in the river off the berth. A tug had always been used previously to turn the vessel when coming alongside the berth but not on leaving and, on this occasion, the Master and pilot agreed that she could swing round without tug assistance, relying on her bow thruster. It is a crucial part of the evidence that the pilot testified that he asked the Master if the bow thruster was working, and he replied that it was.

The vessel encountered difficulties completing the manoeuvre in the river, which expert evidence attributed to bow thruster failure, which resulted in an allision when the bow of the ship hit a dockside crane, causing it to collapse and crushing a shoreside fitter, Shawn Jacobs, who died of his injuries. Captain Schröder was arraigned on an indictment under the Seaman's Manslaughter Act in which the Prosecution alleged the negligence or inattention to duties of Captain Schröder resulted in the death of Mr Jacobs.

During pre-trial case management proceedings, the Judge ruled that the standard of proof under the statute was *simple negligence*, in other words the civil burden was required, rather than the minimum standard required for criminal accountability of *gross negligence*. The Jury even wrestled with this point in their deliberations, and sent two notes to the Judge, seeking clarification and asked if they could add some text to the verdict that they found the Master Guilty of simple negligence rather than gross negligence. The Judge directed them to write Guilty with no further words of explanation.

Captain Schröder was duly convicted and was remanded in custody for sentencing. At the sentencing hearing, some four months later, Judge Granade got as close as she dared to an apology for the injustice of the law, when she said:

> *While I certainly do not discount the terrible consequences that have resulted from this negligence, what he has been convicted of is really a civil offense* [*sic*].[7]

She sentenced him to a term of imprisonment equal to the period he had spent in custody and was therefore free to go.

At least the Master can be forewarned of laws if they are well-defined. There are circumstances, however, in which the law may be unclear, and even the Courts in the Port State have difficulty in drawing conclusions on its application to a ship of a foreign flag. In the 2005 United States case of *Spector v Norwegian Cruise Line*,[8] the United States Supreme Court considered whether domestic American legisla-

7 *United States of America v Wolfgang Schröder* [2007] United States District Court, Alabama Southern District (currently unreported).

8 *Spector v Norwegian Cruise Line Ltd*, 545 US 119 (2005).

tion, in this case the Americans with Disabilities Act 1990, applied to foreign-flag cruise ships in American territorial waters.

The Act itself did not contain a specific provision making its application mandatory to foreign-flag vessels in US waters. The issue arose over the meaning and effect of the Clear Statement Rule, which was defined as a rule of international law that the law of the Flag State ordinarily governs the internal affairs of a ship. As a result, it was argued that, under the Clear Statement Rule, without a clear indication of congressional intent, the Americans with Disabilities Act could not apply to foreign-flag vessels in United States territory. The Lower Court, the Court of Appeals for the Fifth Circuit, had ruled that the Act did not apply to foreign-flag ships because it did not contain a specific provision mandating its application to foreign-flag vessels in US territorial seas. Of the eight Justices, five disagreed with that and held that cruise ships of whatever flag were prima facie bound by a statutory definition of what was *readily achievable* for *public accommodation* and *specified public transportation.*[9]

But then the difficulties started. The majority concluded that the standard required by the Act would be inconsistent with international law, particularly the provisions of SOLAS which address construction and the safety of life at sea, which would place foreign-flag ships in violation of the domestic law as soon as they entered US territorial waters, obviously causing chaos to merchant ship operations, as a result of which the requirements would not be readily achievable, which was a key feature of the Act. But three of those five Justices fell out with the others on the application of the Clear Statement Rule, which, they believed, required that neither the Act in question, nor, indeed, any other Act which did not have a specific maritime application, could apply to the internal order and discipline of a foreign-flag ship without a clear expression of intent that Congress meant that to be the case when it passed the Act in question. In the resultant row four Justices concluded that the Clear Statement Rule merely raises the assumption that Congress does not intend that its statutes should have effect beyond its territorial boundaries. In a complicated decision, it was, at least, possible to identify the key point of the Appeal that the Clear Statement Rule did not invalidate a domestic law which regulated the internal order of a foreign-Flag ship in United States territorial waters; but that the standard which the Act provided must be readily achievable, and what was readily achievable had to be defined so as to avoid conflict with SOLAS.

Revisiting the SOLAS convention, the Master's accountability for the safe navigation of the vessel is derived from SOLAS Ch V Regulations 34:

1 *Prior to proceeding to sea, the master shall ensure that the intended voyage has been planned using the appropriate nautical charts and nautical publications for the area concerned, taking into account the guidelines and recommendations developed by the Organization.*

2 *The voyage plan shall identify a route which:*

9 The Act's own words in italics.

2.1 *takes into account any relevant ships' routeing systems*
2.2 *ensures sufficient sea room for the safe passage of the ship throughout the voyage*
2.3 *anticipates all known navigational hazards and adverse weather conditions;*
2.4 *takes into account the marine environmental protection measures that apply, and avoids, as far as possible, actions and activities which could cause damage to the environment*

But they retain absolute discretion, and it is worth keeping in mind the provision in SOLAS Chapter V Regulation 34-1.

Statute law has been assisted greatly by cases in clarifying the current law, to shed much light on the standards by which an allegation of negligence must be tested, for it is this which brings the Master's accountability into question when things go wrong. This is conveyed articulately in the recent case of *Passarello v Grumbine*[10] in the Superior Court of Pennsylvania, which establishes key principles that, in cases in which the judgment of a professional person is concerned, negligence cannot be established merely because of an unfortunate result which might have occurred despite the exercise of reasonable care. This case involved a claim in negligence against a physician but the rule applies equally to Masters that such professional persons are permitted a broad range of judgment when carrying out their professional duties and so are not liable for errors of judgment unless it has been proved that *an error of judgment was the result of negligence*. Crucially for the case of the Master, it was held that the standard of care to be established in professional negligence cases is objective in nature, because it focuses on the knowledge, skill, and care normally possessed and exercised by the professional in question. Consideration of a mere 'error of judgment' improperly refocuses attention on the professional's state of mind at the time; it is improper because the civil tort of negligence is concerned with consequences, a test which must be objective, rather than the Defendant's state of mind that determines his guilt of a crime, which must be established by a subjective test.

Article 2 of UNCLOS defines maritime sovereignty of a Coastal State beyond any doubt, to extend beyond its land territory to the territorial sea, which Article 3 identifies broadly as the 12-mile limit, within which the State concerned shall enforce its own laws without interference from any other. The problem arises when the Port State's legal process conflicts with the understanding of Justice held by societies in other States, particularly where laws are promulgated in a State, which are inconsistent with its Treaty obligations with other States. Central to this theme is the responsibility and accountability of the Master. They are, of course, the Flag State representative with absolute discretion in their command decisions, but the question of their culpability for matters outside their knowledge or control has

10 *Steven P Passarello and Others v Rowena T Grumbine and Others,* No 1399 WDA 2010; 2011 PA Super 199.

been interpreted very differently, giving rise to tensions between Port and Flag States, from cases such as the *Hebei Spirit* to the *Coral Sea*; in short, some Port Prosecutors have held that the Master must be held guilty even if they were unaware of the mischief, simply because of their position.

Captain Kristo Laptalo was Master of the *Coral Sea,* registered in Nassau under the Bahamas flag. A Croatian national, Captain Laptalo was 58 when, in June 2007, his ship loaded a cargo of 200,000 pallets of bananas at the Ecuadorian port of Guayaquil. A routine search by Ecuadorian police failed to reveal any evidence of illegal drugs having been stowed with the cargo. The charterers initially nominated the port of discharge as Civitavecchia, Italy and the ship sailed on the 6th July. Then, 13 days later, orders were received from the charterers instructing them to steam to the port of Aegion in Greece. More specific orders, to discharge 27,377 pallets at Aegion, came 17 days into the voyage. So, they did.

The cargo was discharged and resting alongside at Aegion when a quality check carried out by the ship's agent revealed that 51.6 kilos of cocaine had been hidden in the cargo. The ship had been cleared to sail and was awaiting the pilot, when Captain Laptalo was informed of the discovery, and he promptly disembarked to inspect the pallets himself.

The Greek authorities then arrested him, together with Lithuanian first mate Konstantin Metelev and Filipino bosun Narciso Carcia. Captain Laptalo was duly indicted on very serious charges of smuggling drugs into Greece and remanded in custody.

At the time of the events, the law of drug trafficking in Greece provided for the criminalisation of import, provision, manufacture, production, sale, delivery, transport, possession and distribution of illegal drugs. That being said, Greece is a party to all major international treaties regarding drug trafficking, organised crime and corruption. Under 2006 law, the import was defined as the illegal entry of drugs in the Greek territory, through its land, sea or air borders, with an intention by the offender to produce the prohibited result (or an acceptance of the result), knowing that is either certain or probable to occur. The offender must at least have acted with intent and have accepted to distribute the drugs

The case duly went to Trial, about a year later, when, among the Prosecution witnesses, the port captain was asked, 'What do you have against those people?' he replied: 'Nothing, but I have 52 kg of drugs and have to arrest somebody.' Far from incriminating Captain Laptalo, the Prosecution evidence suggested that the Defendants could not hide drugs on the ship and that the Master was not culpable. After all, Captain Laptalo did not even know which port of discharge the charterers would nominate when they left Ecuador.

The Prosecution submitted, however, and the Court accepted the argument, that Captain Laptalo as Master had to know everything that was going on board the ship, including the content of the cargo she was carrying, by reason of his position. The Prosecution also submitted the Master must have intended to produce the prohibited result because it was *illogical that someone would send cocaine without any control over it*. They said that the claim by the Ecuadorian police that they had inspected the cargo before the ship sailed proved that the drugs were loaded onto the ship somewhere in the open sea. On 17 July 2008, Captain Laptalo was sentenced to 14 years in prison and a fine of 200,000 euros. The first officer Konstantin Metelev and bosun Narciso Garcia were released. Captain Laptalo appealed against conviction and sentence. At the appeal hearing, the Judicial Council apparently found sympathy with the Defence argument that it would have been physically impossible to access the cargo once it had been loaded. Moreover, it was reported that prosecutors eventually admitted that there was no evidence that Captain Laptalo was responsible for the smuggling. The Judicial Council concluded that neither Captain Laptalo nor any other Master could be prosecuted according to command responsibility without incriminating evidence, observing the principle which we encountered in the case of Captain Holland of the *Capetown Castle* in 1965. At least it corrected the error and clarified the principle to be followed in the future in similar cases, when the Judicial Council reversed the decision against Captain Laptalo.[11]

Concurrently, and possibly without even considering it, the Court brought the decision into line with Article 6(2) of the European Convention on Human Rights, that everyone charged with a criminal offence shall be presumed innocent until proved guilty according to law.

But what happens when the Port State must undertake risk management in confronting a clear scenario in which there is no specific statutory regulation? The danger is that the Court makes it up as it goes along. On 2 April 2012, the Singaporean-flagged *Kota Nebula* departed Shanghai for Ningbo, in Zhejiang. The second officer was officer of the watch at the time of the casualty, when it was alleged that he failed to maintain a proper lookout and proceed with safe speed in a complex navigation situation under poor visibility, when, at about 15.00, she collided with the fishing boat *Zhe Pu Yu 75185* near Zhoushan sea area.

Then, when the bosun realised that the collision had taken place and reported it to the second officer, instead of slowing down or stopping the vessel to undertake rescue measures, the second officer reported the accident to the Master, and continued to make full speed away from the accident location. On receiving notification of the accident, the Master made no attempt to undertake rescue or report the incident to the relevant authorities. He even ordered the crew to destroy evidence of the collision by removing the shattered glass of the fishing boat found on the bow deck.

It was nearly three hours later, that the Zhoushan Maritime Safety Administration (MSA) received a report of the collision, and preliminarily identified the *Kota Nebula* as the suspect vessel. The MSA ordered the *Kota Nebula* to berth and submit to an investigation. The navigation chart, log book and electronic navigation data of the vessel were preserved for further investigation and interviews were carried out by MSA officers with crews on board regarding the suspected collision. Despite the scrape found on both sides of the *Kota Nebula*'s bow, the Master,

11 Unfortunately for Captain Laptalo, the bureaucracy of Greek law had another blow to cast, when, after being acquitted on Appeal, he then was detained for having broken Greek law, according to which non-citizens of the EU can stay in an EU member state no longer than three months.

second officer and duty AB denied the occurrence of any collision during initial interviews. Only on the third day of the investigation did one of the crew admit that he had heard a collision and saw the *Kota Nebula* hit the fishing boat while he was working on deck at the ship's bow. Relevant evidence regarding the condition of the vessel and the bridge at the material time was also available from the electronic data. In the face of the objective evidence against them, the second officer and the Master finally admitted the occurrence of the collision four days later.

Paradoxically, they were pleading Guilty to an offence that had no relevance to marine operations. There was no applicable law for maritime accidents under Chinese law in which seafarers would be criminally accountable for a fatal accident and then leave the scene without reporting it. There was, however, a criminal offence under Chinese law in road traffic accidents in which a driver causes death or personal injury and then leaves the scene of the accident to avoid prosecution. The apparently dishonest conduct of the Master who attempted to pervert the course of justice after the event may well have formed a separate issue, but, in the event, the Court tried and convicted the seafarers for the fatal maritime accident, based on the law and evidence required to establish guilt in a road traffic case. But the circumstantial issues surrounding a maritime collision are hardly relevant in establishing liability for a road traffic offence.

According to the criminal law of the People's Republic of China and the judicial opinion of the Supreme Court, the person bearing the major liability for a road traffic accident shall be sentenced to a term of three to seven years' imprisonment if the liable parties fled from the accident scene after the accident, or if the accident caused the death of more than two people or injured more than five. The second officer, as the seafarer operating the vessel at the time, was held to be the primary liable party, while the Master, who did not report the accident to the relevant authority and ordered the crew to destroy evidence, was held liable for negligent management of the vessel.

It is not as if a European Court would uphold the principles of justice in which the rights of the Defendant stand free from the normative ethics of Society. European society will readily recognise this growing phenomenon of criminalisation, for we have embraced and encouraged it in our own jurisdiction in recent years. The spine has already been chilled with the decision of the European Court of Human Rights in *Mangouras v Spain* that it put the environmental concerns of Port State societies before human rights to identify the seafarers responsible, notwithstanding the demands of the criminal process, *to ensure that they appeared to stand trial and to punish them.*[12]

Advice and Assistance

It is essential that the seafarer facing arrest and prosecution obtains the best possible advice and representation, by a lawyer who is accredited in the State concerned.

12 *Mangouras v Spain* (12050/04); Para 3 Summary of Judgment.

The cost of such representation is likely to be substantial however, and it is therefore they must prepare for such an eventuality in advance, by obtaining a policy of professional indemnity insurance. The cover will give them a sporting chance of a successful defence, or at least the protection of their human rights; but the cover will only start after the insurance contract has been closed and the premium paid; there will be no compulsion on the insurer to underwrite the seafarer's legal costs if they apply for insurance after the incident giving rise to the criminal proceedings. It is a fact of life that the best legal advice and representation can cost more than the State affords a defendant under a legal aid order. Professional indemnity insurance will underwrite the cost of such representation, although it will not indemnify the defendant for fines, because a contract of insurance cannot pay for criminal penalties as a matter of public policy.

Ideally, only the best lawyer will do, and they must be instructed to attend from the point of arrest and questioning. All too often, procedures are not followed, and damaging statements can be made unintentionally that the prosecution can exploit. This can occur even in régimes that one would consider above such things. In overseas jurisdictions, the Flag State's Commissioner or Consul will assist the Master and any seafarers who are nationals of that State; other seafarers must contact their own consular representative. In either event, they will provide a list of lawyers, and the constituent names can be researched and consulted to find the best one for the task, and in maritime cases that can be very specialist. Carrying out some basic research along these lines is crucial because the quality of legal advice and representation depends upon the experience and expertise – and the independence – of the defence team. It is a dangerous thing to instruct a lawyer who has a basic knowledge of the criminal law but lacks experience in maritime criminalisation. This is a specialist field which demands an understanding of how to apply the principles of negligence to the criminal process, and this will often involve searching for the best-experienced lawyer. If time is of the essence, the seafarer must instruct a criminal lawyer to protect their immediate interests, giving them some time and space to find the best lawyer with whom they will go to trial.

Legal representation is only as good as the evidence which the seafarer can deliver. As a result, a key factor over which they have control in their own interests is in the evidence which they can provide to their lawyer. It is then up to them to decide what is relevant and admissible at Trial, how best they can rely on that in discrediting the Prosecution case and, indeed, how expert witnesses may be briefed to deliver their reports, upon which the Courts place great weight.

All that being said, there is a vital factor to remember at all times: Never admit Liability or Guilt. Such an admission can prove an insurmountable obstacle in the seafarer's defence.

16 The Master and Shipboard Management

It may be helpful to preface this chapter with a bullet-point summary of the Master's responsibilities in Flag State shipboard management:

- Safety of navigation and the protection of the marine environment;
- Manning and STCW Requirements;
- Hours of Work and Rest;
- Crew Management within the Maritime Labour Convention;
- Official Log Book;
- GMDSS Log Book;
- Health and Safety, and medical care;
- Accident Reporting;
- Surveys and Audits;
- Stowaways and Refugees;
- Keeping and amending the Continuous Synopsis Record;
- On-board training.

Clearly, the heart of these responsibilities involves the safety of life. Safety management had been a defining feature of shipboard management for generations before the emergence of the International Safety Management Code, and as such relied heavily on the relationship between the Master and the Owner. The following are extracts from Standing Orders given by the Bowater Steamship Company Limited in 1957[1] and mirror the relationship between the Master and the Owner:

> *The Master is at all times the personal representative of the Owners. His authority is supreme in every respect, at all times, both at sea and in port, over all departments and all employees on board ship.*
>
> *The British Statutes and Courts of Law having constantly proclaimed that the Master of a ship is the universally recognized representative of the Owners while the Master remains in command, he cannot divest of his identity and responsibility nor the authority pertaining thereto.*

1 See www.bowatersteamship company.no-ip.com/page86.html.

DOI: 10.4324/9781003361916-16

By comparison, the ISM Code offers little change in substance (although in form it makes substantial changes with the introduction of torrents of paperwork):

> *The Company should ensure that the SMS operating on board the ship contains a clear statement emphasizing the master's authority. The Company should establish in the SMS that the master has the overriding authority and the responsibility to make decisions with respect to safety and pollution prevention and to request the Company's assistance as may be necessary.*

The Master has a special contractual relationship with the Operator of the ship, arising out of their common interest in the success of the marine adventure, which could be relied upon to maintain the bond between them. But the changes in the pattern of ship management, in particular since the 1970s, have seen the outsourcing of skills, so that the business of managing the operation of the ship is often entirely unrelated to the owner, with whom the Master may have their contract of employment. The operator, as manager of the ship, may well have sub-contracted the crewing contract to another business, while they only won the management contract because of a tender which offered the lowest cost, and any additional financial cost would conflict with the manager's bottom-line budget. Indeed, the manager may be operating with the very minimum of resources, far from able to provide the support which the Master might be entitled to expect from the owner of the asset over which they have command. Thus, far from sharing a common interest with the Master, the management company may very well have a vested interest in avoiding legal accountability by dissociating itself from the Master's acts or omissions, for it would derive no financial benefit from such association but could be exposed to risk if the Master's tortious acts led it into vicarious liability. During the course of the twenty-first century, however, legislation has increasingly addressed the obligations of the owner and case law has refined constructions of the distinction between the owner and the operator. In the final Appeal in the case of the *Stema Barge II*,[2] Lord Justice Phillips concluded that the mere provision of the crew did not mean that the vessel was operated by the provider; and that the term Operator *must entail more than the mere operation of the machinery of the vessel (or providing personnel to operate that machinery) ... involving management or control of the vessel*. This, then, gives us the bottom line of the definition which is at the heart of the ISM Code, that the Company with the responsibility means *the owner of the ship or any other organisation or person such as the manager, or the bareboat charterer, who has assumed the responsibility for operation of the ship from the owner of the ship and who on assuming such responsibility has agreed to take over all the duties and responsibilities imposed by the Code.*[3]

Some historical background to ISM is essential in understanding its composition. In this context we can identify its genesis in one case.

2 *Splitt Chartering ApS & Others v Saga Shipholding Norway AS & Others* [2021] (EWCA CIV 1880).
3 SOLAS IX Regulation 1.

P & O Ferries and the *Herald of Free Enterprise*

It is not possible to understand P & O's corporate position without an insight into the story of maritime commerce. This originated in 1824, with the formation of the General Steam Navigation Company. In the course of the next hundred years, it became a household name and, naturally, attracted a great deal of inward investment, thanks to corporate legislation which defined a new business entity, the limited liability company, protecting shareholders whose exposure to claims was limited to the level of their financial shareholding. Following the end of the First World War, P&O could command a great deal of funding but needed European business to fill their ships; the General Steam Navigation Company had the agency business in Europe to fill their ships but needed funding. So it was, that P&O bought the controlling interest in General Steam: the investment aspirations both for General Steam and for P&O were satisfied, and corporate law protected the investors with a future that gave them the confidence that would enable both companies to grow. This underlines the point that it is impossible to discuss the fate of the *Herald* without understanding the financial imperatives which underpin shipping, and the cross-Channel trade.

By the summer of 1986, the board room of P & O Ferries was thinking hard about its long-term strategy, in order to keep its position in the market-place and satisfy the shareholders. Paradoxically, it was this decision which led to the Company taking over the Ownership and operation of the ill-fated *Herald of Free Enterprise*, just a month before her foundering. The *Herald* was one of three sisters, a modern roll-on/roll-off passenger/vehicle ferry grossing 7,950 tonnes, and one of the largest vessels of her type when she left her German builders in 1980. She had been designed at a time when her Owners, Townsend Thoresen, knew that every second and every penny counted in the cut-throat competition on the English Channel. Indeed, so thorough had her design concept been, that the linkspans at either end of her planned service, between Dover and Calais, were especially built to match the levels of the ship's car decks, in order to enable simultaneous loading of both decks and thus minimise the time required for turn-around in port.

The competition just carried on growing on the English Channel, one of the most crowded seaways in the world – and the Dover-Calais run was the most competitive crossing, because it was the shortest – just 22 miles long. While the UK's growing trade with the European Community undoubtedly contributed to the rising demand, competition was heating up thanks to a number of factors. In July 1984, the UK Government announced the privatisation of the former State-owned ferry operator Sealink, which would lead to more pressure still on the competitiveness of the rival ferry operators on the route. Then, in 1986, after generations of aborted attempts to initiate a tunnel project, and in the teeth of bitter opposition from the ferry operators, the French and British governments finally gave permission to build the Channel Tunnel.

In the face of these factors, the board rooms of ferry operators had to consider how best to conduct their prime function: to maximise a yield for their investors. It was against this background that P & O Ferries had to make some bold business decisions. As a short sea shipping company, it had a hugely successful tradition, making the most of its once-mighty foundation in the shape of the General Steam Navigation Company, whose controlling interest had been acquired by P & O in late 1920, and then bought outright in 1972 when P & O remodelled it as P & O Ferries (General European) Limited.[4]

It was the management of the financial risks and opportunities which were uppermost among the concerns in the board room of P & O Ferries; safety management did not feature in their job descriptions. Out of that management of risk, they found a solution, when they resolved to buy out their very formidable rival, Townsend Thoresen, reducing the competition and spreading the overheads. In February of 1987, the deal was completed and the directors of P & O Ferries implemented their plans for maximising the financial yield.

At the time, Townsend's 'Spirit' class of ferries was probably the best-designed for the cross-Channel service. The Spirit-class *Herald of Free Enterprise* and her sisters had enjoyed the best of naval architecture to suit the demands of the operation, which necessitated the vehicle decks to meet the linkspans at Dover and Calais and thus avoid time at either end, allowing turn-arounds to be completed with maximum efficiency.

P & O's own ferries on the Dover–Calais route were doing their job very satisfactorily, however; they did not need Townsend's tonnage there, so it was decided to switch the *Herald of Free Enterprise* to the Zeebrugge route. The only problem was that the linkspan at Zeebrugge had not been designed with the *Herald* in mind, so that, for the vessel's upper vehicle deck to be accessed by the ramp, it was necessary to trim the ship by the head and flood her ballast tanks, to lower the level of the vehicle deck to the linkspan.

When the *Herald* left Zeebrugge on 6 March 1987, not all the water had been pumped out of the bow ballast tanks, causing her to be some 3 feet down at the bow. Mark Stanley, the assistant bosun, was responsible for closing the bow doors but he had been released from duties by the bosun before the sailing time. He duly went to his cabin and fell asleep; tragically, he slept through the 'Harbour Stations' call which ordered the crew to their assigned sailing positions. It was not part of anybody else's duties to ensure that the bow doors were closed before sailing, save the duty of the Master to ensure that the vessel was in all respects safe to proceed to sea. Her design of clamshell bow doors made it impossible for Captain David Lewry to see from the bridge if the doors were opened or closed, though.

The *Herald* sailed at 19.05 local time, with a crew of 80 and some 459 passengers, 81 cars, 3 buses, and 47 trucks. Passing the outer mole 19 minutes later, she increased speed, when a bow wave began to build up under her prow. At 15 knots, with the bow down 3 feet lower than normal, water began to break over the main car deck through the open doors at the rate of 200 tonnes per minute.

4 See Middlemiss, N, 1999, The Navvies, Shield Publications Ltd, Tyne & Wear, pp. 55–56; Robins, N, 2007, Birds of the Sea, Bernard McCall, Bristol, p 112.

In common with other roll on-roll off vessels, the *Herald*'s main vehicle deck lacked transverse bulkheads and, so, the sudden flood of water through the bow doors quickly caused the vessel to become unstable. The *Herald* listed 30 degrees to port almost instantaneously, as water continued to pour in and fill the port wing of the vehicle deck, causing her to capsize 40 seconds later. The *Herald* settled on the sea bed at slightly more than ninety degrees with the starboard half of her hull above water. There had been no chance to launch any of the ship's lifeboats.

At least 150 passengers and 38 members of the crew lost their lives when the vessel capsized, the worst disaster for a British vessel in peacetime since the sinking of the *Titanic* in 1912.

The prevailing legislation at the time for the conduct of an inquiry was the Merchant Shipping Act 1970, defining the statutory provision for a judicial investigation into the loss or presumed loss of a UK-registered ship anywhere in the world, as is the responsibility of the Flag State, or such loss of any ship that foundered in UK territorial waters, as is the responsibility of the Port State. This Formal Investigation was conducted by the Honourable Mr Justice Sheen,[5] whose findings sent the industry into nervous shock.

The purpose of the investigation was to establish findings on the loss of the vessel, with a view to preventing such casualties in the future. It was not the function of the process to establish criminal or civil liability; but the evidence heard in the Inquiry might have been used in litigation to prove – or discredit – such a claim. Mr Justice Sheen, the Admiralty Judge who was appointed Wreck Commissioner for the purpose of presiding over the judicial investigation, summarised his conclusion:

The Court, having carefully inquired into the circumstances attending the above-mentioned shipping casualty, finds, for the reasons stated in the Report, that the capsizing of the HERALD OF FREE ENTERPRISE was partly caused or contributed to by serious negligence in the discharge of their duties by Captain David Lewry (Master), Mr Leslie Sabel (Chief Officer) and Mr Mark Victor Stanley (Assistant bosun), and partly caused or contributed to by the fault of Townsend Car Ferries Limited (the Owners).

The court had no powers of punishment, save the authority to suspend certificates of competence on findings of poor seamanship, and thus suspended *the certificate of the said Captain David Lewry for a period of one year from the 24th July 1987. The Court suspends the certificate of the said Mr Leslie Sabel for a period of two years from the 24th July 1987.*

The Inquiry heard the evidence of a director of the Company, Mr Develin, who, when asked who was responsible for considering matters relating to safety in the navigation of the Company's ships, answered, *Ashore, the system would be to take a consensus of the senior masters*. The Judge took the view that, without a properly qualified marine superintendent, it sounded sensible to rely on such a consensus; the problem revealed by the evidence, though, was that the shore management took very little notice of what they were told by their Masters. In any event, the Masters

5 mv Herald of Free Enterprise. Report of Court No. 8074. Formal Investigation (July 1987).

only met infrequently – indeed, for some two and a half years there had been no meeting at all between Management and Senior Masters, although, latterly, there had been some improvement in this. What really became very clear to the Judge, though, was the frustration felt by the Masters that the Marine department simply did not listen to the complaints or suggestions or wishes of their Masters. And the Judge agreed.

But that was no defence to the allegation against Captain Lewry who, as Master of the vessel, knowingly took a ship to sea in such an unseaworthy state as to endanger life, which came under the provision of section 27 of the 1970 Act, Conduct endangering ships, structures or individuals. As it was not a criminal trial but an inquiry, it was not for the Court to decide the criminality of the case against the Master, but whether there was a case of poor seamanship which would serve the Court's power to make a finding of the Master's fitness to hold a certificate of competency.

The Judge was compelled to address this strictly according to the statutory provision (as summarised above). He explained his findings in full on this:

> *Captain Lewry was Master of the Herald on the 6th March 1987. In that capacity he was responsible for the safety of his ship and every person on board. Captain Lewry took the Herald to sea with the bow doors fully open, with the consequences which have been related. It follows that Captain Lewry must accept personal responsibility for the loss of his ship.*[6]

In judging his conduct, it is right to look at it in perspective. Captain Lewry had served at sea for over 30 years. He had held a Master's Certificate of Competency (Foreign Going) for over 20 years and had held command of a ship for 10 years. Captain Lewry joined the *Herald* on 13 March 1980 as one of five Masters. The Company had issued a set of standing orders which included instructions for Readiness for Sea, which required heads of department to report to the Master immediately they were aware of any deficiency which was likely to cause their departments to be unready for sea in any respect at the due sailing time. In the absence of any such report the Master was advised to assume, at the due sailing time, that the vessel was ready for sea in all respects. As a result, Masters came to rely upon the absence of any report at the time of sailing as satisfying them that their ship was ready for sea in all respects. On 6 March, Captain Lewry saw the Chief Officer come to the Bridge. Captain Lewry did not ask him if the ship was all secure and the Chief Officer did not make a report. Captain Lewry was entitled to assume that the assistant bosun and the Chief Officer were qualified to perform their respective duties, but, in the words of the Judge, he should not have assumed that they had done so. He should have insisted upon receiving a report to that effect. It was apparent to the Judge, however, that the shadow of blame on Captain Lewry should be mitigated by three particular points:

6 Ibid., para 12.1.

1. Captain Lewry merely followed a system which was operated by all the Masters of the *Herald* and approved by the Senior Master, Captain Kirby;
2. The 'Ship's standing orders' issued by the Company made no reference, as they should have done, to opening and closing the bow and stern doors;
3. Company ships had proceeded to sea with bow or stern doors open on five known occasions before the *Herald* casualty.

Some of the incidents in point 3 were known to the management, who had not drawn them to the attention of the other Masters. Captain Lewry had, himself, said in evidence that, if he had been made aware of any of those incidents, he would have instituted a new system on board his ship which would introduce positive reporting to ensure that the doors were closed. The Judge viewed his evidence with a certain caution, however, commenting, rather, that

> *It is possible that he would have done so. But those Masters who were aware of the occasions when ships proceeded to sea with bow or stern doors open did not change their orders.... The fact that other Masters operated the same defective system does not relieve Captain Lewry of his personal responsibility for taking his ship to sea in an unsafe condition. In so doing he was seriously negligent in the discharge of his duties. That negligence was one of the causes contributing to the casualty*[7].

While the function of the proceedings was to investigate the cause of the casualty, it did not have the power to punish – save, under Section 56(4) of the Merchant Shipping Act, which provides that, if, as a result of the investigation, an inquiry is satisfied that a UK-qualified officer has been seriously negligent in the discharge of his duties, and if the inquiry is satisfied that it caused or contributed to the casualty, he may cancel or suspend the officer's certificate. In Captain Lewry's case, the Court took into account the mental and emotional strain which had burdened him as a result of the disaster but, on balance, felt that it would be failing in its duty if it did not suspend his Certificate of Competency. Accordingly, the court suspended Captain Lewry's Master's certificate for one year.

It was not Captain Lewry whom the Judge identified as the villain of the piece, though. While the apparent fault lay with the shipboard management function, that is, the individuals with hands-on control of the crisis – the Master, the Chief Officer and, to a lesser extent, the assistant bosun – the inquiry could not avoid drawing the conclusion, after analysing the exhaustive evidence, that the underlying fault lay within the management control structure, and those responsible for safety as a strategic function of the company. Some safety system had to be rolled out on a company-wide basis, which was down to the responsibility of the company.

In the Judge's opinion, the Company's Board of Directors' ultimate responsibility was to ensure that the safety of their passengers was maintained, which,

7 Ibid., para 12.5.

to the Judge's mind, should have led them to ask themselves, what orders should be given for the safety of their ships? The Board, however, did not appear to have appreciated their responsibility for the safe management of their ships. As a result, not a single director had been charged with the duty of organising safety on the *Herald*. In terms of Board responsibility, this was understandable, if inexcusable – as with most companies, the Board's management function was designed primarily to ensure a profitable yield for the shareholders. Mr Justice Sheen's Report summarised his conclusions on the priority of commercial demands:

11 *Pressure to leave the berth*

11.1 *The Court found some difficulty in finding a clear answer to the question: Why could not the loading officer remain on G deck until the doors were closed before going to his harbour station on the bridge? That operation could be completed in less than three minutes. But the officers always felt under pressure to leave the berth immediately after the completion of loading. The practice was for the officer on the car deck to call the bridge and tell the quartermaster to give the order 'harbour stations' over the Tannoy. Frequently the order 'harbour stations' was given before loading was complete. The order was given as soon as the loading officer decided that by the time the crew arrived at their stations everything would be ready for the ship to proceed to sea. The evidence of Captain Lewry was that on the Zeebrugge run it would have been necessary to delay the order 'harbour stations' until the bow doors had been closed if the Chief Officer was required to remain on G deck until this had been done.*

11.2 *The 'Bridge and Navigational Procedures' guide which was issued by the Company inducted the following:*
Departure from Port: 'a) O.O.W./Master should be on the Bridge approximately 15 minutes before the ship's sailing time;'
That order does not make it clear whether it was the duty of the O.O.W. or the Master to be on the bridge 15 minutes before sailing, or whether the officer was to remain on the bridge thereafter. If the O.O. W. was the loading officer, this order created a conflict in his duties.

The conflict was brought to the attention of Mr Develin by a memorandum dated 21st August 1982 from Captain Hackett, Senior Master of FREE ENTERPRISE VIII in which he said:

Departure from Port: 'It is impractical for the O.O.W. (either the Chief or Second Officer) to be on the Bridge 15 minutes before sailing time. Both are fully committed to loading the ship. At sailing time, the Chief Officer stands by the bow or stern door to see the ramp out and assure papers are on board etc. The Second Officer proceeds to his after mooring station to assure that the propellers are clear and report to bridge.'

The order illustrates the lack of thought given by management to the organisation of the officers' duties.

11.3 *The sense of urgency to sail at the earliest possible moment was exemplified by an internal memorandum sent to assistant managers by Mr D Shipley, who was the operations manager at Zeebrugge. It is dated 18th August 1986 and the relevant parts of it reads as follows:*

'There seems to be a general tendency of satisfaction if the ship has sailed two or three minutes early. Where, a full load is present, then every effort has to be made to sail the ship 15 minutes earlier ...

I expect to read from now onwards, especially where FE8 is concerned, that the ship left 15 minutes early ... put pressure on the first officer if you don't think he is moving fast enough. Have your load ready when the vessel is in and marshal your staff and machines to work efficiently. Let's put the record straight, sailing late out of Zeebrugge isn't on. It's 15 minutes early for us.'

Mr A P Young [witness for the owner] *sought to explain away that memorandum on the basis that the language was used merely for purposes of what he called 'motivation.' But it was entirely in keeping with his own thoughts at that time. On the 13th August 1986 Captain Thorne, the Senior Master of FREE ENTERPRISE VIII, sent a memorandum to Deck Officers with a copy to Mr Young, in which he said:*

'Finally, one of the reasons for such late arrivals is due to late departures from Dover the cause of which is rarely due to any inefficiency on the port of Dover staff – just lack of time available to handle both discharge and loading together with storing (often only 30–40 minutes). This situation can often be assisted by an early sailing from Zeebrugge the previous voyage: Zeebrugge staff MUST be made aware of such necessity immediately upon arrival.'

Mr Young replied:

'I would just like to state that I thoroughly endorse your action.'

The Court was left in no doubt that deck officers were under pressure that no time was to be wasted. The Company sought to say that this disaster could have been avoided if the Chief Officer had waited on G deck another three minutes. That is true. But the Company took no proper steps to ensure that the Chief Officer remained on G deck until the bow doors were closed. On 6 March they were running late. The *Herald* sailed five minutes late. This may have contributed to the Chief officer's decision to leave G deck before the arrival of Mr Stanley, which he anticipated.

This was one of the factors which led to the Judge's comments in the Report, which have subsequently rumbled thunderously through the boardrooms of every shipowner in the country:

> *A full investigation into the circumstances of the disaster leads inexorably to the conclusion that the underlying or cardinal faults lay higher up in the Company. The Board of Directors did not appreciate their responsibility for the safe management of their ships. They did not apply their minds to the question: What orders should be given for the safety of our ships?*
>
> *The directors did not have any proper comprehension of what their duties were. There appears to have been a lack of thought about the way in which the Herald ought to have been organized for the Dover-Zeebrugge run. All concerned in management, from the members of the Board of Directors down to the junior superintendents, were guilty of fault in that all must be regarded as sharing responsibility for the failure of management. From top to bottom the body corporate was infected with the disease of sloppiness.*[8]

While Mr Justice Sheen had exercised his power to deal with Captain Lewry by way of reviewing his certificate of competency, the Judge had no power to order any redress against the Company; recourse would have to follow in a more appropriate Court. And while His Lordship criticised the directors in the *Herald* Inquiry in the most scathing terms possible, the same words, paradoxically, became the directors' salvation. The fact that the evidence led to the conclusion that the directors had not appreciated their responsibility for the safe management of their ships, that they had not applied their minds to the question of safety and their lack of comprehension of what their duties were, showed that no director had assumed any personal responsibility which underpinned a duty of care and, in the absence of that, there could not be any realistic prospect of a conviction for manslaughter against an individual director and, thus, under the essential identification doctrine to establish guilt, there was no prospect of a successful prosecution against the Company for corporate manslaughter. Finally, Mr Justice Sheen commented on the question of a prosecution for a statutory offence that merely regulates and does not legislate, so such a provision does not require the mental element of a guilty mind:

> *Mr Stone, who appeared on behalf of the Department, said, on instructions, that it is not the intention of the Department to prosecute anyone responsible for the fact that the HERALD went to sea with her bow doors open. There is implicit in that statement the suggestion that a statutory offence may have been committed. Mr Steel who appeared on behalf of the Secretary of State, submitted that if a Ro-Ro ferry goes to sea with its bow doors open, that is not an offence under the Merchant Shipping Act 1979 or under the Merchant Shipping (Load Lines) Act 1967 or any other statute. Mr Stone invited the Court to express its opinion as to whether that view is valid.*

8 Ibid., para 14.1.

Neither the Master nor the Owners of the HERALD have been prosecuted. The offence which the Department has in mind has not been formulated. Accordingly, neither the Master nor the Owners have been heard 'in their own defence,' save for some general submissions by Mr Clarke on behalf of the Owners. Accordingly it would be quite unacceptable for this Court to express the view that a statutory offence was committed. The Court is able to deal with this question on this occasion because it is clearly of opinion that no statutory offence has been committed. There are however, four main reasons why it is undesirable that such a question should be raised before a Court of Formal Investigation in the future.

(1) *It is not the function of this Court to answer hypothetical questions;*
(2) *It is not the function of this Court to express its opinion upon a question of construction of a statute, which does not arise in the course of the Investigation;*
(3) *If this Court were to express its opinion upon the construction of a statute that view would not be binding upon a Magistrate's Court;*
(4) *Finally, it might be inferred from a refusal by this Court to answer the question that a statutory offence had in fact been committed.*

This book is not intended to address the Corporate Manslaughter Act; suffice to say, if the *Herald of Free Enterprise* foundered today and was tried on the same evidence, there is no realistic likelihood that the Corporate Manslaughter Act would change the owners' accountability. Rather, it is the enforcement of the ISM Code which will have prominence, and the Merchant Shipping (Safety of Navigation) Regulations 2020, in which Regulation 9(2) specifically creates a criminal offence of violating regulations for safe navigation and avoidance of dangerous situations. Evidence of compliance with the ISM Code could absolve them from accountability; evidence of violation could incriminate them beyond hope.

The whole issue of a management failure demands law and guidance, without which there would be no structure for Flag State (and Port State) enforcement to take place. With that in mind, let us examine the Code more closely.

The purpose of the ISM Code is to provide an international standard for the safe management and operation of ships and for pollution prevention, but it is not a rigid structure, for no two shipping companies or shipowners are the same, and that ships operate under a wide range of different conditions; as a result, the Code is based on general principles and objectives, in producing a ship's safety management system which allows a company to measure its performance against parameters set within a documented system. It thus enables a Company to identify areas for improvement in shipboard safety management and pollution prevention measures.

The ISM Code came into force on 1 July 1998 through SOLAS Chapter IX, Management for the Safe Operation of Ships. The ISM Code provides an international standard for the safe management and operation of ships and for pollution prevention. It has been incorporated into English law following a number of Regulations, most notably the Merchant Shipping (International Safety Management (ISM)

Code) Regulations 2014. Much useful guidance can be obtained from the MCA's Instructions for the guidance of surveyors, otherwise known as MSIS02, which was revised in 2022.[9] As the UK's Flag State administration, the MCA has direct responsibility for the assessment and audit of UK shipping companies and ships against the ISM Code. All UK flag vessels are expected to have the SMS Manual written in or translated into English to enable MCA Auditors to carry out audits.

The Document of Compliance

The first document in the certification process of a ship consists of the Document of Compliance (DOC), which is issued to a Company when the shoreside aspects of the SMS are fully compliant with the requirements of the ISM Code.

The Safety Management Certificate (SMC) audits are conducted by MCA surveyors unless delegated to a Recognised Organisation, which acts as the Flag State's agent.

The benchmarks for compliance are set by international standards, and in the UK are applied by the MCA's Quality Assurance regime, in order to ensure that shipowners and operators meet the standards in SMC audits, in particular certification ISO 9001, 14001, 18001 and 5001. While they are applicable to all organisations regardless of type, size and complexity, they can be applied to shipboard operations. The process necessarily demands a working relationship between the Master, managing the shipboard operation, and the owners ashore. We can summarise the significant points for the purpose of shipboard management as follows:

- ISO 9001 series is designed to ensure that customer requirements for quality are met;
- ISO 14001 provides the elements of an effective environmental management system, minimising the ship's impact through the implementation of documented management systems.

Both standards focus on how the processes are managed, setting the requirements that the management system must satisfy in order to ensure compliance for the SMC.

- 18001 is more properly prefixed as OHSAS 18001, which is the international standard for Occupational Health and Safety Management Systems. By implementing its best-practice processes, the Master demonstrates the risk management requirements identifying and controlling the shipboard health and safety risks, meeting the demands for the audit;
- ISO 50001 sets out the global standard for practical ways to improve energy use through the development and implementation of an energy management system.

9 MSIS 2/Rev 10/22.

During the SMC audit on board a ship, a copy of the ship's DOC from the Flag State should be accepted as evidence that the Company's shore-side management structure complies with the requirements of the ISM Code. A copy of the DOC should be placed on board each of the Company's ships.

The DOC is specific to the ship types operated by the Company and for which the SMS is implemented at the time of audit. The ship types can be classified, regardless of date of construction, as follows:

- Passenger ships including passenger high-speed craft;
- Oil tankers, chemical tankers, gas carriers and cargo high-speed craft of 500 gross tonnes and upwards;
- Other cargo ships and mobile offshore drilling units of 500 gross tonnes and upwards.

That being said, the Code provides that the requirements may be applied to all ships, at the discretion of the Flag State, removing the minimum tonnage limitation as it sees fit.

There are six functional requirements required to be included in every SMS:

- A safety and environmental-protection policy;
- Instructions and procedures to ensure safe operation of ships and protection of the environment in compliance with relevant international and flag state legislation;
- Defined levels of authority and lines of communication between and among shore and shipboard personnel;
- Procedures for reporting accidents and non-conformities with the ISM Code's provisions;
- Procedures to prepare for and respond to emergency situations;
- Procedures for internal audits and management reviews.

A Flag State surveyor (or a surveyor acting as agent on behalf of the Flag State) may, of course, discover deficiencies during the audit, compelling the management team (shipboard and shoreside) to take action to correct the deficiencies, although the Code does not define the time limit for corrections. Equally, there is no time set for a review, but good practice requires that it should be carried out at least annually.

There is a constant imperative in shipping, that compliance must be certified and monitored cost-effectively, as a result of which an Alternative Compliance Scheme (ACS) has been adopted, which streamlines the streamlines the survey and certification process while maintaining standards and minimising duplication of effort with the classification societies identified as Recognised Organisations (ROs). In practical terms, this allows the Flag State to delegate all survey work to the classification societies which it appoints as its agents. All statutory certificates except the Documents of Compliance, the Safety Management Certificate, International Ship Security Certificate and MLC Certificate (which remain the responsibility of the Flag State) are issued by the UK's ROs. The conditions for eligibility under the ACS are that:

- The vessel has not been detained within the previous 36 months;
- During any Port State control inspection within the previous 12 months no inspection report shall have recorded more than 5 deficiencies;
- The vessel is classed with one of the Classification Societies authorised by the Flag State;
- The owner shall permit access by the Flag State (MCA in the UK) to any or all records, files, reports, documents and certificates held or issued by the ACS classification society the vessel is classed with;
- The owner or operator shall notify the MCA one-month in advance of all in water surveys or dry docking dates.

Under paragraph 1.4 of the revised Code,[10] every company should develop, implement and maintain an SMS that includes the following functional requirements:

- A safety and environmental-protection policy;
- Instructions and procedures to ensure safe operation of ships and protection of the environment in compliance with relevant international and flag State legislation;
- Defined levels of authority and lines of communication between, and amongst, shoreside and shipboard personnel;
- Procedures for reporting accidents and non- conformities with the provisions of the Code;
- Procedures to prepare for and respond to emergency situations;
- Procedures for internal audits and management reviews.

The Company's responsibility for providing safe manning is an important feature of the Code, ensuring that the ship is:

- Manned with qualified, certificated and medically fit seafarers in accordance with National and International requirements;
- Appropriately manned in order to encompass all aspects of maintaining safe operations on board;
- Regarding verification of work methods on board, the Company should periodically verify whether all those undertaking delegated ISM related tasks are acting in conformity with the Company's responsibilities under the Code.

The Master has a critical part to play in the ship's safety management procedures. Paragraph 5 sets out the Master's responsibility and authority under ISM, which is dependent on the Company provide clearly written and defined terms in the SMS:

10 Effective from January 2015.

5.1 The Company should clearly define and document the master's responsibility with regard to:

- *Implementing the safety and environmental-protection policy of the Company;*
- *Motivating the crew in the observation of that policy;*
- *Issuing appropriate orders and instructions in a clear and simple manner;*
- *Verifying that specified requirements are observed;*
- *Periodically reviewing the SMS and reporting its deficiencies to the shore-based management.*

From the point at which the SMS is delivered to the ship, the Master's function follows:

- They are required to report any noted deficiencies in the SMS;
- While reviewing the SMS, the Master must review SMS manuals and suggest any edits or corrections;
- They must also draw attention to any requirement mentioned in the SMS manuals that is inconsistent with industry practice or requirements;
- They should make suggestions to improve the ship's SMS and ways that shore-side support can be improved;
- They should also review and comment on the ship's performance on matters related to safety and pollution prevention.

We have already encountered paragraph 5.2:

> *The Company should ensure that the SMS operating on board the ship contains a clear statement emphasizing the master's authority. The Company should establish in the SMS that the master has the overriding authority and the responsibility to make decisions with respect to safety and pollution prevention and to request the Company's assistance as may be necessary.*

In this way, the Master's absolute discretion is underlined; it is a theme constantly running through shipboard management.

The Master is the Flag State representative and the owner's representative and they are thus obliged to ensure that specific risk management is conducted in addition to the generic risk management contained in the SMS. The Master will take whatever action is necessary for the safety of life at sea and the protection of the marine environment; when they are below, however, the risk management function is delegated to the officer of the watch, who is the Master's representative. The Master will ensure that specific risk management is conducted by its provision in the Master's standing orders, which the officer of the watch will be required to sign as evidence that they have received and understood them.

Risk management has a very broad reach under SOLAS. The SMS will form the basis upon which the Master meets their obligation under SOLAS V Regulation 34:

1. *Prior to proceeding to sea, the master shall ensure that the intended voyage has been planned using the appropriate nautical charts and nautical publications for the area concerned, taking into account the guidelines and recommendations developed by the Organization.*
2. *The voyage plan shall identify a route which:*
   - 2.1 *Takes into account any relevant ships' routeing systems;*
   - 2.2 *Ensures sufficient sea room for the safe passage of the ship throughout the voyage;*
   - 2.3 *Anticipates all known navigational hazards and adverse weather conditions;*
   - 2.4 *Takes into account the marine environmental protection measures that apply, and avoids, as far as possible, actions and activities which could cause damage to the environment.*

All that being said, the provisions in the Code merely represent a snapshot in time, and must respond to external stimuli, not the least being the findings and recommendations of the MAIB in casualty reports; just as important, however, is the input made by the Master in the review process, for they are the ones who must implement it and address its shortcomings. New ideas should always be encouraged, in order to identify weaknesses and improve the business of safety management. Just a few have been discussed in recent years, but which may stimulate discussion:

- Streamlining and reducing the paperwork that supports ISM Compliance, particularly the SMS;
- The greater use of technology and IT to reduce paperwork;
- Identifying common areas in the ISM and ISPS Codes, and integrating documentary requirements;
- Motivating seafarers to use the reporting and monitoring systems in the improvement of safety management systems;
- Involving the seafarers in the development and continuous improvement of ISM manuals;
- Increased integrated training for all concerned;
- Exploring measures to reduce the cost of compliance; and improving ISM compliance monitoring and developing performance indicators;
- The impact of Port State control in this area was not explored but certainly appears to merit further study.

The Port Marine Safety Code

In addition to the codes and systems demanded by Flag State control, the Port Marine Safety Code (PMSC) offers a national standard for port safety in the UK with the aim *to improve safety for those who use or work in ports, their ships, passengers and cargoes, and the environment.*

All Harbour Authorities are expected to comply with the Code, although it is not statutory and, so, failure to comply is not an offence; but it cross-references legal duties and, so a breach of the code may provide evidence of civil liability in negligence.

The authorities mist develop and maintain an effective Marine Safety Management System (MSMS), obliging them to publish plans and reports as well as providing information to Masters and operators; in particular they should follow the basic principles:

- Powers, policies, plans and procedures should be based on a formal assessment of hazards and risks and harbour authorities should have a formal MSMS in place, which clearly sets out preparations for emergencies;
- The MSMS should be in place to ensure that all risks are controlled, the MCA emphasises that *the more severe ones must either be eliminated or reduced to the lowest possible level, so far as is reasonably practicable*;
- All parties involved in the safety of navigation must be competent and qualified in accordance with a minimum national standard, which underlines the demand that the MSMS should also document and capture any custom and practices which may have become the standard approach to various port marine operations;
- The MSMS should confirm the roles and responsibilities of key personnel at the organisation, outlining responsibilities and procedures for marine safety within the harbour (including the port approaches), maintaining performance against targets and should be monitored, reviewed and audited on a regular basis;
- Organisations should publish plans and an assessment of their performance in meeting their obligations at least once every three years.

The Port Marine Safety Code was written with the benefit of input of marine pilots, who are particularly exposed to risk because of the nature of boarding and leaving ship, and it is a matter of concern that so many injuries still take place despite guidance and legislation. In June 2022 the Marine Accident Investigation Branch published its annual report in which it highlighted the issue of unsafe pilot ladders, stating that in 2021, *the branch received almost 200 reports about substandard pilot ladders*. Most of the casualties arose out of pilot ladders that were rigged incorrectly, while the others involved ladders that were materially defective. It offered very sound advice:

The crew must inspect the pilot ladder before and after its use to verify that it is in good condition:

- *Ensure the ladder is in date by checking the maker's plate, normally found underneath one of the lower spreaders;*
- *Inspect the ladder's side ropes to ensure that they are undamaged and in good condition;*
- *Check the ladder's steps, making sure they are undamaged, clean, evenly spaced and horizontal;*

- *Replace the ladder if there are any signs of damage, no matter how small. Someone's life may depend on it.*

The Merchant Shipping (Pilot Ladders and Hoists) Regulations 1987 imposes the following obligations on the Master:

6 *The master shall ensure that –*
(a) *Each pilot ladder, accommodation ladder and associated equipment meets the requirements of regulation 7, as appropriate, and is efficient for the purpose of enabling pilots, officials and other persons to embark and disembark safely;*
(b) *Each pilot ladder, accommodation ladder, hoist and associated equipment is properly maintained and stowed and regularly inspected to ensure that, so far as is reasonably practicable, each is safe to use;*
(c) *Each pilot ladder is used only for the embarkation and disembarkation of pilots and by officials and other persons while a ship is arriving at or leaving a port;*
(d) *The rigging of the pilot ladder, accommodation ladder, hoist and associated equipment used for the transfer of pilots and the embarkation and disembarkation of persons thereby is supervised by a responsible officer of the ship.*

Section 11 defines the penalties of violation:

(1) *A master of a ship who contravenes any provision of regulations 6 ... shall be guilty of an offence and liable on summary conviction to a fine not exceeding £1,000 or, on conviction on indictment, to imprisonment for a term not exceeding two years and a fine;*
(3) *An officer who fails to supervise as instructed by the master and required by regulations 6 ... shall be guilty of an offence and liable on summary conviction to a fine not exceeding £500 or on conviction on indictment to imprisonment for a term not exceeding one year and a fine.*

New technologies are constantly evolving in shipping, which include safe and rapid embarkation of crews. At the centre of such technology for offshore installations is the walk to work system from a suitable vessel, which can be envisaged as a potential option in pilotage. In this case, a heave-compensated gangway installed on the pilot vessel then connects to a point on the ship, allowing the pilot to walk safely from one to the other without risking a pilot ladder. It is an embryonic idea, which deserves expert argument, both for and against.

Shipboard Health and the Working Environment

It is not entirely appreciated by seafarers that the foundation statute for occupational health and safety is the Health and Safety at Work etc. Act 1974, section 2 of which states:

(1) It shall be the duty of every employer to ensure, so far as is reasonably practicable, the health, safety and welfare at work of all his employees;
(2) Without prejudice to the generality of an employer's duty under the preceding subsection, the matters to which that duty extends include in particular –
  (a) The provision and maintenance of plant and systems of work that are, so far as is reasonably practicable, safe and without risks to health;
  (b) Arrangements for ensuring, so far as is reasonably practicable, safety and absence of risks to health in connection with the use, handling, storage and transport of articles and substances;
  (c) The provision of such information, instruction, training and supervision as is necessary to ensure, so far as is reasonably practicable, the health and safety at work of his employees;
  (d) So far as is reasonably practicable as regards any place of work under the employer's control, the maintenance of it in a condition that is safe and without risks to health and the provision and maintenance of means of access to and egress from it that are safe and without such risks;
  (e) The provision and maintenance of a working environment for his employees that is, so far as is reasonably practicable, safe, without risks to health, and adequate as regards facilities and arrangements for their welfare at work.

In this context, the 1974 Act applies to the Master and ship's crew when working with shore-based personnel on board ship. Of course, health and safety in marine operations demand very subject-specific regulation, as a result of which the Secretary of State for Transport is placed in a better position to make regulations, which must then be implemented by their department. It means that the 1974 Act applies to all work activities within Great Britain, but the Management of Health and Safety at Work Regulations 1999 do not apply to the master or crew of a sea-going ship or their employer in respect of normal ship-board activities. The applicable legislation, therefore, is the Merchant Shipping and Fishing Vessels (Health and Safety at Work) Regulations 1997.

The MCA regularly monitors and amends the Code of Safe Working Practices for Merchant Seafarers, which is endorsed by the National Maritime Occupational Health and Safety Committee, UK Chamber of Shipping, Nautilus International and the National Union of Rail, Maritime and Transport Workers as best practice guidance for improving health and safety on board ship. It states:

> *The Code is addressed to everyone on a ship regardless of rank or rating, and to those ashore responsible for safety, because the recommendations can be effective only if they are understood by all and if everyone cooperates in their implementation. Those not actually engaged in a job in hand should be aware of what is being done, so that they may avoid putting themselves at risk or causing risk to others by impeding or needlessly interfering with the conduct of their work.*

The Code addresses the areas of risk and guidance in 33 chapters with clarity, cross-referencing with the relevant legislation, which, if violated, may amount to a criminal offence. In any event, a violation of the Code could adduce persuasive evidence of negligence, giving rise to liability in civil proceedings.

The 1974 Act is drafted, amended and enforced by the Health and Safety Executive, while the 1997 regulations are managed by the MCA. In practice, both Government agencies have agreed that, on board ships in ports in Great Britain, the 1974 Act as implemented will not apply and generally the MCA is responsible for enforcing health and safety legislation on ships. Where shore workers and ship's crew work together, however, the 1974 Act does apply and the Health and Safety Executive enforces the law.

In Chapter 8 we were introduced to the STCW Code. MGN 20 sets out detailed guidance on the Merchant Shipping and Fishing Vessels (Health and Safety at Work) Regulations, which came into force on 31 March 1998. A quarter of a century has since passed and, no doubt, a Government review will follow in the fulness of time; but the key elements of the risk assessment process have paramount importance, to which the Appendix in MGN 20 is devoted. The main elements of risk management have been discussed elsewhere in this book, but have been summarised in the guidance to cover:

- Classify work activities;
- Identify hazards and personnel at risk;
- Determine risk;
- Decide if risk is tolerable;
- Prepare action plan (if necessary);
- Review adequacy of action plan.

The management of shipboard health has been expanded to cover issues addressed in the Maritime Labour Convention, particularly arising out of the rights and obligations of seafarers in their employment. In recent years, however, a new issue has arisen which is highly relevant to the health of seafarers, and some States have expressed the view that the MLC does not cover the topic adequately: this involves sexual harassment and bullying.

Any form of discrimination or harassment has been universally acknowledged as unacceptable in the shipboard environment; in the UK, such matters have been addressed by legislation:

- Protection From Harassment Act 1997;
- Sexual Offences Act 2003;
- Equality Act 2010.

This primary legislation forms the rationalisation for dismissal under the Seafarer's Employment Agreement at the very least; at worst if can amount to a criminal offence. Such is not universally applied by Flag States, though, and recent cases have put international law and training under the spotlight.

The behaviour leading to discrimination and harassment have been addressed in the UK's Merchant Navy Code of Conduct as serious misconduct under 7b (XVI):

behaviour which seriously detracts from the social well-being of any other person on board, including but not limited to bullying, harassment, intimidation and coercion.

Notwithstanding the provisions of the MLC, the statutory obligations giving rise to the definition of sexual harassment and bullying, as serious violations of the seafarer's conduct, draw in the requirements of a competent Safety Management System, and the owner's disciplinary code would enhance the Merchant Navy Code of Conduct by harnessing stricter definitions to the Master's disciplinary powers. This would be referenced in the SEA, and could identify such misconduct, for example, as the ITF highlighted in its Guidance On Eliminating Shipboard Harassment And Bullying:

- Physical assault including sexual assault;
- Intimidation;
- Coercion;
- Interference with the work of other seafarers;
- Conduct based on gender affecting the dignity of women and men at work which is unwanted, unreasonable and/or offensive to the recipient.

17 Routines and Emergencies

This chapter follows the previous one with merely a pause, as it continues with the theme of shipboard management, giving the reader a short break in concentration. But only a short one.

Security Management and the ISPS Code

The International Ship and Port Facility Security (ISPS) Code came into force on 1 July 2004 and is applicable to all vessels over 500 gross tonnes operating in international trades, as well as the ports that service them. Its genesis originated in the terrorist attacks which took place on 11 September 2001, when 4 coordinated suicide terrorist attacks carried out by the militant Islamist extremist network al-Qaeda against the United States, revealing a lack of any international co-ordination in security management, whose application to marine operations is obvious.

The code has been implemented in SOLAS under Chapter XI-2 with the following objectives:

- To enable the detection and deterrence of security threats within an international framework;
- To establish roles and responsibilities in security risk management;
- To facilitate collection and exchange of security information;
- To provide a methodology for assessing security risk and compliance;
- To ensure that adequate security measures in place.

The provisions do not extend to the actual response to specific security incidents or activities as they are revealed but enable shipboard and portside teams to:

- Gather and assess information;
- Maintain communication protocols;
- Restrict access, prevent the introduction of unauthorised weapons;
- Provide the means to raise alarms;
- Put in place vessel and port security plans and ensure training and drills are conducted.

DOI: 10.4324/9781003361916-17

The Code is divided into two parts:

Part A: mandatory provisions covering the appointment of security officers for shipping companies, individual ships and port facilities. It also includes security matters to be covered in security plans to be prepared in respect of ships and port facilities;

Part B: guidance and recommendations on preparing ship and port facility security plans.

The Code contains three security levels:

Level 1, normal: the level at which ships and port facilities normally operate.

Level 2 heightened: the level applying for as long as there is a heightened risk of a security incident.

Level 3, exceptional: the level applying for the period of time when there is a probable or imminent risk of a security incident.

In the management of ISPS, there must be some integration into the SMS. For example, under 5.1, it is important to ensure that the company security officer, the Master and the ship security officer (SSO) are given the necessary support to fulfil their duties and responsibilities. Moreover, the hierarchy of command responsibility must still be maintained, achieving consistency with ISM 5.2, ensuring the ship security plan contains a clear statement emphasising the Master's authority.

The Ship Security Assessment must be carried out by persons with appropriate skills to evaluate the security of a ship, and to include an on-scene survey and a number of other elements. The Ship Security Plan (SSP) must be approved by the Administration and carried on board ship, with clear provision for training, drills and exercises on ship security.

Clearly there are two management centres, shoreside, through the Company Security Officer (CSO), and shipboard, through the SSO.

The CSO is a named individual appointed by the company who is responsible for the ship security assessment and for on board survey to confirm the development and implementation of ship security plan as per ISPS code. If any deficiency occurs, CSO is responsible to deal with all the non-conformities and to modify the SSP as per the deficiency.

The SSO is in charge of security of the vessel on board and responsible for the maintenance of ship security as per ISPS code. The SSP is kept on board the vessel defining the duties of crew members at different security levels and the fundamental requirements for dealing with defined security threats. SSO is responsible to the CSO for implementing and maintaining the SSP shipboard.

The Ship Security Alert System (SSAS) addresses the alarm process. Different types of security equipment are kept on board (for example, a metal detector for checking people coming on board). The SSAS does not sound on ship but alarms the shore authority about the security threat.

Implementing the Security Level on the ship is the responsibility of SSO to implement the security level on board in order to comply with the security level set by Port State. If Level 3, a continuous response is to be made to Port State.

Musters, Drills and Emergency Response

Musters and drills are essential parts of emergency planning, preparing crew (and passengers) for safe evacuation, in the event of an emergency on board the ship, with training procedures that familiarise them with escape routes.

In the UK, the Regulations implement the requirements under SOLAS Chapter III, for which MGN 71 gives guidance on the essential procedures. The Merchant Shipping (Musters Training and Decision Support Systems) Regulations 1999 define the requirements for muster lists, the holding of musters and drills, the provision of onboard training and instruction in the use of fire and lifesaving appliances, and the provision of a Decision Support System to Masters of certain passenger ships. Additionally, the Merchant Shipping (Life-Saving Appliances for Ships Other Than Ships of Classes III to VI(A)) Regulations 1999 and the Merchant Shipping (Life-saving Appliances for Passenger Ships of Classes III to VI(A)) Regulations 1999 contain requirements in respect of the provision of training manuals, and for the manning of survival craft and handling of launching arrangements.

MGN 71 covers the following sections:

- Muster Lists;
- Emergency Instructions;
- Emergency Signals;
- Musters and Drills – General;
- Abandon Ship Drills;
- Fire and other Emergency Drills;
- Drills in Closing of Doors, Side Scuttles and Other Openings;
- Survival Craft Muster and Drill;
- Survival Craft Drills held in Port;
- Rescue Boat and Emergency Boat Drills;
- Davit-Launched Life raft Onboard Training;
- Onboard Instruction, Training and Training Manuals;
- Weekly and Monthly Inspection life-saving apparatus;
- Decision Support Systems;
- Records.

Before the ship proceeds to sea prepare a muster list, which must be maintained for the duration of the voyage for which it was prepared, and revise it or prepare a new one, if any change takes place in the crew that necessitates an alteration in the list.

The muster list must specify the following:

- The general emergency alarm signal;
- The action to be taken by crew and passengers when the general emergency alarm signal is sounded;

- How the order to abandon ship will be given;
- Other emergency signals and action to be taken by the crew on hearing them;
- On ro-ro passenger ships and passenger ships built on or after July 1998, the location of assembly stations and the procedures for locating and rescuing passengers trapped in their cabins;
- On other ships, the location of muster stations and the procedures for locating and rescuing passengers trapped in their cabins.

Critical duties assigned to individual members of the crew must be shown, covering:

- Closing of watertight doors, fire doors, valves, scuppers, side scuttles, portholes and similar openings;
- Equipping of survival craft and other life-saving appliances;
- Preparation and launching of survival craft;
- General preparations of other life-saving appliances;
- Muster of any passengers;
- Use of communication equipment;
- Manning of fire parties;
- Special duties assigned in respect of the use of fire-fighting equipment and installations.

Ever since the loss of the *Titanic*, which was made more pertinent still following the case of the *Costa Concordia*, special attention is given to duties assigned to the crew of passenger ships:

- Warning the passengers;
- Seeing that passengers are suitably clad and have donned their lifejackets correctly;
- Mustering passengers at assembly stations or muster stations (as appropriate);
- Keeping order in passageways and on stairways and generally controlling the movements of passengers;
- Ensuring that a supply of blankets (where carried) is taken to survival craft.

The muster list must specify the officer (or substitute if the officer in question is disabled) who is assigned to ensure that life-saving and fire appliances are maintained in good condition and are ready for immediate use. The Master must ensure that:

- Copies of the muster list are exhibited in conspicuous places throughout the ship including the navigating bridge, engine room and crew accommodation spaces;
- Clear instructions to be followed in the event of an emergency are provided for every person on board;
- Illustrations and instructions in English and in any other appropriate languages are posted in passenger cabins and conspicuously displayed at assembly or muster stations (as appropriate) and other passenger spaces to inform passengers of:
  - Their assembly or muster station (as appropriate);

- The essential actions they must take in an emergency;
- The method of donning lifejackets.

Passenger ships must also have a decision support system for emergency management on the bridge. MGN 71 points out that it can be printed on paper, or computer based, and must identify all foreseeable emergency situations, establish emergency procedures for each situation, and provide decisive support to the Master.

Response Management

An emergency situation on the ship must be managed in much the same way as all shipboard risks are managed, but with special awareness of the need for confidence and calmness in the communication management process. The importance of continuous training and practical drills is obvious; but even then, in a real-life situation when the general alarm sounds, despite adequate training, people get panic attacks and sometimes fail to act properly at the time when it is needed most. And before jumping to conclusions, the Master must have clear information of the problem, particularly in a casualty involving an engineering or technical failure.

The Case of the *John I*

This case illustrates the risks that must be anticipated in polar operations, and an effective emergency response planned. Before the voyage starts, special precautions must be taken when a vessel is navigating in ice-covered waters, which includes the risk of some interruption to main and auxiliary sea water engine cooling systems due to ice. Without adequate precautions, the build-up of ice and slush in the sea water cooling system can occur quickly and cause the engine to overheat and shut down. As such, the crew must be aware of the dangers that cold water, ice and slush pose with respect to the sea water cooling system and must adjust its operations accordingly.

On 14 March 2014, the bulk carrier *John I* became disabled off the southwest coast of Newfoundland and Labrador due to flooding in the engine room, and the vessel drifted some 41 miles before grounding on the Rose Blanche Shoals the following day. Although the Master had confirmed that all of the precautions for navigating in ice-covered waters included on the checklist had been taken, some important measures to protect the cooling system were not in place. Furthermore, while the chief engineer had created an onboard checklist for the operation of the sea water cooling system, a copy of the checklist could not be obtained and, therefore, it could not be determined whether the checklist was sufficient to prevent the build-up of ice. The three-way valve was found to be discharging the warmed sea water overboard, suggesting that the crew did not follow the checklist, the checklist did not cover all the precautions necessary, or the checklist gave erroneous instructions.

During this voyage, there were indications that the crew were not adequately familiarised with the cooling system, nor had they properly prepared the cooling system for operating in ice-covered waters:

- The crew inaccurately identified the type of sea water cooling system on board the vessel when initially required to provide this information;
- The warmed sea water leaving the various main engine heat exchangers was not being recirculated to the low sea chest to melt ice;
- The steam valve to the low sea chest had been opened to prevent the build-up of ice and slush, despite the indication in documentation that this is ineffective.

In this case, without the warmed sea water, slush and ice built up in the sea water strainer during the four hours after the vessel began navigating in ice-covered waters, leading to engine overheating, loss of propulsion and potentially a fire. There were no injuries, and all 23 crew members were evacuated by helicopter; but the casualty report made 2 particularly important findings:

1. If crew are not familiar with the measures necessary to prepare and operate a vessel's sea water cooling system when navigating in ice, there is a risk that the main engine will overheat, leading to a loss of propulsion;
2. If all authorities responsible for dealing with an emergency are not involved in a timely and coordinated manner, there is a risk that response options will be limited and the situation will escalate.

A Last Word on Emergency Response

The Master understands the importance of anticipation in risk management; hence they will rely on their experience and training when exercising their absolute discretion, in reaching a decision on that infamous equation of anticipating the likelihood of an unwanted event happening, against the consequences if it does happen. But all they can do is reduce the risk to a level which falls below the threshold of liability; they cannot be clairvoyant. The ultimate illustration of the unexpected in response management lies with an event during the Second World War, involving two very fine ships formerly owned by the General Steam Navigation Company, the *Halcyon* and her sister *Philomel*, which although sold to Khedivial Mail and renamed *Zamalek* and *Zaafaran*, were requisitioned by the Ministry of War Transport which fitted them out as rescue ships. Both ships sailed in the ill-fated Russian Convey PQ17. It turned out to be a disastrous voyage, in which *Zaafaran* was attacked and sunk by enemy aircraft, an ironic fate for a rescue ship, while her officers and crew were rescued by her sister, *Zamalek*.

Personal Injury, Death and Disease

Regulation 4.1 of the Maritime Labour Convention places importance on the provision of onboard health protection and medical care, with standards for measures which aim to meet those which are available to workers ashore, to protect the health of seafarers and ensure their prompt access to medical care on board ship and ashore. The accompanying Standard A4.1 obliges the Flag State to ensure that measures providing for health protection and medical care, including essential dental care, for seafarers working on board ship are set out in enforceable Regulations that include the following minimum standards:

- All ships shall carry a medicine chest, medical equipment and a medical guide;
- Ships carrying 100 or more persons and ordinarily engaged on international voyages of more than 3 days' duration shall carry a qualified medical doctor who is responsible for providing medical care;
- Ships which do not carry a medical doctor shall be required to have either at least one seafarer on board who is in charge of medical care and administering medicine as part of their regular duties or at least one seafarer on board competent to provide medical first aid, having satisfactorily completed training in medical care that meets the STCW requirements, based on the contents of the most recent editions of the International Medical Guide for Ships, the Medical First Aid Guide for Use in Accidents Involving Dangerous Goods, the Document for Guidance under the International Maritime Training Guide, and the medical section of the International Code of Signals as well as similar national guides;
- Given the complex demands which may have to be met in a medical emergency, the Flag State must ensure that the ship has access to a medical advice by radio or satellite communication to ships at sea, including specialist advice, which is available 24 hours a day, free of charge.

In addition, under 4.2, the Flag State shall implement compulsory insurance provisions to ensure seafarers employed on the ships can avail themselves of material assistance and support from the shipowner with respect to the financial consequences of sickness, injury or death occurring while they are serving under a seafarer's employment agreement or arising from their employment under such agreement.

Routine provisions on occupational accidents, injuries and diseases are maintained for the management of occupational safety and health risks in the shipboard workplace, in which the following are listed in Guidance 4.3:

- Structural features of the ship, including means of access and asbestos-related risks;
- Machinery;
- The effects of the extremely low or high temperature of any surfaces with which seafarers may be in contact;
- The effects of noise in the workplace and in shipboard accommodation;
- The effects of vibration in the workplace and in shipboard accommodation;
- The effects of ambient factors, other than those referred to in subparagraphs (e) and (f), in the workplace and in shipboard accommodation, including tobacco smoke;
- Special safety measures on and below deck;
- Loading and unloading equipment;
- Fire prevention and fire-fighting;

- Anchors, chains and lines;
- Dangerous cargo and ballast;
- Personal protective equipment for seafarers;
- Work in enclosed spaces;
- Physical and mental effects of fatigue;
- The effects of drug and alcohol dependency;
- HIV/AIDS protection and prevention;
- Emergency and accident response.

Notwithstanding such comprehensive guidance, the MCA emphasises in its guidance to Masters that every person on board a ship has a responsibility for safety, stating in particular:

> *A ship's safety culture is dependent upon the strong support and encouragement from the ship's senior management. In every ship in which five or more persons are employed the owner or the manager is required to appoint a Safety Officer.*

The Safety Officer plays a crucial part in the ship's health and safety routine, for which they should have suitable training, and should be familiar with the statutory responsibilities for health and safety and with the principles and practice of risk assessment. They should particularly ensure the following:

- The provisions of the Code of Safe Working Practices and the owner's occupational health and safety policies are complied with;
- Occupational health and safety inspections are carried out of each accessible part of the ship in which the crew may be required to work at least once every three months or more frequently if there have been changes in the working conditions;
- Any work is stopped which it is reasonably believed may cause an accident and inform the Master who shall be responsible for deciding when work can safely be resumed;
- The minutes of each safety committee meeting are accessible to all the crew.

On every ship with five or more seafarers on board, the Master is required to appoint a Safety Committee which includes the Safety Officer and each safety representative. The Master is also on the Safety Committee as Chairman and the creation of this committee must be recorded in the Official Log Book. The Safety Committee should meet whenever it chooses, but the Committee should meet regularly, taking into account the pattern of operation of the ship and the arrangement for manning and with sufficient frequency to ensure continuous improvement in safety.

Accident reporting is a headline feature in the Master's shipboard management responsibilities, and the MCA emphasises that, while it is appreciated that your Safety Management System has a procedure covering accidents and injuries on board, there is also a requirement for the Master or Operator to report Accidents and Major Injuries by the quickest means possible and as soon as possible after the occurrence to the Marine Accident Investigation Branch. Chapter 23 deals more on the role of evidence in accident reporting, but MGN 564 offers a valuable summary with guidance on Marine Casualty and Marine Incident Reporting:

The Master must notify the MAIB of any marine casualty or marine incident, as defined in chapter 23, if the ship is within UK waters and carrying passengers to / from the UK, or casualty occurs within the jurisdiction of a UK harbour master.

The MAIB has a 24-hour hotline for reporting accidents, but a dedicated accident report form can be downloaded. Following the accident, the MAIB may require access to additional information and evidence, in respect of which the reader should refer to chapter 23.

The emergency response following the death of a person on board demands attention, and the Master must inform the owner about the deceased person along with other necessary details that are required in the form of evidence. Flag State Regulations make the owner responsible to inform the next-of-kin of the deceased person, but, in fairness, attention must also focus on Port State laws, for if the incident riving rise to the fatality occurs while the ship is in port or at anchor in a Prot State's jurisdiction, the procedures according to the laws of that particular country must be followed. If at the port, the Master should inform the port agent, the emergency medical authority and the owner's P & I Club correspondent; the Port State procedures may be draconian, but it is essential that they be understood and followed.

If the accident giving rise to the fatality takes place at sea, the procedures and guidelines as provided in the SMS and any instructions from the DPA must be followed. Facilities for the preservation of the remains until docking will depend on what is available on the ship, then the port agent at the next port must be informed in advance of arrival so that the necessary information is provided to the local authority.

In addition to a fatal accident, the Master must comply with reporting conditions for quarantinable diseases, whether they know or suspect them, including COVID, cholera, diphtheria, infectious tuberculosis, plague, smallpox, yellow fever, viral haemorrhagic fevers, severe acute respiratory syndromes, novel influenza viruses, and measles. Cases of acute gastroenteritis must also be reported, as they may present a health risk of serious contagion, both on board the ship and being taken ashore. Symptoms include diarrhoea, defined as 3 or more episodes of loose stools in a 24-hour period or what is above normal for the individual, or vomiting accompanied by one or more of the following: 1 or more episodes of loose stools in a 24-hour period, abdominal cramps, headache, muscle aches or fever.

The Master and the Official Log Book

There are few log books which are required under legislation; they are known as statutory logs, and have particular importance under English law because, by their statutory nature they are prima facie evidence of truth of the statements that are contained in it.

The Official Log Book (OLB) is required under section 77(1) Merchant Shipping Act 1995: *Except as provided by regulations under this section an official log book in a form approved by the Secretary of State shall be kept in every United Kingdom ship.* In consequence, they do not have to be corroborated by supporting evidence (such as by affidavit) but they are a document of public record under section 287 of the 1995 Act. It means that a false entry or some other default can have a serious consequence that may lead to the entire log book being held unreliable and rejected in evidence by the Court, and the Master will have to give evidence under oath and tender supporting evidence, in the form of affidavit or other documentary evidence.

As the Flag State representative, it is logical that the Master sign the entries in the OLB; after all, in the event of litigation, it is the Master who must give evidence at the Trial, and they will be cross-examined on the entries made in the OLB. Countless entries may be made in non-Statutory logs, notably the deck log, many of which will not be made by the Master, and then will be entered up in the OLB as a fine copy, which the Master will then sign. Notwithstanding the fact that it is not regulated by legislation, the deck log is an important document that is used to record a wealth of data, scenarios, situations and crises. It is always open to the Master to keep it with the OLB so that entries can be identified by cross-reference, because the deck log may be tendered in evidence, but it will be attached as an exhibit to an affidavit sworn by the individual who made the entry. If there were any error in entry or transcription, or corrected in a fair copy in the OLB, inevitably that will be discovered and revealed under cross-examination, actually weakening the probative value of the OLB at Trial. The sort of question to be asked by one's opponent may be, 'So which log are you asking the Court to accept as genuine?' In their answer, the witness must be damned either way.

The Regulations for official log books are contained in the Merchant Shipping (Official Log Book) Regulations 1981, in particular detailing what entries are to be made, and how they are to be made:

Page 1 – Front Cover

All the entries on page 1 must be made by the Master.

In the first section, the key details of the ship are taken from the Certificate of Registry, namely the ship's name, name, port of registry, official number.

The second section is for the names of successive Masters of the ship. The Master opening the Official Log Book should enter their name and certificate details on the first line, successive Masters should add their details when they take over command. If a Master has been on the ship before and returns while the log book is still in use, they do not need to add their name a second time.

The third section is for the details and address of the registered owner, or the managing owner, as the case may be.

The final section is for the date and place at which the log book is opened.

Pages 2 to 7 – Record of Seamen Employed in the Ship

This section records all seafarers on board, in other words all those in possession of an SEA, and of course this must be consistent with the safe manning document.

The first column gives the reference number of each seafarer in the list of crew, identifying each name with its unique, consecutive number and stating the capacity in which they are employed. If a seafarer leaves the ship and then returns while the log book is still in use, they should be entered again with their new number from the list of crew.

Column 4 gives a cross-reference to an entry made in respect of that seafarer in the narrative section. If there are a number of entries then the page number of each is added, separated by a comma.

Pages 8 and 9 – Births and Deaths

Instructions for completion are at the top of the section. In the section for births, the signature of the mother is required; in the section for deaths, the signature of the Master and another member of the crew are both required.

Pages 10 to 14 – Record of Musters, Boat Drills, etc.

A record must be made of every muster and drill as defined in the Merchant Shipping (Musters, Training and Decision Support Systems) Regulations 1999, for which guidance is given in MGN71.

Every entry must be signed by the Master and by one other crew member, otherwise it will be invalid and will not be accepted as proof that the drills have been carried out. Conditions such as heavy weather may make the operation unsafe and, so, if a muster or drill is not held then an explanation should be entered in column 2. If a drill is postponed or cancelled, then it should take place at the next suitable opportunity.

Pages 15 to 18 – Record of Test Drills and Inspections of Steering Gear

Regulations require steering gear to be tested within 12 hours before sailing (or once per week for ships making one voyage or more per week from the same port) and emergency steering systems must be tested every 3 months.

Pages 19 to 23 – Record of inspections of crew accommodation

This section has subsisted since the requirements for such inspections were defined in merchant shipping legislation and, more recently, in accordance with requirements in the Maritime Labour Convention. The regulations require that the Master, accompanied by a member of the crew, conducts and inspection of the crew accommodation, to ensure that it is being kept clean and that all the requirements of the crew accommodation regulations are being followed, is carried out every seven days. It is acceptable in large ships for the inspections to cover areas of the accommodation on each occasion so long as the whole of the accommodation is inspected in sequence.

Pages 24 to 28 – Record of Inspections of Food and Water

Equally, standards and guidance for food hygiene and fresh water systems are contained in MSN 1845(M). There are no minimum requirements as to the minimum amount of food, but Master (and the owner) must ensure that food and drinking water are provided which are suitable in respect of quantity, quality. Most importantly, the water must be provided free of charge to all seafarers on board the ship, and in the event of a complaint, or if the Master finds the water unsuitable, then bottled water must be made available, again free of charge.

Page 29 – Load Line, Depth of Loading, etc.

The data can be found on the ship's load line certificate, and should be completed at the same time as the OLB is opened, stated on the front cover.

Pages 30 to 39 – Dates of Departure From and Arrival at Each Dock

This section records the date of sailing and the draughts and freeboards of the ship on departure for each voyage and the dates of arrival at the next port, and must be completed at the time of sailing. Normally the person completing the Draught of Water and Freeboard Notice will enter the details in the OLB at the same time for the Master's signature as a final check, then the officer completing the Notice will countersign the entry in the OLB.

Pages 40 to 76 – Narrative Section

All other will be made in this section. A complete list of the categories of entry to be made is contained in the Regulations, but will include:

- Changes of Master;
- The annexing of other documents to the OLB;
- Accidents;
- Casualties;
- Disciplinary matters;
- Discharge of seafarers when they first sign off the list of crew;
- Details of crew left behind;
- Desertions;
- Complaints;
- Promotions and demotions;
- Criminal convictions during a voyage;
- Illness;
- Deaths;

- Appointments of safety officers, representatives and committees;
- Meetings of safety committees;
- Wages disputes;
- Closing of OLB.

If it is not practicable due to its length, or for any other reason for an entry to be contained in the narrative section, it shall be contained in a separate document annexed to the OLB and referred to in an entry in the narrative section.

An error or incorrect entry should not be erased, but should be corrected or cancelled with a further entry. To amend or cancel an incorrect entry, the incorrect entry should be left as made and another entry should be made below it with a reference to the mistake. Obliteration of an entry may be treated as a criminal offence.

Given the redefinition of a voyage under the Maritime Labour Convention, the OLB should be closed and sent, together with the list of crew and GMDSS radio log sheets, at 12-monthly intervals, or at shorter intervals when seafarers have been employed for a fixed term of less than 12 months or for a specific voyage lasting less than 12 months, to the Registry of Shipping and Seamen.

18 The Master and the Owner

The relationship between the Master and the Owner has evolved dramatically in the last two generations, presenting a picture of increasing liability upon the Master even though their responsibilities remain essentially unchanged. Over the same period, the structure of the maritime environment in which they work has changed dramatically, as evidenced by the complex evolution of Fleet Ownership and Management and the resultant challenges in identifying the party liable in a potential action. Paradoxically, the person least able to influence such changes has been the Master, who has seen the key features of their traditional relationship with the ship operator blurring, as the structure of maritime operations has evolved with the demands of social and economic change. The effect of these changes has left the Master with diminishing management influence without losing responsibility. They remain Master Under God, but without God's authority over the management of the ship's affairs. An understanding of this topic thus needs to start with something of a history lesson.

Antiquity

In ages past, when human life was not accorded top priority in the affairs of man, the Master's powers and authority had to underpin his responsibility for the financial investment which the stakeholders had risked in the voyage; hence, with no perceived evidence of any prompting by the law of the day, business practice demanded that he take unfettered responsibility for the safety and wellbeing of his ship and her gear and, once he had signed the bill of lading, for her cargo as well.[1] Any shortcoming could cost him dear, though. In 1541, Judgment was given against two Masters in a civil claim which would be identifiable today as negligence, for the consequences of stranding their vessels; they were ordered to pay damages in compensation, as a Defendant would today,[2] and the Court barred them from future command,[3] which has parallels with current law, by which the Master's

1 Earle, Sailors, p. 47; HCA 13/56, 30 May 1640; 13/88. 19 Sept 1728; 3 Feb 1728/9, fo 93, 7 Nov 1729.

2 The Mariner's Mirror, 56(1970) pp. 131–154 at 144.

3 Today the authority belongs to the Secretary of State for Transport: Section 61 Merchant Shipping Act 1995.

DOI: 10.4324/9781003361916-18

Certificate can be suspended or revoked for serious negligence, but this is not to be regarded as a punishment but, rather, a device for abating the risk of a repetition of the individual's incompetence when clothed with the authority of the Master.

By the turn of the eighteenth century, a hundred years of solid growth in private investment in far-flung colonial adventures had laid the foundation for a complete maritime transport industry to service the demand of those ventures; but it was axiomatic that the investors be persuaded that their money was in safe hands – or at least, as safe as possible under the circumstances of risk. With no established communication, and few trustworthy businessmen in the far-flung loading ports where cargoes had to be negotiated, the venturers had to place their trust in somebody to protect their interests while the vessel was in distant parts, and the Master was the most reliable man on the spot.

It has, therefore, always been on a Master's character, competence and judgment that the entire success of a venture depends. When put in the context of an age in which commercial risks had to be faced with virtually no supporting communication, the loss of a Master in whom the investors had confidence, would naturally have led to a maritime opportunity being turned down, with the downstream consequence, even, of ships being laid up or sold. With nobody else there to assist, such confidence depended heavily upon the ability of the Master to manage the risk in protecting the shareholders' investment, and bring his ship safely to the port of discharge and the successful conclusion of her voyage.

The Master Today

In the twenty first century the investor's risk analysis depends considerably upon the technical specification of the vessel, to minimise the danger of loss or damage; the Master today can rely on very high specifications, with minimum standards defined by SOLAS, while the competence of their crew similarly is underpinned by STCW. But the Master is still the leader in the marine adventure, the Flag State's representative with responsibility for the safety of life at sea and the protection of the marine environment. They are also the owner's representative whose purpose is to make the voyage a commercial success. As the owner's employee, representative and agent, the Master must understand the essentials of commercial risk in which the owner, charterer and cargo-owner are engaged.

In this respect, the Master's position has hardly changed; they are a senior manager in the business, and must ensure that the ship returns a profit that justifies the investment in her. When the owner persuaded their investors that the ship purchase presented a sound financial risk, they employed accounting experts to forecast the essential equation between the acquisition cost of the ship and her gradual depreciation value as an asset, against the financial return on trading her, representing that critical balance between the trading revenue and the operating costs. It is the latter which is so dependent upon the Master's contribution to the business model, for the calculation of ship's operating costs is the key to the success of the company.

Direct operating costs cover what the phrase implies; they include the capital investment costs, management and administration, insurance costs and premiums, and crew costs. Such things are largely uncontrolled by the Master, but a great deal of the direct operating costs include bunkering, planned maintenance, repair and supply costs, as well as canal charges, port costs and charges, stevedoring charges and the numerous bills of other costs that can arise unexpectedly during a voyage. All of these the Master must carefully monitor and control. An effective Master who keeps the direct operating costs within estimates may often be the one whose promotion is favoured. Yet, fluctuating freight rates may still depress the profitability of a voyage, and the downstream consequences of delay may even force consideration of deviation in voyage planning, with downstream consequences on bunkering and crewing costs; such was the experience of ships that were delayed by the grounding of the *Ever Given* in the Suez Canal.

Of course, the Master is also responsible for the consequences of their acts or omissions which may lead to a claim against the owner during the operation of the vessel under their command. The Standard of Duty is the minimum level of performance which a party must meet to avoid fault for the damage of which the other party has complained, and the Master inevitably must take responsibility, and face accountability if they get it wrong. The test of fault poses the question: Is liability for breach of contract strict (meaning fault does not have to be proved), or is it based on proof of fault in the sense of a failure of care, diligence or honesty? If it is fault-based, then the need arises to establish evidence of the lack of care, diligence or honesty as a breach of duty.[4] The owner will rely on the Master to provide convincing evidence.

Naturally, such a failure characterises the Master's contractual obligation to maximise the commercial return for the shipowner, while mitigating risks to the parties which are inherent in merchant ship operations. In this context, the Master's roles as employee, representative and agent of the owner establishes the risk to the owner by association with the Master's accountability for acts or omissions, arising in the course of their employment. In consequence conclusions may be drawn which define the risks in law to which the Master exposes the owner, the charterer and the cargo-owner.

The Master's obligations to the owner can be found in their contract of employment; after all, every seafarer working on a ship must have a written agreement with the owner, known as a seafarer's employment agreement, which was discussed fully in the chapter on the MLC. The agency relationship needs a little further explanation. It is a corner-stones of English Law that the only parties who can sue or be sued on a contract are those who have made valuable commitments to each other in the bargain[5], as a result of which the business of maritime commerce could not take place, because the principal parties would not have direct commitment in a situation which demanded some agreement that would change

4 *Target Holdings Ltd v Redfems* [1996] AC 421.

5 While the Contracts (Rights of Third Parties) Act 1999 alleviated some of the unfairness in the general rule, maritime commerce bad synthesised a solution generations earlier, with precedent leading up to the Carriage of Goods by Sea Act 1992.

their rights and obligations. Applying this to the Master-Owner relationship, for the shipowner, this individual known as the 'agent' logically had to be the same one in whom they had placed trust to bring the ship safely home: the Master. But if the Master, as the Owner's agent, is personally involved in closing the contract with a third party, they must have the comfort that they are not then personally liable to the third party on that contract. Only if the Master had not identified or named the owner as his principal could the third party bring a claim against him – and even that would be an up-hill struggle, for the third party could very easily make enquiries with the Flag State register as to the correct title of the principa1.[6]

An example is the Bill of Lading, which the Master signs strictly as the Carrier's agent. The Master may be held accountable to a third party in negligence if they break a duty of care to that third party who suffers damage as a reasonably foreseeable consequence, notwithstanding any contractual terms agreed between the Owner (or Carrier) and the third party,[7] but a Master acting with the usual authority of their disclosed Principal, the Carrier, will not be liable to the third party in a contract. As the humble Agent, they may have endorsed the contract but liability rests on the Principal for whom they acted – or, rather, on the Principal whom the third party believed they were getting bound into a contract with, so ably demonstrated in the case of the *Starsin*.[8] The Master's contractual liability will be limited to that owed to the Owner and defined according to the express or implied terms of their employment[9].

That being said, the Master has a special contractual relationship with the Owner at Common Law, arising out of their common interest in the success of the marine adventure, which could be relied upon to maintain the bond between them. But the changes in the pattern of ship management over the last thirty years have seen the outsourcing of skills, so that the business managing the operation of the ship is often entirely unrelated to the Owner, giving rise to litigation defining the meaning and liability of the operator, such as the case of the *Stema Barge 11*.[10] They may well have sub-contracted the crewing contract to another business, while they only won the management contract because of a tender which offered the lowest cost, and any additional financial cost would conflict with the manager's bottom-line budget. Indeed, the manager may be operating with the very minimum of resources, far from able to provide the support which the Master might be

6 See *Knight Frank LLP v Aston Du Haney*: CA (Civ Div): 12 April 2011 (currently unreported).

7 As so dramatically demonstrated in Adler v. Dickson [1954] 3 WLR 696, precipitating the Himalaya Clause in the contract for the carriage of goods by sea, the effect of which still holds well today subject to the provisions of the Unfair Contract terms Act 1977.

8 *Owners of cargo lately laden on board the ship or vessel 'starsin' and others v Owners and/or demise charterers of the ship or vessel 'starsin'; Homburg Houtimport BV v Agrosin Private Ltd* Hl [2003] UKHL 12 [2003] 2 WLR 711. [2004] 1 AC 715, [2003] I CLC 921, 2003 AMC 913, [2003] 1 Lloyd's Rep 571, [2003] I All ER(Comrn) 625, [2003] 2 All ER 785, [2003] 1 LLR 571. See above.

9 See *Lister v Romford Ice and Cold Storage Co Ltd* [1956] AC 555.

10 *Splitt Chartering APS -v- Saga Shipholding Norway AS* (the "STEMA BARGE II") [2021] EWCA CIV J880.

entitled to expect from the Owners of the asset over which he has control. Thus, far from sharing a common interest with the Master, the management company may very well have a vested interest in avoiding legal accountability by dissociating itself from the Master's acts or omissions, for it would derive no financial benefit from such association but could be exposed to risk if the Master's tortious acts led it into vicarious liability. This is particularly relevant if the Master's acts or omissions had given rise to criminal liability, in which a Prosecutor may seek to establish that both Master and manager shared common features in the *mens rea* and the *actus reus*. The management company doubtless would be horrified to face the risk that it might share criminal accountability – such had not been contemplated when it tendered for the work – but, after all, that was why the Merchant Shipping Act established criminal liability against them for a dangerously unsafe ship under Section 98 if they had assumed responsibility for safety in the contract with the registered owner (in that situation the owner would actually avoid criminal liability altogether).

Notwithstanding the identity of the manager or operator, the Master today is expected to be a business manager. The successful Master in this context was the one who conducted a risk-benefit analysis in shipboard management designed to maximise the commercial return, and mitigate the dangers, if possible.

The special relationship between Master and Owner has necessarily eroded with changes if Fleet Ownership and Management, but it is still acknowledged as indispensable to maritime operations, and has been embraced and encouraged by international law, acknowledging the Company's role in supporting the Master's authority, most recently through the International Safety Management Code 2002 ('ISM'), which requires the Owners' shore-based management system to support the Master's Responsibility and Authority: *The Company should ensure that the SMS operating on board the ship contains a clear statement emphasizing the master's authority. The Company should establish in the SMS that the master has the overriding authority and the responsibility to make decisions with respect to safety and pollution prevention and to request the Company's assistance as may be necessary.*

In fairness, under English law this merely codified the Common Law position which had evolved with the paternal relationship that had grown up between the Master and the Owner, but ISM levelled up international law. Notwithstanding ISM, the relationship between the Master and owner found its way into statute law long before then, notably following ratification of the Hague Rules 1924, which evolved into the Hague-Visby Rules, adopted by the United Kingdom in the Carriage of Goods By Sea Act 1971. The Hague-Visby Rules provide *inter alia* that the carrier shall be bound before and at the beginning of the voyage to exercise due diligence to make the ship seaworthy and properly man, equip and supply her.[11] It is the Master's personal duty to ensure that the vessel is in all respects safe to proceed to sea, which includes the above requirements – thus, as the Master

11 Article lll(l).

exercises their untrammelled discretion to decide to proceed to sea, they patently make an agency decision which will render the owner accountable to the cargo-owner for any damage.

The core feature arising out of this became known as the Master's Absolute Discretion, and is enshrined in SOLAS under SOLAS V Regulation 34-1. It is a crucial element in the Master's ultimate function of risk management, and the following bullet points may be helpful in illustrating the Master's responsibility in exercising their discretion:

- Risk management and responsibility. The Master must be able to implement, monitor and review the safe operation of the vessel, to assess and manage the risks and review the SMS under ISM 5.1 or make their own judgment under 5.2;
- The dangerously unsafe ship within the context of sections 94 to 98 Merchant Shipping Act 1995;
- The Master-Pilot relationship and intimate awareness of the potential threats to the safety of navigation under pilotage. The operation of the Pilotage Act 1987 demands close interaction between the two, the success of which was observed in the case of the *Höegh Osaka* in 2015, addressed in the chapter on pilotage;
- The safe navigational watch, particularly SOLAS V and the Rules 5 and 19 of the Collision Regulations;
- The Master's discretion in connection with the Safe Port; it is, after all, their decision that will prevail.

The ISM Code obliges the owner to establish a safety management system but the Master has the overriding authority and the responsibility to make decisions with respect to safety of life and protection of the marine environment, through SOLAS V Regulation 34-1. Clearly, therefore, the Master has the authority and responsibility to take decisions in an emergency and to speak with the owner only as they feel it is necessary. However, the ISM Code does not deal with the responsibilities and duties of a Port or Coastal State which may have legislation governing the conduct of a maritime emergency in waters under its jurisdiction or which wishes to exercise its powers to intervene to avoid pollution arising from maritime casualties, beyond the territorial sea.

In these situations, the Master must deal with the emerging event, and while they can take advice from the support team, from the Designated Person Ashore to the P & I Club correspondent, the responsibility still rests with them. Port or Coastal State maritime assistance will provide the point of contact during the resolution of a situation, but the Master's responsibility as Flag State representative will remain unchanged; after all, the Flag State has accredited the Master with that function, not the Port State; indeed, more than one Port or Coastal State may be involved. The situation becomes more complicated still if a Salvor is involved. Clearly confidence must be placed in the Salvor to assess and manage the operation, but the Master's responsibility will not be delegated to them. Indeed, the IMO's own guidance points out that, when a Salvor has been appointed, the Master should cooperate with them to the maximum extent – but the Master's absolute discretion – and accountability – remains.

A summary of the Master's responsibilities and their overlap with the owner may be useful. The Master and the Owner shall ensure that:

- The condition of the ship, including its structure, machinery and equipment, is maintained to regulation standards;
- No material change is made after a survey, except by direct replacement;
- Whenever an accident occurs or a defect is discovered it is reported at the earliest opportunity to Flag State;
- Under section 98 Merchant Shipping Act 1995, if a ship which is in a port is dangerously unsafe, then the Master and the Owner of the ship shall each be guilty of an offence;
- Under section 9(1) The Merchant Shipping (Safety of Navigation) Regulations 2020, any contravention of Regulation 5 relating to the enforcement of the safety of navigation provisions under SOLAS Chapter V, will constitute an offence by the Owner and Master.

A conflict of interests between the Master and the Owner may endanger the special relationship, however, an early example of which can be found in the case of the *Sussex Oak*, which we have examined. Mr Justice Devlin held, obiter, that *The question of safety must be determined at the time when the Master has to make his decision to proceed*, upholding the importance of the Master's absolute discretion; but, while they must anticipate situations as part of their risk management function, the Master is not expected to be clairvoyant. As a result, their professional judgment will be based on factors such as the estimated position which would be reached at the planned time by any well-informed and experienced Master; if a decision is based upon such an estimate the Master's culpability will not be affected by the fact that, in the light of subsequent events, it is proved to be erroneous. At most that would be a mere error of judgment, which does not itself give rise to liability in negligence, which is dependent upon a wrong done and an injury sustained, giving rise to a right to damages; that right does not, by itself, follow someone's estimate of whether a wrong is likely to be done or an injury likely to be sustained.

The same Judge made a ruling that underlined the feature of common sense in the case of *The Stork*.[12] The charterers were obliged to load at safe berths or loading places in accordance with a safe port warranty in the voyage charterparty; however, the vessel was instructed by the charterers to load a cargo of logs in Newfoundland in winter. The loading place was unsheltered, and the vessel dragged her anchors in a heavy wind, in consequence of which the Master took the decision to sail the vessel out of danger. He was unsuccessful, however and the vessel was driven onto a shoal of rocks. Mr Justice Devlin found on the facts that a loading place where a

12 Compania Naviera Maropan S/A v Bowater's Pulp and Paper Mills Limited (*The Stork*): CA 1954 [1955] 2 QB 68, [1954] 2 Lloyds Rep 397, [1955] 2 All ER 241; [1955] 2 WLR 998.

vessel could be blown off her moorings was unsafe. In consultation with the assessor, he found that the Master's decision was not unreasonable and did therefore not constitute a *novus actus interveniens*, thus the breach of the safe port warranty rendered the charterers liable for loss and damage.

It is very apparent that the evolution of the relationship between the Master and the Owner was a model of logic: the Master retains complete responsibility for anything that occurs on or involves their ship, but the liabilities arising out of such operation are covered under the owner's liability insurance. The statutory provisions arising out of the Hague-Visby Rules assured some equity for the Owner, however, in the so-called nautical fault defence, relaxing liability upon them for the Master's negligent acts or omissions over which they had no control and reached its pinnacle – and swansong – with the final appeal in the *Tasman Pioneer* case in 2010.[13] But overall, this apparently paternal, Owner-Master relationship, begged the perception that any suggestion of criminal accountability against the Master would see the vigorous intervention of the Company in their defence. It characterised the high water mark of the relationship, which had been achieved thanks to a sustained period, throughout much of the twentieth century, when efficient global communications connected the Master, wherever the ship may be, with the Company's shore office, whose senior managers and technical support staff were often presided over by a chairman whose life-time experience in shipping and instinct for maritime commerce gave him real advantages in the day-to-day operation of the fleet.

Such issues as seaworthiness are well-defined by Hague-Visby and, therefore, stand as compelling authority for defining a vessel's condition, when interpreting the criminal implications of section 98 Merchant Shipping Act 1995, which renders the Master and the owner criminally liable if a ship in a UK port, or a UK-registered ship in any other port, is dangerously unsafe. Section 94 defines 'dangerously unsafe' in the context of being unfit to go to sea without serious danger to human life because of the condition, or the unsuitability of the ship, her machinery or equipment, or if she is undermanned, overloaded or unsafely loaded, or 'any other matter relevant to the safety of the ship.'

Such a worry does not escape the independent ship manager, for Section 98 provides that, if the owner has passed management control over safety matters either directly, by a charterparty or management agreement, or indirectly, under a series of charterparties or management agreements, then the charterer or manager shall simply stand in the owner's place for the purpose of criminal liability under the Act. In all such cases, the Master retains responsibility for ship safety and, indeed, guards still their unfettered discretion as to whether to proceed to sea; in addition to the provisions of the 1995 Act, the risk under current law raises its head if the Master's act or omission amounts to criminal negligence. As a result, the Master-owner relationship potentially imperils the owner or manager, unless they can mitigate their position by distancing themselves from the Master.

13 *Tasman Orient Line CV v New Zealand China Clays Ltd and Others* [2010] 1 L R 41.

The potential for criminal accountability can be identified most recently in the Bribery Act 2010, which finally came into force in July 2011. Section 1 creates an offence where a person offers, promises or gives a financial or other advantage to another person, in order to induce a person to perform improperly a relevant function or activity, or to reward a person for the improper performance of such a function or activity. Such a function or activity would include any function of a public nature, any activity connected with a business, any activity performed in the course of a person's employment, or any activity performed by or on behalf of the company. However, the Master is described, therefore – as agent, representative or employee – they will be defined within the Act. For better or for worse, inducements to officials in many parts of the world have long been accepted as an occupational hazard of maritime operations, and the close relationship between the Master and the owner conveys a dangerous picture to the shore-based management operation.

That relationship would be a hard one to deny, given the practical reasons so graphically illustrated by the Master's role, and the evolution of Statute Law has created undercurrents in strategic planning that have driven risk management decisions and, whether intentionally or not, are perceived to have eroded the Master-owner relationship. Perhaps most importantly of all in terms of criminal accountability, the downstream consequence of the failure of the prosecution against P & O in the *Herald of Free Enterprise*.

The *Herald* case had dramatic consequence in law. While Mr Justice Sheen had exercised his power to deal with Captain Lewry by way of reviewing his certificate of competency, he Judge had no power to order any redress against the Company; recourse would have to follow in a more appropriate Court. And while His Lordship criticised the directors in the *Herald* Inquiry in the most scathing terms possible, the same words, paradoxically, became the directors' salvation. The fact that the evidence led to the conclusion that the directors had not appreciated their responsibility for the safe management of their ships, that they had not applied their minds to the question of safety and their lack of comprehension of what their duties were, showed that no director had assumed any personal responsibility which underpinned a duty of care and, in the absence of that, there could not be any realistic prospect of a conviction for manslaughter against an individual director and, thus, under the identification doctrine, no prospect of a successful prosecution against the Company for corporate manslaughter.

Mr Justice Taylor had to wrestle with the concept of the controlling mind in the ensuing prosecution of P & O Ferries in the *Herald* case,[14] when he re-stated the law that a corporation may be culpable of the crime of corporate manslaughter where an individual, who is part of the corporation's controlling mind, does an act which fulfils the pre-requisites for the crime of manslaughter. However seriously the disease of sloppiness had taken hold, the mere failure of the management system to prevent a death, in the absence of an individual guilty of manslaughter,

14 *R v P & O European Ferries (Dover) Ltd* [1991] 93 Cr App R 72.

could not, itself, sustain a conviction. In the trial against P & O, therefore, the prosecution was doomed to fail. After a submission by the Defence at the end of the Prosecution case, the Judge ruled that the prosecution was not in a position to satisfy the doctrine of identification.

The erosion of the Master-Owner relationship in recent years owes much to the risk which the shipowner assumes by associating itself with the Master in the situation giving rise to vicarious – and criminal – liability. With the pressing issue of corporate accountability, the Owner's concern to prioritise the shareholders' interests over the Master's presents a serious challenge to any option as being a viable alternative for the protection of the Master which would be acceptable to the shipowner. Nowhere was this observed more keenly than in the case of the *Exxon Valdez*.

The Case of Captain Hazelwood and the *Exxon Valdez*

In the *Exxon Valdez* case, the corporate accountability for the Master's conduct – or what was perceived to be his conduct – was illustrated very clearly indeed. At about 00.09 on 24 March 1989, the vessel, loaded with about 1,263,000 barrels of crude oil, ran aground on Bligh Reef in Prince William Sound, on the coast of Alaska. There were no personal injuries, but about 258,000 barrels of oil spilled into the sea when eight cargo tanks ruptured. Damage to the vessel was estimated at $25 million and the lost cargo cost about $3.4 million – while the clean-up cost during 1989 was $1.85 billion. It was the worst pollution event in American history at that date, contaminating more than 1,300 miles of coastline, destroying the livelihoods of people dependent upon fishing and subsistence hunting in the region and killing hundreds of thousands of birds and marine mammals; as recently as April 2010 scientists had discovered that residual spill was still being ingested by wildlife and would persist in threatening vulnerable species for decades.[15]

The National Transportation Safety Board's investigation concluded that there were five probable causes of the grounding, only one of which incriminated the Owner in that it had failed to supervise the Master and provide a rested and sufficient crew for the vessel.[16] But the determination of Exxon's culpability was reflected in the original order of the Federal Court that it pay $5 billion in punitive damages. A Federal Appeal in 2006 halved it to $2.5 billion and, it must be said, the United States Supreme Court further reduced the punitive award to just over $500 million in 2008. More than $2 billion had been spent on clean-up and recovery, while Exxon paid at least $1 billion in damages overall. But still the litigation was not over.

15 Esler D et al, 2010, Cytochrome P4501A biomarker indication of oil exposure in harlequin ducks up to 20 years after the *Exxon Valdez* oil spill. Environmental Toxicology and Chemistry, Rice University, Houston.

16 Kolstad, J, 1990, Report Ref M-90-26 through 31, National Transportation Safety Board, Washington DC.

It took 26 years finally to resolve the final outcome in Court. On 15 October 2015, a Federal Court in Anchorage heard submissions that State and Federal Governments had decided not to pursue a final $100-million from ExxonMobil over its 1989 oil spill in Prince William Sound. The Judge, H Russel Holland, had presided over the case at its start, and was now closing it. In his final words:

> *My colleagues have been fretting for fourteen years that some of this litigation might outlive my time on this court. Happily that hasn't happened.*

There is no doubt that the Company faced harsh corporate accountability for the spill, while Captain Hazelwood had to accept responsibility as Master, when the Coast Guard suspended his certificate for a period of nine months. He was charged with being drunk at the time of the grounding, although he was acquitted at his Trial, but was convicted of a misdemeanour of negligent discharge of oil, for which he was fined $50,000 and sentenced to 1,000 hours of community service. His employer dismissed him.

Legacy in Corporate Accountability

Unsurprisingly, the Owner of a crude tanker would view the *Exxon Valdez* case as a study in the need for caution – and the accountability for the consequence of a risk management failure. In the case of accountability for their Master's negligence, they felt that they had a sound argument to excuse themselves from liability. Mindful of the Master's unassailable authority in the safe navigation of the vessel, the Owner could argue persuasively that it could not overrule the Master in their duty of care and, therefore, the Owner should be protected from liability in the event of the Master's negligence. This persists as the core feature of the nautical fault defence in the Hague-Visby Rules; what horrifies the shipowning community is the current evolutionary creep of international statutory limitation provisions, by which the Rotterdam Rules sweep away the long-established nautical fault defence, with the result that the carrier will be liable for all or part of the loss, damage or delay if the Claimant proves that the event set forth is subsequent to a fault of the carrier or their Master. If the bill of lading in the *Tasman Pioneer* case[17] had fallen under the Rotterdam Rules instead of Hague-Visby, the Owners would have been hard-pressed to persevere with the argument that their vicarious liability should not apply to the Master's gross misconduct, even though the damage to the deck cargo had occurred as a consequence of the Master's efforts to protect his own interests, rather than theirs.

The shipowner identifies a greater mischief still with the global evolution of the law of criminal negligence against the Master, should the Master incriminate them in a crime under the new Corporate Manslaughter Act,[18] whose origins stemmed

17 *Tasman Orient Line CV New Zealand China Clays Ltd and Others* [2010] 1 Ll R 41.

18 S1 Corporate Manslaughter and Corporate Homicide Act 2007: An organisation to which this section applies is guilty of an offence if the way in which its activities are managed or organised causes

from public and political unhappiness with the corporate positions presented in the *Herald of Free Enterprise* and *Marchioness disasters*, among others. The offence is committed if the way in which the Company's activities are managed or organised causes a person's death and amounts to a gross breach of a relevant duty of care owed by the organisation to the deceased. Liability for the death no longer must be attributed to the conviction of manslaughter against a member of the controlling mind of the Company, but by a 'management failure' involving a person who plays a significant role in the making of decisions about how the activities are to be managed or organised, or the actual managing or organising of the whole or a substantial part of those activities. The Master fits perfectly this definition. If a person is killed, and particularly if the Master is confronted with allegations of criminal negligence, that may be used in evidence against their employer, the shipowner, in order to establish that there was a management failure giving rise to the crime of corporate manslaughter. The UK Government's Sentencing Council[19] published guidelines in 2010 which stated that the fine which would likely be imposed upon the convicted company would seldom be less than £500,000 and could be measured in millions of pounds.

Such threats encourage the owner to distance themselves from the Master as far as they possibly can, for, if the owner is to be held vicariously liable for such negligence, then the consequences in terms of damages may result in punishment which the maritime world had seen first imposed in the *Exxon Valdez* case, involving fines, punishing compensation claims, and plunging share values with which to contend.

The frightful fiend now treading close behind the Master has taken form and substance in the dilemma revealing itself in a very real drama currently confronting the maritime community, arising out of the need for some self-protection against piracy. In a situation in which the Master is responsible for the safety of life and the property of the vessel herself, they are keenly aware of the risks in meeting that responsibility when attacked by pirates – and the shipowner may be held equally accountable by virtue of their relationship with the Master.

a person's death and amounts to a gross breach of a relevant duty of care owed by the organisation to the deceased.

19 Anon, 2010, Corporate Manslaughter & Health and Safety Offences Causing Death – Definitive Guideline, Sentencing Guidelines Council, London. At the present time (December 2011) the only conviction under this Statute resulted in a fine substantially less than this, when Cotswold Geotechnical Holdings Ltd were convicted and fined £385,000 in 2011, the rationale being that it was a very small company which was described in mitigation as being in a parlous financial state. The Judge ordered the fine to be paid in instalments over ten years (currently unreported).

19 Leadership and Shipboard Management

Leadership defines the capacity of an individual to influence people by means of personal skills and qualities, in order to achieve a common goal. Management has a more defined focus, on the implementation of the planning, organising, crewing, directing and controlling of the operation of the ship. In the shipboard scenario the Master must meet their management responsibilities by motivating and engaging the crew, ensuring that they work effectively and collaboratively, possessing a deep understanding of the organisation of the ship, and the drivers that create a successful voyage. Ultimately, the glaring distinction is that management can be delegated, but leadership cannot.

A ship's officer must embrace the qualities of leadership to be found in every textbook on management, with a focus on listening, building relationships, teamwork, inspiring, motivating and directing the crew. Naturally, the officer must be a good leader, for the ship and the safety of life are at stake, and the officer needs to take charge, to be self-reliant, to have initiative and to work as a member of a team.

Many of the qualities which define leadership are found in an individual's suitability, and are grown from there. They must, for example:

- Inspire confidence and authority;
- Remain calm in a crisis;
- Demonstrate care and respect for the crew and the bridge team through everyday actions;
- Assess a situation quickly, make decisions and stick to them.

Leadership and shipboard management demands leading the team by example; in other words, 'Do as I do' rather than 'Do as I say.' The essential feature is to build trust and respect; such things can only be earned, and a crew of seafarers, often from different cultures, needs leadership in order to earn that trust. An interesting question to ask a seafarer is whether they have served with a Master whom they would trust in a mortal crisis to save their lives, and whether they have served with one they would not trust with their little finger.

A great deal of trust and confidence can be earned by knowledge and experience, in particular with relation to safety regulations and the SMS; experience and skills in human resources management will also deliver trust, even though the seafarer is not aware of it.

DOI: 10.4324/9781003361916-19

Human resources skills are important foundations for developing empathy and understanding with seafarers as individuals, identifying and understanding their situation, feelings and motives. But the officer must demonstrate tough empathy: in other words, they must use that empathy to decide what they need – not what they want.

Twenty-first century crews may originate from many national origins, with a range of races and cultures which must be respected. They are also likely to demonstrate different sexual identities which must be respected. These are all features of inclusivity and diversity which are important to respect in any workplace; on board ship, with long periods away from families and loved ones, it may become a matter of life and death, not just the efficient management of the crew.

ISM involves the Master in the function of motivating the crew in shipboard safety, which means creating a sense of community, and involving them in daily decisions, but within a clear discipline framework. Over 80 per cent of maritime incidents are caused by human error, and understanding the contribution and consequences of human and organisational behaviour is key to improving maritime safety, which is highly dependent on the leadership capacity of the senior officers.

At the centre of this, is the function of risk management.

Risk Management

Risk management may be defined as the activity which co-ordinates recognition of risk, risk assessment, developing strategies to manage it, and mitigation of risk using managerial resources. The objective is not to eliminate all risk, but to reduce different risks related to a pre-selected domain to the level accepted by society through statutory authority of common law precedents – in other words, to the threshold of the law of negligence or criminal accountability.

The resources educating and informing readers about risk management run into thousands; in this section we shall confine ourselves to practical issues of risk management in marine operations, and deal with the steps chronologically. We may start with an overview of the process. The bullet points may sound formulaic but, in fact, they are the steps which the Master or officer of the watch will follow, without even thinking about it:

- Identification of the risk in context;
- Mapping out the scope of the risk, to lay the foundation to answer the question: Is it an acceptable risk?
- Consider the objectives of stakeholders, such as crew safety, the owners, insurers, charterers, cargo owners and passengers – and in the twenty-first century, the marine environment;
- Define a framework and an agenda for the management of the risk;
- Develop an analysis of risks involved in the process;
- Mitigation of risks using available technological, human and organizational resources.

Having completed this overview, the Master will proceed to the next stage, of identifying the potential risks. This can take a number of alternative forms, which include identifying the risk by the objectives to be achieved, or identifying them by the scenario in which they present themselves, or identifying them by reference to their intrinsic features, as mapped out in the overview.

The next step is the critical function of the assessment of the risk. Having addressed the issues above, the Master must assess its acceptability. In other words, they must balance an equation, of how likely the undesired event will happen, against the consequence if it does happen.

The Master will then make an informed decision on which treatment option should be adopted:

- Tolerate.

In other words, *Do Nothing*. Having balanced the issues, in particular the objectives to be achieved, the Master may decide that the likelihood of the undesired event is remote by comparison with the consequence, bringing the risk within the risk of acceptability and requiring no action at all. These instances generally should only involve low risk, or repercussions that are easily managed. Such would amount to recklessness and may give rise to liability in negligence, or even criminal accountability.

- Treat.

Treatment involves reducing the risk, in other words taking steps to mitigate or even minimise the consequences of the risk.

- Terminate.

If the consequences outweigh the likelihood, then the risk is deemed too high, and the risk should be terminated by avoiding it; for example, the risk of entering an unsafe port or facing dangerous weather would provide grounds for interrupting or terminating the voyage.

- Transfer.

The alternative is to transfer the risk to another party; which, after all, is the purpose of insurance, and a commercial analysis will often be a determining factor in the successful outcome of the marine adventure. The danger lies in transferring a risk to which the Master failed to give any thought to the consequences, or which they acknowledged the consequences but nevertheless proceeded to take the risk. In this respect, the Master must involve the owners, who will have to give fair presentation to the insurers, or risk the suspension of the policy pursuant to the Insurance Act 2015.

Having decided on the risk treatment option, the Master will create a risk treatment plan. While it may rationalise the assessment and treatment of the risk in detail, ultimately the plan must define two things:

- It must elect appropriate controls or countermeasures to measure each risk;
- It must propose applicable and effective security controls for managing the risks.

It is then essential to follow all of the planned methods for mitigating the effect of the risk. It is by no means the end of the risk management process, however, for a constant review and evaluation of the plan is necessary. Risk management plans will not be perfect; and external circumstances may change which demand some attention. The plan must be reviewed periodically because:

- Statutory Regulations may force changes;
- It is important to evaluate whether the previously selected controls are still applicable and effective;
- It is also important to evaluate the possible risk level changes in the external environment.

STCW 2010, better known as the Manila Amendments, defined substantial new competence requirements related to leadership, teamwork and management skills. Assertiveness training for all seafarers was also included, given its importance not only for those who have to direct operations but also for those in lower grades who may have to communicate on safety matters with the Master or senior officers in the line management structure. There is much content in the Convention but, among other things, attention is given to the seafarer's ability to apply task and workload management, with the knowledge and ability to apply effective resource management, including:

- The allocation, assignment and prioritisation of resources;
- Effective communication on board and ashore;
- Decisions are made which reflect the consideration of team experiences;
- Assertiveness and leadership issues;
- Obtaining and maintaining situation awareness.

Similar skills for applying to decision-making techniques are also addressed in the context of risk management:

- Situation and risk assessment;
- Identify and generate options;
- Selecting course of action;
- Evaluation of outcome effectiveness.

Communication Management

Of all the management skills which must be developed, communication has paramount importance. Communication consists of the transmitting and receiving of full and correct information, with the result that everybody in the process shares the same understanding of the message. It must be managed in a systematic way, with the planning, implementing, monitoring and revision of all the channels of communication within the vessel – and as far as the Master is concerned, between the vessel's owner and the crew.

Communication is the key to shipboard management, leading to the achievement of five basic cultures:

- Listening culture – in particular, listen to their stress and fatigue;
- Learning culture – to ensure that feedback will be collected and acted on;
- Open culture – in particular, dealing with change management;
- Reporting culture – to take action on health and safety concerns;
- Empathetic culture – to respond to what they need.

Communicating and listening clearly are therefore important, but the way in which the message is communicated and the communication of the message itself are also important. Instead of focusing on what you want to say to get your point across, you should focus on what you want the other person to hear. The seafarer may not, in fact, understand the instruction, and may be culturally averse to admitting it, so greater care is needed in such cases.

Communication management demands not just delivering an instruction, but monitoring its execution, and then giving feedback so that performance can be improved. Positive feedback can have an enormous effect which benefits the seafarer and the entire team. Here are some tips:

- Do it now;
- Make it public, but consider the receiver as an individual;
- Be specific;
- Don't wait for the big successes;
- Be sincere.

By the same token, negative feedback can have a disastrous effect. Again, some tips are useful:

- Get your emotions under control;
- Find a private place to give the feedback;
- Focus on their actions, not on the person;
- Be specific;
- Be timely;
- Reaffirm your faith in the person;

- Have dialogue with them to get them to define the positive steps that they can take;
- Get over it; holding a grudge will cause resentment and build barriers that are difficult to break down.

Bridge Team Management

Bridge team management addresses the operational tasks that confront the safe completion of the marine adventure, from the implementation of the passage plan, covering the assessment and management of risks as they arise, enabling the team to apply treatment options and the critical times to abort or commit, until the end of the voyage and debrief meetings. The risk management function must be shared.

Bridge team management demands what it says: it has a central focus on the individuals contributing their part to the team, each member being involved in the process of problem-solving. The officer of the watch has control of safe and effective navigation, but they are not working in isolation, and clear communication is essential so that they all share a common view of the intended passage, and every member should contribute to the process, if necessary reporting issues and asking questions in order to achieve effective problem-solving.

Effective information exchange is vital to the decision-making process. Without it, a wrong decision may result, which can have obviously serious downstream consequences; but there is more to the process. Effective information exchange is vital to situational awareness, so that everybody understands what the emerging issues are and the officer of the watch can assess their impact on the planned voyage. Poor situational awareness has contributed to many casualties; in particular seven constituent factors in situational awareness have been identified:

- Lack of accurate, up-to-date information;
- The situation changes more rapidly than the officer of the watch apprehends, with little time for effective risk analysis;
- New and novel problems emerge, with complexities which are not appreciated at the critical time;
- Bridge team members lack sufficient capability and experience to respond to the problems;
- The officer of the watch is distracted, for example with paperwork demanded by frequent ports of call or with interruptions to their concentration such as mobile phone calls;
- Complacency – a misplaced feeling of confidence that nothing is amiss;
- Fatigue, both factors affecting the team's alertness in identifying and responding to emergent risks.

It is an unpleasant fact that the officer of watch is tempted to stand glued to the ship's navigational aids, or stands in one position instead of moving around the bridge to gather proper situational awareness. Complacency and fatigue are major culprits in such failures. Anticipating and responding correctly to the vessel's changing situation can contribute greatly to the effectiveness of a risk-treatment option.

The officer of the watch is also in charge of the bridge team and while on watch is the Master's representative, and obliged to comply with the Master's Standing Orders. The team is there to support the officer of the watch in the navigation process, who is also responsible to ensure that the ship complies with the Collision Regulations and that all the orders of the Master are followed with utmost safety under all conditions. Clearly the officer of the watch is the decision-maker, and there can only be one decision-maker at any one time, so communication management is important, enabling them to make decisions on the risk treatment option based on the inputs from the team.

The officer of the watch must also be alert to the fitness of their team members. A lookout may not report, or may not be aware of, their own fatigue, but an impairment of their physical or mental capability can lead to a breakdown in the vital information exchange process. The main causes of degraded fitness for duty have been identified through the misuse of alcohol or drugs, even though strict Flag State laws and Company procedures are in place, while injury, illness, stress and worry with personal problems, either from work or family, may cause or contribute to unfitness. The officer of the watch should be alert to the warning signs in their team:[1]

- Inability to concentrate;
- Confusion;
- Degraded situational awareness;
- Being distracted by feeling unwell;
- Poor physical co-ordination;
- Falling asleep;
- Communication failures.

It is sometimes overlooked, that the pilot is also part of the bridge team; but the officer of the watch must also be alert to the pilot's behaviour. In March 2022, *Ever Forward* ran aground in Chesapeake Bay in the United States, while under the navigational control of a pilot. During the investigation by the US Coast Guard, it was revealed that the pilot had made a series of five phone calls on his mobile phone, amounting to over 60 minutes of usage, in which he was distracted. He also sent two text messages and began drafting an email immediately before the grounding occurred regarding issues he experienced with line handlers back at the terminals, which had slightly delayed the vessel's departure. A few minutes before the grounding took place, the pilot had also exited the active navigation of his laptop to view a previous transit.

1 Such problems can hardly be learned effectively in the classroom or bridge simulator, for which there is no substitute for the sea phase.

Her Master was below at the time of the grounding, was unaware of the pilot's behaviour, but the Third Officer, Deck Cadet and an AB at the helm formed the bridge team with the pilot, did nothing. The casualty reported stated:

> *At approximately 20.17, the Third Officer announced on the bridge that the vessel's heading was 161 degrees and speed was approximately 13 knots. [The pilot] verbally acknowledged the Third Officer and took no action. The Third Officer stated that the Pilot was still looking at his phone at this time.*

The ship ran aground a minute later. The report found the incident's causal factors to be the pilot's failure to maintain situational awareness and attention while navigating, but also concluded that a causal factor was inadequate bridge resource management:

> *It is recommended that vessel owners and operators ensure and promote crew awareness of policies regarding the duties and obligations of officers on watch for the safety of the ship, even when a pilot is embarked. International Maritime Organization (IMO) Resolution A.960(23) highlights that efficient pilotage largely depends upon the effectiveness of communications and information exchange between the pilot, master and bridge personnel regarding navigational procedures, local conditions, and ship's procedures.*

The importance of teamwork was highlighted in the casualty of the *Kaami* in March 2020, which grounded on Sgeir Graidach, a straight in northwest Scotland. The MAIB report highlighted the importance of good practice, citing the ICS Bridge Procedures Guide, which provides that communication and teamwork are essential in a bridge team. The lookout had an important role to play in ensuring the safe navigation of the vessel but in this instance, he contributed little to the bridge team. The AB lookout had not received a basic familiarisation with the bridge equipment and had not been given clear expectations of his role, either from the SMS or at the start of the watch from the Chie Mate. As a result, his effectiveness as a member of the bridge team was greatly diminished to the extent there was no communication between him and the Chief Mate and no shared mental model of the navigational situation. He was on the bridge in hours of darkness as it was required by the SMS but, without integration into the bridge team, he was unable to positively contribute to the safe navigation of the vessel. With no useful contribution from the lookout, the Chief Mate became a single point failure – the ultimate breakdown in bridge team management.[2]

The *Kaami* casualty demonstrated the importance of communication once again as a critical factor in effective management. The transfer of information must enable everybody in the team to share the same message, to be conveyed when needed, and acknowledged and understood by the receiver. But the information must also

2 www.assets.publishing.service.gov.uk/media/60acb4bd8fa8f520bde56d16/2021-07-Kaami.pdf.

be accurate, complete and unambiguous, sometimes demanding special care in ensuring that everybody in the team can communicate in the common language on board.

Marine Guidance Note MGN 520 summarises 12 significant factors in defining the human element in maritime safety which dominate bridge team management:

- SITUATIONAL AWARENESS – do you know what's REALLY happening?
- ALERTING – do you REALLY speak up when you should?
- COMMUNICATION – do you REALLY understand each other?
- COMPLACENCY – is everything REALLY OK?
- CULTURE – do you REALLY have a good safety culture?
- LOCAL PRACTICES – efficiency OR dangerous short cuts?
- TEAMWORK – do you work REALLY well together?
- CAPABILITY – is your crew REALLY capable?
- PRESSURE – busy OR dangerously overloaded?
- DISTRACTIONS – multi-tasking OR dangerously distracted?
- FATIGUE – just tired OR dangerously fatigued?
- FIT FOR DUTY – are you REALLY fit to carry out your duties safely?

The Master's Overriding Duty

We have examined the Master's overriding duty to maintain order and discipline, which of course is crucial in the context of this chapter. Historically, discipline was applied in varying levels of zeal on board merchant ships. Captain Hamish Roberts was an Aden Pilot who witnessed first-hand the varying standards, recalling that Alfred Holt ships of the Blue Funnel Line were notable for their discipline, while other companies were decidedly more relaxed, to put it mildly, particularly with alcohol abuse, something which is not unknown in the twenty-first century. Like all things in shipping, Alfred Holt's tradition had a very important purpose: in 1875, their first total loss was followed by a succession of casualties, and the consequent spiralling of premiums demanded by hull and machinery insurers prompted the company to assume the whole of the risk on their vessels. They were taking no chances, building their ships to a standard higher than Lloyd's classification, and demanding order and discipline to minimise any risk. And it worked. The company lost its identity in a series of corporate restructures following changes to post-war shipping patterns, as evidenced by the complex evolution of Fleet Ownership and Management and the resultant challenges in rules of maintaining order and discipline. The effect of these changes has left the Master with diminishing management influence without losing responsibility, in particular their overriding duty is to maintain order and discipline on board. It is sometimes not appreciated that only the Master can perform this duty, because only they are the Flag State representative and the owner's representative, and the duty cannot be delegated, as body else has such authority. But the only two things that the Master has to maintain order and discipline are:

1 – Their skill in leadership
2 – The Seafarer's Employment Agreement, required by the Merchant Shipping (Maritime Labour Convention) (Minimum Requirements for Seafarers etc.) Regulations 2014[3]

While matters of shipboard discipline have been instrumental in the enforcement of maritime conventions, the process continues today, and it is the evolution of moral rules that define the normative ethics of changing societies. Most notably this is apparent in the emerging regulation of shipboard norms of behaviour, which the Master must enforce within their overriding duty.

As Flag State representative, the Master must enforce all the Statutory provisions under current law in this respect, not the least being:

- Protection From Harassment Act 1997;
- Sexual Offences Act 2003;
- Equality Act 2020.

The MLC embraces provisions obliging Member States to issue guidance eliminating shipboard harassment and bullying, and a great deal of work was committed by the ITF and ICS in this respect. Given the previous experience by the IMO and the ILO in the definition of working hours, it would make sense to engage in a process which draws in the requirements defined in the Maritime Labour Certificate, giving the measures some punitive force on shipowners.

Save those States that have not adopted the MLC, the defining features of harassment are incorporated into the Seafarers Employment Agreement, so any strengthening of State requirements can be more simply addressed by amending some of those requirements in order to render disobedience of the provisions serious violations entitling the employer to dismiss the seafarer for the first offence. Such behaviour is already addressed in the UK's Merchant Navy Code of Conduct as serious misconduct under 7b (XVI):

> *behaviour which seriously detracts from the social well-being of any other person on board, including but not limited to bullying, harassment, intimidation and coercion.*

The problem arises when a Member State is not a signatory to the MLC. In that situation, it would perhaps be misconceived if they propose amendments to a Convention to which they are already a signatory but not to one which already is accepted in general practice in international law.

Notwithstanding the provisions of the MLC, the statutory obligations giving rise to the definition of sexual harassment and bullying as serious violations of the seafarer's conduct, draw in the requirements of a competent safety management

3 See MSN 1848.

system, and the owner's disciplinary code would enhance the Merchant Navy Code of Conduct by harnessing stricter definitions to the Master's disciplinary powers. This would be referenced in the SEA, and could identify such misconduct, for example, as the ITF highlighted in its Guidance On Eliminating Shipboard Harassment And Bullying:

- Physical assault including sexual assault;
- Intimidation;
- Coercion;
- Interference with the work of other seafarers;
- Conduct based on gender affecting the dignity of women and men at work which is unwanted, unreasonable and/or offensive to the recipient.

The never-ending demand to meet the standard of law and practice does have a downstream consequence on the Master, who argue that they already have enough paper management to contend with, and can only implement evolving regulations and standards through on-board training; when confronted with multiple layers of guidance and regulation, the result may lead to confusion and error.

A reasonable and cost-effective alternative to the proposal would be welcome, such as one which sets out the basic knowledge and understanding in the employer's handbook on procedures, and is applied to amending the Code of Safe Working Practices, which would take little but cost-effective change in the chapters on Occupational health and safety and Company and worker responsibilities. This also conveniently cross-references the provisions on disciplinary issues in the SEA giving rise to dismissal, and obviate the risk that the seafarer could allege unfair dismissal on the grounds that they had not been told.

Dispute Resolution

The whole structure of shipboard management relies on consensus, so that everybody understands and agrees the critical issues of their employment and the resolution of complaints. This presents leadership and management with its ultimate challenge in the resolution of disputes on board the ship, largely because it involves learning the technique of dispute resolution, which is very difficult to learn from a text book. MSN 1849 addresses the fundamental issues of dispute resolution from the MLC, giving guidance on the requirements of the Merchant Shipping (Maritime Labour Convention) (Survey and Certification) Regulations 2013 for dealing with complaints procedures. The Regulation compels every ship to which to which the MLC applies to have an on-board complaints procedure which must:

- Seek to resolve the complaint at the lowest level possible;
- Enable a seafarer to complain directly to the master and appropriate external authorities;
- Include the right of the seafarer to be accompanied or represented when making a complaint;

- Ensure that the seafarer does not suffer any detriment for making a complaint;
- And in all cases seafarers must have the right to lodge a complaint directly with the Master and the MCA.

It is inevitable that disputes arise in which the parties themselves cannot reach an agreement; communication breaks down, and a state of deadlock can only be broken by litigation. But then the complainant and the Master have to face the facts: if they intend to pursue their rights, they will be faced with a long process that may end up in litigation, and once that process has been commenced, it may be very hard to stop, with potential consequences in costs, and in the process can cause intolerable stress, as well as tying up key personnel who should be better employed do the job for which they are paid. Moreover, the complainant may actually be a very good seafarer, who has cost the employer a lot in training, and a good replacement can be hard to find. Moreover, an unresolved dispute on a long voyage can have a disastrous effect on the morale and well-being of the crew.

How Does It Work?

The whole process concentrates on the advantages of flexibility in resolving a dispute. There are as many answers to this question as there are disputes, for each turns on what is important to those parties. There are virtually no cases in shipboard management for which the process is not suitable, for its life-blood merely depends on the will of both parties to find a compromise, however hard they may be pressing their case. Once again, communication management is key, for once a dispute becomes a crisis, communication breaks down and escalation rapidly follows, possibly involving impossible demands on crew Management and the Master's time.

The need is clear: to find an alternative route to manage the dispute, a route which explores a practical solution, avoiding the uncertainty, the cost and delays inevitable in escalation. The solution in shipboard dispute resolution involves an entirely confidential process and, rather than presenting the adversarial approach of litigation, concentrates on a flexible approach to achieving an agreement to end the dispute. By working towards a common goal of a solution, the Master can identify what is important to both of them; very often, they have priorities which they would not dream of disclosing, unless the process were confidential and Without Prejudice should the dispute escalate.

In this situation, the Master is somewhat in the position of a Mediator between the seafarer and the employer. The environment should be informal and non-confrontational, the language and tone conversational and the process conducted in a calm atmosphere – all essential ingredients in focusing on a resolution of the dispute, in which they can explore a compromise which may not be ideal for one or the other but is something which everybody can live with.

In the end, the dispute resolution process needs to be recorded in the OLB and a report sent to the shore office. A Master who can resolve a dispute before it becomes a crisis inevitably will come to the attention of the employer, which will count in their favour in their career.

20 Port State Control

In Chapter 15 we examined the Master's Responsibility towards the Port State. In this chapter we need to discuss further the role and function of the Port State, in terms of its routine procedures in global marine operations.

Port State Control (PSC) describes the power of the Port State to regulate and inspect ships of other flags in its waters, and if necessary to prevent a ship from proceeding to sea and consists of three broad areas:

- Enforcement of international regulations;
- Arrest and detention procedures;
- Places of refuge.

Enforcement of International Regulations

The process of inspection of foreign-flag ships in the Port State takes place to check:

- That the condition of the ship and her equipment comply with the requirements of international Conventions;
- That the ship is manned and operated in compliance with the Conventions;
- To ensure maritime safety and security and prevent pollution.

Article 218 (1) of UNCLOS defines the power:

> *When a vessel is voluntarily within a port or at an off-shore terminal of a State, that State may undertake investigations and, where the evidence so warrants, institute proceedings in respect of any discharge from the vessel outside the internal waters, territorial sea or exclusive economic zone of that State in violation of applicable international rules and standards established through the competent international organization or general diplomatic conference.*

Article 219 addresses measures relating to seaworthiness of vessels to avoid pollution:

DOI: 10.4324/9781003361916-20

States which, upon request or on their own initiative, have ascertained that a vessel within one of their ports or at one of their off-shore terminals is in violation of applicable international rules and standards relating to seaworthiness of vessels and thereby threatens damage to the marine environment shall, as far as practicable, take administrative measures to prevent the vessel from sailing. Such States may permit the vessel to proceed only to the nearest appropriate repair yard and, upon removal of the causes of the violation, shall permit the vessel to continue immediately.

From this point, we can identify the link with the survey requirements required under Conventions, described in Chapter 4.

Ship Certificates and Documents That Must Be Produced in a Port State Control (PSC) Inspection

The IMO's Procedures For Port State Control[1] list 50 certificates and documents which should be checked as a minimum during the inspection. Naturally they will not apply to all ships, but it is as well to list them for the sake of completeness:

1. International Tonnage Certificate (TONNAGE 1969 Article 7);
2. Reports of previous port State control inspections;
3. Passenger Ship Safety Certificate (SOLAS 1974 Regulation I/12);
4. Cargo Ship Safety Construction Certificate (SOLAS 1974 Regulation I/12);
5. Cargo Ship Safety Equipment Certificate (SOLAS 1974 Regulation I/12);
6. Cargo Ship Safety Radio Certificate (SOLAS 1974 Regulation I/12);
7. Cargo Ship Safety Certificate (SOLAS 1974 Regulation I/12);
8. Exemption Certificate (SOLAS 1974 Regulation I/12);
9. Minimum safe manning document (SOLAS 1974 Regulation V/14.2);
10. International Load Line Certificate (1966) (LL 1966/LL PROT 1988 Article 16.1);
11. International Load Line Exemption Certificate (LL 1966/LL PROT 1988 Article 16.2);
12. International Oil Pollution Prevention Certificate (MARPOL Annex I Regulation 7.1);
13. International Pollution Prevention Certificate for the Carriage of Noxious Liquid Substances in Bulk (NLS) (MARPOL Annex II Regulation 9.1);
14. International Sewage Pollution Prevention Certificate (MARPOL Annex IV Regulation 5.1 and MEPC.1/Circ.408);
15. International Air Pollution Prevention Certificate (MARPOL Annex VI Regulation 6.1);
16. International Energy Efficiency Certificate (MARPOL Annex VI Regulation 6);

1 A 32/Res.1155 28 January 2022.

17 International Ballast Water Management Certificate (BWM 2004 Article 9.1(a) and Regulation E-2);
18 International Anti-Fouling System Certificate (AFS 2001 annex 4 Regulation 2);
19 Declaration on AFS (AFS 2001 annex 4 Regulation 5);
20 International Ship Security Certificate or Interim International Ship Security Certificate (ISPS Code part A/19 and appendices);
21 Certificates for masters, officers or ratings (STCW 1978 Article VI and Regulation I/2, and STCW Code section A-I/2);
22 Copy of Document of Compliance or a copy of the Interim Document of Compliance (SOLAS 1974 Regulation IX/4.2 and ISM Code paragraphs 13 and 14);
23 Safety Management Certificate or an Interim Safety Management Certificate (SOLAS 1974 Regulation IX/4.3 and ISM Code paragraphs 13 and 14);
24 International Certificate of Fitness for the Carriage of Liquefied Gases in Bulk, or the Certificate of Fitness for the Carriage of Liquefied Gases in Bulk, whichever is appropriate (IGC Code section 1.4 or GC Code section 1.6);
25 International Certificate of Fitness for the Carriage of Dangerous Chemicals in Bulk, or the Certificate of Fitness for the Carriage of Dangerous Chemicals in Bulk, whichever is appropriate (IBC Code section 1.5 or BCH Code section 1.6);
26 International Certificate of Fitness for the Carriage of INF Cargo (SOLAS 1974 Regulation VII/16 and INF Code section 1.3);
27 Certificate of insurance or other financial security in respect of civil liability for oil pollution damage (CLC 69/92 Article VII.2);
28 Certificate of insurance or other financial security in respect of civil liability for bunker oil pollution damage (BUNKERS 2001 Article 7.2);
29 Certificate of insurance or other financial security in respect of liability for the removal of wrecks (Nairobi WRC 2007 Article 12);
30 High-Speed Craft Safety Certificate and Permit to Operate High-Speed Craft (SOLAS 1974 Regulation X/3.2 and 1994/2000 HSC Code paragraph 1.8.1 and section 1.9);
31 Document of Compliance with the special requirements for ships carrying dangerous goods (SOLAS 1974 Regulation II-2/19.4);
32 Document of authorization for the carriage of grain and grain loading manual (SOLAS 1974 Regulation VI/9 and Grain Code section 3);
33 Condition Assessment Scheme (CAS) Statement of Compliance, CAS Final Report and Review Record (MARPOL Annex I Regulations 20 and 21; Resolution MEPC.94(46), as amended by Resolutions MEPC.99(48), MEPC.112(50), MEPC.131(53), MEPC.155(55) and MEPC.236(65));
34 Continuous Synopsis Record (SOLAS 1974 Regulation XI-1/5);
35 Oil Record Book, parts I and II (MARPOL Annex I Regulations 17 and 36);
36 Cargo Record Book (MARPOL Annex II Regulation 15);
37 Garbage Record Book (MARPOL Annex V Regulation 10);

38 Garbage Management Plan (MARPOL Annex V Regulation 10 and Resolution MEPC.220(63));
39 Logbook and the recordings of the tier and on/off status of marine diesel engines (MARPOL Annex VI Regulation 13.5.3);
40 Logbook for fuel oil changeover (MARPOL Annex VI Regulation 14.6);
41 Ozone-depleting Substances Record Book (MARPOL Annex VI Regulation 12.6);
42 Ballast Water Record Book (BWM 2004 Article 9.1 (b) and Regulation B-2);
43 Fixed gas fire-extinguishing systems – cargo spaces Exemption Certificate and any list of cargoes (SOLAS 1974 Regulation II-2/10.7.1.4);
44 Dangerous goods manifest or stowage plan (SOLAS 1974 Regulations VII/4 and VII/7-2 and MARPOL Annex III Regulation 5);
45 For oil tankers, the record of oil discharge monitoring and control system for the last ballast voyage (MARPOL Annex I Regulation 31.2);
46 Search and rescue cooperation plan for passenger ships trading on fixed routes (SOLAS 1974 Regulation V/7.3);
47 For passenger ships, List of operational limitations (SOLAS 1974 Regulation V/30.2);
48 Nautical charts and nautical publications (SOLAS 1974 Regulations V/19.2.1.4 and V/27);
49 Records of hours of rest and table of shipboard working arrangements (STCW Code section A-VIII/1.5 and 1.7, ILO Convention No.180 Articles 5.7 and 8.1 and MLC 2006 Standards A.2.3.10 and A.2.3.12); and
50 Unattended machinery spaces (UMS) evidence (SOLAS 1974 Regulation II-I/46.3).

In addition, another 47 certificates and documents are required to be on board as may be applicable, including by mere example:

- Construction drawings (SOLAS 1974 Regulation II-1/3-7);
- Ship Construction File (SOLAS 1974 Regulation II-1/3-10);
- Manoeuvring booklet and information (SOLAS 1974 Regulation II-1/28);
- Stability information (SOLAS 1974 Regulations II-1/5 and II-1/5-1, and LL 1966/LL PROT 1988 Regulation 10);
- Subdivision and stability information (MARPOL Annex I Regulation 28);
- Damage control plans and booklets (SOLAS 1974 Regulation II-1/19 and MSC.1/Circ.1245, as amended);
- Ship Structure Access Manual (SOLAS 1974 Regulation II-1/3-6).

It is also important that ships produce their Maritime Labour Convention documentation.

Memoranda for Port State Control Inspections

Port States have gathered in regional groups in order to co-ordinate and harmonise their functions and share findings. Currently, there are ten PSC regimes, comprising eight regional Memoranda of Understanding (MoUs), and one Agreement on covering another specific region:

- Europe and the north Atlantic (Paris MoU);
- Asia and the Pacific (Tokyo MoU);
- Latin America (Acuerdo de Viña del Mar);
- Caribbean region (Caribbean MoU);
- West and Central Africa (Abuja MoU);
- Black Sea (Black Sea MoU);
- Mediterranean Sea (Mediterranean MoU);
- Indian Ocean (Indian Ocean MoU);
- Persian Gulf (Riyadh MoU);
- The United States Coast Guard controls the functions in the tenth PSC regime.

Note that some member countries belong to more than one PSC regime.

Their representatives attend IMO meetings and, in particular, deliver a great deal of data on their annual activities to every session of the Sub-Committee on Implementation of IMO Instruments, which informs the process of supporting the assessment of the fitness of and compliance with IMO standards, and the IMO rule-making process.

The Paris MoU on PSC consists of 27 participating maritime Administrations and covers the waters of the European coastal States and the North Atlantic basin from North America to Europe. It followed a faltering start to the process in 1978, when its commencement coincided with a massive oil spill occurred off the coast of Brittany as a result of the grounding of the Very Large Crude Carrier *Amoco Cadiz*. This event caused public outrage in Europe which promptly led to demands for far more stringent regulations than the Hague Memorandum offered. This pressure resulted in a more comprehensive memorandum which covered:

- Safety of life at sea;
- Prevention of pollution by ships;
- Living and working conditions on board ships.

Subsequently a new Memorandum of Understanding on Port State Control was signed in January 1982 by 14 European countries at a Ministerial Conference held in Paris, entering into force on 1 July 1982. Since then, this Paris MoU has been amended several times to accommodate new safety and marine environment requirements stemming from the IMO and requirements related to working and living conditions of seafarers.

The mission of the Paris MoU is to eliminate the operation of sub-standard ships through a harmonised system of Port State Control. The current member States of the Paris MoU are:

Belgium, Bulgaria, Canada, Croatia, Cyprus, Denmark, Estonia, Finland, France, Germany, Greece, Iceland, Ireland, Italy, Latvia, Lithuania, Malta, the Netherlands,

Norway, Poland, Portugal, Romania, Slovenia, Spain, Sweden and the United Kingdom. The Russian Federation is currently suspended until further notice.[2]

Annually more than 17,000 inspections take place on board foreign-flag ships in the Paris MoU ports, ensuring that these ships meet international safety, security and environmental standards, and that crew members have adequate living and working conditions. The prime responsibility for compliance with the requirements laid down in the international maritime conventions lies with the shipowner-operator, but responsibility for ensuring such compliance remains with their Flag State.

The Inspection Process

Ships will be subject to inspection according to their Risk Profile, which is calculated according to the following criteria:

- Type of ship;
- Age of ship;
- Flag;
- Recognised Organisation (inspection, survey and certification);
- Company performance;
- Number of deficiencies;
- Number of detentions.

A line or two on Company Performance may be helpful. This factor is based on the company's performance in the Paris MOU region appertaining to number of deficiencies per inspection and number of detentions in the preceding three-year period.

The frequency of inspection depends on the ship's individual risk profile, and applied in three broad categories:

- High-Risk ships will be due periodic inspections every five to six months;
- Standard risk: every 10 to 12 months;
- Low risk: every 24 to 36 months.

A useful interactive risk profile calculator can be found on the Maris MoU website: www.parismou.org/inspections-risk/library-faq/ship-risk-profile.

The frequency of inspections depends on the inspection window for each category. When the window opens, the ships is designated a Priority II vessel and may be inspected during that period. When the window closes, she becomes Priority I vessel and must be inspected.

2 Russia's suspension was announced on 20 May 2020 following its invasion of Ukraine in February, contrary to international legislation; but international legislation has proved not to trouble Russia in maritime issues.

Thus, for a high-risk ship, she may be inspected in accordance with the Priority II discretionary designation. Once an inspection has taken place she could expect an inspection free period of at least five months. If, however, she is not inspected within the fifth month discretionary window, she becomes a Priority I ship and must be inspected at the next Paris MOU port.

For a Standard Risk ship, a similar process applies. Once an inspection has taken place she could expect an inspection free period of at least ten months. If, however, she is not inspected within the window of 10 to 12 months following her last inspection, she becomes a Priority I ship and must be inspected at the next Paris MOU port.

For a low-risk ship, once an inspection has taken place she could expect an inspection free period of at least 24 months. The ship could be inspected within the following 12 months but will know that after 36 months she will be inspected at the next Paris MOU port.

A Priority I inspection can be postponed in limited circumstances, associated with the workload demands on the PSC in question, but only to another port in the same Member State or a port in another Member State provided that they agree in advance to undertake the inspection.

The type of Inspection falls into three types:

- Expanded;
- Initial;
- More detailed.

High-risk ships, regardless of type, will undergo, as a minimum, an expanded inspection; standard-risk and low-risk ships will undergo an initial or more detailed inspection.

An expanded Inspection is a thoroughly prescriptive inspection that covers specific items on different ship types. It includes a check of the overall condition of the ship, including the human element where relevant. Subject to their practical feasibility or any constraints relating to the safety of persons, the ship or the port, verification of the specific items in the risk areas for each ship type must be part of an expanded inspection.

All high-risk ships and ships of a risk type which are more than 12 years old are eligible for an expanded inspection. Ships in this category include:

- Bulk carriers;
- Oil tankers;
- Gas carriers;
- NLS tankers;
- Chemical tankers;
- Passenger ships.

Ships requiring an expanded inspection must give notice of arrival in a UK port or anchorage to the port authority at least 72 hours before arrival, enabling the port authorities to have surveyors available.

In respect of inspections carried out on UK-flag ships, the port authority must forward the information to the MCA via the MCA Consolidated European Reporting System.

The exhaustive process in an expanded inspection demands that the ship will be subject to operational delays while the process takes place. As a result, the ship's operator – and Master – must set aside sufficient time in the operating schedule to allow an expanded inspection to be carried out; the ship is required to remain until the inspection is completed.

An Initial Inspection reflects the reduced risk category of the ship, involving merely the Port State to:

- Check the certificates and documents listed in Annex 10 of the MoU text;
- Check that the overall condition and hygiene of the ship – including navigation bridge, accommodation and galley, decks including forecastle, cargo holds/area and engine room – meets accepted international rules and standards;
- Verify, if it has not previously been done, whether any deficiencies found by an Authority at a previous inspection have been rectified in accordance with the time specified in the inspection report.

A More Detailed Inspection will be carried out whenever there are clear grounds encountered during an initial inspection for believing that the condition of the ship or of her equipment or crew does not substantially meet the relevant requirements of a relevant instrument. Clear grounds exist when a PSC officer finds evidence, which in their professional judgement warrants a more detailed inspection of the ship, her equipment or its crew. The absence of valid certificates or documents is considered a clear ground; other examples of clear grounds can be found in Annex 9, paragraph 6 of the MoU text. A more detailed inspection will also be carried out on ships flying a flag that has not yet ratified all of the Relevant Instruments of the Paris MoU.

A more detailed inspection will include an in-depth examination in:

- The area(s) where clear grounds were established;
- The areas relevant to any overriding or unexpected factors;
- Other areas at random.

The more detailed inspection will take account of the human elements covered by the Conventions and include operational controls as appropriate.

Additional Inspections may be carried out between periodic inspections due to Overriding or Unexpected Factors, such as a report from a pilot, a ship involved in a collision, grounding or stranding on her way into port.

An Overriding Factor is a factor that is considered serious enough to trigger an additional inspection at Priority I level, notably in respect of ships entering Port State waters:

- Having been reported by another Member State;

- Having been accused of an alleged violation of the provisions on the discharge of harmful substances and effluents.

Its effect will automatically trigger the ship to be designated Priority I and must be inspected.

An Unexpected Factor is a factor that could indicate a serious threat to the safety of the ship and the crew or to the environment and may be inspected at the discretion of the PSC administration. Examples include:

- A ship reported by a pilot;
- A ship which did not comply with the reporting requirements;
- A ship operated in a manner to pose a danger.

An unexpected factor will cause the ship to become Priority II vessel and may be inspected at the discretion of the PSC administration.

The Paris MoU recognises that inspections cause delay and expense, which is best avoided off-berth and, so ships may be inspected in an anchorage within the port jurisdiction where a ship-port interface takes place, enabling operations to continue involving movement of persons or goods or the provision of port services or bunkering.

Refusal of Access

Refusal of Access consists of a ban on an individual ship, rather than the registered owner. Once banned, a transfer of company, flag or change in other involved parties does not revoke a ban or otherwise shorten the applicable periods mentioned. There are three reasons for which a ship to be refused access to ports in the Paris MoU region:

- When a ship has been detained 3 times, within a period of 36 months this applies to ships flying the flag of a State on the black list of the Paris MoU or when a ship has been detained 3 times, within a period of 24 months this applies to ships flying the flag of a State on the grey list of the Paris MoU;
- When a ship jumps a detention;
- When a ship does not call at the agreed repair yard following a detention.

Banning includes all ship types registered with a black or grey listed flag, according to the Paris MOU listing[3]. Banning will be based on the number of detentions within a specified period. The minimum time of banning is 3 months for the first ban, and 12 months for the second ban. A detention after a second ban could lead to possible permanent exclusion from EU ports and anchorages.

3 Attributing black, grey or white flag status.

Arrest and Detention

Arrest

The main purpose of arresting a vessel is to stop the Defendant owner from removing the vessel from the jurisdiction of the Court before the Claimant has managed to get Judgment on their claim. In this way a successful Claimant has the comfort of some asset that can be held at the Order of the Court and then made the subject of an Order for Sale if the Judgment Debt is not satisfied. But the arrest itself does not give the Claimant any property rights in her.

It is thus an instrument available in a dispute between private parties, rather than the State, in which one is seeking compensation from the other. That being said, the arrest is granted by an Order of the Court, and carried out by a Court officer, the Admiralty Marshal or their agent (generally the Customs Officer in the port concerned). The process is covered by Part 61 Civil Procedure Rules (CPR), and the appropriate Practice Directions for the Admiralty Court. The ship is arrested either:

- By service on her of an arrest warrant;
- Where she is not reasonably practicable to serve the warrant, by service of a notice of the issue of the warrant –
  - (a) In the manner set out in paragraph 3.6(1) of the Practice Direction to Part 61 CPR;
  - (b) By giving notice to those in charge of the property.

Case management is a priority factor in English courts, which have a duty to meet the overriding objective of enabling the court to deal with cases justly and at proportionate cost. The Practice Direction to Part 61 states that, when a claim is commenced, the Registrar responsible for the management of cases will issue a direction in writing stating routine matters for hearing the case, including the appropriate Court and place of Trial. The arrest documentation is then sent to the Admiralty Marshal who undertakes responsibility for the arrest, but not the costs, which must be borne by the Applicant, and must form part of the Judgment debt if they are to be recovered.

Detention

Detention describes the power of the Port State to prevent a vessel from proceeding to sea, so it is fundamentally different from an arrest in civil proceedings. The authority in English law is derived from section 95 of the Merchant Shipping Act 1995:

1. Where a ship in a port in the United Kingdom appears to a relevant inspector to be a dangerously unsafe ship the ship may be detained;
2. The power of detention conferred by subsection (1) above is exercisable in relation to foreign ships as well as United Kingdom ships;

3. The officer detaining the ship shall serve on the master of the ship a detention notice which shall –
   (a) State that the relevant inspector is of the opinion that the ship is a dangerously unsafe ship;
   (b) Specify the matters which, in the relevant inspector's opinion, make the ship a dangerously unsafe ship;
   (c) Prohibit the ship from going to sea until it is released by a competent authority.

The case of Club Cruise Entertainment v Dept for Transport [2008], referred to in Chapter 4, illustrates the obligations and pitfalls in a Port State detention.

A Port State detention also has an interface with the Paris MoU, but the powers of detention are still defined by Statute, in section 95, following the criteria set out above:

- A ship which is unsafe to proceed to sea will be detained upon the first inspection, irrespective of the time the ship is scheduled to stay in port;
- The deficiencies on a ship are so serious that they will have to be rectified before the ship sails.

Detention can involve not just the use but also the abuse of power, which may suit the Port State very well, but undermine global maritime confidence in the process of the protection of seafarers' rights and the respect for the rights of another Flag State, which the next case study serves to illustrate. This case demonstrates graphically the fateful interplay between the Master's Responsibility and Port State Control.

The Case of the *Heroic Idun*

Just after midnight on 8 August 2022, the two-year old crude tanker *Heroic Idun* arrived at Nigeria's Akpo offshore terminal in accordance with voyage orders. The vessel submitted all the documents that they had received with a request to complete and return and proceeded to tender Notice of Readiness. It then transpired that not all Nigerian National Petroleum Corporation clearances and Nigerian Navy clearances were in order, as the amount of cargo to be loaded had not been confirmed, and the vessel was requested to leave her anchorage and stand away from Akpo Terminal. For the next three days the Master re-tendered Notice of Readiness daily to the charterers who were requesting vessel readiness to load at Akpo if called at short notice. They duly complied with all orders.

The Master did everything right; he sent the necessary protests, and hove to with engines ready to proceed to the terminal. In the meantime, contingency plans were readied to meet a piracy attack, as the ship was in a notoriously vulnerable area. At about 21.00 that evening, the officer of the watch picked up VHF communications that a vessel was approaching with the intent of intercepting the tanker. The Master was called to the bridge and after endeavouring but failing to clarify the legitimacy of the fast-approaching vessel, the Master had to decide whether to follow an order received from Port State authorities to follow the alleged Navy vessel to Bonny Fairway Anchorage and was given a maximum of ten minutes to comply.

Based on a lack of positive identification and confirmation of motive, the Master implemented best management practices in accordance with Best Management Practice for West Africa, which involved evading the assailant by increasing to full speed, sending a distress alert, activating SSAS, bringing the fire hoses up to pressure in defence, mustering the crew in the citadel with only three persons remaining on the bridge, and alerting the war risk insurers contingency team. After a pursuit of some one and a half hours, the assailant broke off the pursuit, and she remained hove to for further orders.

The *Heroic Idun* was then seized by an Equatorial Guinea naval vessel at gun point, at the request of its Nigerian counterpart, and ordered to sail to the Port of Luba. All 26 crew were taken into custody on 13 August, and forcibly removed by the Nigerian Navy from Equatorial Guinea on 10 November, even though they had no legal right to do so – there had been no Flag State consultation and there was no extradition procedure in place between the two countries.

The crew were then charged with conspiracy in the theft of oil and falsifying a claim of a piracy attack, in breach of Nigeria's Suppression of Piracy and Other Maritime Offences Act. They were denied bail, but in name alone, for they were remanded under arrest on board the ship. The Naval Commander representing the Chief of Policy and Plans, subsequently listed the offences allegedly committed by the vessel to include:

- Attempting to deal in export crude oil without license or authorisation;
- Entering a restricted zone around an oilfield without authorisation and thus violating Nigeria's Exclusive Economic Zone regulations;
- Falsely accusing a Nigerian Navy Ship of piracy on International Maritime reporting platforms after having communicated with the Nigerian Navy Ship without ambiguity about her identity, therefore violating sections of the Suppression of Piracy and Other Maritime Offences Act 2019;
- Violating all lawful instructions at sea from Maritime Law Authorities as well as Nigeria's Miscellaneous Act and other associated national and international laws ascribed to by Nigeria and violation of Custom and Immigration Laws as acceded by Nigeria regarding the operations of Akpo Oil Terminal being an Oil installation in the Nigerian Exclusive Economic Zone.

Defence lawyers have expressed pious hopes that talks with Nigeria's Director of Public Prosecutions and the Attorney-General can bring the episode to a close without further escalation, while proceedings are underway in the Supreme Court declaring the rendition of the crew from Equatorial Guinea as unlawful, while the Flag State, the Marshall Islands has joined in the process, commencing arbitration proceedings against Equatorial Guinea under the jurisdiction provided under UNCLOS.

The storm of outrage from the international maritime community will not change a thing, though; Nigeria is a sovereign State under the United Nations charter. Nigerian criminal law relies heavily on its Criminal Code, based on English Common Law and legal practice, and Customary Law, following the customs and traditions of the people, and nobody else has the right to interfere in their administration of justice. Of course, nobody is fooled, either; Nigeria was pursuing the Master and crew to meet a domestic political agenda, and showed every sign of crowing about its success in this case as its fight against piracy and oil theft. It is yet another illustration of the phenomenon of criminalisation that has been developing for years.

Trial proceedings had stumblingly commenced in December 2022, after the Master and crew were indicted on obscure charges of conspiracy in the theft of oil and falsely claiming a piracy attack in order to escape, allegedly breaching Nigeria's Suppression of Piracy and Other Maritime Offences Act. This blatant demonstration of criminalisation lacked a shred of corroborative evidence to support the Prosecution case, but it very nearly succeeded against them, as the Trial had been listed for hearing and then adjourned a number of times. The problem for the seafarers, was that the case proceeded in accordance with the Rules of the Nigerian criminal process; other maritime States could protest and argue as much as they liked but, as a sovereign State, nobody else had any power to intervene.

It was only on 21 April 2023 when the Court in Port Harcourt ordered the prosecution to be ended and the crew released. Had the case proceeded, it would have been difficult to establish how there could have been any conspiracy at all, as the operators of the Akpo terminal were not charged with any complicity, and neither were the owner, manager and charterer. But the decisions of Courts in many countries can be very capricious, and a convenient scapegoat in foreign crews is often irresistible to Port States.

Places of Refuge

The issue of places of refuge for vessels in distress has been brought high in the maritime agenda due to much publicity following a number of incidents, including the *Erika* in 1999, the *Prestige* in 2002, the *Napoli* in 2007 and the *Flaminia* in 2012. These cases raised much controversy on whether or not the existing rules were sufficient to regulate the situation of a ship in need of assistance, and the accountability of parties, from the Master to the Charterer. The December 2003 IMO Guidelines on Places of Refuge for Ships in Need of Assistance were adopted, recommending that Coastal States develop procedures that would enable an efficient and objective risk assessment in order to allow the ship into a place of refuge and contain elements that should be taken into consideration while making such assessments. Even though a ship in need of assistance defines a situation that could give rise to its loss or an environmental or navigational hazard and a Place of Refuge as a port, the part of a port or another protective berth or anchorage or any other sheltered area identified by a Member State for accommodating ships in distress,[4] the critical issue of the safety of the ship herself remains enslaved to Coastal State priorities.

Article 20 of the 2002 EU directive on vessel traffic monitoring requires Member States to set up national plans to address the issue of places of refuge for vessels in distress. The place of refuge requirements were further amended in 2009,[5] providing for a more elaborate content of plans of places of refuge and a prominent role of competent authority in relation to the situation assessment and decision making. But the decision to grant access to a place of refuge could involve a political decision, which would involve the Coastal State having the power to consider balancing the interests of the ship in distress with those of the environment, which was the point of controversy encountered with virtually all the recent cases in which a ship was refused access; once the safety of life had been secured, the ship herself could be denied access if the Coastal State accorded greater importance to the cost of environmental damage, including the consequential costs of financial compensation.

In the face of that, Article 11 of Chapter II the International Convention On Salvage, 1989, particularly requires the Coastal State to take into account the need for co-operation in the salvage operation of a ship which is in such distress that the safety of life or of the ship is at stake – but it then appends the escape clause *as well as preventing damage to the environment in general*. Unfortunately other Conventions do not help, and UNCLOS is actually silent on this point, limiting itself to the provision for search and rescue services.[6] By contrast, the Port or Coastal State can rely on numerous provisions allowing it to guard against marine environmental pollution.

In the case of the *Prestige*, therefore, Spain arraigned Captain Mangouras on a charge of initially defying its instructions which it gave, not for the safety of life or the ship but for its own political purpose of reducing environmental risk, apparently choosing to ignore the long-accustomed practice of granting safe refuge. The European Court of Human Rights in his case held that his rights were made subservient to the political demands of Spanish governance, giving priority over his human rights to *the growing and legitimate concern both in Europe and internationally in relation to environmental offences and the tendency to use criminal law as a means of enforcing the environmental obligations imposed by European and international law*.[7]

4 Definitions falling in EU Directive 2002/59.
5 Directive 2009/17.
6 Article 98.
7 *Mangouras v Spain* (12050/04). The author's reading of the text of the Judgment, which is in French.

21 Pilotage

Compulsory pilotage was implemented through Port State laws as a result of commercial pressure, which forced its introduction into English Statute Law in the early years of the nineteenth century, as a means by which the Port State could manage the risk to life and property presented by the massive growth in Britain's brave new maritime commerce, which had been helped so ably by the Napoleonic Wars. The risks to safe navigation in local waters was reposed in the knowledge and skills of a pilot experienced in the particular waters of a locality; as such pilotage became an important in the risk management process and, as a result, the Pilotage Act 1812 introduced the concept by statute. A century later, the relationship between those involved in pilotage changed dramatically with the Pilotage Act 1913, expressly overriding any conflicting provision in primary or secondary legislation, and providing that the Owner and Master of a vessel navigating in a compulsory navigation area shall be answerable for any loss or damage caused by the navigation of the vessel or by any fault of the navigation of the vessel in the same manner as he would if pilotage were not compulsory. This has been taken forward into current law by Section 16 of the Pilotage Act 1987, which provides that the fact that a ship is being navigated in a compulsory pilotage area shall not affect any liability of the Owner or Master of the ship for any loss or damage caused by the ship or by the manner in which it is navigated.

Compulsory Pilotage and the Master-Pilot Relationship

Section 15(1) of the 1987 Act certainly perpetuates the requirement that a ship which is being navigated in a compulsory navigation area shall be under the pilotage of an authorised pilot unless the Master or Mate possesses a pilotage exemption certificate in respect of that area and ship. This section defines the obligation for compulsory pilotage in any ship in UK territorial waters:

1 *A ship which is being navigated in an area and in circumstances in which pilotage is compulsory for it by virtue of a pilotage direction shall be under the pilotage of an authorised pilot accompanied by such an assistant, if any, as is required by virtue of the direction; or under the pilotage of a deck officer possessing a pilotage exemption certificate in respect of that area and ship.*

DOI: 10.4324/9781003361916-21

The critical obligation in criminal law follows in the next subsection:

2 *If any ship is not under pilotage as required by subsection (1) above after an authorised pilot has offered to take charge of the ship, the master of the ship shall be guilty of an offence.*

To avoid any confusion, subsection 3 provides that the Master commits an offence if *the ship is navigated in an area in which a pilotage direction applies to it, and the competent harbour authority which gave the direction has not been given pilotage notification.*

In compulsory pilotage situations the legislation calls for the Master to hand over the navigation of the ship to a licensed pilot, whose duties will involve:

- Directing the course of the ship;
- Directing the speed of the ship;
- Making necessary signals;
- Directing tugs;
- Directing where and when the ship will come to rest.

The question of responsibility becomes blurred, however, because the pilot is not the Flag State representative, but the Master, and the Master's Authority under Flag State jurisdiction remains unfettered. They remain in command at all times, so their personal liability for safe navigation continues.

As a result, the Master retains the power to dismiss the pilot if the pilot demonstrates unfitness or manifest incompetence or hazards the vessel or other vessels persons or property for any reason. The procedure would oblige the Master to challenge the pilot and, if they remain concerned that the pilot is standing the ship into danger, the Master must inform the pilot of their dismissal and request that the pilot take the ship to a safe place to await another pilot. Only in order to avoid some imminent danger would the Master be able to rely on SOLAS V Regulation 34-1 by intervening and assume conduct of the navigation of the ship before another pilot comes aboard. But the Master will have to support their case with good evidence. Clear and unequivocal conversations on the VDR can make the world of difference.

However blurred the lines of responsibility may appear at first sight, in fact it makes sense, and it works. As the Master remains in command at all times, so their responsibility for safe navigation continues regardless of the pilot aboard. If they discharge their obligations, well and good; but if they do not justify their conduct in the case of a negligent Pilot, they will be held liable for the consequences. Parliament clearly intended to underpin the Master's authority and in the debate in the House of Lords on the Pilotage Bill in June 1986, Lord Strathcona said:

> *It seems odd to legislate in great detail as to who should command a ship at sea and then apparently abandon all control once the ship comes into a pilotage area.*[1]

1 *HL Deb 25 June 1986 vol 477 cc377-407.*

Within three years this argument would be tested. In the case of the *Esso Bernicia*,[2] Lord Jauncey underlined the importance of associating good law with common sense. Lord Jauncey drew the sensible conclusion of English law that the Master, like any individual who has a personal duty of care such as that envisaged in *Donoghue v Stevenson*, which of course forms the foundation of accountability in gross negligence under *R v Adomako*, cannot walk away from their responsibility under that duty simply by delegating the performance of the task to somebody else, and it does not matter how the somebody else has been put there – whether an employee under a contract of service, or an independent contractor (such as a voluntary pilot), or whether the engagement has been imposed by a Statute (in this case the Pilotage Act 1987). Thus, while the pilot has command and control of the navigation of the ship in compulsory waters, the Master will still have the responsibility for the safety of the ship and observe their contractual obligations to their employer, the shipowner, with whom the duty ultimately rests.

Paradoxically, this concurrently offers salvation to the shipowner under the nautical fault defence of the Hague-Visby Rules in the event of damaged cargo: the Master's discretion in navigation must prevail supporting the Merchant Shipping (Safety of Navigation) Regulations 2002 (amended by SI 2011 No 2978) and thus the employer in this instance cannot be responsible for its employee's negligence over whom it has no control.[3] More recently, criminal accountability has been implemented in the Merchant Shipping (Safety of Navigation) Regulations 2020, which creates a criminal offence of breaches of SOLAS Chapter V violating provisions for safe navigation and the avoidance of dangerous situations; glaringly, however, the offence is committed by the Master, not the pilot. Had this law been in place in 1996, the consequence for the Master in the next case might have been very different.

The Case of the *Sea Empress*

One of the most serious pollution casualties in recent times serves to underpin the rationale for the relationship between the Master and the Pilot. The Liberian-registered tanker *Sea Empress* was less than three years old when she loaded her cargo of Forties light crude oil at Hound Point, in the Firth of Forth and sailed from there for Milford Haven on 13 February 1996. Two days later, under the navigation of the compulsory pilot, the bows had passed the Middle Channel Rocks Light on approach to Milford Haven when there was a shuddering vibration, followed by a sound from the deck below of liquid being forced under pressure, accompanied by a strong smell of oil. The Marine Accident Investigation Branch concluded in its report that the immediate cause of the grounding was pilot error, namely his failure

2 *Esso Petroleum Company Ltd v Hall Russell & Company Ltd* [1989] 1 Ll R. 8.

3 See *Tasman Orient Line CV v New Zealand China Clays Ltd and Others* [2010] 2 Ll R 13. Worryingly for the shipowner, the Rotterdam Rules have abandoned this defence, although these are far from implementation due to the low number of ratifications.

to take appropriate and effective action to keep the vessel in the deepest part of the Channel. But the Pilot and the Master had not discussed and agreed a pilotage passage plan, as a consequence of which neither the Master nor the Chief Officer knew what the Pilot's intentions were. Moreover, the Master failed to follow the standing orders of his managers with respect to pilotage matters and, when it became clear to the Master that the Pilot was hazarding the vessel, the Master wrongly kept quiet. Although the MAIB's reports are not prepared with a view to establish the liability of a party in litigation, the facts which it finds certainly are of value in such matters. For such reasons, the MAIB found fault with the Master, and critical conclusions in the MAIB's report can lead to consequences in civil and, more importantly, in criminal proceedings.[4]

The *Sea Empress* case illustrates the essential feature subsisting in maritime law that the Master's authority remains unfettered. They retain the power to take the navigation out of the hands of the pilot if the pilot demonstrates manifest incompetence or hazards the vessel or other vessels persons or property for any reason. But if they do so, they cannot proceed an inch without the authority of the harbour authority, as Section 15(3) of the 1987 Act demands. The downstream consequence, of course, raises issues of criminal liability under the 2020 Regulations.

The Risk Management Function

It is, therefore, the management function of transferring the risk, which is essential in compulsory pilotage, and even then, the Master must ensure that they always keep the navigation of the vessel under scrutiny. If the pilot is incompetent and must be dismissed, or if they become incapacitated, then the Master must advise VTS of the facts and seek directions. They after all will be the ones who will have the knowledge of the appropriate place of safety and, in any event, must have in place contingency plans for dealing with ships that cannot respond due to Pilot incapacity or navigation defect on the ship. It must also be borne in mind that the Master's decision of a place of safety may not take into account the hazards presented to third parties in the circumstances of the particular case and in any event could lead to all sorts of insurance problems.[5]

Section 16 of the 1987 Act makes the point clearly that the fact that a ship is being navigated in a compulsory pilotage area *shall not affect any liability of the owner or master of the ship for any loss or damage caused by the ship or by the manner in which it is navigated.* This clearly is intended to address civil liability, demanding that the Master maintains command of the voyage within the

4 The report of the Chief Inspector of Marine Accidents into the grounding and subsequent salvage of the tanker SEA EMPRESS at Milford Haven between 15 and 21 February 1996, HMSO.

5 While the Master's discretion to act remains unfettered, he must still report to VTS any way in accordance with the Merchant Shipping (Vessel Traffic Monitoring and Reporting Requirements) Regulations 2004 on the reporting of incidents at sea and the incapacity of a Pilot would meet the definition of an incident in section 12(2)(b).

parameters of their experience and knowledge of the area, but the pilot may be held to account for criminal misconduct. Section 21 of the 1987 Act provides:

> *If the pilot of a ship ... does any act which causes or is likely to cause the loss or destruction of, or serious damage to, the ship or its machinery, navigational equipment or safety equipment, or the death of, or serious injury to, a person on board the ship; or ... omits to do anything required to preserve the ship or its machinery, navigational equipment or safety equipment from loss, destruction or serious damage or to preserve any person on board the ship from death or serious injury, and the act or omission is deliberate or amounts to a breach or neglect of duty or he is under the influence of drink or a drug at the time of the act or omission, he shall be guilty of an offence.*

If the pilot is incompetent and must be dismissed, or if he becomes incapacitated, then the Master must advise VTS of the facts and seek directions. They after all will be the ones who will have the knowledge of the appropriate place of safety and, in any event, must have in place contingency plans for dealing with ships that cannot respond due to Pilot incapacity or navigation defect on the ship. It must also be borne in mind that the Master's decision of a place of safety may not take into account the hazards presented to third parties in the circumstances of the particular case and in any event could lead to all sorts of insurance problems.[6]

That being said, the harbour authority has to balance the availability of resources, with commercial considerations of cost, often making it necessary to provide the pilotage service by a vessel traffic manager ashore. In some States, the provisions of 'shore pilotage' is offered which permits a relaxation of the requirement to have a pilot on board, enabling a process to give directions much as an air traffic controller. It is a dangerous step, and the Port State knows it; in many cases they will offer the Master shore pilotage but with the proviso that if the Master accepts, the Port State will not admit any liability for consequences. The alternative, of course, would be to lose time on the voyage while awaiting a pilot on board, and risk the ship being deemed off-hire.

Moreover, the risk to navigation in shore pilotage can be high; the pilot may have all manner of electronic instruments to deliver information to them, but that is all they have, to give them the speed, rate of turn, course and position. With this, they must give instructions to the crew on the bridge and, of course, the tugs. The bridge team may well not know the pilot – to them he is a remote voice which makes it difficult for all the parties involved, from the pilot to the bridge team and the tugs, to work to the model of safe navigation envisaged by the 1987 Act. The consequence is that, given any situation or emerging situation, the pilot is limited

6 While the Master's discretion to act remains unfettered, he must still report to VTS any way in accordance with the Merchant Shipping (Vessel Traffic Monitoring and Reporting Requirements) Regulations 2004 on the reporting of incidents at sea and the incapacity of a Pilot would meet the definition of an incident in section 12(2)(b).

to the information that can be received on a computer screen and from the radio communication with a bridge team, whose facial expressions and demeanour of incomprehension he is unable to detect.

Meanwhile, the Master remains accountable, which serves to demonstrate the Master's need to respond to situations in which he is exposed to liability as a result of statutory provision that makes pilotage compulsory – except where no pilot is available, making it necessary to control vessel traffic movements remotely and, thus, offering the Master a service equivalent to that of the air traffic controller. While it is apparent that vessel traffic management has an important part to play in safety control, the Master's responsibility to discharge their duty of care remains unassailable, even though the person upon whom they rely – the vessel traffic controller – is performing the pilotage function simply with the use of electronic aids. The object lesson in incompetent Port State traffic monitoring and management became only too clear in the case of the grounding of the *Wakashio* in 2020.

While the Master's management of the safe navigation of the vessel has clearly been eroded by compulsory pilotage, they unquestionably remain accountable – they would have to be, of course, for in the Master reposes the Flag State's confidence to protect their sovereign interests. That does not mean to say that they are *absolutely* liable, and they can rebut the charge with the benefit of argument supported by the evidence. If the pilot is negligent, the Master must account for himself but, if they could not have prevented the casualty in accordance with the normal principles of negligence, they will not be to blame. Had the Master of the *Sea Empress* followed the Company's standing orders for pilotage procedures, had he drawn his concerns to the pilot's attention and received satisfactory replies, then his culpability in consequent pollution offences, usually such a source of fear for the master in such circumstances, could not be established, according to the demands of international law for a fair trial.[7] How the Port State views that may be a different matter, particularly in the scenario in which some Port State's environment has been damaged by a marine pollution event, while the vessel was in a compulsory pilotage area but, necessarily, remaining under the responsibility of the Master.

Pilotage and the Master's Absolute Discretion

Much light has been cast on the Master's absolute discretion, the metamorphosis of which appears well-defined by Convention in SOLAS Chapter V Regulation 34-1. On the face of it, the Master never loses control of his command; and he cannot share it either. Compulsory pilotage was implemented by Port State laws because of commercial pressure on navigation in confined waters; in the UK, the Pilotage Act 1987 clearly defines the requirements and powers for compulsory pilotage, but what happens when the Master must exercise their absolute discretion, as implemented in UK law by the Merchant Shipping (Safety of Navigation) (Amendment)

7 See European Convention on Human Rights 1950, Art 6.

Regulations 2011?[8] The Master has no authority to assume the conduct of the navigation of the vessel in a compulsory pilotage area but is bound to challenge the pilot if they consider the pilot is standing the ship into danger. They should express their opinion to the pilot on important matters of navigation and manoeuvring and warn the pilot if it appears that the pilot is taking or proposing to take any action of which the Master disapproves and may insist that the pilot takes all reasonable precautions. If, however, the Master apprehends that the pilot is incapable through illness, drink, drugs or fatigue – as Captain Corner discovered in the St Lawrence River[9] – or fails to take action despite the Master's challenge, then, in reliance upon the Master's absolute discretion under SOLAS V Reg 34-1 in an emergency for the immediate protection of the safety of life at sea or the protection of the marine environment. The Master may then take emergency action to abate or mitigate the imminent danger, and then, as the Owner's representative, will follow a strict procedure:

1. They must inform the pilot he is dismissed and request him to take the ship to a safe anchorage where they can await another pilot;
2. They must then contact the pilotage authority and request another pilot.

It is important that the dismissal of the pilot does not give the Master the right to assume the duties of the pilot. The Master must await arrival of another pilot (unless they or the Mate hold a pilotage exemption certificate).

In reality, everybody should rely on the foundation of the bridge team, and the Master and pilot should, in most cases, strive to work together as a fundamental part of that team. An example of good crisis management in this context can be found in the case of the *Höegh Osaka*. This dedicated roll-on roll-off vehicle carrier was built in 2000 Tsuneishi Shipyard in Japan. Originally in the management of AP Møller, in 2008 she was sold to Höegh Autocarriers and renamed *Höegh Osaka* under the management of Wallem Shipmanagement, Singapore.

The Case of the *Höegh Osaka*

On 3 January 2015 *Höegh Osaka* she already had some cargo on board when she was alongside in Southampton, loading a cargo of buses, construction equipment and Range Rover cars. More cargo was to be loaded at Bremerhaven, Germany, her next port of call, when she would proceed to Hamburg to load more cargo and bunkers.

A pilot embarked at 19.30 and the ship sailed at 20.06, carrying 1,400 vehicles and about 70 pieces of construction equipment. Twenty minutes after departure, the chief mate and the deck cadet went to the ship's control centre to commence

8 SI 2011 No 2978.
9 See Daniels, S, 2022, Responsibility and Accountability in Maritime Law, Informa Law from Routledge, Abingdon, p. 163.

the calculation of the ship's departure stability. Due to a large number of changes between the planned load and the actual load, the chief officer decided to re-enter all of the cargo figures rather than amend the departure stability condition that he had used for his calculation earlier in the day. As *Hoegh Osaka* proceeded along Southampton Water, the Master telephoned the chief mate and told him that he thought the ship did 'not feel right.' The chief mate replied, 'I'm working on it.' However, When the chief mate had entered the cargo figures into the ship's loading computer, he became concerned that the indicated static stability was less than his earlier departure stability calculation had predicted. He sent the deck cadet to take soundings of the three aft peak tanks in preparation for loading additional ballast water. The chief mate began setting up the ballast system using the mimic panel in the ship's control centre, anticipating that he would require an additional 300 tonnes of ballast in the aft peak tanks

At 20.59, the pilot gave the first helm order to starboard to start the Calshot turn, at which time the ship was making 10 knots. The bridge team was supporting the pilotage, and the Master was moving around the bridge to maintain an overview of the operation. The Calshot turn was completed without incident, the ship heeling to port and returning upright as expected. At 21.02, as *Hoegh Osaka* entered the Thorn Channel, the pilot requested that the ship's speed be increased and she duly increased speed to 12 knots. At 21.09, she made a port turn at the West Bramble Buoy and developed a severe list. The pilot gave the order to stop engines a minute later, and expressed doubts in respect of the static stability of the ship. As the list increased, the ship's propeller and rudder came clear of the water. The ship grounded on the Bramble Bank off the Isle of Wight at 21.15.

The action that was taken most likely avoided more serious loss in the common peril, but the Chief Inspector of Marine Accidents made the comment that raised issues of negligence at the time of the ship's departure:

> *The MAIB's investigation found that Hoegh Osaka's stability did not meet the minimum international requirements for ships proceeding to sea. The cargo loading plan had not been adjusted for a change to the ship's usual journey pattern and the number of vehicles due to be loaded according to the pre stowage plan was significantly different from than that of the final tally. The estimated weight of cargo was also less than the actual weight. Crucially, the assumed distribution of ballast on board, bore no resemblance to reality, which resulted in the ship leaving Southampton with a higher centre of gravity than normal. This accident is a stark reminder of what can happen when shortcuts are taken in the interest of expediency*

Criminal Liability Against the Pilot – the Case of the *Cosco Busan*

A striking case in which confidence was misplaced in the pilot and the Master merely followed their instruction can be found in the *Cosco Busan* casualty. At 08.07 on 7 November 2007, the Hong Kong-registered container ship *Cosco Busan* left her berth in the Port of Oakland, United States, heading for Busan, South Korea, with an all-Chinese crew. She was in a compulsory pilotage area and, therefore, needed a pilot.

John Cota was appropriately licensed by the Coast Guard and California as a Bar Pilot. He was a member of the San Francisco Bar Pilots and had been employed in the San Francisco Bay pilotage area since 1981. What he had not told anybody, was that his ability was impaired because of his use of prescription drugs while piloting the container vessel, which rendered him unable to use the radar and electronic navigation charts correctly. At the very least, he had been required to declare the use of prescription drugs on annual forms submitted to the US Coast Guard.

According to the prosecution case, Captain Cota made the decision to leave in heavy fog, while the pilots of six other large commercial vessels decided not to depart in the heavy fog which reduced visibility to less than half a nautical mile. Indeed, the fog was so thick that the bow of the vessel was not visible from the bridge. It must be said that there was no effective Master-Pilot exchange and Cota took no steps to review the transit plan in the circumstances of the restricted visibility. But the Master did not stop him.

In his defence, Cota claimed that he found both radar unreliable, but he did not notify the Master or the Coast Guard that a required piece of equipment that was needed to navigate the ship safely had failed. In fact, evidence was adduced in rebuttal by captured images of the radar retained on the ship's computer show that the radar was fully operational. Moreover, the VDR recording showed that Cota was confused regarding the operation of the electronic chart system upon which he chose to rely including the meaning of two red triangles, representing buoys marking the tower of the bridge that he eventually hit.

At 08.27, the *Cosco Busan* was about a third of a mile from the San Francisco–Oakland Bay Bridge, when a VTS operator ashore noticed that she was deviating from her passage plan and was out of position to make an approach to the bridge's Delta–Echo span. The VTS operator radioed the pilot. The pilot reported to VTS that he was *steering 280*, when the ship's actual heading was 262. The VTS operator did not communicate further with the pilot. At no time did Cota – or indeed, any of the crew – consult the ship's paper chart or take a single positional fix to verify the ship's position. But still the Master did nothing. The casualty report subsequently stated that the Master did not feel comfortable challenging the pilot because of the pilot's off-hand manner; once again, we encounter the factor of cultural issues which interfere in communication management. On the other hand, Masters must deal with all nationalities and should have maintained effective bridge team management, something which would arise in future cases, not least being that of *Costa Concordia*.

At 08.29, the bosun used his radio to report, in Mandarin, *The bridge column. The bridge column.* The Master replied (in Mandarin), *Oh, I see it. I see it.* Clearly the imperative of the working language in English was not observed; but the pilot then said, *Yeah, I see it.* Despite the language barrier, the pilot clearly understood.

About ten seconds later, the pilot ordered the rudder (which had been at hard starboard) to mid-ships. After another five seconds, the pilot ordered hard port rudder. The forward port side of the vessel allided with the corner of the fendering system at the base of the Delta tower at 08.30, which compromised the forward port side of the hull with a gash, 212 feet long by 10 feet high by 8 feet deep, breaching 2 bunker tanks and a ballast tank.

The National Transportation Safety Board's casualty report determined the causes of the casualty thus:

- The pilot's degraded cognitive performance from his use of prescription medications, despite his completely clean post-accident drug test;
- The absence of a comprehensive pre-departure master/pilot exchange and a lack of effective communication between Pilot John Cota and Master, Captain Mao Cai Sun during the accident voyage; and
- Captain Sun's ineffective oversight of Cota's piloting performance and the vessel's progress.

The Trial against Cota proceeded, not on an indictment of endangering the safety of life or the ship by deliberate or negligent conduct, but according to a plea bargaining agreement in which he pleaded Guilty to negligently causing the discharge of a harmful quantity of oil in violation of the Clean Water Act, as amended by the Oil Spill Act 1990 (implemented following the *Exxon Valdez* disaster in 1989); as well as violating the Migratory Bird Treaty Act, by causing the death of protected species of migratory birds. The logical explanation is that the risk society in California gave priority to environmental protection over seafarer's lives. Yet, the submission made by the Prosecution dwelt on intentional *and* (not or) negligent acts, presumably of seamanship:

> *he made a series of intentional and negligent acts and omissions, both before and leading up to the incident that produced a disaster that, as widespread as it was, could have had even worse consequences ... Captain Cota abandoned ship by not following required safety procedures which then resulted in an environmental disaster.*

In July 2009 Cota was sentenced to serve ten months in a federal prison.[10] In fact this was the maximum in the range agreed in the plea-bargaining agreement.

The prosecution of the pilot, rather than the Master, does remain exceptional, and we must bear in mind that the Master remains in command of the vessel at all times, which serves to demonstrate the Master's need to respond to situations in which they are exposed to liability as a result of statutory provision that makes pilotage compulsory. That does not mean to say that they are *absolutely* liable. If the pilot is negligent, the Master must account for their part but, if they could not have prevented the casualty in accordance with the normal principles of negligence, they will not be to blame. Had the Masters of the *Sea Empress* and the *Cosco Busan* followed the Company's standing orders for pilotage procedures, had

10 See www.justice.gov/opa/pr/prison-sentence-cosco-busan-pilot.

they drawn their concerns to the pilot's attention and received satisfactory replies, then their culpability in consequent pollution offences, usually such a source of fear for the Master in such circumstances, could not be established, according to the demands of international law for a fair trial.[11] How the Port State views that may be a different matter, particularly in the scenario in which some Port State's environment has been damaged by a marine pollution event, while the vessel was in a compulsory pilotage area but, necessarily, remaining under the responsibility of the Master.

The priority accorded to the environmental case was underlined by the US Attorney for the Northern District of California, who said *The court's sentence of John Cota should serve as a deterrent to shipping companies and mariners who think violating the environmental laws that protect our nation's waterways will go undetected or unpunished. They will be vigorously prosecuted.*[12]

As a postscript, a federal grand jury also indicted Fleet Management Ltd of Hong Kong, the company that operated *Cosco Busan*. The indictment alleged six counts of falsifying documents to interfere with a federal investigation and two counts of criminal negligence for allegedly helping to cause the spill. Following a dispute resolution process, the Defendant company paid $10 million in fines and restitution.

Bridge Team Mismanagement – The Case of the *Ever Forward*

The importance of the bridge team is evident in a more recent case. On 13 March 2022, at approximately 18.12 Eastern Standard Time (EST), the Hong Kong flagged containership *Ever Forward* departed Seagirt Marine Terminal in Baltimore, Maryland *en route* to Norfolk, Virginia with a licensed Maryland State Pilot, in direction and control of the vessel. The vessel's departure was slightly delayed due to a line handling issue at the facility.

The pilot was on the bridge with the Master and the bridge team until approximately 1930, when the Master departed the bridge to get dinner. At approximately 19.50, the bridge team completed a scheduled watch relief, and a new Third Officer and Deck Cadet reported to the bridge. At this time, the bridge team was comprised of the pilot, the Third Officer, Deck Cadet and an Able-Bodied Seaman who was at the helm. At approximately 2.017, the vessel passed its charted waypoint, marking a turn to approximately 180 degrees True that needed to be executed in accordance with the voyage plan. No order was given to turn the vessel and the helmsman maintained the previously ordered course of 161 degrees True. At 20.18, the pilot realised that the vessel was past its turn and ordered 15 degrees rudder to starboard. The vessel grounded outside the Craighill Channel, east of Lighted Buoy 16.

The pilot immediately attempted to use astern propulsion to free the vessel. Soon after, the Master returned to the bridge and performed a series of safety checks

11 See European Convention on Human Rights 1950, Art 6.

12 See www.justice.gov/opa/pr/prison-sentence-cosco-busan-pilot.

in accordance with the vessel's Safety Management System (SMS), prior to continuing efforts to free the vessel. After all safety checks were completed, the *Ever Forward* bridge team and the pilot continued to attempt to free the vessel using astern propulsion and bow thrusters. At approximately 20.31, the Master notified the vessel's shoreside representative that the *Ever Forward* required assistance. At approximately 21.01, the pilot notified U.S. Coast Guard Sector Maryland-National Capital Region of the grounding. At approximately 22.50 and after being relieved by another licensed Maryland State Pilot, the pilot departed the grounded vessel.

During the outbound transit, the pilot was solely relying on his Portable Pilot Unit (PPU) to navigate the *Ever Forward.* Just prior to the grounding, the pilot exited the active navigation of his PPU to view a previous transit. The pilot also made a series of 5 phone calls amounting to over 60 minutes of time during the course of his outbound transit. He also sent two text messages and began drafting an email immediately before the grounding occurred regarding issues he experienced with facility line handlers.

As a result of its investigation, the U.S. Coast Guard determined that the initiating event for this casualty was the grounding. No mechanical issues or equipment failures contributed to this marine casualty. The causal factors that contributed to this casualty include:

1. Failure to maintain situational awareness and attention while navigating;
2. Inadequate bridge resource management.

During the investigation, the pilot confirmed that he solely relied on his PPU to navigate and did not use any ship's equipment or charts. While approaching a critical turn, the pilot was taking a screenshot on his PPU of a previous trip to text another member of the Maryland Pilots Association in regard to an ongoing issue with line handlers. The pilot then began to draft an email on his cell phone in order to follow-up with a text message. The PPU operator manual states that the PPU automatically records all active vessel movements unless a replay of a previous trip is begun in the middle of an active trip. The PPU will then stop recording the active trip and save the active vessel movement up until the point the PPU user navigated away from the active trip to view a previous one. It will then save that active trip into a file and start a new, separate file once the user returns to the active trip screen. This means that there will be a data gap in the active trip for the duration of time that a user views a previously recorded trip. In this incident, the pilot's PPU had two saved files with a gap in recording from 2015 to 2019, approximately the time that the pilot stated he was viewing a previous recording to retrieve information to identify the line handler issue. Since the pilot stated that he used no navigational equipment aside from his personal PPU, and the PPU recording was gapped from 2015 to 2019, the evidence shows that for this duration of time, the pilot was not actively engaged in navigating the vessel immediately prior to the grounding.

Furthermore, during the vessel's outbound transit, the pilot made or received five phone calls from his personal cell phone. AT&T records indicated that the calls totalled approximately 61 minutes of the 126-minute voyage up to the grounding.

The longest personal call placed was over 55 minutes, starting at 1903 and ending at 1958. The pilot also made a work call regarding the line handler issues that had been previously encountered, something not urgent and unrelated to the current safe navigation of *Ever Forward*. Further, he sent two text messages at 2007 and 2015, a critical time period leading up to when the turn south into the lower Craighill Channel should have been executed. The Third Officer observed the pilot looking at his phone at 2017, approximately one minute before the vessel ran aground. Although the pilot did not disclose the purpose of all of the calls, he stated that due to the duration of time pilots are onboard vessels, it is not unusual to complete various personal tasks while underway. However, when the pilot was interviewed, he stated that he was not in the practice of making personal calls while in transit and would only feel comfortable doing so in an emergency situation.

All that being said, bridge management failures were also identified. A key aspect to effective bridge resource management includes using all available resources, both human and electronic. The only equipment the pilot used to navigate the vessel was his PPU. He stated that he was not aware that there were paper charts on the bridge and that he was intentionally in the practice of not using the ship's installed navigation equipment, including the ship's ECDIS. This was due to his avowed distrust of equipment besides his PPU. He also stated he found the navigational buoys to be unhelpful. Since it was a clear night and his view was unobstructed, the pilot should easily have been able to view the available navigational aids that marked the channel's turn south, a lighted gated pair of lateral buoys. The pilot's lack of awareness and decision not to use ship's charts, navigation aids and other available bridge navigation systems demonstrates an over-reliance on the singular PPU system. This overreliance on a single navigational tool limited the pilot's ability to accurately and quickly make a full appraisal of the situation and safely navigate the vessel. Had the pilot used all available means to determine the ship's location, the grounding likely would not have occurred.

The management function demands that the members work as a team. Immediately prior to the grounding, the Third Officer, a Chinese national, believed that the vessel had missed the waypoint to turn. However, instead of directly telling the pilot that the turn had been missed, he repeated the heading multiple times in an attempt to prompt the pilot of the vessel's situation. The *Ever Forward*'s SMS states that if the vessel experiences difficulty maintaining course or any doubts arise in regard to the vessel's situation, the officer on watch shall call the Master. After the Third Officer's attempts to prompt the pilot, he did not immediately notify the Master. Had the Third Officer immediately notified the Master, the likelihood of an alternate outcome was low due to the short amount of time between the point when the turn south was missed and the grounding. Without substantive input from the bridge team, the pilot continued to underutilise the available resources for navigation and continued to look at his cell phone. The Third Officer acknowledged that, as the expert on local waters, he was hesitant to question the pilot's expertise and familiarity with the channel. This may have in part been due to the Third Officer fearing he may offend the pilot or cultural differences regarding seniority. When interviewed, the pilot, the Master and the Third Officer all agreed that the pilot was in direction and control of the vessel until he had completed the transit. Nevertheless, as noted in the ship's SMS, the presence of a pilot does not relieve a bridge team of its shared responsibilities for safe navigation. Despite cultural differences or seniority, the Third Officer and others on the bridge should have been more assertive to let the pilot know the waypoint had been passed and turn missed. Had the bridge team been more assertive and notified the pilot of the missed turn, there may have been enough time to avoid or minimise the significance of the grounding.

If it is any consolation, the pilot had his Certificate of Competency suspended.

22 Piracy and Stowaways

Piracy and Armed Robbery Against Ships

Piracy is defined by UNCLOS Article 101 as consisting of any illegal acts of violence or detention committed for private ends by persons on a private ship, whether they call themselves crew or passengers, and directed against another ship either on the high seas, or at least in a place outside the jurisdiction of any State. This definition has been incorporated into English law by virtue of section 26 Merchant Shipping and Maritime Security Act 1997 and, accordingly, applies to the venerable statutory provisions which are enforced globally against a person who commits an act of piracy; it matters not which is the Flag State of the pirate ship or the innocent vessel.[1] According to the legal theory of English criminal law, the offender may be arrested, tried and punished, in this case, in the Crown Court,[2] even though the alleged offence took place in international waters. If the offending activity took place within the jurisdiction of UK territorial waters, then the Defendant will be arraigned on the charge in domestic law of robbery, under the Theft Act 1968[3] and tried in the Crown Court, irrespective of which State had allocated its flag to the innocent vessel.[4] In terms of Sovereign State jurisdiction, this is an obvious example of the common-sense application of the clear statement rule.[5]

1 Section 2 Piracy Act 1837: Whosoever, with intent to commit or at the time of or immediately before or immediately after committing the crime of piracy in respect of any ship or vessel, shall assault, with intent to murder, any person being on board of or belonging to such ship or vessel, or shall stab, cut, or wound any such person, or unlawfully do any act by which the life of such person may be endangered, shall be guilty of felony, and being convicted thereof shall be liable to imprisonment for life. The sentence was amended from death by the Crime and Disorder Act 1998, bringing consistency with the Human Rights Act 1988 (the right to life).

2 See section 6 Courts Act 1971.

3 Section 8(1) Theft Act 1968: person is guilty of robbery if he steals, and immediately before or at the time of doing so, and in order to do so, he uses force on any person or puts or seeks to put any person in fear of being then and there subjected to force.

4 Section 2 Territorial Waters Jurisdiction Act 1878: An offence committed by a person, whether or not he is a subject of Her Majesty, on the open sea within the territorial waters of Her Majesty's dominions, is an offence … Although it may have been committed on board or by means of a foreign ship, and the person who committed such offence may be arrested, tried and punished accordingly.

5 A less common-sense example may be argued in the case of *Spector v Norwegian Cruise Line Ltd* 545 US 119 (2005).

DOI: 10.4324/9781003361916-22

Within the jurisdiction of the Sovereign State, all the laws must be applied – the Prosecution cannot pick and choose which laws they will uphold, and if the elements of other crimes are apparent, then the issues must be tried. The point is that any action taken by the innocent party resulting in death or personal injury to the assailant may be subject to accountability in the same jurisdiction. As a result, the Master of the innocent vessel will remain accountable to the laws of the Flag State, or the Port State under the clear statement rule for the death of the individual, and if a defence such as self-defence failed, then the Master would be exposed to a sentence for murder, if malice aforethought is established, or manslaughter if it is not. Even if the defence is successful and the Master is acquitted, they may have spent years on remand in custody in circumstances or conditions which would be unrecognisable to the reader of the IMO's Guidelines on the fair treatment of seafarers. To the shipowner, the contract of employment may well incriminate them on the basis of the Master's defence that they were protecting the property and employees of the owner as their employee, representative and agent and the resultant death occurred because of a management failure to preserve the assailant from death during the offending activity.[6]

The issue of self-defence is fraught with difficulty. Section 3 Criminal Law Act 1967 states that *a person may use such force as is reasonable in the circumstances in the prevention of crime, or in effecting or assisting in the lawful arrest of offenders or suspected offenders or of persons unlawfully at large*. On the face of it, unlawful boarding and violent robbery on board the ship will support such an argument of self-defence, but the question of whether the force used was reasonable in the circumstances would likely lead to a Trial, when the verdict would be in the hands of the jury. In that circumstance, the jury would have to consider whether the degree of force was reasonable, so if the Master had an alternative to killing the pirates, that would be a matter which would weigh heavily in the jury's deliberations – and juries can be notoriously capricious in their decisions. In the light of this, the decision of a flight to the citadel or non-lethal use of force (as we shall meet with the case of Captain Stapleton) is likely to be preferable to a conscious decision that may lead to a long and uncertain Trial.

That being said, under section 13 Firearms Act 1968, the Master may, without holding a personal firearms certificate, have in their possession a firearm or ammunition on board a ship, but only as part of the equipment of the ship. As such this has traditionally been defined to mean distress flares and, in any event, is dependent upon how the MCA would view the provision of firearms for approval in the ship's security plan, as required by the International Port Facility Security Code (ISPS). The prevailing Marine Guidance Note[7] containing guidance on this issue explained

6 S1 Corporate Manslaughter and Corporate Homicide Act 2007: see below. the owner is guilty of an offence if the way in which its activities are managed or organised causes a person's death and amounts to a gross breach of a relevant duty of care owed by the organisation to the deceased.

7 Measures to Counter Piracy, Armed Robbery and other Acts of Violence against Merchant Shipping, MGN 298(M), published October 2005: *The carrying and use of firearms for personal protection or protection of a ship is strongly discouraged and will not be authorised by the British Government.*

the hazards somewhat dramatically in its strong discouragement of carrying and using firearms on board at all.[8]

Even if the Master were held lawfully to be in possession of such weapons while on board the vessel, when she comes alongside in the port of another State, the question begs itself as to what will be the consequence in law. While a Flag State has the power to make laws granting powers permitting their merchant ships to carry firearms, the acknowledgement of such by a Port State may be open to question. As one example, the Master of a merchant ship arriving at a South African port, which has firearms on board, must apply for a permit from the South African Police 21 days prior to their arrival in South Africa.[9] How the procedure is to work in practice remains somewhat unclear; for example, when the charterer had not even nominated her port of discharge at the time when she had left her port of loading.

Over all this, hangs the Master's absolute discretion under SOLAS V 34-1, which means that they must maintain that right to make the final decision for the safety of life, which cannot be delegated to somebody else. If, in a pirate attack, a member of the crew fired a weapon and some personal injury was inflicted, whether intended or not, and whether or not due to the crew's inexperience with a firearm, the Master would still be held accountable, very possibly for criminal negligence or a homicide offence. Worse still for the shipowner, they would be incriminated as the Master's employer, for whom they were playing a significant role in the making of decisions about how the shipowner's activities were managed or organised, and such management failure could result in the dread consequence of a conviction for corporate manslaughter, with all that entails in the form of fines, subsequent compensation claims and the publicity ultimately affecting the share price.

Flag State Protection? How the Flag State Sees It

The Flag State's overall responsibility is defined, in the terms of UNCLOS, for the implementation and enforcement of those international maritime regulations to

Carriage of arms on board ship may escalate an already dangerous situation, and any firearms on board may themselves become an attractive target for an attacker. The use of firearms requires special training and aptitudes and the risk of accidents with firearms carried on board ship is great. In some jurisdictions killing a national may have unforeseen consequences even for a person who believes that they have acted in self-defence. MGN 440 post-dates this (2010) but confines itself to links to relevant websites.

8 The small matter of insurance will also be a relevant issue to the shipowner. While an insurance product for corporate manslaughter claims arising out of the use of armed guards was launched in July 2011, it necessarily can only cover the legal costs which the shipowner might incur in defending a claim. The insurer would certainly not cover the risk of payment of a fine in a criminal conviction. While Protection and Indemnity cover can extend to the lawful payment of ransom demands, its extension to other claims in a piracy situation are very limited. Perhaps the most useful recent case was *Masefield AG v Amlin Corporate Member Ltd* [2010] EWHC 280 in which the High Court held, that kidnap and ransom cover is a longstanding and important feature of the insurance market, and can be enforced, while the payments of ransom were recoverable strictly as a sue and labour expense. But while this may comfort the shipowner, it does little to assist the Master.

9 Firearms Control Act 2000.

which it has committed itself, in respect of all ships to which it has allocated the right to fly its flag. The potential consequences on the Flag State for management failure has demanded some accountability; the question has to do with how the State renders that into blame. It may be that the Master must be held liable for that; in which case the question to be raised is how the Master's position can be justified or defended in law if lethal force is employed. The Master's judgment call is inextricably linked with their duty to protect the Flag State responsibility for the ship herself, to which the flag has been allocated. The very fact of that allocation brings the vessel within the protection of that State and, necessarily, all the State's laws by which it controls its subjects. When addressing the human rights of individuals to go about their lawful business it would naturally be preferable to have such laws codified by statute but, in a Common Law system, Common Law rights and obligations have been defined in Judgments and, by their evolution, the Master has some guidance for divining their accountability.

The UK shares the unhappy feature with many States, that it must balance Flag State laws with international Conventions, as a result of which its general guidance is uncertain. Given the principles of law which we have highlighted, it acknowledges the option for shipowners to employ armed guards on board their vessels outside Port State jurisdictions, in order to protect human life from a piracy attack, but only within the context of Flag State law and only in exceptional circumstances:

- When the ship is transiting the high seas throughout a high risk area (which may be classified or declassified, according to recent piracy attacks);
- The latest best management practice is being followed fully but, on its own, is not deemed by the shipping company and the ship's master as enough to protect against acts of piracy;
- The use of armed guards is assessed to reduce the risk to the lives and wellbeing of those on board the ship.

In summary, though, the Government's advice is *it's not advisable to carry firearms. If you do, the [Master] must make sure they're allowed by the flag state and host country. Penalties for the use of firearms can be severe in some countries.* In other words, the UK Government would not assist in the event of some consequence arising out of their use.

The Case of the *Enrica Lexie*

The *Enrica Lexie* is a crude oil tanker, at the time of the incident registered under the Italian flag.[10] In 2012 she was sailing under charter from Singapore to Egypt with a crew of 34 including 19 Indians. The voyage would take her through waters which exposed her to the risk of piracy, because of which the Government ordered six marines from the Italian Navy to join the ship for the purpose of defending her

10 In 2018 she was renamed *Olympic Sky* and registered under the Marshall Islands flag.

against the risk of a pirate attack. Two of the marines were named as Salvatore Girone and Massimiliano Latorre.

At 16.30 on 15 February 2012, the ship's position was 20.5 nautical miles off the Indian coast; in other words, within the area of India's exclusive economic zone. The ship was outside the sovereign jurisdiction of India, although she remained bound to the sovereign jurisdiction of the Flag State. At that time, a fishing vessel, *St Antony*, was returning from an innocent fishing expedition in the Laccadive Sea, under the command of its skipper, Freddie Louis, who gave evidence that men on board the *Enrica Lexie* began firing at them without provocation for approximately two minutes. Indian nationals Ajesh Binki and Valentine aboard the *St Antony* were allegedly killed as a result of the gunshot wounds. At all times it was the case of the Italian marines that they believed that the *St Antony* was conducting a piracy attack on her.

After the incident, the *Enrica Lexie* was intercepted in the Lakshadweep archipelago, a group of islands in the Laccadive Sea, between 120 and 270 nautical miles off the southwestern coast of India, in an area administered as a union territory and district of India. She was detained by the Indian Coast Guard and compelled to proceed to the port of Kochi. The matter rapidly gained international exposure, when Italian Foreign Minister, Giulio Terzi, alleged through an Italian newspaper that the ship had been detained because of a subterfuge by the local police, who had required her Master to head for the port of Kochi to contribute to the identification of some suspected pirates. This allegation was subsequently rejected by India's Foreign Minister, Salman Khurshid; in any event, the two marines were held in custody for interrogation on charges of homicide under section 302 of the Indian Penal Code. Following the post mortems which were carried out the following day, Kerala Police charged the two marines with murder, and were remanded in custody. They were subsequently released on bail, but Italy strongly objected to any trial at all on the grounds that India had no sovereign jurisdiction over the Accused for the alleged offences.

The incident rapidly descended into a dispute, in which Italy alleged that India had violated UNCLOS in several crucial areas:

> Article 87(1) *The high seas are open to all States, whether coastal or land-locked. Freedom of the high seas is exercised under the conditions laid down by this Convention and by other rules of international law. It comprises, inter alia, both for coastal and land-locked States: (a) freedom of navigation;*

> Article 92(1) *Ships shall sail under the flag of one State only and, save in exceptional cases expressly provided for in international treaties or in this Convention, shall be subject to its exclusive jurisdiction on the high seas.*

> Article 97(1) *In the event of a collision or any other incident of navigation concerning a ship on the high seas, involving the penal or disciplinary responsibility of the master or of any other person in the service of the ship, no penal or disciplinary proceedings may be instituted against such person*

> *except before the judicial or administrative authorities either of the flag State or of the State of which such person is a national.*
>
> Article 97(3) *No arrest or detention of the ship, even as a measure of investigation, shall be ordered by any authorities other than those of the flag State.*

Given the unsubstantiated evidence that the *St Antony* was a pirate vessel, Italy's further allegation was somewhat misconceived that India had violated its obligations to co-operate in the repression of piracy under Article 100: *All States shall cooperate to the fullest possible extent in the repression of piracy on the high seas or in any other place outside the jurisdiction of any State*. Consequently, submitted Italy, India was in breach of Article 300 *States Parties shall fulfil in good faith the obligations assumed under this Convention and shall exercise the rights, jurisdiction and freedoms recognized in this Convention in a manner which would not constitute an abuse of right.*

These were, of course, profoundly serious issues and, with no resolution in sight, Italy proceeded to refer the case to the International Tribunal for the Law of the Sea (ITLOS), an independent judicial body established by UNCLOS for resolving disputes rapidly, or at least more rapidly than the International Court of Justice. In the meantime, time was pressing, with no sign of protection for the human rights of the Accused, as a result of which, in December 2015, Italy filed a Request for the Prescription of Provisional Measures pursuant to Article 290, paragraph 1 of UNCLOS:

> *If a dispute has been duly submitted to a court or tribunal which considers that prima facie it has jurisdiction under this Part or Part XI, section 5, the court or tribunal may prescribe any provisional measures which it considers appropriate under the circumstances to preserve the respective rights of the parties to the dispute or to prevent serious harm to the marine environment, pending the final decision.*

In April 2016, ITLOS adopted an Order in respect of Italy's Request, thus securing the protection of the marines' freedoms, and commenced the process by taking submissions from both sides to resolve the issue as to whether India had the right to subject them to a prosecution under their judicial process. In accordance with the Tribunal's relaxed case-management processes vaguely described as a procedural calendar, the Parties subsequently exchanged written pleadings on the Tribunal's jurisdiction and the merits of the case.

On 2 July 2020, the Tribunal published its award, and unanimously held that India had not acted in breach of Article 87 and had not violated Article 92. It further held that Article 97 was not applicable to this case, and that India had not violated Article 100 of the Convention and that therefore Article 300 cannot be invoked.

The Tribunal found unanimously, however, that Italy as Flag State had interfered with the *St Antony*'s rights to freedom of navigation.

By a majority decision, the Tribunal upheld Italy's sovereign rights and found that the marines were entitled to immunity in relation to the acts that they committed during the incident and that India was, therefore, precluded from exercising its jurisdiction over the Marines.

By a majority decision, the Tribunal took note of Italy's expressed commitment as Flag State to resume its criminal investigation into the allegations of homicide and, therefore, India must take the necessary steps to cease to exercise its criminal jurisdiction over the Marines, and that no other remedies are required.

The Tribunal concluded that, because of its finding that Italy was in breach of Article 87(1)(a), which we have defined above, then Italy was now entitled to payment of compensation as a civil remedy for *the loss of life, physical harm, material damage to property ... and moral harm suffered by the captain and other crew members of the 'St Antony,' which by its nature cannot be made good through restitution.*

The Tribunal went on to say that it retained jurisdiction to resolve a dispute if the Parties sought an award for the quantum of damages in compensation.

The Tribunal's decision, effectively exonerating India from liability for breaching Articles 87, 92 and 97, and imposing liability on Italy, may very well serve to confuse the law rather than clarify it, because, in effect, the two positions in which the Parties find themselves as a result may be difficult to reconcile.

The case reminds us that the responsibility of the seafarer, indeed, their accountability, is derived primarily from the laws of the Flag State. What, therefore, would have been the position of the Master, if they had been held accountable with the marines for the deaths of the individuals on board the *St Antony*? We are back on the treadmill of the Master as Flag State representative, who will be accountable for failure to discharge their duties within that responsibility. It is therefore down to the Master to maintain their Flag State responsibility for the safety of life, whether the Flag State will provide protection and, as we have seen, that protection may well come at a price.

The Master's Dilemma

The importance of maintaining the unassailability of the Master's absolute discretion is a key feature of any guidance, for, naturally, the Master will remain responsible for all consequences, from the very possession of a firearm to the death of an individual, hence the IMO cautioned the shipowner to ensure that the command and control structure linking the ship operator, the Master, the ship's officers and the contract security team leader has been clearly defined and *documented* – for the purpose of establishing the critical evidence should a Trial follow some event.

For all the complexities of the Master's position in the efficient shipboard management of such security risks, exposure to Flag State law remains if the vessel is attacked in international waters, and the Government's licence will carry little weight with the authorities in other Port States. In response to the UK Government's announcement of its intention to permit private armed security on board merchant ships, the Egyptian Government promptly announced that it would not permit armed merchant vessels to proceed through the Suez Canal, whether or not they possessed a licence issued by the Flag State.

This starkly highlights the point that tensions between Flag State and Port State have not gone away – and the Master's criminal accountability may just be underlined further, if the defence of a vessel results in the breach of Port State laws, exposing the Master to risk of prosecution and, quite possibly, imprisonment – let alone breaches of Flag State obligations, for the Master will still be held to account for the deaths of individuals according to Flag State laws.

Given the definition of piracy under Article 101 of UNCLOS, it necessarily follows that the act – and the process – must take place outside the sovereign jurisdiction of a Port or Coastal State. If within the jurisdiction of a State, then that State's own laws will prevail (such as, for example, armed robbery in the UK).

How then is the Master to maintain the safety of their ship and crew in accordance with their Flag State obligations? The solution on the face of it is to defend her with such reasonable force as Flag State laws permit. If the Master uses excessive force under Flag State law and a pirate is killed on board his ship, then the defence of self-defence would fail if they were to be tried for murder. As Master of the vessel, with responsibility and, therefore, accountability under Flag State law, they would be exposed to criminal liability if defensive measures were used which might not be protected under the law. Captain Stapleton had acted very wisely.

Whatever Flag State laws permit or restrict, has little bearing if the ship is in another State's territorial waters. If the vessel's private army of armed guards infringed the laws of any Port State which they visited, then the local jurisdiction's laws would certainly be enforced, bringing to account the shipowner as well as the Flag State, for both of whom, of course, the Master is representative – and the first target for criminal accountability.

In the long-running and bitter history of piracy attributable to the failure of Somalia's jurisdictional control over its people, shipowners are losing patience with the constraints imposed upon them by the current law, and are turning increasingly to the use of privately contracted armed guards on board their ships, thus taking the law into their own hands to defend themselves against a threat which they perceive to be incapable of control by the rule of law. The IMO's guidance published in 2011 and circulated to Member Governments, doubtless was written with a view to urge extreme caution upon shipowners in using privately contracted armed security personnel and if it were intended to discourage the practice, will probably succeed beyond its wildest dreams.

The guidance emphasises the importance of the Master's position, as being central to the shipboard management role in maintaining Flag State law on board the vessel, the sovereign territory over which other States have no prima facie right in which to intervene – unless, of course, their laws have been broken and, very possibly, their nationals have been killed. In either case, the Master may optimistically take some comfort in their human rights of being able to defend themselves and, indeed, they may be acquitted at the eventual trial. But, they would have to go through that accountability process in the first place and, in the meantime, may be held in custody in some foreign jurisdiction whose accommodation for Defendants awaiting trial is inconsistent with what a Master may feel entitled to expect. And then, they may still be found Guilty at the trial. No criminal defence can ever be certain.

To summarise, the Master's responsibility to the Flag State is born of necessity, in order that the Flag State can maintain management control. The Master has assumed that responsibility by virtue of their acceptance of the role, and by their seeking accreditation with that Flag State in the first place. By contrast, the position in which the Master has found themselves accountable under Port and Coastal State jurisdiction has proved a key factor in the analysis of criminalisation. Such is the Master's dilemma.

Problems and Solutions: The Story of Captain Stapleton of the *Teignbank*

When the China Navigation Company, acquired the Bank Line from Andrew Weir Shipping in 2006, the assets which passed to the new owners included the *Teignbank*, a multi-purpose cargo ship that had been converted for round-the-world service from an Arctic freighter built for the Soviet Union in 1984. China Navigation renamed her *Boularibank* but, with the global economic downturn, her last round-the-world service was scheduled for the spring of 2009. She was on this last run, under the command of her UK-certificated Master, Captain Peter Stapleton, with a mainly Russian crew of 31 including 4 British cadets, and carrying 11 passengers and the Master's wife, when, on 28 April, 120 miles northeast of Socotra Island at the entrance to the Gulf of Aden, Captain Stapleton saw, on the radar, a green blip travelling in the wrong direction. It might have been innocent fishermen – but turned out to be Somali pirates, and two skiffs were launched from the mother vessel, closing rapidly on the *Boularibank* at a speed of some 26 knots. Captain Stapleton realised that they could not out-run the pirates, so he carried out evasive manoeuvres, while under fire from the assailants' assault rifles and rocket-grenades, one of which exploded above the bridge.[11]

Captain Stapleton was, of course, acutely aware of the risk to the lives of the ship's company and the passengers – the safety of life being the overwhelming issue in his responsibility as Master. He was also aware that current law left him naked to do more than prepare to repel the pirates with the sort of force to which merchant ships are limited both by convention and by domestic laws. Risk-management procedures were put in place in accordance with these limitations, which involved turning the fire hoses on the attackers, and bundles of heavy timber baulks were hung on ropes over the ship's side behind the forecastle, while container twist locks were made ready to throw; then the outside staircases were blocked by ropes, all

11 A host of sources exists for this event, some of which tend to dramatise it more than others. Recommended reference is made to:

Andrew Weir Shipping Ltd, Ocean Liner Museum, UK

International Transport Workers Federation

Linington, A, 2010, Nautilus Telegraph, Nautilus International, London.

outside watertight doors were closed, and the passengers were ordered to hide in the corridors behind the wheelhouse. Captain Stapleton then steered his 22-year-old ship on a zig-zag course, creating a wash to keep the pirates' boats away.

The attack failed and the pirates broke off. Captain Stapleton was later awarded the UK Merchant Navy Medal for exceptional bravery during the attack. A Russian destroyer captured 29 suspected pirates shortly afterwards; but there was little more that the naval protection force could do. The pirates were disarmed, and then had to be released. That is the current law and, for the Master, it is a minefield which could lead to their accountability for the most serious crimes if they get it wrong.

Stowaways

MGN 70[12] offers guidance with a definition of a stowaway as *a person who is secreted on a ship, or in cargo which is subsequently loaded on the ship, without the consent of the shipowner or the master or any other responsible person and who is detected on board the ship after it has departed from a port, or in the cargo while unloading it in the port of arrival, and is reported as a stowaway by the master to the appropriate authorities.*

Naturally, preventive measures are an essential feature of the ship's security, and emphasis is placed on meeting the current law and guidance, including:

- Convention on Facilitation of International Maritime Traffic (FAL);
- International Ship and Port Facility Security Code (ISPS);
- International Convention for the Safety of Life at Sea (SOLAS);
- Ship and Port Facility (Security) Regulations 2004;
- The Merchant Shipping Act 1995.

Part A of the ISPS Code contains mandatory requirements & guidance outlining maritime and port security requirements to which SOLAS signatories, their port authorities and shipping companies must adhere.

Shipowners and Masters must take all reasonable precautions to prevent stowaways gaining access to vessels, ensuring the following:

- That ships have responsibilities under the ISPS Code for controlling access to the ship; controlling the embarkation of persons and their effects; monitoring restricted areas to ensure that only authorised persons have access and monitoring of deck areas and areas surrounding the ship;
- That shipowners and Masters, as well as other responsible persons have security arrangements in place which, as far as practicable, will prevent intending stowaways from getting aboard to the ships, and, if this fails, as far as practicable, will detect them before the ship leaves port;

12 Currently MGN 70 (M) Amendment 1.

- That vessels due to leave a port have undergone a thorough search in accordance with a specific plan or schedule with priorities given to places where stowaways might hide taking into account the specific ship type and its operations. Search methods which are likely to harm secreted stowaways should not be used;
- To implement restricted areas on board vessels.

Part B of the ISPS Code gives guidance on risk-management identifying and implementing measures to guard against security violations:

- Ensuring the performance of all ship security duties;
- Controlling access to the ship;
- Controlling the embarkation of persons and their effects;
- Monitoring restricted areas to ensure that only authorized persons have access;
- Monitoring of deck areas and areas surrounding the ship;
- Supervising the handling of cargo and ship's stores;
- Ensuring that security communication is readily available.

The risk of incidents with stowaways naturally rises in port, which forms an important part of risk-management in ship security plans; in practical terms, the Master should ensure that heightened precautions are taken, including:

- Maintaining a gangway watch, prohibiting stevedores from certain areas and having a watch kept on them;
- Checking everyone embarking and disembarking;
- Sealing off certain parts of the ship to prevent access and reduce the areas and compartments that may need to be searched;
- Conducting searches of vehicles and loose cargo;
- Posting a lookout to prevent people climbing aboard;
- Making an extensive, systematic and detailed search of the ship immediately before departure, especially from any high-risk port or place, where the use of dogs may be advisable.

The all-important audit trail demands routine procedures to be implemented, with a checklist or lists based on the ship and cargo. And confirmation that a thorough search has been made of all areas of the ship by crew parties with an officer in charge of each party. Checklists then must be returned to the Master/Chief Mate. The discovery of a stowaway must be recorded in the narrative section of the Official Log Book and, so, an entry should be made in the OLB as a public document, attaching the checklists with full details of the date, time, spaces searched, and names and ranks of searchers.

It is essential that the Master communicates with the P & I correspondent in the next port of call, because the Master will be obliged to report the stowaway and a financial penalty will follow. In this respect, a security bond for each stowaway on board must be evidenced in documentary form, and port authorities will enforce these bonds if the stowaways are found missing from the ship at the time of outward clearance.

23 The Role of Evidence in Criminal Proceedings

Article 6 of the European Convention on Human Rights summarises the importance of a fair trial:

> *In the determination of his civil rights and obligations or of any criminal charge against him, everyone is entitled to a fair and public hearing within a reasonable time by an independent and impartial tribunal established by law.*

It follows, therefore, that the legal process must be devoted to these tenets; indeed, the Criminal Procedure Rules 2020 starts with defining the overriding objective of the Court process:

1.1(1)*The overriding objective of this procedural code is that criminal cases be dealt with justly.*

The section follows with a more detailed explanation of what that means:

(2) *Dealing with a criminal case justly includes –*

- a) *Acquitting the innocent and convicting the guilty;*
- b) *Dealing with the prosecution and the defence fairly;*
- c) *Recognising the rights of a defendant, particularly those under Article 6 of the European Convention on Human Rights;*
- d) *Respecting the interests of witnesses, victims and jurors and keeping them informed of the progress of the case;*
- e) *Dealing with the case efficiently and expeditiously;*
- f) *Ensuring that appropriate information is available to the court when bail and sentence are considered;*
- g) *Dealing with the case in ways that take into account –*
  - i. *The gravity of the offence alleged;*
  - ii. *The complexity of what is in issue;*
  - iii. *The severity of the consequences for the defendant and others affected;*
  - iv. *The needs of other cases.*

The importance of evidence in a fair trial is critical, and in the English Crown Court each juror must swear an oath upon being called: *I swear by almighty God*

DOI: 10.4324/9781003361916-23

that I will faithfully try the defendant and give a true verdict according to the evidence.[1]

While the judge should properly direct the jury as to the issues of fact that must be established to satisfy the criteria for the offence, they should never give meaningless directions, particularly where such directions may reflect the judge's own opinions;[2] it is not the judge who delivers a verdict in criminal law, but the jury. That being said, the judge should look for any possible defence arising from the evidence, and raise it, even if the Defence has not.

The Evaluation of Evidence

This is what the burden and standard of proof are all about. The general rule is that the burden is firmly on the Prosecution to adduce evidence upon which a reasonable jury could convict,[3] and remains there throughout the Trial.[4]

The standard of proof is somewhat different, and defines to what degree the evidence which is advanced by the Prosecution must be persuasive. While the Prosecution is not obliged to make the jury feel certain of the defendant's guilt, the standard of proof requires the Prosecution to persuade the jury beyond reasonable doubt that the Defendant committed all elements of the crime; they need not be absolutely certain, but on the evaluation of the evidence they must be sure. Of course, the distinction between being certain and being sure can be a very fine one, and in such cases the judge will wish to direct the jury in more detail on what constitutes reasonable doubt.

It is for the Prosecution and the Defence to present the evidence, and discredit the probative value of the other's, but it is for the jury to reach their verdict on that evidence.

So, What Must the Evidence Establish?

The evidence must establish beyond reasonable doubt the two elements of a crime upon which a conviction must subsist:

1 The *actus reus*, containing all the elements in the definition of the crime except the Defendant's mental element;
2 The *mens rea*, establishing the Defendant's intention to commit the crime, according to its defined terms.

1 A juror may elect a variation depending on their religion, or an affirmation if they decline to swear by a religion.
2 *R v Aziz* [1996] 1 AC 41, HL.
3 *R v Hunt* [1987] AC 352.
4 *Woolmington v DPP* [1935] AC 462.

This was qualified by section 8 Criminal Justice Act 1967, which provides that, when assessing whether the Defendant had the necessary *mens rea*, the Jury shall not be bound to infer that the Defendant intended or foresaw the result of his actions merely because it is the natural and probable result of those actions, but by the subjective test of whether he actually did intend or foresee that such result would ensue, but the Jury must apply the test objectively by *drawing such inferences from the evidence as appears proper in the circumstances* (the Statute's own words).

This reference to the 1967 Act illustrates the point that it is up to Parliament as to how it qualifies the requirement of *mens rea* in general; how particular issues are refined, may be established by decided cases. A notable example of this in context is recklessness, qualifying the requirement of intent, which will incriminate a person in a particular offence depending on his awareness of a risk given the circumstances or the result that may be apprehended from the circumstances.

In criminal accountability, the Prosecution must persuade the jury that the evidence establishes beyond reasonable doubt that the Defendant's *mens rea* coincides with the *actus reus* required for the crime. If ever there is an illustrative authority which blends instruction with entertainment, it is the non-marine case of *R v Deller*.[5] The Defendant persuaded a third party to purchase his car by representing that it was free from encumbrances. Deller, however, had previously borrowed money from a finance company which had taken a mortgage over the car as security and, so, he believed that he was telling a lie – satisfying the mental element of dishonesty. When it transpired that the car was mortgaged and, therefore, very unfree from encumbrances, he was charged with obtaining property by false pretences by intentionally misrepresenting a past or existing fact, contrary to section 32 of the Larceny Act 1916.

But it then transpired that the bill of sale for the transaction had not been registered in accordance with legal requirements and, therefore, the mortgage was void. The car, therefore, had been free from encumbrances all along, so the *actus reus* for the crime was not present, and Mr Deller's conviction was quashed on appeal.

The requirement of *mens rea* remains the key issue in determining criminal accountability; this most ancient of bastions in criminal law was upheld by Lord Reid in *Sweet v Parsley*,[6] in the presumption that Parliament does not intend to make criminals of people who are not blameworthy for what they did, quoting the venerable Brett J in a case a century old but had stood the test of time:

> *Upon all the cases I think it is proved that there can be no conviction for crime in England in the absence of a criminal mind or mens rea.*[7]

The demands made by the requirement of *mens rea* on criminal liability require some qualification of the general principle, if a person, who does not intend to cause a harmful result, takes an unjustifiable risk of causing it. Such is the foundation of

5 *R v Deller* [1952] 36 Cr App Rep 184.
6 *Sweet v Parsley* [1970] AC 132, at p. 148.
7 *R v Prince* (1875) LR 2 CCR 154.

recklessness, in which either the Defendant was aware of its existence or, in the case of an obvious risk, the Defendant failed to give any thought to the possibility of its existence.

Central to the laws of evidence is the concept of its probative value. Evidence will not be admitted by a court unless it goes some way to show, either directly or indirectly, that a fact in dispute did or did not exist. However, courts will not listen to everything that is relevant. Relevance and admissibility are separate concepts. The Rules of Evidence have evolved over generations to establish the Defendant's guilt; basically, it must satisfy four questions:

1 *Can the evidence be used in Court?*
    1 Prosecutors should consider whether there is any question over the admissibility of certain evidence. In doing so, prosecutors should assess:
    2 The likelihood of that evidence being held as inadmissible by the Court, for example if it violates the privilege against self-incrimination, legal professional privilege, litigation privilege, without prejudice negotiations and public policy immunity;
    3 The importance of that evidence in relation to the evidence as a whole;
    4 Evidence excluded under the hearsay rule requires a little explanation. The object of this rule is to limit a witness's evidence to proving the facts asserted to things which the witness perceived with their own five senses: that is to say, things which they had seen, heard, felt, smelt or tasted. This rule is subject to a number of exceptions best left to the advice of the Defendant's legal team; for example, a confession by a Defendant is hearsay but is nonetheless admissible, if it was not obtained through oppression or other dubious means;

2 *Is the evidence reliable?*
    - Prosecutors should consider whether there are any reasons to question the reliability of the evidence, including its accuracy or integrity.

3 *Is the evidence credible?*
    - Prosecutors should consider whether there are any reasons to doubt the credibility of the evidence.

4 *Is there any other material that might affect the sufficiency of evidence?*
    - Prosecutors must consider at this stage and throughout the case whether there is any material that may affect the assessment of the sufficiency of evidence, including examined and unexamined material in the possession of the police, and material that may be obtained through further reasonable lines of inquiry.

The Analysis of Evidence and the Master's role in an Accident

The Master is responsible in law for the safety of that ship and all aboard her. They cannot delegate or contract out of this responsibility, and thus play a crucial role in the delivery of evidence in an accident:

- The loss or abandonment of the ship;
- Death, serious injury, or the loss of a person from a ship;

- Stranding or disabling of a ship;
- Material damage to the ship, another ship or marine structure;
- Serious pollution.

Each Flag State undertakes to investigate any casualty occurring to ships under its flag, and as Representative of the Flag State, the Master must ensure compliance with SOLAS Chapter I Regulation 21:

(a) *Each Administration undertakes to conduct an investigation of any casualty occurring to any of its ships subject to the provisions of the present Convention when it judges that such an investigation may assist in determining what changes in the present regulations might be desirable.*

Chapter XI Regulation 1 contains additional requirements for the investigation of marine casualties and incidents:

> *Taking into account regulation I/21, each Administration shall conduct investigations of marine casualties and incidents, in accordance with the provisions of the present Convention, as supplemented by the provisions of the Code of the International Standards and Recommended Practices for a Safety Investigation into a Marine Casualty or Marine Incident (Casualty Investigation Code) adopted by resolution MSC.255(84).*

Flag States also have obligations to investigate incidents involving harmful substances under MARPOL Article 8, requiring a report to be made *without delay to the fullest extent possible.* Articles 12 applies to casualties to ships and states:

1. *Each Administration undertakes to investigate of any casualty occurring to any of its ships subject to the provisions of the regulations if such casualty has produced a major deleterious effect upon the marine environment;*
2. *Each Party to the Convention undertakes to supply the Organization with information concerning the findings of such investigation, when it judges that such information may assist in determining what changes in the present Convention might be desirable.*

The International Convention on Load Lines 1966 devotes Article 23 to Casualties:

1. *Each Administration undertakes to investigate of any casualty occurring to ships for which it is responsible and which are subject to the provisions of the present Convention when it judges that such an investigation may assist in determining what changes in the Convention might be desirable;*
2. *Each contracting Government undertakes to supply the Organization with the pertinent information concerning the findings of such investigations. No reports or recommendations of the Organization based upon such information*

> *shall disclose the identity or nationality of the ships concerned or in any manner fix or imply responsibility upon any ship or person.*

The Marine Accident Investigation Branch (MAIB) examines and investigates all types of marine accidents to or on board UK ships worldwide, and other ships in UK territorial waters. Their powers and obligations are defined by the Merchant Shipping (Accident Reporting and Investigation) Regulations 2012, with powers devolved by Parliament under the Merchant Shipping Act 1995; as a result, their powers are limited, for when Parliament says 'Jump,' their only question is 'How high?'

So, what is an accident? Accidents are classified as *Very Serious Marine Casualties*, *Serious Marine Casualties*, *Marine Casualties* or *Marine Incidents*, depending on their severity. An accident for the purpose of the Regulations means any occurrence on board a ship or involving a ship whereby:

(a) There is loss of life or major injury to any person on board, or any person is lost or falls overboard from, the ship or one of its ship's boats;
(b) A ship –
  (i) Causes any loss of life, major injury or material damage;
  (ii) Is lost or presumed to be lost;
  (iii) Is abandoned;
  (iv) Is materially damaged by fire, explosion, weather or other cause;
  (v) Grounds;
  (vi) Is in collision;
  (vii) Is disabled;
  (viii) Causes significant harm to the environment.
(c) Any of the following occur –
  (i) A collapse or bursting of any pressure vessel, pipeline or valve;
  (ii) A collapse or failure of any lifting equipment, access equipment, hatch-cover, staging or boatswain's chair or any associated load-bearing parts;
  (iii) A collapse of cargo, unintended movement of cargo or ballast sufficient to cause a list, or loss of cargo overboard;
  (iv) A snagging of fishing gear which results in the vessel heeling to a dangerous angle;
  (v) A contact by a person with loose asbestos fibre except when full protective clothing is worn;
  (vi) An escape of any harmful substance or agent, if the occurrence, taking into account its circumstances, might have been liable to cause serious injury or to cause damage to the health of any person.

Major injury means –

(a) Any fracture, other than to a finger, thumb or toe;
(b) Any loss of a limb or part of a limb;

(c) Dislocation of the shoulder, hip, knee or spine;
(d) Loss of sight, whether temporary or permanent;
(e) Penetrating injury to the eye;
(f) Any other injury –
  (i) Leading to hypothermia or to unconsciousness;
  (ii) Requiring resuscitation;
  (iii) Requiring admittance to a hospital or other medical facility as an inpatient for more than 24 hours.

Serious injury means any injury, other than a major injury, to a person employed or carried in a ship which occurs on board or during access which results in incapacity for more than three consecutive days, excluding the day of the accident, or as a result of which the person concerned is put ashore and the ship sails without that person, unless the incapacity is known or advised to be of three consecutive days or less, excluding the day of the accident.

When an accident occurs, the Master or senior surviving officer must send a report to the Chief Inspector as soon as is practicable following the accident. The owner must also send a report to the Chief Inspector as soon as is practicable following the accident unless the owner has ascertained that the report has already been made by the Master or senior surviving officer.

Initial reports of accidents should include as much of the following as possible:

(a) Name of vessel and IMO and official number;
(b) Name and address of owners;
(c) Name of the master;
(d) Date and time of the accident;
(e) Where from and where bound;
(f) Latitude and longitude or geographical position in which the accident occurred;
(g) Part of ship where accident occurred if on board;
(h) Weather conditions;
(i) Name and port of registry of any other ship involved;
(j) Number of people killed or injured together with their names, addresses and gender;
(k) Brief details of the accident, including sequence of events leading to the accident, extent of damage and whether accident caused pollution or hazard to navigation;
(l) If the vessel is fitted with a voyage data recorder, the make and model of the recorder.

Follow-up accident reports and initial reports of serious injuries should include the above information as well as the conclusions of any on-board examination covering the cause, how a future similar incident might be avoided, and what action has been taken or recommended.

The MAIB is emphatically not an enforcement or prosecution agency. The Prosecution of Offences Act 1985 established the Crown Prosecution Service, giving the Crown Prosecutor the power to conduct criminal proceedings, within the limits defined by the Director of Public Prosecutions. The MCA's Enforcement Unit considers all reports of significant breaches of maritime legislation, notably offences involving:

- Pollution;
- Collision regulations;
- Unsafe operations – Owners;
- Conduct endangering – Master and Crew;
- Carriage of Dangerous Goods;
- Fraud – Seafarer documentation.

It has a range of administrative sanctions it can take against companies or individuals before it decides to prosecute, but as soon as criminal proceedings are started the control over the sanction is passed to the court, and their function is limited to the delivery of evidence.

The Master and the Privilege Against Self-Incrimination

Privilege against self-incrimination excuses a person from being compelled to give evidence either by documents or providing information which might incriminate them in any potential or current criminal proceedings in England and Wales. It has been reinforced by section 14(1) Civil Evidence Act 1968, which provides that a party may claim privilege against self-incrimination if compelled to disclose information that would tend to expose them to criminal proceedings for an offence or the recovery of a penalty.

Section 267 Merchant Shipping Act 1995 sets out the Secretary of State's powers to investigate the following categories of marine accidents:

a) *any accident involving a ship or ship's boat where, at the time of the accident – (i)the ship is a United Kingdom ship, or (ii)the ship, or (in the case of an accident involving a ship's boat) that boat, is within United Kingdom waters;*
b) *such other accidents involving ships or ships' boats as the Secretary of State may determine.*

Having been given the authority, the Secretary of State will define the procedures more fully in a Statutory Instrument. The Merchant Shipping (Accident Reporting and Investigation) Regulations 2012 set out the procedural rules by which the MAIB conducts an investigation. The Regulations also define restrictions on the use of the report following its publication. Regulation 14(4) provides that, where information has been obtained by an investigator exercising the powers of an inspector under the Act, any part of a document or analysis it contains is inadmissible in judicial proceedings whose purpose is to attribute liability unless permission of a court is granted.

Every MAIB report duly carries the following notices:

> *The United Kingdom Merchant Shipping (Accident Reporting and Investigation) Regulations 2012 – Regulation 5: 'The sole objective of the investigation of an accident under the Merchant Shipping (Accident Reporting and Investigation) Regulations 2012 shall be the prevention of future accidents through the ascertainment of its causes and circumstances. It shall not be the purpose of an investigation to determine liability nor, except so far as is necessary to achieve its objective, to apportion blame.'*
>
> *This report is not written with litigation in mind and, pursuant to Regulation 14(14) of the Merchant Shipping (Accident Reporting and Investigation) Regulations 2012, shall be inadmissible in any judicial proceedings whose purpose, or one of whose purposes is to attribute or apportion liability or blame.*

But the lines have been blurred.

In the 2014 decision in *Hoyle v Rogers*[8] the Court of Appeal upheld the lower court's decision that the AAIB report, containing all the opinions and analysis, could now be admitted in proceedings, giving rise to three issues:

1. In accordance with normal rules of evidence, the maker of a report ordered to be admitted under UK law in Part 32 of the Civil Procedure Rules, must be available for cross-examination; otherwise the robustness of assertions of fact or opinion contained in the report would be undermined as unsafe. The effect is that the confidentiality of the investigators contributing to the report may be more cautious about the statements they make, diluting their contribution to air safety;
2. As we have seen above, such opinions which could lead to a Court's finding of negligence in civil proceedings may subsequently underpin a decision to arraign a Defendant on charges of criminal negligence;
3. The downstream consequence is that interviewees in the investigation process may be reluctant to co-operate with the investigating authorities and, despite State regulations compelling their co-operation, would be justified by their privilege against self-incrimination, entitling them to be cautioned before an interview and to have independent legal advice throughout the interview, so that they may have counsel on their right to silence. The further dilution of the value of such investigations to air safety is obvious.

8 *Scott Hoyle v Julia Mary Rogers and Nicola Lucinda Rogers and Secretary of State for Transport (1st Intervener) and International Air Transport Association (2nd Intervener)* [2014] 3 WLR 148, [2014] CP Rep 30, [2014] EWCA Civ 257, [2014] 3 All ER 550.

European Regulation No 376/2014 has been vaunted as a guardian of the rights of individuals against such abuse but, even at such a delicate stage in its nascent development, its value in this context must be cast in doubt. Article 15.2 provides that information derived from occurrence reports shall be used only for the purpose for which it has been collected and that Member States *shall not make available or use the information on occurrences in order to attribute blame or liability ... or for any purpose other than the maintenance or improvement of aviation safety.* The case of *Hoyle v Rogers* puts such a noble provision firmly in its place. Most pertinently, Article 16 provides in paragraph 10 that the protection afforded to individuals shall not apply *in cases of wilful misconduct* or *where there has been a manifest, severe and serious disregard of an obvious risk and profound failure of professional responsibility to take such care as is evidently required in the circumstances, causing foreseeable damage to a person or property, or which seriously compromises the level of aviation safety.*

This does nothing more than underline the principle that a State's criminal law shall remain inalienable within its sovereign jurisdiction. There can be no qualification of this, so the mischief of criminal negligence and its uncertain application between different regimes remains unaltered. However unjust it may seem to the rest of the world, the rest of the world cannot do anything about it.

The potential for abuse in the prosecution of Offenders was first observed by the civil aviation industry in the early years of the twenty-first century, prompting the development in Europe of a Just Culture policy, as an essential feature in improving aviation safety through more and better reporting of aviation occurrences – the very issues which define the remit of the MAIB. As a result, the Eurocontrol Just Culture Task Force was established, developing a Model Policy regarding criminal investigation and prosecution of civil aviation incidents and accidents. However its success has been measured, so similar safeguard has been established in marine accidents.

The Just Culture concept has received the unimpeachable authority of the European Court of Human Rights which held in a marine case alleging criminal negligence:

> *The Court ... noted in that connection the States' powers and obligations regarding the prevention of marine pollution and the unanimous determination among States and European and international organisations to identify those responsible, to ensure that they appeared to stand trial and to punish them.*[9]

Since the case of *Hoyle v Rogers* there has been growing concern about the risk to interviewees answering MAIB questions that might incriminate them in criminal culpability and civil liability. The decision in this case meant that the interviewee

9 *Mangouras v Spain* (12050/04); Para 3 Summary of Judgment.

would no longer have the benefit of the right against self-incrimination, nullifying the right set out in IMO Casualty Investigation Code:

> 24.1 *If a person is required by law to provide evidence that may incriminate them, for the purposes of a marine safety investigation, the evidence should, so far as national laws allow, be prevented from admission into evidence in civil or criminal proceedings against the individual.*
>
> 24.2 *A person from whom evidence is sought should be informed about the nature and basis of the investigation. A person from whom evidence is sought should be informed, and allowed access to legal advice, regarding:*
>
> 1. *Any potential risk that they may incriminate themselves in any proceedings subsequent to the marine safety investigation;*
> 2. *Any right not to self-incriminate or to remain silent;*
> 3. *Any protections afforded to the person to prevent the evidence being used against them if they provide the evidence to the marine safety investigation.*

The lack of understanding throughout the industry is understandable but cannot be accepted from those who seek to direct the learning of others. At the risk of saying the same thing in a different way, the downstream consequence of *Hoyle v Rogers* is that interviewees in the investigation process may be reluctant to co-operate with the investigating authorities and, despite State regulations compelling their co-operation, would be justified by their privilege against self-incrimination, entitling them to be cautioned before an interview and to have independent legal advice throughout the interview, so that they may have counsel on their right to silence.

The apparent confusion was partially rectified more recently in the case of the *Ocean Perfect*[10] in which the Commercial Court ruled that reports of the MAIB are inadmissible as evidence as to liability without the express permission of the Court.

In the Merchant Shipping (Accident Reporting and Investigation) Regulations 2012, Regulation 11 (5) actually acknowledges the right of an interviewee to be advised by a solicitor during the questioning process, naturally enabling the solicitor to advise their client that they are not obliged to answer a particular question, for that specific reason. It states:

> *Any person, not being a solicitor or other professional legal adviser acting solely on behalf of the person required to attend, who either has been allowed by an inspector to be present; or has been nominated to be present by a person required to attend, at a witness interview before an inspector, may at any time be excluded from being present by the inspector with the agreement of the Chief Inspector, if both the inspector and Chief Inspector have substantial reason to believe that the person's presence would hamper*

10 *Ocean Prefect Shipping Limited v. Dampskibsselskabet Norden AS (Ocean Prefect)* [2019] EWHC 3368 (Comm).

the investigation with the result that the objective in regulation 5 is likely to be hindered and future safety thereby endangered; and the Chief Inspector is satisfied, having regard to all the circumstances, that it is proper to exclude that person.

Sentencing Guidelines

While the strict liability offences provided in UNCLOS and MARPOL clearly are intended to deliver redress, the way in which that redress is carried out is a matter for the judicial processes of the individual States – and they may go far beyond the Convention limitations of a fine. In the UK, the Sentencing Guidelines Council published a helpful paper in 2004, addressing overarching and general principles relating to the sentencing of offenders. In 2018 new, additional guidelines were issued to Judges which increase prison sentences for Defendants convicted of gross negligence manslaughter in a workplace setting – which includes the shipboard scenario.

In this situation we shall deal with how the evidence in a case will lead to the sentencing of an offender after conviction.

Criminal procedure broadly compels the Court to take into account five purposes of sentencing when dealing with convicted offenders: the punishment of offenders, the reduction of crime (including its reduction by deterrence), the reform and rehabilitation of offenders, the protection of the public and the making of reparation by offenders to persons affected by their offence. The application of those purposes in the context of the seafarer in fact underpins the relevance of all save the reform of offenders, which is not a matter with which the Port State is likely to concern itself.

The overarching obligation on the Court is to pass a sentence that is fair and proportionate when considered with the seriousness of the offence. The seriousness of an offence is determined by two main parameters: the culpability of the offender and the harm caused or risked being caused by the offence.

Culpability

Culpability, or blameworthiness on the part of the offender, will be determined by such factors as motivation, whether the offence was planned or spontaneous or whether the offender was in a position of trust – or responsibility. Such features manifestly lend themselves to considering the position of a seafarer in a casualty event and, thus, the relevance to the task in context is compelling. Sentencing in cases of gross negligence manslaughter follows section 125(1) of the Coroners and Justice Act 2009, which provides that every Court must consider the appropriate sentencing guidelines, even though the factors indicate a lower culpability, where there was no intention by the Defendant to cause any harm and no obvious risk of anything more than minor harm. This would address the category into which the seafarer would fall.

In cases of non-fatal accidents, culpability has been analysed by the Council to have four levels, which determine the seriousness attached to the *mens rea* of the offender and can be paraphrased to apply in seafarers as follows:

- The seafarer had the intention to cause harm, with the highest culpability when the offence itself was planned. The worse the harm intended, the greater the seriousness;
- The seafarer was reckless as to whether harm would be caused, that is, where they appreciated that at least some harm would be caused but proceeded any way, giving no thought to the consequences even though the extent of the risk would be obvious to most seafarers in that position;
- The seafarer had knowledge of the specific risks entailed by their actions even though they did not intend to cause the harm that resulted;
- The seafarer was guilty of negligence. (Sadly, the word 'negligence' is not defined by the Council.)

Harm

Harm must always be judged in the light of, and, therefore, must follow the determination of, culpability. The Council has analysed the parameter of harm to cover three types:

- Harm to the individual, who may suffer death, personal injury, psychological stress or financial loss; in other words, issues which are personal to the victim in question, and cause a particular impact which the Court should reasonably take into account when determining the seriousness of the offence;
- Harm to the community, which widens the impact from the individual considered above to the well-being or otherwise of the local society, or society at large;
- Other types of harm, which the Council had difficulty in characterising but, in the context of a pollution casualty, may describe the effect on wildlife and the marine environment but there may be human victims as well who suffer financially or psychologically as a result of the environmental damage, or the suffering inflicted upon animals because of the casualty which gave rise to the offence.

The Council acknowledged that some conduct is criminalised purely by the normative ethics of society, in particular when public feeling is inflamed by the consequences of the behaviour, which can influence public perception of the harm caused. This returns us to the issue of discrimination between the human rights to which all individuals are entitled.

Environmental Offences

Separately, the Sentencing Advisory Panel's first advice to the Court of Appeal addressed the issue of formulating guidelines for environmental offences, with the overall aim to promote fairness and consistency in sentencing. The panel addressed its guidance in relation to five specific environmental statutes, one of which involved a maritime context in the Water Resources Act 1991, controlling, *inter alia*, pollution in coastal and territorial waters. In this work, aggravating factors were more particularised in determining the culpability of the offender, and the results can enhance and develop the work of the Sentencing Guidelines Council for a more reliable approach to sentencing, as a model for the punishment of the convicted seafarer. Building on the foundation of the combined work published to date, the factors determining culpability include:

- The offence is shown to have been a deliberate or reckless breach by the Defendant of their obligations in law by reason of their responsibility, both as to Flag State law and such Port State laws which have been promulgated as a result of the authority and powers under UNCLOS and MARPOL;
- With reference to the conduct which led to the casualty event, the Defendant acted from a financial or commercial motive, whether of profit or of cost-saving on behalf of the owner or charterer;
- The Defendant failed to respond to advice, caution or warning from the relevant regulatory authority; in the case of the Master, this must always be tempered with the Master's discretion under SOLAS V r 34-1;
- The seafarer ignored Company Standing Orders, or ignored the concerns expressed by others.

It should be mentioned that reckless demands that the seafarer is shown to have had knowledge of the specific risks involved, apprehending the risk that a crime could occur as a result of their action and, nevertheless, proceeded to take that risk.

The harm to be considered in the light of culpability can equally be addressed with a model which relates to the actual or potential extent of the damage caused:

- The pollutant spilled was noxious, widespread or pervasive, and / or liable to spread widely or have long-lasting effects, affecting the water column, the sea bed and or the coastline;
- Human health, animal health, or flora were adversely affected, especially where a protected species was affected, where a site designated for nature conservation was affected, or where the event took place in a pristine environment or a special sea area under MARPOL, demanding increased awareness of the risk of damage;
- Extensive clean-up, site restoration or animal rehabilitation operations were required, again demanding increasing awareness of the hazards to effective clean-up such as the geography and weather hampering operations in the sea area;
- Other lawful activities were prevented or significantly interfered with, such as fishing, leisure and tourism.

24 Essentials of Contract Law

Introduction

The fulcrum on which the whole of maritime commerce turns, is the law of contract. In the growth years of the Industrial Revolution in the nineteenth century, the discovery of ocean routes reduced the risk and expense of international trade, making private investment viable and encouraging shipowners to commission vessels which would enable them to embark on the key function which defines the initial step in the trade cycle of getting the goods to the market-place.

Nineteenth-century London was an incredibly litigious place, and the mighty business of the General Steam Navigation Company, founded by Hall and Brockelbank in 1824, would participate in more, even, than most businesses.[1] For the partners in a shipowning business, the risk was very real indeed. In the nascent years of Britain's maritime Empire in the eighteenth century, shipowners had become increasingly worried by the risk of legal claims against them, giving rise to damages that could ruin them. As a result, a petition was presented to Parliament, and passed without a division (a vote), to regulate claims for the loss of goods arising out of the accountability of the Master or crew of the ship carrying them, by limiting the quantum of damage to the value of the vessel, her equipment, and any freight due for the voyage. In other words, a Judgment creditor could not seek to enforce Judgment on any other goods or money owned by the shipowners in question.

The profitability of the marine venture necessarily presents the driving force behind maritime commerce; if there were no profit in it, there would be no business case for building a vessel in the first place. In this way, we can identify that modern contract law has evolved to meet the priorities of the parties, but the statutory limitation rules, which today can be found in Hague-Visby, had origins that grew at the same time.

1 In research, the Author identified 36 cases appearing in law reports involving the General Steam Navigation Company, and another 32 case files survive in the custody of the National Archives. On the likely basis that not all case files will have been preserved, and mindful of the legendary statistic in the legal profession that ninety per cent of cases settle before getting to Court, the actual total of disputes must have been staggering.

DOI: 10.4324/9781003361916-24

The essential features of a contract are surprisingly simple, and very flexible; they have to be, in order to meet the demands of the parties in endless scenarios in maritime commerce; performance of the term provides the evidence that underpins the standard of duty owed between commercial parties in relationships, which are thus very personal to them.

A contract is all about the need to ensure that parties know what they have got into; all it does is provide evidence of an agreement made by the exchange of commercial promises, managed by terms and recognised as a legal obligation. Naturally, there is an advantage in having such evidence in writing, signed by the parties, but there are few cases in which a written contract is demanded by law.

During the course of commercial activities involving ships, many legal questions will arise. They will be handled by the parties and their advisers as part of their daily business, without any wish to get involved in litigation. Inevitably, however, disputes will occur. Most disputes are resolved by negotiation before the relationship between the parties breaks down, taking into account many priorities that the law cannot address, such as the importance of privacy in commercial activity and its effect on the reputation and share value of the business, with the result that the wider commercial considerations are met, keeping existing trading arrangements alive, and the desire to avoid the expense and delay involved in going to Court.

The role of the law in this context is to define the basic obligations of the parties, which provide a basis for negotiation, so if there is some argument during performance, and the parties simply cannot resolve the matter by negotiation, it is then that the legal process will resolve the dispute for them, delivering a decision which can be enforceable, whether they like it or not. Therefore, a contract dispute can be resolved by the parties according to a framework that they construct themselves; but the moment that proceedings are commenced, control of the resolution process is lost, because it has passed to the Court or the Arbitrator, over which the parties have no influence.

In civil cases, the Claimant must persuade the Court that it has proved on The Balance of Probabilities by the weight of evidence that the Defendant is in breach of the body of law pleaded against him (or vice versa in a Counterclaim). Lord Denning famously described the burden as *Being more certain than not*; in other words, the balance is established at 51 per cent to 49 per cent.

The Court will hear oral evidence from witnesses but, most importantly, it will be guided by documentary evidence, such as the written contract or subsequent variations, protests, correspondence, notes or memoranda. Each side is expected to present its own case and protect its own interests to the fullest (subject to professional rules and duties to assist the Courts in reaching fair and just conclusions, e.g., submissions of authorities). The Judge is entirely impartial, and each party has the right to answer the allegations made against it and to make submissions to the Judge on all matters which are presented to them. The probative value of the evidence is therefore essential.

Contract cases in maritime trade invariably have an international element. The process of globalisation transforms both the concept and practice of state sovereignty, in which the case must be determined according to the law of a particular jurisdiction, to be settled by the law by which the parties agreed to abide. The contract is instrumental in the transfer of risk in international trade and, therefore, the parties are free to decide which jurisdiction manages the risk best for them; it is a question of whose jurisdiction they trust the most. And there's the rub; because the 'home' court of one party will be a 'foreign' court to the other, resulting in a lack of confidence by at least one party in a fair resolution, from the time when proceedings are issued. A party to an international contract which does not contain a jurisdiction clause to define which law is to be followed runs the risk that one party must be forced to submit to a court of foreign jurisdiction and employ lawyers who are qualified in that jurisdiction, but whose advice and culture may be quite alien to the party concerned. The element of trust, therefore, is everything, and it is a fact, that the vast majority of international contracts are formed under English law, so that disputes are resolved in English civil courts or English arbitrators.

The Conflict of Laws

The very international nature of maritime commerce therefore demands the answer to a preliminary question: whose law should be applied to the case at hand? The issue arises where a contract contains a foreign element where a relevant fact or party has a connection with a foreign country, but there is no evidence that they had agreed on the jurisdiction of disputes at the time the contract was closed. The inevitable result of such an issue, leads to a situation known as forum shopping. The key elements are:

- The Claimant wants its case heard in the Court thought most likely to provide a favourable Judgment;
- The Claimant believes the Defendant or his key witnesses will not be able to travel to the state selected, opening the opportunity for the Claimant to get Judgment in Default;
- The Court or body of law or rules of evidence are most likely to favour the Claimant's priorities.

In this case, the Court's task is to determine whether their first instance forum is the natural forum, in other words, where there is a real and substantial connection between the venue and the cause of action to provide some protection against the Defendant from being pursued in jurisdictions having little or no connection with the transaction or the parties. In so deciding, the Court may decline to hear, or may even transfer a case, if that Court is not the most convenient for the case.

The Case of *Solano v Gulf King*

The case of *Solano v Gulf King*[2] illustrates very well the key issues in forum shopping, and the approach taken by the Court. Ten Nicaraguan seafarers, whose contracts

2 Raymundo Cerrato Solano V Gulf King 55, Inc; Gulf King Services, Inc; Gulf King 55 In Rem (2000) 212 F3d 902 (United States Court Of Appeals, 5th Circuit.

were all closed in brought work-related personal injury actions against the Defendant vessel owners under United States law. The Defendant owners of the Gulf King vessels were Delaware-registered corporations with their principal place of business in Texas. The owners of 96 per cent of the stock of the corporations were United States citizens and Texas residents. Gulf King owned 43 shrimping vessels, 34 of which operated exclusively in Nicaraguan waters, and the fleet managers and Masters answered to and were in regular daily contact with Gulf King management in Texas. Gulf King financed its vessels primarily through two loans: one from the United States Small Business Administration and one from the United States Department of Commerce, National Marine Fishery Service. Because both loans were made by United States agencies, the Plaintiffs characterised Gulf King as *owing it all to United States taxpayers*. Moreover, the entire catch from the Nicaraguan vessels were imported to the United States and sold to American consumers.

Each Claimant asserted causes of action based on the Jones Act,[3] and the general maritime laws of the United States for personal injuries suffered while working on the vessels. None asserted any action against any Defendant based on the laws of Nicaragua or any other country, whose laws and judgment enforcement of damages procedures were inferior to those in the United States.

Each vessel was documented under the laws of the United States and flew the American flag as Flag State; but then, confusingly, each also flew the Nicaraguan flag above the American flag, in accordance with Nicaraguan law. This is in flagrant breach of Article 92 of UNCLOS which states:

> *Ships shall sail under the flag of one State only and, save in exceptional cases expressly provided for in international treaties or in this Convention, shall be subject to its exclusive jurisdiction on the high seas.*

The United States has not ratified UNCLOS, however and, at the time of the case, neither had Nicaragua.

The fishing licences were issued by the Nicaraguan State, which required safety inspections before the licences were granted, the vessels sailed for the whole period in Nicaraguan waters, and were not subject to United States Coast Guard safety requirements or inspections. There was no doubt, however, that the structure for awarding damages and the quantum of those damages were more beneficial to the Claimants in US Courts, where they could also enforce Judgment more easily, given the domicile of the Defendants' assets.

Unsurprisingly, Gulf King applied for Summary Judgment claiming that Nicaraguan law governs the claims, not United States law. The key issues for consideration involved the following principles:

- The parties were not both based in the same jurisdiction;
- Each party only had substantial assets in the country where it was resident;

3 46 U.S.C. § 688 (1994).

- The employment contracts were closed in a different country to that where they were performed, with no clause defining jurisdiction;
- All or part of the performance was to take place in a different jurisdiction to that in which the case was being heard.

The Appeal Court held:

> *When we discount the law of the flag and allegiance of the Defendants' factors which favour application of United States law, and accord more weight to the Plaintiffs' citizenship and residence, the place of the employment contracts and the place of injury, all of which were in Nicaragua, it is clear that the calculus ultimately dictates application of Nicaraguan law.*

In a nod to the motivation for the Defendants' choice of venue, the Court observed:

> *We note, further, that the District Court's assumption that the application of United States law would allow the Plaintiffs a more generous recovery, while almost certainly correct, was not a valid consideration in its choice-of-law analysis. The fact that the law of another forum may be more or less favourable to a Plaintiff, does not determine choice of law.*

Mention should be made that, under English law, the Contracts (Applicable Law) Act 1990 adopted the Rome Convention, providing that:

> *A contract shall be governed by the law chosen by the parties – either expressly or demonstrated with reasonable certainty by the terms.*
>
> *If not so chosen, the contract shall be governed by the law of the country with which it is most closely connected.*

Finally, it is necessary to mention a word about the enforceability of Conventions by or against individuals. Generally speaking, a Convention is enforceable between the States which have ratified it, but if it is to be enforced against individuals or legal bodies, it must be executed in domestic legislation in that State; the exception arises where the State concerned expressly states otherwise. Staying in the United States jurisdiction, the Court held in *Bowater v Patterson*:[4]

> *When the wording of a treaty is sufficiently explicit to permit its application without additional implementing statutes, and the States Parties intended it to be self-executing, all of which the Court found in this treaty, it can be enforced without domestic legislation.*

4 *The Bowater Steamship Company Ltd, Petitioner, v Earl Patterson, Etc et al.*, US Supreme Court 1962/206/371 US860/83 S Ct 116/9 L Ed 2d 98 /6-25-1962.

This case is addressed in more detail in the chapter on Sources of Law.

The Anatomy of a Contract

A contract is nothing more than an agreement, in other words, a voluntary assent between two or more parties, made by the exchange of commercial promises, managed by terms and recognised as a legal obligation. The whole essence of a contract lies in this concept of an agreement, or a bargain, by which an agreement is reached by mutual commitments.

The Bargain

The essence of the contract, therefore, is that it is a bargain. It does not matter whether it is a good bargain or a bad bargain; if reached between the parties in good faith without deceit, it will be binding in English law.

The concept of bargain is an ancient one, and the Courts historically will not step into the shoes of one party or another to decide whether they achieved a good bargain; and this has recently been upheld in the non-marine case of *Mott Macdonald v Trant*.[5] In this case, an exclusion clause in the contract limited the value of any claim against Mott MacDonald to £500,000, and Trant's counterclaim for a far higher sum against them was thus limited to that sum. The Court held, that the exclusion clause was in the clearest of terms, excluding liability for certain categories of loss, even if the excluded losses resulted from a deliberate or wilful breach. It mattered not whether that was a good or a bad bargain, and the parties were stuck with it.

The Element of Good Faith

Good faith is said to have two elements:

- Adherence to reasonable commercial standards of fair dealing;
- Faithfulness to the agreed common purpose of the contract and to the reasonable expectations of the parties arising from it.

The concept of good faith is ill-defined but has been upheld in numerous cases. The problem with its definition lies in the fact that it is an element which takes different forms in different commercial contexts, but it is an important factor, nevertheless, because an obligation of good faith must be upheld when applying the intention of the parties to the performance of the contract. As a result, the Court can imply a term demanding good faith, even if it is not expressed in the contract.

In the 2013 case of *Yam Seng v ITC*,[6] the Defendants entered into a distribution contract, by which they gave rights to Yam Seng to distribute fragrances in Asia

5 *Mott Macdonald Ltd v Trant Engineering Ltd* [2021] EWHC 754.
6 Yam Seng PTE Ltd v International Trade Corporation Ltd [2013] EWHC 111 (QB).

branded *Manchester United*. The Claimant, however, alleged breach of contract as orders were not shipped promptly, and pleaded that the Defendants offered the same products for sale at a lower price in Asia, as well as providing false information it knew the Claimant would rely on for marketing. Yam Seng duly sought a declaration that there was an implied term for good faith in the performance of the contract and that the term was breached.

The case was heard in the High Court, in which Legatt J recognised that, although the general view is that good faith is not recognised in English contract law because its very nature created uncertainty, nevertheless, English law proceeds incrementally, and embodies an ethos that parties are free to pursue their own self-interest without breaching the contract. Good faith was introduced into English law via European directives which led to the Unfair Terms in Consumer Contracts Regulations 1999, and, for all its nebulous character, has been recognised in other common law countries such as the United States, Australia and Canada, showing that it is, at least, capable of definition in other legal systems.

Accordingly, the Court held, that the duty of good faith was an implied term, which was breached by the Defendants in this case. It should not create a universal precedent, however. Leggatt concluded:

> *Under English law, a duty of good faith is implied by law as an incident of certain categories of contract, for example, contracts of employment and contracts between partners or others whose relationship is characterized as a fiduciary one. I doubt that English law has reached the stage, however, where it is ready to recognise a requirement of good faith as a duty implied by law, even as a default rule, into all commercial contracts. Nevertheless, there seems to me to be no difficulty, following the established methodology of English law for the implication of terms in fact, in implying such a duty in any ordinary commercial contract based on the presumed intention of the parties.*

That being said, the character of a bargain has been modified over the passage of time, as new commercial agreements developed that dispensed with the negotiation of terms; rather, it is the agreement which is voluntary, so the offeree who accepts terms on a 'take it or leave it' basis, still accepts the agreement as voluntary.

The Standard Form Contract

The concept of a standard form contract is defined as a contract between two parties, where the terms and conditions of the contract are set by one of the parties, and the other party has little or no ability to negotiate more favourable terms; hence the phrase, that the offeror proposes it on a take it or leave it basis. In reality, it is still a voluntary agreement, because the offeree can simply leave it.

A Bill of Lading is not, in itself, a contract, but is evidence of the contract between the carrier and the shipper. In this respect, it represents evidence of standard terms; either the shipper accepts them or not.

The exception to its enforceability under English law was introduced by section 3 Section 3 Unfair Contract Terms Act 1977, which provides that, when one party agrees to contract on the other's standard terms, the other cannot exclude or restrict any liability if they are the party in breach of contract; and the other party cannot claim to be entitled –

(i) *To render a contractual performance substantially different from that which was reasonably expected of him;*
(ii) *In respect of the whole or any part of his contractual obligation, to render no performance at all, except in so far as (in any of the cases mentioned above in this subsection) the contract term satisfies the requirement of reasonableness.*

Implied Terms

Terms may be implied into a contract, either by common law decisions in precedent cases, or by a history of usage in the industry, or by Statute.

In the case of *Attorney General of Belize and others v Belize Telecom,*[7] the Court had to trade the fine line of implying terms to give business efficacy to a contract, without crossing the line of its authority, and stepping into the shoes of either party in a contract, and impose terms upon them.

In this case, the Court held that *in order for a term to be implied it must be necessary for business efficacy or alternatively be so obvious as to go without saying. In practice, it will be a rare case where one of those conditions is satisfied but not the other*. The Belize case was followed in *Mediterranean Salvage v Seamar Trading,*[8] in which Lord Clarke MR held, *The correct approach to the question when to imply a term into a contract or other instrument, including therefore a charterparty, has recently been considered by Lord Hoffmann, giving the judgment of the Judicial Committee of the Privy Council, which also comprised Lord Rodger, Baroness Hale, Lord Carswell and Lord Brown, in Attorney General of Belize v Belize Telecom Ltd [2009] UKPC 10 ... His analysis in the Belize case is extensive. It repays detailed study but for present purposes it is I think sufficient to say that the implication of a term is an exercise in the construction of the contract as a whole.* He proceeded to quote Lord Steyn[9] that, *If a term is to be implied, it could only be a term implied from the language of [the instrument] read in its commercial setting.*

Terms Implied by Statute

Looking, once again, into the genesis of commercial law, the British Empire was absolutely dependent upon maritime commerce, at a time when the confidence of merchant venturers needed underpinning – and the law satisfied that need, with a structure of commercial law that established the rights and obligations in which risk was transferred in an agreement. As early as the eighteenth century, the Lord

7 *Attorney General of Belize v Belize Telecom Ltd* [2009] UKPC 10.
8 *Mediterranean Salvage & Towage Ltd v Seamar Trading & Commerce Inc (The Reborn)* [2009] EWCA Civ 531.
9 *Equitable Life Assurance Society v Hyman* [2002] 1 AC 408, at 459.

Chief Justice of the day, Lord Mansfield, laid this foundation in a series of test cases which defined the rights and obligations in the stressful venture in which the shipowner, the cargo-owner and their insurers all trusted in the utmost good faith to make a profitable living out of the carriage of goods by sea.[10] It was, thus, the common law, settled by judges case by case, creating precedents. By which commercial law evolved; but the times were a-changing.

By the dawn of the age of the steamship, Britain's exports had increased by nearly 300 per cent in just two decades, and British merchant venturers had profited exceptionally well from the disablement of foreign competition; but Parliament was uneasy about the evolution of maritime law based solely on judicial precedents; hard cases can influence the body of law, but inevitably, judicial opinions can be revisited by judges in subsequent cases and put the law into different words according to their understanding. This demonstrated the need for Parliament to take control of the law by precise words in statutory form[11] for trust to be steadied in maritime trade, with statutory regulation of the ships and commercial agreements to which the State had to uphold for the benefit of all concerned. In the chapter on Bills of Lading we shall examine the genesis of statutory control with the Bills of Lading Act 1855, which imposed statutory terms for the carriage of goods by sea, demonstrating the importance of terms implied by Statute; and since then statutory control of terms has evolved to play an ever-increasing role, notably in limiting liability and contractual defences by exclusions.

Statutory Limitation Rules

These rules find compulsory application in the Carriage of Goods by Sea Act 1971 which introduces terms into the contract pursuant to the Hague-Visby Rules, whether the parties like it or not. Section 1 of the Act applies the Rules in their chronological context, starting with the International Convention for the unification of certain rules of law relating to bills of lading signed at Brussels in 1924, as amended by the Protocol signed at Brussels in 1968 and the Brussels Protocol of 1979, inserted by the Merchant Shipping Act 1981.Article II of the Rules sets out the general principle:

> *Subject to the provisions of Article VI, under every contract of carriage of goods by sea the carrier, in relation to the loading, handling, stowage, carriage, custody, care and discharge of such goods, shall be subject to the responsibilities and liabilities, and entitled to the rights and immunities hereinafter set forth.*

10 Crowhurst, P,1977, The Defence of British trade, 1689-1815, Dawson & Sons, Folkestone, p. 81.

11 See Posner, R, 1993, The Problems of Jurisprudence, Harvard University Press, Cambridge Ma, p. 248; note also Posner raises a pertinent point (p. 262) about statute law, in that the Court's function, to interpret the Will of Parliament, relies on letting the plain meaning of the words in a statute dictate the interpretation of the text.

Accordingly, the Carriage of Goods by Sea Act 1971 Has the following statutory effect:

- It applies whether or not the bill of lading refers to the Rules, to the carriage of goods by sea from a port in the UK; it includes coasting voyages so long as the contract of carriage provides expressly or by implication that a bill of lading will be issued.
- It applies to carriage between any ports in different States, provided that the bill of lading is issued in a State that has ratified the Protocol; carriage from a port in a contracting State to a port in another State; or from a port in any State to a port in another State, where the parties to the contract have agreed on its being governed by the law of a State that has adopted the Hague-Visby Rules or enacted legislation giving effect to them.
- It applies where the contract is governed by UK law and the parties agree that a bill of lading or a non-negotiable receipt subject to the Rules shall be issued.
- It specifically does not apply to deck cargo and live animals in accordance with the Rules.

Article III of the Rules define the broad duties, including the following:

- The carrier shall be bound before and at the beginning of the voyage to exercise due diligence to make the ship seaworthy;
- To properly man, equip and supply the ship;
- To make the holds, refrigerating and cool chambers, and all other parts of the ship in which goods are carried, fit and safe for their reception, carriage and preservation.

However, it is not all bad. Article IV of the Rules provides certain defences:

> *Neither the carrier nor the ship shall be liable for loss or damage arising or resulting from unseaworthiness unless caused by want of due diligence on the part of the carrier to make the ship seaworthy, and to secure that the ship is properly manned, equipped and supplied, and to make the holds, refrigerating and cool chambers and all other parts of the ship in which goods are carried fit and safe for their reception, carriage and preservation in accordance with the provisions of paragraph 1 of Article III. Whenever loss or damage has resulted from unseaworthiness the burden of proving the exercise of due diligence shall be on the carrier or other person claiming exemption under this article.*

The Rules then apply the Nautical Fault Defence, of universal importance to the carriage of goods by sea:

> *Neither the carrier nor the ship shall be responsible for loss or damage arising or resulting from ... (a) Act, neglect, or default of the master, mariner, pilot, or the servants of the carrier in the navigation or in the management of the ship.*

The Sale of Goods Act 1979

The Sale of Goods Act has a far wider remit than the Carriage of Goods by Sea Act, defining the contract of sale, its formalities, subject-matter, and, particularly, implies terms about risk:

- Risk of theft;
- Risk of loss or damage;
- Risk of non-conformity.

The key provision on risk is contained section 20:

> *Unless otherwise agreed, the goods remain at the seller's risk until the property in them is transferred to the buyer, but when the property in them is transferred to the buyer the goods are at the buyer's risk whether delivery has been made or not.*
>
> *But where delivery has been delayed through the fault of either buyer or seller the goods are at the risk of the party at fault as regards any loss which might not have occurred but for such fault.*
>
> *Nothing in this section affects the duties or liabilities of either seller or buyer as a bailee or custodian of the goods of the other party.*

The Sale of Goods (Amendment) Act 1995 added provisions on Undivided shares in goods forming part of a bulk cargo. This section applies to a contract for the sale of a specified quantity of unascertained goods if:

- The goods or some of them form part of a bulk which is identified either in the contract or by subsequent agreement between the parties;
- The buyer has paid the price for some or all of the goods which are the subject of the contract and which form part of the bulk.

The 1995 provides that, in this case, *then (unless the parties agree otherwise), as soon as the conditions specified above are met or at such later time as the parties may agree –*

(a) *Property in an undivided share in the bulk is transferred to the buyer;*
(b) *The buyer becomes an owner in common of the bulk.*

Part IV of the Act addresses delivery. In particular, section 32 addresses delivery to the Carrier:

- *Where, in pursuance of a contract of sale, the seller is authorised or required to send the goods to the buyer, delivery of the goods to a carrier (whether named by the buyer or not) for the purpose of transmission to the buyer is prima facie deemed to be a delivery of the goods to the buyer;*

- *Unless otherwise authorised by the buyer, the seller must make such contract with the carrier on behalf of the buyer as may be reasonable having regard to the nature of the goods and the other circumstances of the case; and if the seller omits to do so, and the goods are lost or damaged in course of transit, the buyer may decline to treat the delivery to the carrier as a delivery to himself or may hold the seller responsible in damages;*
- *Unless otherwise agreed, where goods are sent by the seller to the buyer by a route involving sea transit, under circumstances in which it is usual to insure, the seller must give such notice to the buyer as may enable him to insure them during their sea transit; and if the seller fails to do so, the goods are at his risk during such sea transit.*

There is just one issue to remember here: these provisions are concerned with the sale contract, and should not be confused with the contract of affreightment, which is regulated with terms implied by the Carriage of Goods by Sea Act 1971.

Terms Implied by Custom or Usage

Where there is clear and sufficient factual evidence that a custom operates within an industry, the courts have the power to imply a term giving effect to the custom. Such terms implied by custom or usage meet the definition of what is standard in the industry, so they are generally well known and accepted. Generally applied tests will apply such a term on particular conditions:

- It is notorious, certain and reasonable;
- It is not contrary to the general law;
- It is more than a mere trade practice.

The very uncertain ground on which such terms sit, make them highly problematic to apply, and risk expensive litigation that may result in failure due to the fact that the tests that the Court may apply are uncertain and, in any event would demand prior acceptance by the parties based on their regular and consistent trading with each other.

Tackling Ambiguities: The Case of Compulsory Pilotage

We have devoted a chapter to pilotage but it has close relevance in the law of contract. Compulsory pilotage was implemented by Port State laws as a result of commercial pressure. Its origins in some jurisdictions can be traced back centuries,[12] but that pressure forced its introduction into English Statute Law in the early years

12 See Quick, G, Undated, The Role of the Pilot in Risk Management, International Organisation of Masters, Mates & Pilots of Maryland, USA. Retrievable at www.impahq.org/technology/article_1228231036.pdf.

of the nineteenth century, as a means by which the Port State could manage the risk to life and property presented by the massive growth in Britain's brave new maritime commerce, which had been helped so ably by the Napoleonic Wars. The developing laws of ship construction would be of little help to an expensive new merchant frigate whose back was broken on dangerous rocks and her cargo lost, simply because her Master did not possess knowledge of the local waters, and the power-mongers in the new era of post-war economic regeneration, the investors, the traders, the exporters and the insurers, persuaded Parliament to mitigate the losses of navigating in dangerous waters as the ships arrived or sailed from port. The solution was seen in the knowledge and skills of a pilot experienced in the particular waters of a locality; such expertise was identified as a crucial asset by the Port State in the risk management process and, as a result, the Pilotage Act 1812 introduced the concept by statute.

The nineteenth-century view taken of the liabilities between the parties was changed by the Pilotage Act 1913, expressly overriding any conflicting provision in primary or secondary legislation, and providing that the Owner and Master of a vessel navigating in a compulsory navigation area shall be answerable for any loss or damage caused by the navigation of the vessel or by any fault of the navigation of the vessel in the same manner as he would if pilotage were not compulsory. This has been taken forward into current law by Section 16 of the Pilotage Act 1987, which provides that the fact that a ship is being navigated in a compulsory pilotage area shall not affect any liability of the Owner or Master of the ship for any loss or damage caused by the ship or by the manner in which it is navigated. It may be argued that this actually relaxes the Master's and owner's liability somewhat, as it rows back from the sterner wording of the 1913 Act providing that the Owner and Master 'shall be answerable for any loss.' It starkly emphasises the departure from the principles of voluntary commitment in settling terms.

Section 15(1) of the 1987 Act, which perpetuates the requirement that a ship which is being navigated in a compulsory navigation area shall be under the pilotage of an authorised pilot, creating a statutory obligation, but the relationship is a commercial one so that, if the Master apprehends that the pilot is standing the ship into danger, they may dismiss the pilot and demand a new one, for, unless the pilotage authority cannot offer one, the Master would proceed with the voyage in violation of the Statute, creating a criminal offence. In practice, the pilotage authority will hasten to offer a new pilot, for fear of losing the trust of port users, if that cannot be done, the ship is relieved of its statutory obligation and, of course, would be unwilling to remit the contractual fee.

The consequence is that the arrangement between the shipowner and the competent harbour authority providing the pilot is not a voluntary one. Paradoxically, this concurrently offers salvation to the shipowner under the nautical fault defence of the Hague-Visby Rules in the event of damaged cargo: the Master's discretion in navigation must prevail supporting the Merchant Shipping Safety of Navigation Regulations and thus the employer in this instance cannot be responsible for its employee's negligence over whom it has no control. The Master may not have navigational control but will still be in command at all times and, therefore, will still have contractual liability to their employer for any breach of the standard of duty giving rise to negligence. Section 16 provides:

> *The fact that a ship is being navigated in an area and in circumstances in which pilotage is compulsory for it shall not affect any liability of the owner or master of the ship for any loss or damage caused by the ship or by the manner in which it is navigated.*

Clearly the parties intend a contractual relationship even given the statutory obligation. The Port of London Authority's Directions state:

> *The PLA will seek a contractual agreement with the owner or operator of the vessel regarding the management of navigation on board the vessel and procedures relating to the use of PECs in the London Pilotage District.*[13]

Moreover, section 22 of the 1987 Act strictly applies a limitation clause for any negligence:

> *The liability of an authorised pilot for any loss or damage caused by any act or omission of his whilst acting as such a pilot shall not exceed £1,000 and the amount of the pilotage charges in respect of the voyage during which the liability arose.*

In the case of *The Cavendish*,[14] it was held, that a harbour authority is not vicariously liable for a pilot's negligence, averring that a pilot is an independent professional person, even though the port provides their services, and can insist on their employment. Section 2 of the 1987 Act imposes a duty on a harbour authority as to whether to provide pilotage services, but the pilotage authority pointedly is not obliged to conduct the pilotage itself but merely to supply a properly authorised pilot, so the authority is not vicariously liable to a shipowner for damage caused by such a pilot's negligence.

To summarise, the obligation to engage a pilot is statutory, for which the shipowner must pay, and the limitation of the pilot's liability is also statutory, effectively imposing contractual terms over which the shipowner has no control. The Master cannot be overruled, however, and thus the question arises as to the Master's powers in the contract for the provision of the pilotage service. In consequence, the Master's position as representative, employee and agent of the owner will give authority to the Master to dismiss the pilot if the pilot stands the ship into danger; they cannot continue without a pilot, however and, so, will have to anchor or heave to until another pilot is supplied. The contractual fee, no doubt, will be a matter in dispute at a later stage.

13 PLA, Pilotage Directions 2017 as amended, p. 13.
14 *Oceangas (Gibraltar) Ltd v Port Of London Authority (The Cavendish)* [1993] 2 Ll R 292.

25 Contract Formation

The very nature of maritime trade demands enormous flexibility as to how contracts are formed, and in most cases of a voluntary agreement only four elements must be proved:

5. Offer: an expression that Offeror is willing to enter into a binding agreement as soon as the terms are accepted by the Offeree;
6. Acceptance: an unconditional acceptance of the Offeror's terms;
7. Consideration: a promise must be 'bought' in the idea of a voluntary bargain;
8. Intention to create legal relations: there must be evidence that the parties intended the agreement to be subject to the law of contract.

There are very few contracts which must be evidenced in writing and, paradoxically, the marine industry has its fair share of them, including the following:

- The carriage of goods by sea provides terms which shall attach to the Bill of Lading
- The registration of a UK ship demands evidence of ownership in the form of a Bill of Sale
- A seafarer must have a written Seafarer's Employment Agreement

The general rule, therefore, is that a contract does not have to be in writing; but the challenge is to prove that the key elements are all satisfied. If one is missing, the contract is unenforceable.

The Offer

An offer is an expression of willingness to contract made with the intention that it shall become binding on the offeror as soon as it is accepted by the person to whom it is addressed. Certain general principles have evolved in contract law which describe the face of the offer:

- It must be communicated in some way; this maty be in writing, orally or by conduct but, in any event, it must enable the offeree to accept or reject it.
- It must be clear and definite in substance, and not a mere invitation to treat.

DOI: 10.4324/9781003361916-25

- That being said, it may be made to a particular person, to a group of persons, or to the world at large.

An offer may be described as being bilateral or unilateral. Most contracts in maritime trade will be bilateral, in that it will be an expression of willingness in which both parties are committed to be bound by the transaction and have a contractual obligation to perform in accordance with their respective promises. In a contract for the supply of goods or services in maritime law, the offeror submits their draft contract to the buyer, who may seek amendments of some terms, or else confirms agreement and the contract is then closed. Whichever party expresses a willingness to be bound unconditionally by their proposals, will be deemed to have made an offer (or a counter-offer, which amounts to the same thing).

In the case of *The Leonidas*,[1] the Claimant shipowner had been negotiating with Trafigura to fix a charterparty, and reached the stage at which they had reached an agreement in principle, subject to a provision which was generally accepted in chartering cases to indicate a precondition, which, until lifted, prevented the acceptance of an offer. In this case, in a telephone call when negotiating the charter of a vessel, the Charterers lifted all outstanding subs except one. But that one was sufficient to defeat the contract, and the Court held accordingly.

There are instances in which a contract may be defined as unilateral, in which case the offer must be distinguished from an invitation to treat. If that is the case, the transaction will require the settlement of critical terms by negotiation. A wealth of entertaining cases defined these general principles, not the least being *Carlill v Carbolic Smoke Ball Company*.[2] In that case the alleged offeror was the manufacturer of a product guaranteed to prevent influenza, consisting of a rubber ball filled with carbolic acid, with a tube attached that was inserted into a user's nose. It duly placed an advertisement in a number of newspapers, guaranteeing the product's reliability by stating:

> *£100 REWARD will be paid by the CARBOLIC SMOKE BALL CO. to any Person who contracts the Increasing Epidemic, INFLUENZA, Colds, or any Diseases caused by taking Cold, after having used the CARBOLIC SMOKE BALL according to the printed directions supplied with each Ball.*

It added:

> *£1,000 is deposited with the ALLIANCE BANK, Regent Street, showing our sincerity in the matter.*

Louisa Carlill saw the advertisement, bought one of the balls and promptly contracted influenza. She commenced proceedings against the manufacturer, which

1 *Nautica Marine Ltd v. Trafigura Trading LLC(The Leonidas)* [2020] EWHC 1986 (Comm).
2 *Carlill v Carbolic Smoke Ball Company* [1892] EWCA Civ 1.

entered a defence that the advertisement was not intended to amount to an offer, but was a mere advertising puff. Incredibly, this case ended up in the Court of Appeal, where the company's arguments were rejected and it was held that the offer was not an invitation to treat to all the world but an offer restricted to those who acted upon the terms contained in the advertisement. By satisfying those conditions, Ms Carlill had duly accepted and by purchasing or merely using the smoke ball constituted good consideration, because it was a distinct detriment incurred at the behest of the company and, furthermore, more people buying smoke balls by relying on the advertisement was a clear benefit to Carbolic. the fact that the company claimed to have deposited the money with the Alliance Bank showed the serious intention to be legally bound.

Acceptance

An acceptance represents a final and unqualified assent to the terms of the offer. As such, therefore, a statement by a party declaring that it intends to close a contract is insufficient for the establishment of a contract. Equally, a mere acknowledgement of an offer would not be an acceptance, unless the terms expressly contained a statement that the sender agreed to the terms of the offer, thereby accepting it.

The adjective 'unqualified' is essential: the acceptance must be identical to the offer, otherwise it becomes a counter-offer, and a ping-pong between offeror and offeree will proceed until the unqualified assent is reached. It therefore follows that the terms must be agreed at the time when the contract is closed, unless the parties agree that some terms can be agreed later – but that demands clear consent.

It therefore follows, that the certainty of terms is essential in the offer, without which there cannot be an acceptance, subject to any provision for procedural mechanics to make the contract work. In *Didymi v Atlantic Lines*,[3] a charterparty contained a clause covering the rate of hire for a five-year time charter:

> *30(1) The ... speed and fuel consumption of the vessel as stipulated in this charter-party are representations by the owners. Should the actual performance of the vessel taken on an average basis throughout the duration of this charter-party show any failure to satisfy one or more of such representations, the hire shall be equitably decreased by an amount to be mutually agreed between owners and charterers.*

The Court had to address the question whether this provided sufficient certainty to give rise to a binding obligation on the parties, rather than a procedural question of how the right in question might be determined. It was argued that the clause was not enforceable, because it was only an agreement to agree but the Court held, that the obligation was sufficiently defined by the reference to the word *equitably* and that the provision for mutual agreement was no more than procedural mechanics.

3 *Didymi Corporation v Atlantic Lines And Navigation Company Inc (The Didymi)* [1988] 2 Ll R 108.

The parties must, however, have agreed on the key terms at the time when the contract was closed. In the case of *Olley v Marlborough Court Hotel*,[4] the Claimant had paid for a week's stay at the defendant hotel, and having completed the formalities went to her room. In the room, a notice was displayed stating that the proprietors would not be responsible for any items lost or stolen, unless they were handed to them for safekeeping. Ms Olley left the room and deposited her key on the board in reception before leaving the hotel. The key was stolen, however, and several items were taken from her room. Ms Olley commenced proceedings against the hotel on the grounds that they had been negligent in failing to keep the key safely. She further claimed that the contract contained an implied term that the hotel would take reasonable care of her property in her bedroom. In her particulars of claim she pleaded that the hotel's failure to keep the key safely amounted to a breach of that contract. The hotel argued the guests were bound by the terms displayed on the notice in the bedrooms, and therefore, the hotel had effectively excluded liability for any negligence. The Court, however, held, that the exclusion clause had not been incorporated into the contract terms because the contract was concluded at reception, and the notice purporting to exclude liability was not visible until after the contract was formed, when she entered her room. Mrs Olley was therefore successful.

Validity

There are some issues which have an effect on the validity of the offer and acceptance.

Capacity of minors

In general terms, a minor has very limited capacity to enter into a contract, which means that a minor has the right to avoid the contract, meaning that the minor can repudiate the contract when they attain the age of 18. That being said, minors remain contractually bound to pay for necessaries, that is, things that fall within the definition in section 3 of the Sale of Goods Act 1973 as goods suitable to the condition in life of the minor and their actual requirements at the time of sale, although even then they may only have to pay a reasonable price.

Nevertheless, the maritime Labour Convention defines the minimum age requirements for seafarers at 16.[5]

Bankruptcy and Insolvency

Under sections 36 to 38 of the Insolvency Act 1967, a bankrupt is disqualified from doing or participating in an array of matters. As such, a bankrupt individual

4 *Olley v Marlborough Court Ltd* [1949] 1 KB 532.

5 See Chapter 14: The employment of seafarers.

or insolvent business lacks capacity to enter into a contract, rendering it unenforceable. This demands some qualification, which can be found in *Foo Fatt Chuen v Jacobsen Cheong Weng*[6] in which the Court held:

> *On the facts of this case, there was sufficient evidence to establish elements of an entering into, or carrying on of a business by the very terms of the relevant agreements. It was plain that the legislative intent of section 38(1)(d)*[7] *of the Act was not to condone any act of the undischarged bankrupt in relation to the entry into or the carrying on of a business, or in relation to directly or indirectly taking part in the management of a company unless he had the prior permission of the DGI. A similar reasoning should apply in relation to the effects of the prohibition under s 38(1)(e) of the Act. Thus, although this court was not sitting as a bankruptcy court nevertheless it was held that since there had been a breach of section 38(1)(d) of the Act this court could not ignore the legal effects of illegality on the agreements.*

The Insolvency Act 1986 addressed the capacity of insolvent companies to enter a contract; this statute was amended by the Corporate Insolvency and Governance Act 2020. Naturally, a limited company would lack the capacity to enter into a binding contract if the act is ultra vires, but a criminal offence is committed by trading while insolvent, as that would amount to a fraud. Section 993 Companies 2006 states:

> *If any business of a company is carried on with intent to defraud creditors of the company or creditors of any other person, or for any fraudulent purpose, every person who is knowingly a party to the carrying on of the business in that manner commits an offence.*
>
> *This applies whether or not the company has been, or is in the course of being, wound up.*

Consideration

A contract must be characterised with the exchange of consideration, which was long ago defined as *some right, interest, profit or benefit accruing to one party, or some forbearance, detriment, loss or responsibility given, suffered or undertaken by the other.*[8]

The principle is that, if a promise is to be legally binding then it must be 'bought' with something of value given by the promise.

6 *Foo Fatt Chuen v Jacobsen Cheong Weng Hin & Ors* [2012].
7 Insolvency Act 1967.
8 *Currie v Misa* (1875) Ll R 10 Ex 153.

In the case of *Stilk v Myrick*,[9] the Claimant was a seaman, who signed articles for a round voyage from London to the Baltic and back, for which he was to be paid £5 per month. All the seamen had been bound by the terms of their contract to perform all their services under all the emergencies of the voyage, until that voyage should be completed.

While the vessel was alongside in Cronstadt, two sailors deserted. The Master was concerned that the vessel had to be worked to continue the voyage and, in order to ensure this, agreed with the nine remaining seamen to split the defaulters' wages among the remaining sailors, equally, if new hands could not be signed on and the ship made it back to London.

The Claimant was not paid the additional wages promised. He sued, arguing that the Defendant had agreed to pay the wages of the two deserters in exchange for performing the additional work that was necessary – essentially, that there had been a fresh exchange of promises.

The Defendant argued that the seamen who remained had a duty to ensure that the ship was worked *under all the emergencies of the voyage, until that voyage should be completed*, submitting that the desertion of the two crew members had to be considered an emergency of the voyage as much as death, and those who remained were bound by the terms of their original contract to exert themselves to the utmost to bring the ship in safely to her port. Held, by Lord Ellenborough:

> *Here, I say, the agreement is void for want of consideration. There was no consideration for the ulterior pay promised to the mariners who remained with the ship. Before they sailed from London they had undertaken to do all that they could under all the emergencies of the voyage. They had sold all their services till the voyage should be completed. If they had been at liberty to quit the vessel at Cronstadt, the case would have been quite different; or if the captain had capriciously discharged the two men who were wanting, the others might not have been compellable to take the whole duty upon themselves, and their agreeing to do so might have been a sufficient consideration for the promise of an advance of wages. But the desertion of a part of the crew is to be considered an emergency of the voyage as much as their death; and those who remain are bound by the terms of their original contract to exert themselves to the utmost to bring the ship in safety to her destined port. Therefore, without looking to the policy of this agreement, I think it is void for want of consideration, and that the plaintiff can only recover at the rate of £5 a month.*

This decision has influenced subsequent cases, and was cited more recently in *Williams v Roffey*.[10] The appellant Company, Roffey Brothers, were builders who were contracted to refurbish 27 flats belonging to a housing corporation. The con-

9 *Stilk v Myrik* [1809] EWHC KB J58; (1809) 170 ER 1168; KB.
10 *Williams v Roffey Bros & Nicholls (Contractors) Ltd* [1991] 1 QB 1.

tract had a penalty clause for late completion. The appellants subcontracted some work to Williams, a carpenter. When Williams fell behind with his work the appellants offered him bonus payment to finish on time. Williams carried on working until the payments stopped. He sued the appellants for breach of contract.

The appellants argued that the agreement to pay extra was unenforceable as Williams had provided no consideration; the appellants only received the practical benefit of avoiding the penalty clause, and did not receive any benefit in law. Williams was only agreeing to do what he was already bound to do, and in this context the appellants relied on *Stilk v Myrick*.

The Court of Appeal held that the principle in *Stilk v Myrick* had been refined since then. Gildwell LJ said a promise to make bonus payments to complete work on time was enforceable if the promisor obtained a practical benefit and the promise was not given under duress of by fraud. It was the appellants' own idea to offer the extra payment, and they gained a practical benefit by avoiding the penalty clause.

Will Non-Payment of Part Mean a Failure of Consideration and Fundamental Breach?

In the case of the *Astra*,[11] Flaux J held that payment of hire was a condition of the contract and so one missed payment was enough for a ship owner to terminate and claim damages. This was overturned by the Court of Appeal, however, in *Grand China Logistics v Spar*,[12] which resolved that whether any particular term in any particular time charterparty is a condition or not is a pure question of interpretation of the charterparty concerned; and the term as to payment of hire in the time charterparties involved, is not a condition but rather an innominate term as in this case the construction of the relevant term of each charterparty did not make it clear that it was to be regarded as a condition.

Privity: The Downstream Consequence of Consideration

The timeless rule in contract law is that consideration must move from the party entitled to sue on the contract; in other words, only the offeror and the offeree can sue or be sued. Many of the defining cases are non-marine, such as *Tweddle v Atkinson*, which will be addressed in the chapter on Agency. The key issue in this chapter is that the general principle survives, as held in the case of *Port Line v Ben Line*.[13] Port line time chartered a vessel from Silver Line, which sold the vessel to Ben Line during the period of the time charter. The vessel was subsequently requisitioned and Port Line sued the new owners. It was held, that because a time charterer, like a voyage charterer has no proprietary interest in the ship, it has no contractual interest in her as an asset; the reason is very logical, because, having

11 *The Astra* [2013] EWHC 865.

12 *Grand China Logistics Holding (Group) Co Ltd v Spar Shipping* AS [2016] EWCA Civ 982.

13 *Port Line v Ben Line* [1958] 2 QB 146.

given no contractual consideration in the vessel as an asset, they have no privity in that contract as a result. Port Line had not given any consideration in the contract for the sale of the ship, and therefore their claim failed.

The general rule was relaxed by an exception defined in the Contracts (Rights of Third Parties) Act 1999, which provided under section 1:

> *Subject to the provisions of this Act, a person who is not a party to a contract may in his own right enforce a term of the contract if–*
>
> (a) *The contract expressly provides that he may;*
> (b) *Subject to subsection (2), the term purports to confer a benefit on him.*

In the case of *Dolphin Maritime Aviation v Sveriges*[14] the Court interpreted the meaning of *purports to confer a benefit* to mean that the term in question must be one of the purposes of the bargain and not merely incidental to it. In this case, a cargo of steel was damaged during the voyage, and having indemnified the cargo owner, their insurer assumed their rights of subrogation and sued the Carrier, who had given a contractual letter of undertaking to the insurer promising that for non-arrest of the ship they would pay the cargo owner or their agent. The Carrier, however, paid the insurer instead and the cargo owner sued the Carrier on the letter of undertaking. The Court emphasised the importance of the test in the 1999 Act, that one of the purposes of the bargain of the parties, rather than one of its incidental effects, must be to benefit the third party. In this case, the letter of undertaking was merely the means by which the carrier could underwrite their obligation to the insurer; paying the cargo owner was not the purpose and, in any event, neither the insurer nor the carrier intended to confer on the cargo owner any benefit under the letter of undertaking.

Subsection 2 of the 1999 Act, however, stated that subsection (1)(b) above does not apply *if on a proper construction of the contract it appears that the parties did not intend the term to be enforceable by the third party*.

It would be essential for the third party to be expressly identified in the contract by name or in some other way clearly inhering the right, but does not confer on them a right to enforce a term of a contract otherwise than the strict terms defined in the contract.

However, in accordance with section 6, no rights are conferred on a third party in the case of a contract for the carriage of goods by sea; such rights are defined in the Carriage of Goods by Sea Act 1992, which provides under section 2:

> *Subject to the following provisions of this section, a person who becomes—*
>
> (a) *The lawful holder of a bill of lading;*
> (b) *The person who (without being an original party to the contract of carriage) is the person to whom delivery of the goods to which a sea waybill relates is to be made by the carrier in accordance with that contract;*

14 *Dolphin Maritime & Aviation Services Ltd v Sveriges Angfartygs Assurans Forening (The Swedish Club)* [2009] EWHC 716 (Comm).

(c) *The person to whom delivery of the goods to which a ship's delivery order relates is to be made in accordance with the undertaking contained in the order, shall (by virtue of becoming the holder of the bill or, as the case may be, the person to whom delivery is to be made) have transferred to and vested in him all rights of suit under the contract of carriage as if he had been a party to that contract.*

This provision works well in simple cases, but complications need more definition in terms of Court judgments. In *Standard Chartered Bank v Dorchester LNG*,[15] the Court of Appeal held, it was not helpful to seek to identify the *real and effective cause of the transfer*, but rather that the court should *simply identify the arrangement, if any, pursuant to which the transfer was made.*

Intention to Create Legal Relations

The intention to create legal relations is defined as an intention to enter a legally binding agreement or contract; as such it is one of the necessary elements in formation of a contract, because it establishes the readiness of a party to accept the legal sequences of having entered into an agreement. Without such an intention, the parties cannot sue or be sued on the contract.

However, in the commercial context of merchant shipping, there is a presumption or intention to be legally binding, which can only be rebutted by evidence to the contrary. In *Kleinwort Benson v Malaysia Mining Corporation*,[16] the Claimant bank agreed a loan to a subsidiary of the Defendant company, and asked the defendant company for a guarantee. The defendant replied that it was not their policy to guarantee loans to subsidiaries but, instead, offered a letter of comfort stating:

It is our policy to ensure that the business of MMC (Metals) is at all times in a position to meet its liabilities under the arrangements.

The bank accepted the letter but charged a higher rate of interest. Then the market collapsed and MMC went into liquidation. The bank sought to claim the balance of monies from the Defendant on the letter, but on appeal, the Court held, that there was no intention to create a legally binding agreement in the statement, which was not meant to act as guarantee, but merely stated the current position, without giving any assurance of not future intention.

So When Is the Binding Contract Closed? The Case Of the *Ever Given*

Appearances can be deceptive, even in the law, and the apparent presence of all the elements for a binding contract may yet fail to reach the threshold on which the Courts

15 *Standard Chartered Bank v Dorchester LNG (2) Limited (The Erin Schulte)* [2014] EWCA Civ 1382.

16 *Kleinwort Benson Ltd v Malaysian Mining Corporation*, [1989] 1 WLR 379.

will determine that the parties are bound. It is a dangerous thing to discuss a case study which has not exhausted the appeal process, but the 2023 case of the *Ever Given*[17] nevertheless illustrates the importance of taking an objective view of the negotiation process as a whole, rather than a selective choice of a point in the correspondence.

On 23 March 2021, the Ultra Large Container Vessel *Ever Given* famously grounded in the Suez Canal, and remained stranded for six days, blocking the Canal in both directions, which had a serious downstream consequence on maritime trade. On the day of the grounding, the Owners sought assistance from Smit, initially in the form of technical advice, but the salvors subsequently contributed a great deal more to the effort to refloat the vessel, and anticipated the conclusion of a contract, which was to be based on a standard form Wreckhire 2010 but subject to amendments, for which negotiations followed rapidly. The Court heard evidence in the exchanges of e-mails, broadly sent on the morning of 26 March, which reached consensus on the critical term of remuneration for Smit's services. The parties then continued to negotiate the terms amending the standard form, in which the Owners sent substantial proposed amendments which the salvors rejected, notably leaving unaddressed the time the vessel was to be refloated. At 11.35on 26 March, the Owners sent an email to Smit:

> *We refer to our telephone conversation subsequent to my previous email and my further conversation with Japan. As agreed over phone, I am please* [*sic*] *to confirm as below on behalf of Owners of Ever Given. Owners agree to the following:*
>
> *The tugs, dredgers, equipment engaged by SCA and their subsequent salvage claim are separate to the Smit's offer of assistance.*
>
> a) *SMIT personnel and equipment to be paid on Scopic 2020 rates*
> b) *Any hired personnel and equipment, out of pocket expenses of SMIT to be paid on Scopic 2020 rate + 15% uplift*
> c) *Refloatation Bonus of 35% of Gross invoice value irrespective of the type of assistance rendered.*
>
> ci) *Refloatation bonus not to be calculated on amounts chargeable for quarantine or isolation waiting period.*
> cii) *Refloatation bonus to SMIT will be applicable if refloatation attempt by SCA on 26 March 2021 is unsuccessful.*
>
> *We look forward to your confirmation. We can then start ironing out the wreck hire draft agreement so that the same can be signed at the earliest.*

Five minutes later, the Managing Director of Smit replied:

> *Thank you Captain and confirmed which is very much appreciated. I shall inform our teams accordingly and we shall follow up with the drafting of the*

17 *Smit Salvage BV & Others v Luster Maritime SA & Another* (The *Ever Given*) [2023] EWHC 697 (Admlty).

> *contract upon receipt of your/your client's feedback to our draft as sent last night.*

The draft Proposal to which this email referred, set out, under a heading of *Commercial terms and conditions on daily hire basis*, what it described as a summary of the *main terms and conditions* of Smit's proposal, in the form of seven bullet points and continued with sections providing Smit's thoughts on Optional transition to Lloyd's Open Form, Support and coordination with SCA, and Operational scenarios of refloating by tugs only, refloating with tugs in combination with dredging, and refloating with tugs in combination with cargo lightering (with three options for consideration).

The Owner's case was that by these e-mails the parties had reached consensus as to all of the essential terms of a contract and intimated a mutual intention to be bound immediately thereby, notwithstanding their mutual intention to agree and sign a more detailed written contract in the future. The salvors were equally certain that no binding agreement had been concluded because the parties had not intended immediately to be bound. Smit argued that, notwithstanding the conclusion of critical terms, the parties had intended only to be bound upon the conclusion and signature of the amended standard form contract.

Baker, J, held, that by the exchange of emails relied on by the Owners, upon their terms read objectively

and in context, no actual conclusion on negotiated terms had been reached by the parties:

> *By that exchange, agreement was reached, after a period of uncertainty ... on the remuneration terms for a contract that was being negotiated. However, the parties made clear to each other that they were still negotiating, indeed the detailed work of negotiating the contract terms by which they would be bound was only thus able to commence, albeit there was room for the view that it ought not to require much time to complete ... The parties did not communicate to each other an intention to be bound in the absence of completing that work of negotiating and agreeing a detailed set of contract terms. The tenor of their exchanges, to the contrary, was that they did not intend to be so bound. In the event, that work was not completed, as the counter-proposal on detailed terms later sent by Captain Sen* [on behalf of the Owners] *put the parties some considerable distance apart, and that gap was never closed.*

The Judge concluded that no contract as alleged had been concluded and that, therefore, under the terms of the Salvage Convention and/or at common law for the work carried out, Smit were entitled to a salvage award, rather than the quantum of a contract claim.[18]

18 This decision may be subject to Appeal.

The Terms of the Contract

A very useful overview of the contract terms may be summarised in that the nature and extent of the parties' obligations is determined by:

- The terms of the contract;
- The manner in which the terms formed part of the contract, whether they were expressly provided for or implied by custom, by the courts or by statute;
- The relative importance of those terms.

A Condition

This is a fundamental term of the contract, by which, if there is a failure in its observance, causes the contract to be substantially different to that which the parties originally intended. Its breach entitles the innocent party to the right to treat the contract as repudiated. The breach of a condition is said to go to the root of the contract, entitling the innocent party to claim damages to put them into the position they would have been in had the contract been performed as promised.

In the ancient case of *Poussard v Spiers*[19] an opera singer was taken ill and could not perform for the first three days of the engagement. The Defendant hired another singer to cover her, who proved a success and, when the Claimant sought to take up her position, the Defendant refused. In those days, such cases were heard in the High Court by a jury and in his case, the jury found that the Claimant was in breach of a condition, bringing the contract to an end. This finds its parallel in maritime law, in the case of a vessel that fails to reach the port of loading at the stated time, entitling the charterer to cancel, in other words to terminate the contract by the Carrier's fundamental breach. For the charterer this makes sense, for they must account to the buyer of the cargo for any delay in delivery or damage to the cargo occasioned by delay.

A Warranty

This term is not fundamental to the contract, but only collateral to it. The aggrieved party has no specific right to repudiate – so he must perform his part of the contract.

In the case of *Wills v Amber*,[20] a four-berth motor boat had been sold, subject to an innocent statement by the seller that the hull was sound; this was held to be a warranty, even though the buyer had entered into the contract in reliance upon it, when in fact the hull was rotten. The Court reasoned that the contract was not substantially different to that which the parties originally intended.

An Intermediate Term

This term remains unclassified until the seriousness of a breach can be judged. If the benefit goes to the root of the contract, the relevant term will be classified as a condition.

19 Poussard v Spiers (1875) LR 1 QBD 410.
20 *Wills v Amber* [1954] 1 Lloyd's Rep 253.

In the case of the *Hong Kong Fir*,[21] a time charter was fixed on 26 December 1956 between the owners of the *Hong Kong Fir* and the defendant charterers, for period of 24 months from 13 February 1957. The Charterparty provided that the vessel was capable of steaming *12½ knots in good weather and smooth water* and:

1. *The Owners let, and the Charterers hire the Vessel for a period of 24 (Twenty-Four) calendar months (with one month more or less at Charterers' option), from the time (not a Sunday or a legal Holiday unless taken over) the Vessel is delivered and placed at the disposal of the Charterers ... she being in every way fitted for ordinary cargo service.*
3. *The Owners to provide and pay for all provisions and wages, for insurance of the Vessel, for all deck and engine-room stores and maintain her in a thoroughly efficient state in hull and machinery during service.*

Further, by Clause 13:

> *The Owners only to be responsible for delay in delivery of the Vessel or for delay during the currency of the Charter and for loss or damage to goods on board, if such delay or loss has been caused by want of due diligence on the part of the Owners or their Manager in making the Vessel seaworthy and fitted for the voyage or any other personal act or omission or default of the Owners or their Manager or their servants.*

While on a voyage from Liverpool to Osaka, from 13 February to 25 May 1957, the vessel was at sea for 8½ weeks and off hire, under repair (costing £21,400) for 5 weeks; at Osaka, 15 weeks (until 15 September), and repairs costing £37,500, were required to make her seaworthy.

The Charterers repudiated the contract on the grounds that the Owners were in breach of such condition as to entitle them to bring the contract to an end. The Owners then commenced proceedings on the grounds that the Charterers had wrongfully repudiated the contract, in that they had failed to meet the required standard of duty which led to the breach of the contract by reason of their fault.

The charterers counterclaimed under two particular heads:

(1) That shipowners were in breach of charter in that they failed;
  (a) To deliver seaworthy vessel;
  (b) To maintain her;
  (c) To deliver vessel capable of 12½ knots in good weather and smooth water.
(2) That shipowners failed to remedy breaches within a reasonable or a frustrating time.

The main issue was whether the undoubtedly serious unseaworthiness had had an effect sufficiently grave to entitle the charterers to repudiate.

21 *Hong Kong Fir Shipping v Kawasaki Kisen Kaisha* [1962] 2 QB 26.

On the facts, given that the charterer had had the substantial benefit of the contract for some 80 per cent of the time period, the Court held, that the breach was adequately remedied by damages; in other words, it was a mere warranty.

The *Hong Kong Fir* decision was met with some alarm in the shipping world because certainty is crucial, and lawyers rushed to perfect terms in charterparty agreements to create more certainty. The problem was the delay element; one must wait and see the effect of the breach, but the enormous costs involved in chartering mean that parties cannot afford the luxury of waiting and seeing and, thus, the industry demanded better service from the law.

This followed in the case of the *Mihalis Angelos*.[22] This case concerned the question of certainty in Readiness and Cancellation terms, which must be classified as Conditions. In this case, the owners fixed the charterparty, in which clause 1 contained an expected readiness clause for *about July 1, 1965*. There was also a cancelling clause if the vessel were not ready to load by 20 July. The owners had no reasonable grounds to expect the vessel to be ready to load on 1 July though, or indeed for the next two weeks. Eventually the ship could not have been ready for trading until 25 July. The Court held, that the expected readiness clause was a condition of the contract, the breach of which entitled the charterers to cancel on 17 July 17; further, that, even had that not been the case, the charterer would have been entitled to cancel under the cancellation clause, and the owners would have been entitled to nominal damages only.

More recently, the *Hong Kong Fir* case was confirmed in the Australian case of *Koompahtoo Land Council v Sanpine*,[23] which defined three senses of repudiation:

a) Conduct which evinces an unwillingness or an inability to render substantial performance of the contract;
b) Any breach of contract which justifies termination by the other party;
c) Termination by the party relying on the other party's default (which the majority said is a usage best avoided).

22 *Maredelanto Compania Naviera SA v Bergbau-Handel GmbH (The Mihalis Angelos)* [1970] 3 All E.R. 125.
23 *Koompahtoo Local Aboriginal Land Council v Sanpine Pty Ltd* [2007] HCA 71.

26 Contract – What Can Possibly Go Wrong?

Misrepresentation

A misrepresentation concerns a statement of fact (distinctly not an opinion) that is not true but persuades a party to enter into a contract, leading them to suffer damage. It can be made by an agent or employee on the part of their principal or employer; hence a Master can make a representation in a contract on behalf of the shipowner, which may in fact turn out to be a misrepresentation. This is an area of contract law in which the UK Government has implemented legislation with the Misrepresentation Act 1967, amending a much old statute, the Sale of Goods Act 1893.

There are three types of misrepresentation, namely innocent misrepresentation, negligent misrepresentation and fraudulent misrepresentation.

Innocent Misrepresentation

When the maker of the statement innocently gives false information, that is, it is not fraudulent or negligent, but the information induces the other party to enter into a contract, then there will be an innocent misrepresentation.

In this case, there are circumstances in which the Court can intervene in order to remedy the situation; this can be achieved by rescission and then putting the parties back into the position they would have been in, but for the misrepresentation, or else it can award damages in lieu of rescission, but it cannot do both.

Negligent Misrepresentation

If the statement is made carelessly or without reasonable grounds for believing it to be true, then this can constitute a negligent misrepresentation. The Claimant must prove that the statement was not true and in defending a claim, the party making the statement will have to prove that they believed the statement and demonstrate that this belief was reasonable.

The consequence of a negligent misrepresentation can lead to an Order for rescission of the contract, an equitable remedy (at the discretion of the Court) which allows a contractual party to cancel the contract; or the Claimant may seek damages in compensation for loss, even if that loss were not foreseeable.

DOI: 10.4324/9781003361916-26

Fraudulent Misrepresentation

Fraudulent misrepresentation is founded on a deliberate deceit practised upon the innocent party, and naturally is regarded as the most serious type of misrepresentation, which may attract a criminal consequence in addition to any civil case. In this case, the Claimant must establish that the untrue statement was made knowingly or recklessly, that they relied upon it and that it induced them to enter into the contract. Proof of loss and damage is naturally essential, although the losses do not have to be reasonably foreseeable.

Because of the seriousness of the allegation, the standard of proof is high, and the criminal element will require that the Court is satisfied beyond reasonable doubt that the person making the statement knew it was false or had no belief in its truth or was reckless as to whether it was true or false. The Claimant would also have to show that the Defendant intended that the Claimant to rely on the representation and that, had it not been for the fraud, the Claimant would not have entered into the contract.

If the court finds fraudulent misrepresentation, then it can order rescission of the contract and damages for any losses caused. More serious criminal charges may follow, depending on the assessment of the Defendant's guilty mind.

Fraudulent Misrepresentation: The Kyslant Case

The case of fraudulent misrepresentation against Lord Kylsant[1] was actually prosecuted as a criminal case, indeed it was one of the most notorious cases of the twentieth century; but it demands an understanding of the background in shipping, and the anatomy of fraudulent misrepresentation.

The Royal Mail Steam Packet Company was a British shipping company founded in 1839 by James MacQueen, and since 1902 had been managed by its Chairman Lord Kylsant, who had acquired many UK shipping companies to create a very substantial organisation indeed. In the years following the First World War, the White Star Line had been enjoying prosperity on the North Atlantic, with a higher average number of passengers than any competitor on the run to New York. JP Morgan's International Mercantile Marine, which owned the company, was deeply suspicious of the advantages that their British-flag ships lent to the combine, though, and had been planning to sell White Star for a number of years. Lord Kylsant stepped in and, in November 1926, announced that he had purchased the whole share capital of White Star. This made his group the largest shipping empire in the world, and White Star was to be the jewel in his crown.

On 10 November 1928, The *Vestris*, owned by Lamport + Holt, one of the companies in Kylsant's group, left New York bound for the River Plate with 128 passengers and 198 crew. She had not been made properly ready for sea, however, and, the next day, ran into a severe storm that flooded her boat deck and swept

1 *R v Kylsant and Another* (1931) 48 TLR 62.

away two of her lifeboats. Part of her cargo and bunker coal shifted, causing the ship to list to starboard and, at about 19.30 that evening, a heavy wave caused her to make a lurch further to starboard. The failure to make her seaworthy proved fatal and the ship took on water faster than her pumps could remove it. By next morning she was rapidly shipping water and was almost on her beam ends when the Master ordered a distress call to be sent, and with no hope of assistance he gave the order to abandon ship. With the ship listing to starboard and the weather battering her on her port side, he ordered the port lifeboats to be launched first; but the boats were still in their falls as the ship sank, killing 11 of the 128 passengers and 198 crew on board.

The publicity for the company proved disastrous, as shareholders took flight, and Lamport + Holt became insolvent. It then had a domino effect upon Royal Mail and the other companies in the Kylsant group, though, for the other constituents had cross-shareholdings with Lamport + Holt, which meant that their balance sheets were affected by the shares that they had lost and. The spark that lit the powder, however, followed a year later, this time in circumstances beyond Kylsant's control. On 24 October 1929, share prices took a tumble on the New York Stock Exchange and, five days later, they fell hard again. It was the beginning of the Wall Street Crash, and, instead of investing in companies such as Kylsant's, people drew out whatever money they had left.

On the face of it, Kylsant could have employed a phrase which is much vaunted by politicians today – that he had not done anything wrong. The process of cross-shareholding involved companies investing in others within the group, so that, when the profits of a company in one trade rose, the dividend could be enjoyed by the others; but with the loss of the *Vestris* and the Stock Market collapse, he resorted to subterfuge to calm a nervous market. He published a shareholder prospectus that conveyed the assurance that the company was making handsome profits, when, in fact, the process of cross-shareholding was concealing losses, and it was no sudden thing. In February 1931, the Government's accountant, William McLintock, investigating the group's finances, reported that that Royal Mail Steam Packet Company had liabilities in excess of £10,000,000, revealing the cross-trading process that for several years the Royal Mail Steam Packet group had been paying dividends to stockholders despite trading at a loss.

The Government now had a political headache, because the group had brought ruin to thousands of shareholders, who were demanding a head to hang. Accordingly, Lord Kylsant was arrested and charged with making false statements with regard to company accounts for 1926 and 1927, contrary to section 84 of the Larceny Act 1861. The company auditor, Harold Morland, was charged with aiding and abetting the same offences. Lord Kylsant was also charged with issuing a document (the prospectus issued for the 1928 debenture stock issue) with intent to deceive, contrary to section 84 of the Larceny Act 1861. Both defendants pleaded Not Guilty, and well they might, because the constituent requirements for the crimes were not met in the words in the prospectus, which were not actually false in themselves; it was up to the reader to form what impression they liked, and that was not a crime by the Defendants. But the People would not be denied.

The Trial at the Central Criminal Court took place in July 1931 and, inevitably, he was convicted and his subsequent appeal dismissed. He served ten months in Wormwood Scrubs prison before being released in August 1932.

Of course, his career was over but, far worse, the Royal Mail Steam Packet Company was financially ruined. A company so vast could not be allowed to fail, though and so much of Britain's shipping industry was involved that arrangements were made to guarantee the continuation of operations after it was liquidated. Consequently, Royal Mail Lines Limited was created in 1932 and took over the assets, concentrating on its traditional routes to the east coast of South America, the West Indies and Caribbean, and the Southampton–Lisbon–Brazil–Uruguay–Argentina route continued, restoring trust in the Royal Mail name and, in the words of one Argentinian correspondent, *The word of an Englishman.*

Fraudulent Misrepresentation in a Charterparty

In the case *of SK Shipping Europe Capital Maritime*[2] the charterer alleged that it was induced to enter into the charterparty by fraudulent misrepresentations made by the Owner as to the vessel's fuel consumption, and claimed rescission and/or damages. In the alternative, the charterer claimed that, if the charterparty claimed to be entitled to and did terminate the Charterparty by reason of the Owner's breaches of the Charterparty. The Court noted, in particular:

> *The Owner denied any misrepresentation 'entitling rescission of the Charterparty' or that it was in breach of the Charterparty. On the same date, it sent a further email with a proposal to adjust the rate of hire for the turbocharger incident. It said that it was going to try and obtain more performance data, suggesting that the parties meet once that data was available. In return, the Charterer repeated its allegations, including those of misrepresentation, in further emails of 30 July, 1 August and 11 August 2017, and reserved the right to rescind or terminate the VLCC charterparties. The first of these messages stated:*
>
> *The Vessels' actual consumption is so substantially different from that represented and guaranteed that no further analysis is required to evidence the fact of misrepresentation ... The fact is had the Vessels been truthfully described at the time of contracting, the Charterers would never have fixed them.*

For their part, the owners sought damages alleging the charterer's repudiatory breach, and that the Fifth Defendant guaranteed the Charterer's obligations and liabilities under the Charterparty. The court was asked to consider whether an offer of a speed and consumption warranty was a representation of the vessel's

2 *SK Shipping Europe Plc -v- (among others) (3) Capital VLCC 3 Corp and (5) Capital Maritime and Trading Corp* [2020] EWHC 3448 (Comm).

performance which induced charterers to enter into the charterparty. The judge made clear in this case that the mere offer of a speed and consumption warranty, and in particular of a continuing warranty, should not of itself be held to involve an implicit representation as to a vessel's current or recent performance.

The Court summarised the law relating to actionable misrepresentations as follows:

1 Evidence that the representation was made, namely:
   i) A representation as a statement of fact made by the representor to the representee on which the representee is intended and entitled to rely as a positive assertion that the fact is true;
   ii) Determining the construction of the statement in context, and interpreting the statement objectively according to the impact it might be expected to have on a reasonable representee in the position and with the known characteristics of those to whom the representation is being made;
   iii) A statement of opinion is not in itself actionable but is invariably regarded as incorporating an assertion that the maker does actually hold that opinion. Further, at least where the facts are not equally well known to both sides, a statement of opinion by one who knows the facts best may carry with it a further implication of fact, namely that the representor by expressing that opinion impliedly states that he believes that facts exist which reasonably justify it;
   iv) Silence by itself cannot found a claim in misrepresentation. But an express statement may impliedly represent something. In relation to implied representations the 'court has to consider what a reasonable person would have inferred was being implicitly represented by the representor's words and conduct in their context';
   v) In a deceit case it is also necessary that the representor should understand that he is making the implied representation and that it had the misleading sense alleged. A person cannot make a fraudulent statement unless he is aware that he is making that statement. To establish liability in deceit it is necessary 'to show that the representor intended his statement to be understood by the representee in the sense in which it was false.'

2 The representation must be false:
   A representation may be true without being entirely correct, provided that it is substantially correct and the difference between what is represented and what is actually correct would not have been likely to induce a reasonable person in the position of the claimant to enter into the contracts.

3 The statement must have been made fraudulently:
   i) One of the two mental states established in Derry v Peek (1889) 14 App Cas 337 must be established: the statement must have been made knowing it is untrue, or recklessly, not caring whether it is true or not.
   ii) The requirements for proving that a misrepresentation was made fraudulently must not be watered down into something akin to negligence, however gross. However, the unreasonableness of the grounds of the belief,

though not of itself supporting an action for deceit, will be evidence from which fraud may be inferred.

iii) Actionable fraud involves an intention on the part of the representor to induce the representee to act as he did. It is not necessary for the representor to intend to induce the specific action taken by the representee in reliance on the misrepresentation. It is only necessary that there should be an intention that the representation should be acted on.

iv) The standard of proof in a case of fraud is the balance of probabilities.

4 The representee must have relied on the misrepresentation:

The representee must show that he in fact understood the statement in the sense (so far as material) which the court ascribes to it, and that, having that understanding, he relied on it. The general principles applicable where a misrepresentation is said to have induced the making of a contract are set out in Chitty on Contracts (33rd) paras. 7-036 to 7-042. In this regard, it is important to keep two distinctions well in mind: the distinction between fraudulent and non-fraudulent misrepresentations; and the distinction between what the misrepresentee must establish in order to be in a position to rescind a contract for a pre-contractual misrepresentation and what must be shown in order to be able to recover damages for loss suffered as a result of entering into a contract.

Performance and the Standard of Duty

The Standard of Duty is the key feature which defines contractual performance. This is illustrated in the case of the Master's obligations. Consider, therefore, the relationship between the Master and the owner in Contract:

1 The Master is the Employee of the Owner (or in the case of a bareboat charter, an employee of the Charterer);
2 They are the Representative of the Owner;
3 They are the Agent of the Owner.

Of course, the Master's obligation extends beyond their contractual position, for they have responsibilities to the Flag state, as well as responsibilities in the law of negligence. The Master has a duty to take the standard of care, reasonably expected of such a professional in his position, to guard against acts or omissions which might cause loss or damage to persons and the breach of such duty of care which results in damage will give rise to a claim for damages. Thus, in terms of their employment, the Master is entitled to disobey instructions which may affect the navigation or safety of the vessel; once again the Master's absolute discretion will underline their standard of duty, as defined by SOLAS Chapter V Reg 34-1.

This further extends the perception in Current Law that contractual liability has evolved a close identity with the tort of negligence and the overlap between the standard of duty and the duty of care in negligence. The following questions give the foundation to the argument:

- Is liability for breach of contract strict, or is it based on fault in the sense of want of care, diligence or honesty?
- If it is fault-based, is that due to want of care, diligence or honesty – in which case, is Tort taking over?

The downstream consequence is the need to address the basis for a claim – if in Contract, its purpose is to restore the innocent party to the position in which they would have been in had the contract been performed as intended at the time it was made.

The question of performance must be determined by the seriousness of the breach, entitling the innocent party to treat the contract at an end; but, in its turn, the innocent party must demonstrate its determination of the contract, if it is to make a claim for damages that would put it back in the position it expected had the contract been performed.

The case of Suisse Atlantique

In the well-known case of Suisse Atlantique[3] a two-year time charter was fixed for the *General Guisan* to export coal from Europe to the United States, based on back-to-back voyages, for which the owners were to be paid an agreed freight rate according to the amount of cargo carried. If the laytime were exceeded, the charterers were to pay demurrage of $1,000 per day. Serious delays occurred because the charterers had difficulty both in getting cargo to the port, and in loading and unloading efficiently. Nevertheless, the shipowner did not cancel the contract, but allowed the charter to continue for the remainder of the two years. In all, only eight round trips were made, whereas the owners claimed that, without delays, a further six trips were feasible. The total demurrage payable amounted to only $150,000. The owners sued for damages, arguing that their claim should not be limited to the demurrage amount because the charterer's gross delays amounted to a fundamental breach of the contract, and claimed the additional sum in damages against the charterers alleging that, if loading and discharging had been completed within laytime, nine or six additional voyages would have been possible.

The House of Lords observed that since the charterparty did not prescribe a minimum number of voyages, there was no inherent breach by the charterers undertaking only 8 voyages rather than the 17 that the owners claimed were possible. Rather, if the delays meant that the charterer had exceeded laytime, then demurrage would be payable; and since the demurrage clause plainly showed that the parties had contemplated the possibility of delay, it followed that the delays did not amount to fundamental breach.

Perhaps fatally, though, the Owners had deliberately kept the contract alive by reminding the charterers of the demurrage provisions. Lord Wilberforce reasoned that the fact that the Plaintiffs allowed the Defendants to continue with voyages

3 *Suisse Atlantique v Rotterdamsche Kolen Centrale* [1967] 1 AC 361.

after several delays in loading at ports shows that this term was not so fundamental as to qualify for termination grounds.

Frustration

International marine operations naturally involve the risk assessment of hazards from weather, tides, and all manner of evils over which the shipowner has no control. It would therefore be iniquitous to require them to meet compensation in such circumstances. In this situation, it is relevant to consider the case of Target Holdings v Redferns[4] in which Lord Browne-Wilkinson said[5] that liability was *fault-based*. He was concerned not so much with the Standard of Duty but with the rule that the Defendant *was only liable for the consequences of the legal wrong*.

In this context, therefore, we must consider the consequence of a breach of the contractual duty:

I. Was the contractual obligation broken?
II. If so, was it the fault of the Defendant?

It is this two-part question which defines the landscape of the Standard of Duty, and asks the question, what if no fault attaches to non-performance?

It has been asserted that failure to perform is not a breach where a supervening event either discharges a contract under Frustration or provides a party with an excuse for non-performance. In fact, this is wrong; failure to perform remains a breach under these circumstances, but the defaulting party is not liable for the consequences of that breach if they are not at fault.

This, indeed, upholds the principle in English law that holds parties who have contracted to do something accountable even where subsequent events make performance challenging or expensive. Nevertheless, two exceptions can often be invoked, frustration and force majeure.

Frustration has been approached with extreme caution by the Courts, because, after all, it is axiomatic to the argument that one of the parties has broken their promise of performance, and contract law upholds the absolute nature of promises. However, since *Taylor v Caldwell*[6] a doctrine has evolved which mitigates the rigour of the Law's strict position when frustrating events occur which:

- Were not contemplated when the contract was made;
- Fundamentally change the contract;
- Are events for which neither party was responsible;
- Result in a situation to which neither party would have wished to be bound.

In such an event the 'doctrine of frustration' may mitigate the general rule and excuse the parties from further performance of their obligations.

4 *Target Holdings Ltd v Redferns* [1995] UKHL 10; [1996] AC 421.
5 At p. 432.
6 *Taylor v Caldwell* (1863) 3 B & S 826; 122 ER 309; [1863] EWHC QB J1

It is important to note that under English law force majeure only applies if there is a specific clause within a contract that provides for it, while frustration is a common law doctrine. There has been renewed interest on force majeure, in particular, because of the COVID-19 pandemic.

Force majeure clauses are routine provisions in marine contracts; although their defined terms may vary, the general principles must be defined:

1. The clause must define the event forecast, which must be outside either party's control. Typical examples of such force majeure events define them as weather, piracy, war and strikes and, as we have noted, COVID restrictions; if not defined the Court would have to divine what the parties intended.
2. It must be established that the frustrating event prevented, hindered or delayed the shipowner from discharging their performance obligations under the contract.
3. At the time when the frustrating event emerged, no reasonable steps were possible to avoid the consequences, and all reasonable efforts to mitigate the frustrating event were taken.

In the case of *Seadrill Ghana Operations v Tullow*[7] Teare J held that, *ultimately, the question of whether a force majeure event must be the sole cause of the failure to perform is one of construction of the clause itself.*

In this case, the clause required the event to be the sole effective cause. In fact, the event relied upon was not the sole effective cause of the defendant's inability to perform. Furthermore, the contract required the Defendant to use reasonable endeavours to circumvent the force majeure event, but had
failed to do so. Teare J concluded:

> *Tullow failed to discharge its obligation to use 'reasonable endeavours' to circumvent the force majeure event.*

The Quantum of Damages

Liability for breach of contract must be followed by the appropriate measure of damages, the Common Law remedy which is available as of right, with the purpose to put the innocent party back into the position in which they would have been, had the contract been performed. The principles for the award of damages were discussed by Baron Alderson in *Hadley v Baxendale*[8] thus:

> *Where two parties have made a contract which one of them has broken, the damages which the other party ought to receive in respect of such breach of contract should be such as may fairly and reasonably be considered*

7 *Seadrill Ghana Operations Limited v Tullow Ghana Limited* [2018] EWHC 1640 (Comm).
8 *Hadley v Baxendale* (1854) 9 Exch 341 as developed in the Heron II [1969] 1 AC 350

either arising naturally, that is, according to the usual course of things, from such breach of contract itself, or such as may reasonably be supposed to have been in the contemplation of both parties, at the time they made the contract, as the probable result of the breach of it. Now, if the special circumstances under which the contract was actually made were communicated by the plaintiffs to the defendants, and thus known to both parties, the damages resulting from the breach of such a contract, which they would reasonably contemplate, would be the amount of injury which would ordinarily follow from a breach of contract under these special circumstances so known and communicated. But, on the other hand, if these special circumstances were wholly unknown to the party breaking the contract, he, at the most, could only be supposed to have had in his contemplation the amount of injury which would arise generally, and in the great multitude of cases not affected by any special circumstances, from such a breach of contract.

The case of the *Golden Victory*

The case of the *Golden Victory* involved a VLCC, built in 1999 and capable of lifting 300,155 tonnes of crude. Her owners, Golden Strait Corporation, fixed a charter to Nippon Yusen Kubishka Kaisha for seven years, with the earliest date of redelivery of December 2005. The charterparty contained a war clause providing that the charterers should have the right to cancel the charter if war broke out between certain countries, including the US, UK and Iraq.

The charter commenced amidst the interesting times in which Iraq had found itself and the charterers redelivered the vessel on 17 December 2001. History has, of course, branded the redelivery as premature – the Iraq war did not commence for another 14 months. Indeed, in the following arbitration proceedings, it was accepted in evidence that, at the time of redelivery, neither party considered the risk of war with Iraq inevitable or even probable, but that it was merely *a possibility*. In any event, as a result the owners accepted redelivery as a repudiatory breach terminating the charter, which had a period of just less than four years to run and sought damages in compensation for the entire period outstanding. The charterers contended that if they had not repudiated, the war clause would have entitled them to cancel the charter on the outbreak of the war, and so the owners' claim for damages only ran for the 14 months between the date of termination and the start of the war, not the remaining 4-year period of the charter.

The arbitrator duly found as a fact that, at the time when the charterparty was terminated in December 2001, a reasonably well-informed person would have considered such a war as *merely a possibility* but not *inevitable* or even *probable*. He also found that, if the charter had still been running when the Iraq war began, the charterers would have cancelled it under the war clause. In his award he held that the charterers only had to pay damages for the 14-month period from termination to the beginning of the Iraq war based on the difference between the charter rate and the (lower) market rate.

The owners' appeals to the Commercial Court and thence to the Court of Appeal were dismissed. They then appealed to the House of Lords.[9]

All five Law Lords accepted that, as a general rule, damages for breach of contract are assessed based on what is known at the date of the breach, but that the court could depart from this rule where it judged it necessary to do so to compensate the victim properly. But they differed about whether the court was justified in departing from the general rule in the case of commercial contracts.

The majority, led by Lord Scott, held that the owners' right to damages stopped when war broke out. Lord Scott said that, if the damages were assessed based on what was known at the time of breach – rather than what was known at the time of assessment of damages – the owners would be overcompensated.

The minority, led by Lord Bingham, strongly affirmed the general rule of English law, that damages for breach of contract are assessed at the date of the breach. He observed that the charterers had not challenged this rule, but merely disputed its applicability in this instance. They had submitted that there was no need for the arbitrator to speculate about what might have happened when assessing damages, when what actually happened was known. In the minority Judgment, their Dissenting Lordships would have awarded damages for the entire four years. They said that contracts were made to be performed, not broken; that, on the date of termination, the owners became entitled to be compensated for the value of a charterparty with just under four years to run; that the charterers ought to have paid damages promptly following termination and they should not benefit from the delay; and that the idea that a party's accrued rights could be changed by subsequent events militated against certainty and predictability in commercial transactions.

This case was followed with somewhat indecent haste by the *Achilleas*. Her time charterers had agreed to redeliver the ship to the owners by 2 May 2004. On the preceding 21 April, the owners agreed to charter the vessel to new charterers for her next employment on terms that they could cancel the charterparty if the vessel were not available by 8 May.

By 5 May, though, it had become obvious that she would not be redelivered within the next three days, so the owners negotiated an extension of the new charterparty's cancelling date to 11 May. The problem was that, by then, the charter rates had fallen dramatically and they were forced to reduce the daily charter rate from $39,500 to $31,500 in exchange for the extension.

The owners claimed damages for loss of the original terms of the new charterparty at the difference between the original rate and the reduced rate, which resulted in a quantum of nearly $1,365,000. The charterers admitted breach of the charterparty, but contended that they only had to pay damages at the market rate for the six days the owners were deprived of the use of the vessel, that is, $158,301.

It was common ground that the owners' loss of the original terms of the new charterparty was caused by the charterers' breach and that, at the time the charterparty

9 *Golden Strait Corporation v Nippon Yusen Kubishka Kaisha (the Golden Victory)* [2007] UKHL 12, [2007] 2 AC 353; [2007] 2 Ll R 164.

was fixed, it was foreseeable that the late return of the vessel was likely to result in the type of loss which in fact occurred, namely, loss of the vessel's next employment. The principles defined in *Hadley v Baxendale*, therefore, would reasonably have entitled the owners of the Achilleas to claim the entire loss as the measure of damages to restore them to the position that would have been expected at the time when the contract was made. Indeed, this was the result in the arbitration, in the Commercial Court and in the Court of Appeal.

When the final appeal was heard in the House of Lords,[10] though, Lords Hoffman, Hope and Walker held that the foreseeability of the type of loss suffered was not the correct test. In Lord Hoffman's opinion, the question was not simply, what was a probable loss, but what the parties had in mind, or what was in their contemplation, regarding the nature of the business transaction. On the facts, the charterers could not be taken to have assumed responsibility for the loss of a following charterparty over whose timing, duration and hire rate they could have no knowledge or control and which, depending on market fluctuations, could result in an enormous claim for a minor breach.

Lord Rodger and Baroness Hale decided the case more narrowly:

> *it is important not to lose sight of the basic point that, in the absence of special knowledge, a party entering into a contract can only be supposed to contemplate the losses which are likely to result from the breach in question – in other words, those losses which will generally happen in the ordinary course of things if the breach occurs. Those are the losses for which the party in breach is held responsible – the stated rationale being that, other losses not having been in contemplation, the parties had no opportunity to provide for them.*

10 *Transfield Shipping Inc v Mercator Shipping Inc, the Achilleas* [2008] UKHL 48.

27 Agency

Introduction

As the era of deep-sea maritime trade was blooming in the nineteenth century, it became commercially essential that the investors be persuaded that their money was in safe hands – or at least, as safe as possible under the circumstances of all the risks that stalked the opportunities for profit. With no established communication, and few trustworthy businessmen in the far-flung loading ports where cargoes had to be negotiated, the venturers had to place their trust in somebody to protect their interests, and the Master was the most reliable man on the spot. If his ship were arrested, he had to secure her release. If supplies ran out or gear was lost or broken, he had to arrange for their replacement, and raise the necessary funds if need be.[1] Besides, the Master often had a financial stake in the adventure himself. Slowly, but with undeniable logic, the Master's contractual relationship was developing into partner, employee, and Agent.

This was a critical object-lesson in the evolution of the relationship between the Master and the Owners, which illustrates well the principles which define the modern law of Agency. While there seem to be as many examples of an Agent in maritime trades as there are tradespeople, the concept can be described simply as the relationship that exists between two persons when one, called the Agent, is considered in law to represent the other, called the Principal, in such a way as to be able to affect the Principal's legal position in respect of third parties by the making of contracts or the disposition of property. The ancient case of *Tweddle v Atkinson*[2] was not a marine action but, nevertheless, demonstrates the issue of Privity. The Claimant (known before 1999 as the Plaintiff) was the son of the late John Tweddle, who had arranged with the equally late William Guy that a marriage portion would be given to the Claimant as part of the marriage arrangement. Although he was the individual who was to be the beneficiary under the contractual arrangement, he was neither the offeror nor the offeree. The Court delivered the clear general principle that parties who have not personally closed the contract do not derive any rights from that agreement nor are they subject to any burdens imposed by it.

1 HCA 13/78, 24 Oct 1676.

2 *Tweddle v Atkinson* (1861)1 B & S 393; 121 ER 762.

DOI: 10.4324/9781003361916-27

The Concept

The birth of the law of Agency was essential in order to cure what would otherwise have been a fatal problem for contracts in maritime commerce; it is one of the corner-stones of English Law that the only parties who can sue on a contract are those who have made valuable commitments to each other in the bargain.[3] The commercial logic was articulated by Blackburn J in *Ireland v Livingston*,[4] in describing the process by which cargo is to be delivered by the seller to the buyer (more properly described for the purpose of this exercise as the consignee, because the obligation for the carriage of the goods must be discharged by the Carrier to the person entitled to receive them). Once the contract of sale is agreed, the seller raises an invoice to the consignee, containing the sale price, the premium for the cargo insurance and the freight, the contractual fee for the carriage by sea which must be paid upon delivery at the port of discharge. Although the seller is the party who has closed the contract with the Carrier, the benefit of the contract, therefore, goes to the consignee. By the same token, when the ship duly discharges the cargo it is the consignee who will have to pay the freight, in accordance with the contract with the Carrier; unless, of course, that cargo is not delivered, in which case the contractual obligation will not have been met to deliver the cargo and, so, the consideration under that contract, the freight, cannot *prima facie* be demanded against the consignee. If the non-delivery is in consequence of some breach of the contract for the carriage of goods for which the Carrier is held liable, then the consignee will recover the value of the cargo from the Carrier; if the Carrier is not liable, then the consignee will call upon the cargo insurance policy which the seller had arranged on the consignee's behalf, and who passed on the premium in his invoice. In substance, therefore, Justice Blackburn explained, the consignee enjoys the same rights and obligations as if he had been the original contracting party with the Carrier (and, indeed, the cargo insurer). By the same token, unless the seller expressly assumed some personal liability to the Carrier (who could then choose whom to sue), the seller would not enjoy any such rights and obligations.

The effect of the concept is that the Agent is an individual in whom his Principal could place his trust and so would not get him into trouble; or, indeed, would get him out of trouble as quickly as he had got into it. In the chapter on the Master-Owner relationship, we learned that, from the shipowner's perspective, this individual known as the Agent logically had to be the same one in whom he had placed his trust to bring the ship safely home: the Master. From the viewpoint of the Master, the critical feature is that, having closed a contract on behalf of the owner, he is not then personally liable to the third party on that contract. Only if the Master had not identified or named the owner as his Principal could the third party bring a claim against him – and even that would be an up-hill struggle, for the third party

3 While the Contracts (Rights of Third Parties) Act 1999 alleviated some of the unfairness in the general rule, maritime commerce had synthesised a solution generations earlier, with precedent leading up to the Carriage of Goods by Sea Act 1992.

4 *Ireland v Livingston* (1872) *LR 5 395*.

could very easily make enquiries with the Flag State register as to the correct title of the Principal[5].

The Agent's Duties in Law

Primarily, the parties have the same rights and obligations to each other as any other contracting parties. Hence, the Agent will be liable for failing to carry out their Principal's instructions and represent their interests, in the circumstance in which the Principal has little or no control over how the Agent actually manages their affairs. This can be summarised in twelve, fundamental requirements:

1 The Duty to Perform the Promised Task

The contract is a voluntary one, in which both parties are aware of their obligations at the time when the offer was accepted and the contract closed. Consequently, the Agent must perform their duty precisely as the agreement requires, accomplishing the promised task, subject only to facts of frustration or *force majeure.*

2 The Duty to Meet All the Contractual Obligations

This takes us one step further than the duty to perform the promised task, and obliges the parties to comply with all the terms expressed in the contract, as well as the obligations imposed by statute.

In addition, the Commercial Agents (Council Directive) Regulations 1993 govern the relationship between an Agent and their Principal when goods are being sold. Patently, therefore, this does not apply to the Master or port Agent, but to a self-employed intermediary who has a continuing authority to negotiate the sale or purchase of goods on behalf of the Principal.

3 The Duty Not to Deny the Principal's Title

Naturally, the Agent has all the executive powers over the Principal's property that their authority permits in the contract, which may be very extensive indeed. As a result, the Agent must not exceed those powers, which demands that they can do whatever the contract permits, except to hold themselves out as owners of the Principal's property. This may involve binding the Principal in some third party agreement that transfers the Principal's title to the property to the third party, or indeed raising money or collateral benefit by offering the Principal's property as security. The ship manager may well convey to the world at large that they have all executive authority over the vessel, which might imply to third parties that they have the power to sell her or raise money by way of a mortgage on her, but as they are not the registered owner with the vessel as an asset in their balance sheet, they

5 See *Knight Frank LLP v Aston Du Haney*: CA (Civ Div): 12 April 2011 (currently unreported).

would be in breach of the agency agreement and, indeed, would be committing a fraudulent misrepresentation.

4 The Principal's Best Interests

The Agent's primary duty is to act in the best interests of their Principal. If the Agent is the Master, or a port Agent, the Principal will likely be the shipowner. Thus, where an Agent is appointed to facilitate or negotiate a transaction on behalf of the Principal, the Agent owes a duty to the Principal to act in the Principal's best interests within the authority of their appointment.

In practice, this is likely to be defined in the contract between the Principal and the Agent, with terms expressed as conditions that the Agent has a duty to act in the best interests of the Principal, demanding that the Agent uses due diligence and skill to negotiate terms of a transaction on behalf of their Principal with a third party to the greatest advantage of their Principal in the circumstances.

5 No Conflict of Interest

An Agent has consciously committed to the relationship with the Principal and, therefore, should not thereafter accept appointment to act for another Principal if the interests of the first conflict with those of the second. The exception arises if the Agent fully discloses to each Principal the Agent's interests under the two appointments and the fact that they act for both Principals at the same time, receiving the clear consent of each Principal to the dual agency with evidence that would stand scrutiny in Court.

The Agent's duty to avoid a conflict of interest applies equally to cases where the personal interests of the Agent conflict – or even *potentially* conflict – with their duties to the Principal. In default of full disclosure to the Principal, the Agent will be in breach of their duty of trust to the Principal and, thus, liable to account for any profit that the Agent has made from such transaction, and other remedies may be available in the shape of an injunction or damages arising out of the breach of duty.

6 No Secret Profit

The Agent owes a Common Law duty to the Principal not to make any profit or acquire any benefit in the course and in the matter of his agency without the knowledge and consent of his Principal. An Agent who has made a secret profit is liable to account to the Principal for such profit in addition to other remedies that the Court may order. However, the Agent may satisfy this duty if they make full disclosure of all the relevant facts to the Principal and the Principal consents to the making and retention of such profit by the Agent.

In such circumstances, a port Agent may obtain a benefit through their position as Agent for the shipowner; having been appointed to oversee the provision of goods or services for the shipowner in some distant port, they may obtain secret monetary or other benefit from the supplier for placing purchase orders with the supplier. Moreover, an Agent who, without lawful authority or reasonable excuse, solicits or accepts any advantage in relation to his Principal's affairs or business in the course of their agency shall be guilty of an offence under the Bribery Act 2010.

7 Use of Information or Knowledge

An Agent who acquires information or knowledge which they have been employed by the Principal to collect or discover, or which they have otherwise acquired for the use of their Principal should not make use of the same for their personal gain. The obvious example is where the Agent has been made aware of confidential commercial information about the shipowner, such as freight rates; they must not disclose such information or, indeed, allow any advantage to a competitor who could benefit, for example, by offering lower freight rates. It would generally be applicable in circumstances in which the Agent receives some benefit or reward for disclosure of the information, which, again, would amount to a secret profit.

8 Duty of Confidentiality

The Agent is automatically placed in a fiduciary relationship with the Principal, in other words, a position of trust is created which demands that the Agent in good faith on their behalf and respects the position of confidence in which they find themselves. This goes a step further with the use of information and knowledge, insofar as the Agent must not disclose any information concerning the Principal or any confidential information entrusted to them to any third party in the absence of the Principal's consent.

Such confidential information may be described as any information which is not readily available to the public, and thus may be quite broad. As such, for the benefit of certainty, express provision should be made for this in the agency agreement defining the information what constitutes a trade secret and what other information is to be included.

This obligation persists even after the agency relationship has ended, compelling the Agent to continue to keep confidential any information concerning the Principal or any confidential information entrusted to them by the Principal, unless the Principal consents to disclosure or unless the information has ceased to be confidential.

This duty is modified by the Principal's instructions; thus the Principal may instruct the Agent to disclose information of any defined sort, such as information to port authorities or instructions and advice between a lawyer and the Agent acting on the Principal's behalf.

9 Duty to Use Care and Skill

The Agent must meet the standard of duty in discharging their duties with due care and skill, in accordance with the normal rules of liability in negligence, subject to the higher duty demanded of the Agent in their profession, trade or calling. This demands performance with the degree of care and skill expected of a reasonable, average member of the relevant profession, trade or calling meets the requisite standard.

10 Duty to Account to the Principal

An Agent who receives any money or property from or on behalf of their Principal is bound to keep it separate from their own and hold it as a trustee, not a beneficiary. In this way, the Agent should keep clear and open accounts which are designated as separate from the interests of the Agent, and render such accounts to the Principal on demand.

Again, this duty will subsist even after the agency has finished. At that termination of the relationship, the Agent must return to the Principal all accounts of monies had and received, all documents and property originally given to the Agent by the Principal and documents prepared by the Agent on the instruction and at the expense of the Principal.

11 Duty Not to Delegate

The agency agreement constitutes a personal contract for services; thus, the Agent is not permitted to delegate their authority or duty under the agreement to any third party, in whole or in part, except with the authority and consent of the Principal. As a result, the Agent has normally no implied authority to employ deputies or sub-Agents to carry out their duties.

If the agreement permits the Agent to delegate to a third party, that sub-Agent will not have contractual privity with the Principal, and thus the Principal will not be bound to any contractual duties closed with the sub-Agent. In turn, if the Principal suffers loss and damage as a result of the acts or omissions of the sub-Agent, they will be entitled to sue the Agent on the main contract, and enforce judgment against the Agent. How the Agent seeks to pursue the sub-Agent is not a matter which will trouble the Principal.

12 Duty of Obedience

It is a fundamental rule of Common Law that the Agent has a duty to obey the lawful and reasonable instructions of the Principal under the agreement. Where the Principal's instructions are clear, the Agent does not normally have any discretion and must follow those instructions, unless an Agent is a professional person regulated by some authority, and the Principal relies on the Agent to exercise their professional skill and discretion in accomplishing the performance of their duties.

By the same token, if the Principal's instructions are ambiguous or if the Agent is not certain as to their meanings, the Agent should clarify such instructions with the Principal before acting.

Examples of Maritime Agencies

The Master

We have devoted a chapter to the Master-Owner relationship, defining the very purpose and effect of agency, committing the Owner in contract, although not themselves risking liability in the agreement. The Master may be held accountable to a third party in *negligence* if they break a duty of care to that third party who suffers damage as a reasonably foreseeable consequence, notwithstanding any contractual terms agreed between the Owner and the third party,[6] but a Master acting with the usual authority of their disclosed Principal, the Owner, will not be liable to the third party in a *contract*. As the humble Agent, they may have endorsed the contract but liability rests on the Principal for whom they acted – or, rather, on the Principal whom the third party believed they were getting bound into a contract with, so ably demonstrated in the case of the *Starsin*.[7] The Master's contractual liability will be limited to that owed to the Owner and defined according to the express or implied terms of their employment.[8]

The Case of the *Starsin*

In 1995, while the *Starsin* was on time charter to Continental Pacific Shipping Limited (CPS), bills of lading on CPS' liner form were issued for the carriage of 17 parcels of timber and plywood. The carriage was between ports in Malaysia and Antwerp/Avonmouth; but the cargoes were damaged. Receivers sued the owners for breach of contract, or alternatively in tort in the event that the bills of lading were charterers' bills. The Court of Appeal defined the central issues:

1. Whether the Owners or Charterers were the Carriers under the bills of lading;
2. What, if any, protection the Himalaya clause in the bills of lading affords the Owners;
3. Depending on the answer to 2, the question may arise whether the Owners can be sued in tort.

The issue was whether the bills of lading were charterers' or owners' bills. The terms of each of the 17 bills reveal inconsistent provisions. CPS were the charterers. The signature box on the face or front of a specimen Bill of Lading prominently carried a signature *As Agent for Continental Pacific Shipping (The Carrier)*. The face of the Bill of Lading contained essential commercial provisions such as the identity of the shippers, the name of the vessel and a description of the cargo, as well as a reference to the contract of carriage, the latter being set out in the box commencing with the word *Shipped*. Clause 1(c) is consistent with what appears on the face of the Bill of Lading: it provides that the *Carrier* is *the party on whose*

6 As so dramatically demonstrated in *Adler v. Dickson* [1954] 3 WLR 696, precipitating the Himalaya Clause in the contract for the carriage of goods by sea, the effect of which still holds well today subject to the provisions of the Unfair Contract terms Act 1977.

7 *Owners of cargo lately laden on board the ship or vessel 'starsin' and others v Owners and/or demise charterers of the ship or vessel 'starsin'; Homburg Houtimport BV v Agrosin Private Ltd HL* [2003] UKHL 12 [2003] 2 WLR 711, [2004] 1 AC 715, [2003] 1 CLC 921, 2003 AMC 913, [2003] 1 Lloyd's Rep 571, [2003] 1 All ER (Comm) 625, [2003] 2 All ER 785, [2003] 1 LLR 571. See above.

8 See *Lister v Romford Ice and Cold Storage Co Ltd* [1956] AC 555.

behalf this Bill of Lading has been signed. So far the document is in harmony; but tucked away in barely legible, tiny print on the back of the Bill of Lading are two clauses which contradict the contractual position revealed by the face of the bill. Clause 33 provides that the contract evidenced by the Bill of Lading was *between the merchant and the owner of the vessel named herein (or substitute)*. Clause 35, a demise clause, provides that the Bill of Lading shall only take effect as a contract of carriage *with the owners or demise charterers.*

The Judge embarked on a rhetorical question worthy of Cicero:

> *How is the problem to be addressed? For my part there is only one principled answer. It must be approached objectively in the way in which a reasonable person, versed in the shipping trade, would read the bill. The reasonable expectations of such a person must be decisive. In my view he would give greater weight to words specially chosen, such as the words which appear above the signature, rather than standard form printed conditions. Moreover, I have no doubt that in any event he would, as between provisions on the face of the bill and those on the reverse side of the bill, give predominant effect to those on the face of the bill. Given the speed at which international trade is transacted, there is little time for examining the impact of barely legible printed conditions at the time of the issue of the Bill of Lading. In order to find out who the Carrier is it makes business common sense for a shipper to turn to the face of the bill, and in particular to the signature box, rather than clauses at the bottom of column two of the reverse side of the bill.*

Taking advantage of their knowledge of the way in which the market works, two commercial judges – Colman J and Rix LJ in the Court of Appeal – adopted the mercantile view. The majority in the Court of Appeal, however – Morritt V-C and Chadwick LJ – in effect gave preponderant effect to the standard template, or boilerplate clauses, on the back of the Bill of Lading. These may have stood the test of time in litigation on their definition, but, realistically, commercial integrity that comes with good faith is promoted by giving greater effect to the front of the Bill of Lading, on which commercial parties focus, rather than the small print on the back. The signature which they see is that of the Master, acting as Agent for whomever is stated on the face of the bill, be that the shipowner or the charterer.

Statutory Provision

The relationship between the Master and owner found its way into statute law, notably following ratification of the Hague Rules 1924, which evolved into the Hague-Visby Rules, adopted by the United Kingdom in the Carriage of Goods By Sea Act 1971. The Hague-Visby Rules provide inter alia that the Carrier shall be bound before and at the beginning of the voyage to exercise due diligence to make the ship seaworthy and properly man, equip and supply her.[9] It is the Master's personal duty

9 Article III(1).

to ensure that the vessel is in all respects safe to proceed to sea, which includes the above requirements – thus, as the Master exercises their absolute discretion in deciding to proceed to sea, they patently make an agency decision which will render the owner accountable to the cargo-owner for any damage. Such issues as seaworthiness are well-defined by Hague-Visby and, therefore, stand as compelling authority for defining a vessel's condition, when interpreting the criminal implications of section 98 Merchant Shipping Act 1995, which renders the Master and the owner criminally liable if a ship in a UK port, or a UK-registered ship in any other port, is dangerously unsafe. Section 94 defines 'dangerously unsafe' in the context of being unfit to go to sea without serious danger to human life because of the condition, or the unsuitability of the ship, her machinery or equipment, or if she is undermanned, overloaded or unsafely loaded, or 'any other matter relevant to the safety of the ship.'

Section 98 provides that, if the owner has passed management control over safety matters either directly, by a charterparty or management agreement, or indirectly, under a series of charterparties or management agreements, then the charterer or manager shall simply stand in the owner's place. In all such cases, the Master retains responsibility for ship safety and, indeed, guards still their unfettered discretion as to whether to proceed to sea; in addition to the provisions of the 1995 Act, the risk under current law raises its head if the Master's act or omission amounts to criminal negligence. As a result, the Master-owner relationship potentially imperils the owner or manager, unless they can mitigate their position by distancing themselves from the Master. In the law of Agency, that presents a remote possibility, unless the Master acted without apparent or ostensible authority.

The potential for criminal accountability takes the Agency relationship further, and can be identified in the Bribery Act 2010, which came into force in 2011. Section 1 creates an offence where a person offers, promises or gives a financial or other advantage to another person, in order to induce a person to perform improperly a relevant function or activity, or to reward a person for the improper performance of such a function or activity. Such a function or activity would include any function of a public nature, any activity connected with a business, any activity performed in the course of a person's employment, or any activity performed by or on behalf of the company. However the Master is described, therefore – as Agent, representative or employee – they will be defined within the Act. For better or for worse, inducements to officials in many parts of the world have long been accepted as an occupational hazard of maritime operations, and the close relationship between the Master and the owner conveys a dangerous picture to the shore-based management operation.

That relationship would be a hard one to deny, given the practical reasons so graphically illustrated by the Master's rôle, and the evolution of Statute Law has created undercurrents in strategic planning that have driven risk management decisions and, whether intentionally or not, are perceived to have eroded the Master-owner relationship.

In fact, the Master may also enter into a relationship as Agent for the cargo owner. The Master, as the Carrier's representative, is the bailee of the cargo, and as such is responsible for the proper care and delivery in good condition of the goods. Any relationship in law demands the consent of both parties, but as bailee the Master may be confronted with a risk assessment which demands that some decision is made over the cargo that may risk loss or damage in part in order to save the whole, in circumstances in which the cargo owner may not have received the intelligence of the situation to give any consent. Even though they have not appointed the Master as such, the Master will necessarily be an Agent of necessity in such circumstances. By extension of the analogy, the Master may be described as an Agent of necessity for all the stakeholders in a marine adventure when resorting to a general average act, in which the extraordinary sacrifice or expenditure is voluntarily and reasonably made or incurred by the Master in time of peril for the purpose of preserving the property imperilled in the common adventure.

Ship Management

Ship Managers act as Agents for shipowners, in precisely the way summarised above. Ship Managers often carry out a wide range of services in relation to various functions in marine operations management and, as such, it is important that the parameters of the relationship are expressly defined in the agency agreement.

Accordingly, standard form agreements contain boilerplate terms identifying the manager and the owner separately and stating that the manager carries out services as Agents for and on behalf of the owner. This confers a consequent benefit on the manager, who is thus protected from claims brought by third parties, for the Agent has no liability in cases in which the Principal is disclosed to the third party. Indeed, under standard form agreements the terms are well tried and tested, and the manager is only liable if the loss is caused by their negligence or wilful default. In this situation, the manager is able to limit their liability to a risk computed according to their management fee, provided that the loss has not resulted from the manager's personal act or omission committed with the intent to cause such loss and with recklessness as to whether such loss would occur.

That being said, the manager may have an insurable interest in the vessel and, therefore, may be entitled to insurance protection over her. In any event, they would certainly be entitled to professional indemnity insurance against risks involved in her management.

The Port Agent

The Port Agent is generally the ship's sole Agent at the particular port and, therefore, stands in the shoes of the owner or operator, with the apparent or ostensible authority to do whatever business the owner or operator has in that port or determined area.

The Port Agent thus undertakes to act as the owner's representative in consideration of a fee defined in the agreement. The agreement will define the Agent's authority, either in express terms or in a generic phrase describing the usual operations incident to the carrying out of shipping trade; in any event, they will be accountable to the Master, who is the owner's representative or Agent on the spot.

The range of services will thus include the following authority:

- To deal with Port State officials and the port authority;
- To make all arrangements for the vessel;
- To accept statements incident to the arrival, stay and departure of the vessel;
- To conclude in the name of the owner or operator, contracts of carriage, contracts of marine insurance and contracts of cargo handling;
- To issue bills of lading;
- To receive and to pay all amounts incident to the call of the vessel at the port and to the carriage of cargo or of passengers;
- To pursue, in the name of the owner or operator, claims arising from contracts of carriage and marine accidents.

Shipbroking

A shipbroker is an Agent who acts as an intermediary or negotiator between shipowners and charterers, or between buyers and sellers of vessels. Some brokerage firms have developed into large companies, incorporating departments specialising in shipping's various sectors. The physical shipping markets are not regulated by central government authorities but, since the nineteenth century, the Baltic Exchange in London has set out a Code of Conduct which defines market standards. The Baltic Code provides guidance to shipbrokers and their Principals on ethical conduct in the physical freight and freight derivatives markets, and plays an important role by providing guidance and acting as a reference point.

It is worthwhile clarifying the work of the two broad types of shipbrokers.

13 Sale and Purchase Brokers

These Agents manage the sale and purchase of existing vessels in the second-hand market or newbuildings, as their Principals, the owning company, may require. They will consider the various factors:

- Financial management priorities;
- Market sales;
- Vessel values;
- Market trends and activity.

Shipbrokers are experts on the shipping market and global maritime economy; shipowners will rely on their advice, which will be framed in the context of the maritime economic cycle, and the law of supply and demand which drives the cycle. The resultant strengths and weaknesses impact on freight rates because they are determined by the interaction of supply and demand: an increase in the availability of deadweight tonnage will lower freight rates if not accompanied by increased demand by charterers, and an increase in demand will raise freight rates unless accompanied by increased availability of tonnage. With the shipbroker's advice, the owner has a sporting chance of achieving a bottom line in profit and loss which provides earnings levels over, or at least not below, the operating costs.

In order to deliver the best advice, the broker will scour the market for buyers, or for suitable sales candidates, and negotiate the main points of the sale transaction: price, survey and delivery.

The sale of a ship is one of the few contracts which must be evidenced in writing, which needs the professional involvement of a lawyer acting for each side, and the shipbroker will liaise with their client's solicitor – but always as the owner's Agent.

14 Dry Cargo Brokers

These Agents are specialists in the chartering of bulk Carriers, and are appointed by the Principal shipowner who either is looking for employment for a ship, or a charterer with a cargo to be shipped. Dry cargo brokers maintain large databases of vessel positions, cargoes and rates, paying constant attention to the direction of the markets so as to advise their clients accurately as to how to maximise profits or minimise expenses. Their expertise also enables them to negotiate key terms such as freight, laytime and demurrage.

Each size of vessel suits different types of cargo and trade routes, but dry cargo brokers must also consider versatility in maximising performance with minimum time costs; so, for example, they will favour the open hatch bulk Carrier, designed to offer direct access to the hold through hatches which extend the full width of the vessel. As a result, large cargo units can be lowered into place. Such vessels are versatile, able to load cargoes such as forest products but also heavy units are easier to handle than in a conventional bulk Carrier; but open hatch ships are more expensive, because there is extra steel necessary to widen the hatches and give structural strength, and the freight rate must, ultimately, deliver a profit margin that makes the purchase and operating costs worthwhile. The broker must balance all these matters in their advice, which demands a broad range of knowledge and daily intelligence reports.

15 Tanker Broking

Like dry cargo brokers, these Agents specialise in negotiating charterparties with terms including positioning, lay-time, freight and demurrage, but they require different skillsets to dry cargo brokers, demanding different knowledge and applied data. They may specialise in crude oil, gas, oil products or chemical tankers, and the nature of the commodity demands particular skills in forecasting supply and demand.

Tanker chartering involves challenges that the broker must confront, not the least being that the values of the cargoes are significantly higher than those in most other trades, and must take into account foreign exchange rates, interest rates, commodity prices and equity prices. Tanker owners are exposed to fluctuations in all kinds of financial prices, as a natural by-product of their operations, and the effect of changes in these prices on reported earnings can be overwhelming. As a result, the tanker broker must be able to manage their instructions with exceptional skill and, often, an appetite for risk; once again, there is a heavy dependence on daily intelligence reports, in an industry which is notorious for its cut-throat competition.

28 Charterparties

The Organisation of Charter Shipping

A charterparty is mere jargon for a contract between the charterer and the ship-owner. Like any other contract, it is an agreement made by the exchange of commercial promises – managed by terms – and recognised as a legal obligation. It does not even have to be in writing; few sorts of contracts do, essentially those which are defined under statute law.

The parties are free thus to make their own bargain and the terms of the contract must be decided by the parties to the contract. But once the bargain has been struck, the law is resolute and unyielding in the absolute nature of the standard to which the parties will be held. In the quintessential case on frustration,[1] Blackburn J held,

> *There seems no doubt that, where there is a positive contract to do a thing not in itself unlawful, the contractor must perform it or pay damages for not doing it, although, in consequence of unforeseen accident, the performance of his contract has become unexpectedly burdensome, or even impossible.*

That being said, in the case of a charterparty for the carriage of goods by sea, the statutory limitation rules will introduce terms into the agreement whether the parties like it or not; so, for example, in UK law, the Hague-Visby Rules have been incorporated into the Carriage of Goods by Sea Act 1971, which define the Carrier's duties, out of which they cannot contract, as well as important defences in the international carriage of goods by sea. Article X of the Hague-Visby Rules states that they will apply to every Bill of Lading if:

- The Bill of Lading is issued in a contracting state;
- The carriage is from a port in a contracting state;
- The contract contained in or evidenced by the Bill of Lading provides that these Rules, or legislation of any State giving effect to them, are to govern the contract.

The carriage of cargoes represents the most common instance of charterparties, in which the cargo Owner hires the ship from her Owner, either for a certain length

1 *Taylor v Caldwell* [1863] EWHC J1 (QB); (1863) 3 B & S 826, 122 ER 309 (6 May 1863).

DOI: 10.4324/9781003361916-28

of time – when it is called a time charter – or for a certain voyage, when it is called a voyage charter. It plays an essential part in international sale contracts, standing alongside the contract for the sale of the cargo, in which the agreed terms of delivery are defined, but that is a matter between the buyer and seller to which the Carrier is not a party, thus the rights and obligations in loading and delivery must be defined in the charterparty. It is such a fundamental issue, that standard terms have been devised for incorporation into sale contracts, which have stood the test of time. Of these, some of the most frequently used are:

Free On Board (abbreviated to FOB)

This term means that the seller delivers when the goods cross the ship's rail at the named port of loading; as a result of which the buyer must fix the charter and will be responsible for all costs and risks to the goods from that point. All that the seller does after delivery to the port is to clear the goods for export.

Cost and Freight (CFR)

Under this option, the seller delivers when the goods cross the ship's rail in the port of shipment, and must clear goods for export; it is the seller who must fix the charter and pay the costs of carriage and freight in order to bring the goods to the named port of discharge; but then the risk of loss or damage, as well as any additional costs due to events occurring after the time of delivery, are all transferred from the seller to buyer, so the buyer must arrange insurance.

Cost, Insurance, Freight (CIF)

The seller delivers when the goods cross the ship's rail in the port of shipment, and the seller must clear the goods for export. Again, it is the seller who fixes the charter and must pay the cost and freight necessary to bring the goods to the named port of discharge; but the seller must take out a policy of insurance for the cargo and assign the benefit to the buyer, covering the risk of loss and damage between loading and discharge.

It is essential to understand that the charterparty evidences the hire of the ship, it is not intended to be a contract for the carriage of goods by sea; those terms will be contained in the Bill of Lading, subject to the statutory limitation provisions, to be found in the Hague-Visby Rules, introduced into English law by the Carriage of Goods by Sea Act 1971.

Clearly, the cargo Owner is concerned merely with the safe delivery of the cargo in accordance with the contract of sale, subject to their obligations under the statutory limitation rules:

- To pay the freight;
- To pack the goods sufficiently for the journey;
- To describe the goods honestly and accurately;

- Not to ship dangerous cargoes (unless agreed with the Carrier);
- To have the goods ready for shipment once the Carrier gives notice of readiness to load the cargo.

The charterparty evidences the hire of the whole ship, generally either for a single voyage to deliver the cargoes sold by the trader, or for a period of time if the cargoes traded exceed the deadweight tonnage limited by a single voyage. The Carrier supplies the vessel, crew and bunkers, and the charterer will be responsible to the Carrier for the due release of the ship, without damage, at the end of the charter in accordance with the charterparty terms. Thus, the charterparty serves the sale of bulk cargoes, which, indeed, account for a vast percentage of global maritime trade. While a charterer can make choices on the deadweight tonnage of a ship that suits them best, if they have no wish to fill the ship with their own cargo, they can agree with the Owner to sub-charter space – but the charterer will still remain responsible for meeting all the obligations in the charterparty.

The charterer may want to fix a charter with the Owner for other purposes, not least being to satisfy a demand for tonnage in the fleet. In this way the concept is used to transfer possession (although not Ownership) to another shipowner. This will often be to take advantage of an emerging market, when the charterer is short of tonnage. An example of how this can work in the complicated business of shipping can be found in the charter of the *Saxon Star*.

Columbus California had been completed in 1976 for Hamburg Südamerikanische Dampfschifffahrts-Gesellschaft and, in 1983 was chartered by Blue Star Line who renamed her *Saxon Star*, in what appears to have been a series of back-to-back voyage charters to meet Blue Star's commitment to the BHLR consortium with three other UK companies, Houlder Brothers, Lamport + Holt and Royal Mail Line, running between Europe and South America. Clearly, however, Hamburg Süd had a deeper interest, because at the same time they also chartered her sister *Monte Sarmiento* to Royal Mail, who renamed her *Avon*, on the same service sailing out of Southampton, and they were both returned to Hamburg Süd in 1986, when the four members of BHLR joined Hamburg Süd and six other European operators in a new consortium on the same run.

As an aside, to complete the picture of these fixtures in the complex business of shipping, at this time Lamport + Holt was owned by the Vestey group which owned the Blue Star Line, while Royal Mail was acquired by Furness Withy, who also owned Houlder Brothers; Furness Withy, in turn, had been taken over by C Y Tung of Hong Kong in 1975. Then, in 1990, the Tung group sold Furness Withy to Rudolf Oetker who controlled Hamburg Süd. In November 2017, the Oetker group sold Hamburg Süd to Maersk Line. Meanwhile, Blue Star was bought by P&O Nedlloyd in 1998, who in turn were bought by Maersk in 2005.

The Bareboat Charter

A frequent option that may attract lower charter rates in return for more flexibility in operation than that afforded in a voyage or time charter, is to fix a bareboat (or demise) charter. It is an option which follows the circumstances presented by maritime trade at any given time, suiting both the Owner and the charterer. In most cases of marine operations, the ship is a depreciating asset, whose newbuild value therefore must depreciate over her trading life. As a result, a straightforward accounting practice gives her a depreciation rate as an asset over a given time (a general cargo ship will have an anticipated trading life of 20 years), so she must earn a profit stream which meets her asset value at any given time. The alternatives to operating her demand making more profitable use of the asset value by bareboat chartering for a rate irrespective of her trading profit, which will be balanced against the options in global trading of selling the asset, either to another company for further trading or to a breaker for scrap. In this way, an investor may buy a ship at a time when asset values are running high in the balance sheet, and bareboat charter her to an operator who identifies a strong profit margin in her operation, for the charter rate will not involves sharing the freight earned, but will be a simple premium agreed at the time the contract is made. The charterer then insures the ship and manages all the costs, including any liabilities. In fact, the only thing that the charterer cannot do is claim that the ship is actually theirs.

The charterer is in a position similar to that of a leaseholder, and risk forfeiture if they fail to comply with the terms of the bareboat charter. Equally, the bareboat charterer can exercise all the rights of the Owner except that which compromises the Owner's title to her. So the duties and rights of the Owner are performed and maintained by the charterer; the Master signs Bills of Lading as the charterer's agent, and the Owner cannot interfere in the management of the vessel in any way, unless the terms of the charterparty permit them to do so. The real contention arrives when the charterer defaults on their obligations, leaving the Owner with no option but to seek to mitigate their loss and recover the vessel, with what compensation that they can obtain.

The Case of the *Jotunheim*

The case of the *Jotunheim*[2] illustrates the risks involved. The Claimant Owners chartered the *Jotunheim* to the Defendants under a bareboat charter for forty-eight months, at the end of which Ownership would transfer to the Defendants; this is a common practice in bareboat chartering, equating to a hire purchase agreement. On expiry of the charter, provided that the charterers had fulfilled their obligations, payment of the last month's hire instalment was to constitute the final part of the purchase price, so the vessel would then belong to the charterers, subject to a specific term:

> *It is hereby agreed between seller and buyers that in case of buyers' default for non-payment of hire monies due to Owner or non-performance of any of*

2 *More OG Romsdal Fylkesbatar AS v The Demised Charterers of the Ship Jotunheim* [2005] 1 Ll R 181.

the agreed terms within the realm of this agreement the vessel will return back to the sellers free of all expense incurred, if any ... Should buyers default seller will not be obliged to pay back any money paid down during the bareboat period. If the hire paid down during the bareboat period does not cover the sellers' losses, they shall be entitled to claim further compensation for their losses and for all expenses.

The vessel was delivered in December 2003 but problems soon arose over payment of the hire. The first and second month's payments were made five days late. The first was short by 17 cents, the second by $41.17. The Owner complained and asked for the shortfall to be made up by the February payment; but twice in February they chased for payment by fax, on the second occasion threatening that, unless hire was paid that day, they would take the vessel back. The charterer, however, could only promise payment *next week*. Upon subsequent default of payment, the Owner's brokers informed the charterer by fax on 24 February that the Owner proposed to withdraw from the charter, which they did later that day. The February payment was, nevertheless, made on 26 February (short by $142.67) and a further payment was made on 2 March of $88.50.

The default, therefore, was not severe, but the Owner argued that, under the clause above, they were entitled to the immediate return of the vessel on the charterer's default, without notice. In the alternative, if notice were required, it was given by fax on the 24 February.

The demise charterers argued, among other things, that they should be entitled to relief from forfeiture. Such relief is not available when the Owner exercises a right of withdrawal under a time charter because a time charter is a contract for services; it does not transfer any right to possession and is not a contract susceptible to an order for specific performance. But the same did not apply to this bareboat charter, under which the demise charterers had been given contractual and possessory rights in the vessel and had the right to have Ownership transferred to them at the end of the charter period.

A great deal, therefore, turned on the issue of the relief from forfeiture. In the 1973 case of *Shiloh Spinners Limited v Harding*[3] the House of Lords identified situations in which the court could grant relief from forfeiture, which included where it was possible to state that the object of the transaction and the inclusion of the right to forfeit were essentially to secure the payment of monies. The charterers argued that this situation fell into the first category, and that the purpose of including the right to withdraw was to secure the hire payments and the deposits.

The Court had to take into account such things as the conduct of the defaulting party, the gravity of the breach and the disparity between the value of the property and the damage caused by the breach. In this case, the conduct of the demise charterers had been poor, demonstrating bad faith in deliberately flouting

3 *Shiloh Spinners Limited v Harding* [1973] AC 69.

their obligations to pay on time and pay in full despite protests from the Owners. The Court determined that, although the shortfalls were small, they demonstrated a cavalier disregard for the strict obligations of the contract. This was not a case in which a significant part of the charter period had passed, but showed that the charterers were unsatisfactory payers. Although the direct effects of late payment and underpayment were small, it was the attitude that underlay it that gave cause for concern. The Judge duly found that this was one of those cases where granting relief from forfeiture was not appropriate.

The organisation of charter shipping is completed with a picture of how the charterparty works within the process of international trade.

The pattern of trade is illustrated simply in the case of a trader in a bulk commodity:

- The Trader, A, follows the markets and global current affairs to establish the point at which they can buy the parcel at the lowest price and sell it to a buyer at the highest price. This may take place even before the commodity has been extracted or harvested;
- The Buyer, B, identifies the demand for the commodity which dictates the price at which they can sell it;
- The User, C, will source the cheapest supply, which B hopes will be them;
- But the cargo has got to get from the port of loading to the port of discharge. This will be expressed in the sale contract as a contractual term, defining who charters, and how. In this way, the charterparty terms are fixed.

This will likely be concluded as soon as the price is right in the sale of the commodity, so the charterparty is often closed well in advance of the time fixed for loading, when the vessel will likely be on the high seas or at the port of loading or discharge in performance of her current charter obligations.

The ordinary form of charterparty will therefore define the terms of the Carrier's performance, which can be examined in chronological order.

Critical Charterparty Terms

1 The Carrier's Obligations as to Seaworthiness

In a charterparty for the carriage of goods by sea, the Carrier must comply with the statutory limitation rules, even if they are absent from the charterparty. Article III of the Hague-Visby Rules provides:

> *The Carrier shall be bound before and at the beginning of the voyage to exercise due diligence to:*
>
> (a) *Make the ship seaworthy;*
> (b) *Properly man, equip and supply the ship;*
> (c) *Make the holds, refrigerating and cool chambers, and all other parts of the ship in which goods are carried, fit and safe for their reception, carriage and preservation.*

The application of the Hague-Visby Rules forms a topic which is discussed throughout this book, but for the benefit of this chapter may be summarised by Lord Hamblen in the recent case of the CMA *CGM Libra*:[4]

> *The Carrier cannot escape from its responsibilities under article III rule 1 of the Hague Rules by delegating them to its servants or agents qua navigators, or qua managers, or qua engineers or qua ship repairers. If the task of making the vessel seaworthy has been entrusted by the Carrier to those servants or agents then (if relevant) they are acting qua Carriers and under article III rule 1 of the Hague Rules the Carrier is responsible for any causative failure by them to exercise due diligence.*

Lord Hamblen's conclusion is worth quoting for its summary of the Carrier's duty under the charterparty:

> *The Carrier's obligation under the Hague Rules is not subject to a category-based distinction between a vessel's quality of seaworthiness or navigability and the crew's act of navigating. The crew's failure to navigate the ship safely is capable of constituting a lack of due diligence by the Carrier. It makes no difference that the delegated task of making the vessel seaworthy involves navigation. In particular:*
>
> (i) *On the proper interpretation of the Hague Rules, the article IV rule 2 exception of act, neglect or default in the navigation or management of the vessel cannot be relied upon in relation to a causative breach of the Carrier's obligation to exercise due diligence to make the vessel seaworthy;*
> (ii) *If the vessel is unseaworthy, it makes no difference whether negligent navigation or management is the cause of the unseaworthiness or is itself the unseaworthiness;*
> (iii) *The concept of unseaworthiness is not subject to an attribute threshold requiring there to be an attribute of the vessel which threatens the safety of the vessel or her cargo;*
> (iv) *Save for exceptional cases at the boundaries of seaworthiness, the well-established prudent Owner test, namely whether a prudent Owner would have required the relevant defect to be made good before sending the vessel to sea had he known of it, is an appropriate test of seaworthiness, well suited to adapt to differing and changing standards;*
> (v) *The fact that a defect is remediable may mean that a vessel is not unseaworthy. This is likely to depend on whether it would reasonably be expected to be put right before any danger to vessel or cargo arose;*

4 *Alize 1954 and another v Allianz Elementar Versicherungs AG and others* [2021] UKSC 51 On appeal from: [2020] EWCA Civ 293.

(vi) *Given the 'essential importance' of passage planning for the 'safety ... of navigation,' applying the prudent Owner test, a vessel is likely to be unseaworthy if she begins her voyage without a passage plan or if she does so with a defective passage plan which endangers the safety of the vessel;*

(vii) *The fact that the defective passage plan involves neglect or default in 'the navigation of the ship' within the Article IV rule 2(a) exception is no defence to a claim for loss or damage caused by unseaworthiness;*

(viii) *The obligation on the Carrier to exercise due diligence to make the vessel seaworthy requires that due diligence be exercised in the work of making the vessel seaworthy, regardless of who is engaged to carry out that task;*

(ix) *The Carrier may not be liable for lack of due diligence which occurs before he has responsibility for the vessel or for lack of due diligence which occurs before he has responsibility for the cargo. The Carrier may nevertheless be liable if the defect or danger would be reasonably discoverable by the exercise of due diligence once the vessel or cargo has come within his control;*

(x) *The Carrier is liable for a failure to exercise due diligence by the master and deck officers of his vessel in the preparation of a passage plan for the vessel's voyage. The fact that navigation is the responsibility of the master and involves the exercise by the master and deck officers of their specialist skill and judgment makes no difference;*

(xi) *The Carrier's seaworthiness obligation in relation to passage planning is not limited to providing a proper system for such planning.*

2 The Preliminary Voyage

This is also known as the positioning voyage, when the vessel will be sent to the port of loading.

The charterer must calculate the date at which the vessel will reach her loading port so that the cargo is prepared in time, because time for loading will start once the Master has delivered the Notice of Readiness. For this reason, statements on the position of the vessel at the time of chartering are Conditions – in other words, they go to the root of the contract, and are so fundamental to the contract that their breach gives rise to the right to repudiate and claim damages. In the same way, the shipowner is obliged to prosecute the preliminary voyage with due or reasonable despatch.

Given that the charterparty will be fixed in advance, sometimes well in advance, the risks and uncertainties that can arise in the simple process of the voyage make it difficult to predict precisely when the ship will arrive at the nominated loading port, particularly when she is still committed to completing an earlier charter at that moment. Consequently, the Carrier is reluctant to agree a contractual date that they might not be able to keep, so most voyage charters will impose no absolute contractual obligation to do so. The charterer may be placed in an impossible position as a result of delay, however, for the trader will have sold the cargo to the buyer, who may well have already sold it to the end-user, and fluctuations in commodity rates may risk the profitability of the deal. Alternatively, the charterer may have sub-chartered space in the ship to another trader, with equally worrying consequences on them.

If the ship does not arrive in time for the due loading date, the charterer must be notified, and will need to know as early as possible whether to make alternative arrangements.

Naturally, the risk cannot be eliminated, but it can be managed by terms in the contract. Accordingly, the Carrier will address a provision in the contract for *expected readiness to load*, as well as agreeing to proceed to the port of loading with *due diligence* or *due despatch.*

In addition, the charterparty will incorporate a clause under which gives the charterer the right to terminate the charterparty for anticipated late arrival; this is the cancellation clause, containing a provision for the Cancelling Date, the latest date for the charterer to exercise the option.

3 The Cancelling Date

The purpose of a cancelling clause in a voyage or time charterparty is to fix a definite date by which, if the Carrier fails to deliver the vessel to the charterer, the charterer is entitled to wait no longer for the vessel to be delivered. The consequence of its breach, therefore, makes it a term in the law of contract.

Notwithstanding the Carrier's obligation to complete the preliminary voyage with due despatch, if they *anticipate* that, despite the exercise of due diligence, the ship will not be ready to load by the Cancelling Date, they must notify the charterer without delay stating the expected date of the vessel's readiness to load and asking whether the charterers will exercise their option of cancelling the charterparty, or agree to a new Cancelling Date. That being said, the condition is usually hedged with limitation clauses that protect the Carrier from an action for damages for delay. Thus, the charterer can exercise their contractual right to cancel, but this does not give them the right to treat the Owner as in repudiatory breach and claim damages, unless they can establish that the Carrier has breached some other fundamental condition, giving rise to loss.

Once the Cancelling Date has matured, the charterer may exercise his right to cancel if the ship is not ready; but if she is not then at the load port, the charterer probably need not cancel immediately, according to a case that was reported in 1910[5] but still holds good law. In the absence of express provision, the charterer will usually be entitled to wait until the ship has arrived before making his decision. Once the ship has arrived at the loading port, however, the charterer must generally exercise their right of cancellation promptly, since they are then under an obligation to load the cargo once Notice of Readiness has been given.

4 Nomination of Loading Port

The charterparty evidences the hire of the ship, thus it is for the charterer to nominate the ports of loading and discharge. In fact, given the uncertainty of the cargo's

5 *Moel Tryvan v Andrew Weir* [1910] 2KB 844.

destination at the time of loading (a cargo can be sold and re-sold any number of times during a voyage), the charterparty may give the charterer the option to name a port, or instruct the Carrier to proceed to a geographical range of ports. Naturally, the option must be exercised within a reasonable time, which is stipulated in the contract. If the charterer fails to give the orders within the contractual period, this would entitle the Carrier to repudiate the contract, although if the cargo is already in board, the complexities arising out of this can be imagined.

5 Safe Port

Some ports are notoriously dangerous to shipping under certain conditions of weather and season, therefore the Owner protects his vessel with a provision contained as a warranty, for example, that:

> *The Vessel shall be employed in lawful trades within Institute Warranty Limits (IWL) ... between safe ports or safe places where she can safely enter, lie always afloat, and depart.*[6]

The key issue is that this term is a warranty; its breach is not so fundamental that it brings the contract to an end, but damage arising from the breach will entitle the Carrier to compensation.

The case of *The Stork*[7] addressed the safe port warranty within the context of contract law, giving useful guidance that where, in breach of a charterparty, the charterer orders a vessel to proceed to an unsafe port, the conduct of her Master in obeying the order will be judged sympathetically, in context and will not lightly be treated as unreasonable. In this case, the vessel was instructed by the voyage charterers to load a cargo of logs in Newfoundland in winter. The loading place was unsheltered, however, which placed risks on the charterer, who was obliged under the contract to load at safe berths or loading places. The vessel dragged her anchors in a heavy wind and the Master took the decision to sail the vessel out of danger. He was unsuccessful, however and the vessel was driven onto a shoal of rocks. Devlin J found on the facts that a loading place where a vessel could be blown off her moorings was unsafe, and found that the Master's decision was not unreasonable and did therefore not constitute a novus actus interveniens, stating that *There must be an obligation to nominate at least one loading place, and there must be implicit in that some condition about safety to prevent the making of a derisory nomination.*

The definition of a safe port was addressed in the famous case of the *Eastern City*,[8] which followed just three years later, when the finding *obiter* of Sellers LJ held has become a mantra:

6 Gentime warranty.

7 *Compania Naviera Maropan S/A v Bowater's Pulp and Paper Mills Limited (The Stork): CA 1954* [1955] 2 QB 68, [1954] 2 Lloyds Rep 397, [1955] 2 All ER 241 [1955] 2 WLR 998.

8 *The Eastern City, Leeds Shipping Company Ltd v Societe Francaise Bunge* [1958] 2 Lloyd's Rep 127.

A port will not be safe unless, in the relevant period of time, the particular ship can reach it, use it and return from it without, in the absence of some abnormal occurrence, being exposed to danger which cannot be avoided by good navigation and seamanship.

The case of *The Stork* clearly addressed the issue of the Master's navigation, in which there was no element of negligence. Where a ship is ordered to an unsafe port and the Master acts negligently in entering or remaining in the port, this will present an intervening act in causation which will free the charterer liability for breaching the safe port warranty. The emphasis is on the Master's duty of care: only if the negligence is sufficiently serious to sever the causal connection between the order and the damage to the vessel, will the charterer be excused from liability.

The Case of the *Star B*

The case of the *Star B*[9] illustrates this point well. Slebent Shipping, the Owners, fixed the *Star B* under a time charter dated 27 October 1999 to Associated Transport Line, as charterers. While operating under this charterparty in late November 1999, the vessel performed a voyage with timber and general cargo from Brazil for discharge in San Juan, Puerto Rico, Rio Haina (Dominican Republic) and Kingston, Jamaica. As a result of congestion at Rio Haina, the charterers ordered the vessel to discharge her Rio Haina cargo at the nearby port of Boca Chica. While attempting to enter the channel to Boca Chica, under pilotage (for which the Owners remained liable in civil proceedings), the vessel ran aground and was not refloated until the following day. Thereafter, she entered the port, discharged her cargo and departed without further incident.

Slebent Shipping claimed that the grounding had caused substantial damage to the vessel's hull, stern tube and controllable pitch propeller and accordingly brought arbitration proceedings against the charterers, on the basis that the latter, in ordering the vessel to Boca Chica, were in breach of the safe port warranty contained in the charterparty. The case was referred to arbitration, to be held under the jurisdiction of English law, although for the convenience of the parties it was held in New York.

The tribunal unanimously found that there was evidence to support the Owners' contention that at Boca Chica, there were deficiencies in the entrance buoys, the range markers, the charts, the navigation guides and with the pilot sufficient to render the port unsafe at the time in question. On the other hand, the tribunal found that there was also sufficient evidence to support the charterers' argument that the grounding could have been averted by the exercise of good seamanship.

9 *Slebent Shipping Company Ltd v Associated Transport Line LLC, the Star B Award of the Society of Maritime Arbitrators of New York 19 November 2003.*

A majority of the panel found that *the actions of the master on the passage [to Boca Chica] and in attempting to enter Boca Chica on that date were so egregiously negligent and unseamanlike that they overcame any safe port deficiencies and led directly to the vessel's grounding.* In consequence, the majority denied the Owners' claim.

The noun 'majority' should not be lost here: Mr. Arnold dissented on the grounds that it failed to reflect that a contributing cause of the grounding was a breach of the charterparty warranty of a safe port, preferring the rule under United States law that liability should be apportioned between the parties, given that the safe port warranty had been broken. This, however, would present insurmountable difficulties coming into conflict with the Master's absolute discretion; nobody can overrule their professional judgment for safe navigation, but in consequence negligent navigation must break the chain of causation arising out of a breach of the safe port warranty.

6 Notice of Readiness

It necessarily follows that the vessel must be fit to load as soon as the Master tenders Notice of Readiness. The crew must therefore have cleaned the holds (and in the case of a reefer cargo, cooled them) to the satisfaction of a cargo surveyor. Consequently, this term in the charterparty requires that, on arrival at the port of loading, the vessel's holds shall be clean and in all respects ready to receive the intended cargo, failing which the vessel will be off-hire from the time of rejection until she is deemed ready.

There are three requirements to be met in order to tender a valid Notice of Readiness:

- The vessel must have reached the agreed place;
- The vessel must be physically ready;
- The vessel must be legally ready.

In order for the vessel to be an arrived ship, having reached the port of loading, the Notice of Readiness must be tendered when the ship has arrived, either in the port or at the berth depending on the charterparty term. The obligation is a severe one, for she must be ready in all respects to load the whole cargo. This includes not just clean holds but also all equipment required for the cargo operations, including hatches, cargo gear and equipment. It does not mean that hatches must be open (a serious failing for a reefer cargo in hot weather) but does mean that the vessel must be ready and able to load without delay whenever the charterer gives the order. It also means that the ship has cleared customs on entry, that she has met immigration and police approval, and complied with Port State health pratique.

In summary, the Notice of Readiness is confirmation that the vessel is ready in all respects to receive her cargo, triggering the time for loading, and a resultant claim for demurrage if such time overruns. As a result, a great deal hinges upon it.

The Case of the *Posidon*

The case of the *Posidon*[10] involved a voyage charter to load a cargo of carbon black feedstock at Galveston and Houston in the US Gulf, for delivery to Singapore and Thailand, via Port Elizabeth. The vessel's previous cargo had been a cargo of crude oil from Indonesia, which was discharged at Norco, Louisiana, on the Mississippi River. The charterparty contained a clause which provided:

> *It is understood that vessel's last cargo is Low Sulphur Waxy Residue, and the ship will tender at load port with all tanks ... well drained and stripped free of any liquid and pumpable cargo residues ... Cargo tanks to be cleaned to the satisfaction of Charterers' independent inspector, bearing in mind the above.*

This cargo is notoriously difficult to clean out of the tanks, as it has to be heated to be discharged and some will always remain on board beneath the vessel's heating coils. The Carrier did what they could but it took 22 days to clean and load the vessel's tanks at Galveston. The Master grew increasingly anxious about the time for cleaning and ended the operation early for fear of missing the Cancelling Date in the charterparty. As a result, 2,436 barrels of unpumpable residues remained in the tanks.

While the ship was still at Norco, the charterers telexed the Owners declaring that the condition of the vessel's tanks was *far from acceptable* and requested that they be cleaned with very hot water under pressure. The Owners instructed the Master to comply with these instructions during the voyage from Norco to Galveston. On arrival at Galveston, the Owners gave Notice of Readiness to load under Tauber's charterparty, saying that the unpumpable residues had been reduced to about 900 barrels and that, given the specific terms of the in the charterparty, the vessel met the agreed condition of readiness. However, Tauber's surveyors at Galveston found the tanks *far from ready to load* and, at the charterers' request, the ship continued cleaning efforts with fresh water, but without satisfactory results. Tauber then took charge of the cleaning operations, at first employing sub-contractors, but their efforts proved ineffective, and the charterers had to try to remove the rest with buckets and manual labour. After ten days of futile effort, the sub-contractors' operation was terminated and the charterers opted for a new method, by washing the tanks with heated carbon black as a solvent. This worked well, however, and readiness was finally approved, allowing loading to start that day. The vessel then moved to Houston for the completion of loading and sailed on her overseas voyage, which was completed without incident.

The Owners claimed that they had met the charterparty clauses and, on arrival at Galveston, the vessel's tanks were well drained and stripped free of any liquid and

10 *Giant Shipping Ltd as Owners of MT Posidon v Tauber Oil Company* New York Society of Maritime Arbitrators 8 April 2002.

pumpable cargo residues, as required by the charterparty. Any additional cleaning that had been carried out on the charterers' express instructions. They duly claimed $625,957 for demurrage; Tauber promptly counterclaimed for $971,492 for the extra cleaning costs incurred at Galveston, as a result of the Master's termination of the stripping operation too soon at Norco, allowing 2,436 barrels of the former cargo to remain on board.

A majority of the Arbitrators found that the Owners' demurrage claim failed, as they did not present a ship ready to load upon arrival at Galveston, since, at that point, the vessel's tanks were not *well drained and stripped free of any liquid and pumpable cargo residues ... They were not suitable for loading carbon black feedstock*. It was not until the charterers took the decision to flush out the residues with heated carbon black that adequate cleaning was effected, and the majority held that laytime was delayed and that the Owners' demurrage claim was accordingly reduced to $259,481.

The Arbitrators held, that the Owners were obliged to take all reasonable measures to ensure that the tanks were well drained and stripped, even if they met the charterparty description of being *free of any liquid and pumpable residues*. As a consequence, when the ship arrived at her loading port with an excessive amount of cargo remaining on board, she was not in a condition to give a valid notice of readiness and laytime could only commence once loading began.

The Arbitrators' award also held against the charterers, however, because, once they had assumed responsibility for the further tank cleaning operations, they were responsible for the consequences of engaging incompetent contractors. By so doing, they failed to mitigate their damages arising from the Owners' breach of contract in tendering the vessel for loading in a discrepant condition. As a consequence, the charterers could not recover the amounts they had paid the contractors and the Owners were entitled to damages for detention for the time the contractors spent in their fruitless efforts to clean the ship's tanks.

7 Loading

The charterer is obliged to provide the cargo within the definitions and exceptions containing in the charterparty. This generally will mean that the cargo must be delivered to the ship's rail, in the apparent order and condition stated precisely on the face of the Bill of Lading.

The charterparty usually provides for the option as to whether the vessel's own handling gear is to be used. If the charterer refuses to load, the Carrier may treat this as a repudiatory breach of contract, or they can simply await the expiry of the time allowed for loading in the charterparty. The only potential problem with this is that, if they wait, some frustrating event may intervene to terminate the contract automatically, and the Carrier will be left with no redress against the charterer.

Time Taken for Loading

Time is invariably an important factor in modern shipping. Freight rates can fluctuate, and overheads incurred while a ship is in port gnaw away at the Owner's profits in a voyage charter (not, of course, in a time charter). Provision for adjustment of revenue is made through clauses providing for:

8 Laytime

This defines the period which the charterer can use for loading and discharge. The lay-days begin to run against the charterer as soon as the ship arrives and gives the charterer Notice of Readiness.

A perennial problem with loading concerns congestion in the port delaying loading, even though it is no fault of either Carrier or charterer. A solution which mitigates the risk involves a provision clarifying whether the charterparty is to be a berth of port charterparty:

1. In a berth charterparty, provision is made for the ship to proceed to a named berth or quay in the port where she will receive or discharge the cargo. As soon as the ship arrives at the berth and gives notice of readiness, the lay-days start running against the charterer who must start loading or discharging straight away;
2. A port charterparty merely provides that the ship proceed to a named port, where a suitable loading-spot will be allocated and agreed when one is made available. The contractual effect is that the duty to start loading or discharging starts after laytime has started (on arrival).

If the contractual laytime period expires before loading or discharge is complete, then the charterer is liable to pay the Owner demurrage. The question then arises, as to who must bear the cost of waiting time. In a berth charterparty, it is the shipowner, as lay-time only starts when she comes alongside. In a port charterparty, the situation is more complicated, for the allocated berth may be occupied on the vessel's arrival, but the Master is entitled to give Notice of Readiness, and laytime or demurrage shall then count as if she were in berth and in all respects ready for loading. In *Oldendorff v Trade Export*,[11] Lord Reid held, that before a ship can be said to have arrived at a port she must, if she cannot proceed immediately to a berth, have reached a position where she is at the immediate and effective disposition of the charterer. If she is at a place where waiting ships usually lie, she will be in such a position unless in some extraordinary circumstances proof of which would lie in the charterer.

In the absence of an express provision, there is an implied term that a charterparty may be held to include an indemnity requiring the charterer to indemnify the Owner against the consequences of complying with the charterer's orders, although this does not cover reasonably foreseeable risks in trading operations that the Carrier accepted at the time that the charterparty was fixed. In the case of *Action Navigation v Bottiglieri Navigation*,[12] the Court held, that the risk of hull fouling

11 *S L Oldendorff & Co GmbH v Trade Export S A* [1974] AC 479.
12 *Action Navigation Inc v Bottigliere Di Navigazione SPA (The Kitsa)* [2005] 1 Ll R 432.

arising from the vessel's stay in a warm water port was such a risk and that the Owners were, therefore, not entitled to an indemnity from the charterers in respect of cleaning costs.

9 Demurrage

This constitutes the compensation which the charterer must pay to the Owner for the lost time, outside the period of lay-days defined in the charterparty, during which the ship is going nowhere but the crew still has to be paid and port dues met, while the ship cannot undertake another charter.

It is fundamentally important that demurrage is defined in terms of liquidated damages, representing a genuine pre-estimate of the Owner's loss. Any element of profit on top of this, would amount to a penalty in law, and penalties are not recoverable, meaning that the shipowner could not recover anything at all.

The Case of the *Paragon*

In the case of *The Paragon*,[13] the Owners time-chartered their vessel to the Charterers on terms that they would hire the vessel *from the time of delivery, for about minimum 3 to about 5 months (about means +/- 15 days)*. The vessel was delivered on 29 November 2006. Allowing for the plus 15 days' margin, the last possible day for lawful redelivery was 14 May 2007. The last voyage under the charter took 77 days, with the vessel being redelivered on 20 May 2007, which was 6.166 days beyond the final terminal date.

The Charterers paid hire at the charter rate for the duration of the charter up until the last redelivery date on 14 May 2007 and at the market rate for the 6.166 days the vessel was overdue. The Owners also claimed hire based on the market rate for 30 days before the latest date for redelivery in reliance on clause 101 of the charter, which stated:

> *The Charterers hereby undertake the obligation/responsibility to make thorough investigations and every arrangement in order to ensure that the last voyage of this Charter will in no way exceed the maximum period under this Charter Party. If, however, Charterers fail to comply with this obligation and the last voyage will exceed the maximum period, should the market rise above the Charter Party rate in the meantime, it is hereby agreed that the charter hire will be adjusted to reflect the prevailing market level from the 30th day prior to the maximum period [d]ate until actual redelivery of the vessel to the Owners.*

At this time, hire rates were rising, so the additional claim was at a market rate of $46,083.82 per day, as opposed to the charter rate of $29,500 per day. On this

13 *Lansat Shipping Co Ltd v Glencore Grain BV, The Paragon* [2009] EWHC 551.

basis, the Owners claimed $471,603.32 over and above what the Charterers had already paid.

In this case, the clause which provided for the hire rate for the final 30 days of the time charter period to be increased to the higher prevailing market rate upon late redelivery of the vessel beyond the final terminal date of the charter period, amounted to a penalty and was consequently unenforceable under English law, as the clause's primary purpose was to act as a deterrent to late redelivery by the charterers and not as a genuine pre-estimate of damage resulting from the breach of contract. The critical factor is that, if the Court finds that the sum is not a genuine pre-estimate but a penalty, such a sum will not be enforceable; but, of course, the Court has no power to step into the parties' shoes and re-define the bargain to settle what would be a genuine pre-estimate.

The Case of the *Eternal Bliss* and its Consequences

More recently, the Court of Appeal overturned a Judgment in the Commercial Court of the High Court and ruled that, unless otherwise provided in the charter-party, demurrage at the agreed rate is the only remedy available to an Owner in the event of losses arising from a voyage charterer's failure to complete loading or discharging of cargo within the permitted lay-time. In the case of the *Eternal Bliss*,[14] the vessel loaded a cargo of soybeans from Brazil to China, the charterparty providing that, in the event that lay-time was exceeded, demurrage was to be paid at a daily rate. On arrival at the discharge port, the vessel waited at the anchorage for 31 days due to port congestion and a lack of warehouse space ashore. On discharge, and due to the delay, the condition of the cargo was found to have deteriorated. The consignee of the cargo pursued a claim against the Owner for losses arising from the damaged cargo. Given the law, for reasons which are not entirely clear, the Owner settled the consignee's claim and sought to recover the amount incurred from the charterer in arbitration, as damages for failure to complete discharge within the laytime permitted under the charterparty. The charterer refused to pay such damages, arguing that demurrage was the only remedy to which the Owner was entitled in the event of discharge time exceeding the permitted laytime.

The case ended up in the Court of Appeal, where Males LJ held, that demurrage *liquidates the whole of the damages arising from a charterer's breach of charter in failing to complete cargo operations within the laytime and not merely some of them. Accordingly, if a shipowner seeks to recover damages in addition to demurrage arising from delay, it must prove a breach of a separate obligation.*

Taking the Court's decision a stage further, what are the Owner's rights if the period of actual loading or discharge has gone so far beyond the laytime that the Owner cannot be expected to be content with his right to demurrage, but ought to be allowed to order his vessel away in order to meet a more profitable bargain?

14 *K Line Pte Limited v Priminds Shipping (HK) Co Limited (The Eternal Bliss)* [2021] EWCA Civ 1712.

In this situation, the contract must necessarily be described as at an end, because it has ended up as having an entirely different character to that which the parties had contemplated when they fixed the charterparty. In these circumstances the Owner is not bound to accept the liquidated damages fixed in the demurrage clause, because there is no longer a contract to which the liquidated damages clause can be attached. In effect, the Owner is claiming damages, bringing all the clauses in the contract to an end by reason of the charterer's breach. In order to do this, though, it is necessary for the Owner to transmit to the charterer notice of termination by reason of the charterer's repudiatory breach. If they do not do so, the charterparty will run on and the Owner will only be able to recover the quantum agreed for demurrage.

This had been the decision in the case of *Suisse Atlantique*[15] in 1967, and clearly remains the case still. In December 1956, the Owners chartered their vessel to the charterers for two years to carry coal from the USA to Europe on consecutive voyages. The charterers agreed to load and discharge at specified rates, any extension of time being paid for at the rate of $1,000 per day. By September 1957, there had been such a massive delay as to entitle the Owners to repudiate the contract, but in October they agreed to let the charter run on. The charterers then made another eight round voyages. In the end, the Owners, who had suffered damage in excess of the agreed demurrage, claimed their entire loss. The Court held, that the Owner's claim must fail, and the charterers need only pay $1,000 demurrage for each day lost. Had the Owners repudiated the charter in 1957, as they were entitled to do, they would have terminated the contract – which obviously included the demurrage clause – and could have recovered all the damages suffered according to the normal rules of contract.

15 *Suisse Atlantique v Rotterdamsche Kolen Centrale* [1967] 1 AC 361.

29 The Bill of Lading

The Roman Empire depended heavily on maritime trade, which was a much more efficient way of importing grain from Egypt, the absolute staple for maintaining a quiet population, and the alternative transport by land was unacceptable (beyond a certain distance, approximately 25 mils, oxen and horses eat more grain than they can carry). As a result, maritime trade developed exponentially with the prosperity of Rome; and with it an embryonic form of marine insurance. The risks inherent in shipping were naturally grave, particularly from heavy weather, piracy and dishonesty (not much different from today, then), as a result of which a system of financial protection was developed, involving a policy of insurance in the form of a loan. Naturally it was essential to prove that the trader had delivered the cargo into the Carrier's care, so a receipt was produced as evidence, some of which have survived today in the form of clay or wooden tablets and, remarkably, share much the same character as today's Bill of Lading.

The importance of the Bill of Lading as evidence in the carriage of goods by sea was acknowledged by the UK Parliament, which appreciated the need for some statutory regulation, in order to manage the business of maritime commerce, and give confidence to traders that they could rely on the law to limit their exposure to the risks inherent in the carriage of goods by sea, which demanded that the Carrier's contractual standard of duty, and any exceptions, had to be contained in a documentary Bill of Lading; for all the complexities of the jargon, it was a contract, nevertheless, and subject to the terms which the parties agreed; upon that basis, fault could be established in negligence if the Plaintiff could persuade the Court of the Carrier's failure fully to perform their pre-existing duty in contract. As a result, statutory regulation emerged with the Bills of Lading Act 1855:

> *Every Consignee of Goods named in a Bill of Lading, and every Endorsee of a Bill of Lading to whom the Property in the Goods therein mentioned shall pass, upon or by reason of such Consignment or Endorsement, shall have transferred to and vested in him all Rights of Suit, and be subject to the same Liabilities in respect of such Goods as if the Contract contained in the Bill of Lading had been made with himself.*
>
> *Nothing herein contained shall prejudice or affect any Right, of Stoppage in transit, or any Right to claim Freight against the original Shipper or Owner, or any Liability of the Consignee or Endorsee by reason or in*

DOI: 10.4324/9781003361916-29

> *consequence of being such Consignee or Endorsee, or of his Receipt of the Goods by reason or in consequence of such Consignment or Endorsement.*

The authority in the Master's signature was crucial to the process, even in 1855:

> *Every Bill of Lading in the Hands of a Consignee or Endorsee, for valuable Consideration representing Goods to have been shipped on board a Vessel shall be conclusive Evidence of such Shipment, as against the Master or other Person signing the same, notwithstanding that such Goods or some Part thereof may not have been so shipped, unless such Holder of the Bill of Lading shall have had actual Notice at the Time of receiving the same that the Goods had not been in fact laden on board; Provided that the Master or other Person so signing may exonerate himself in respect of such Misrepresentation by showing that it was caused without any Default on his Part, and wholly by the Fraud of the Shipper, or of the Holder, or some Person under whom the Holder claims.*

Given the importance of maritime trade, this proved to be an incredibly long-lived statute, and was only replaced by the Carriage of Goods by Sea Act in 1992. Section 4 defines the representations in Bills of Lading:

> *A Bill of Lading which –*
>
> (a) *represents goods to have been shipped on board a vessel or to have been received for shipment on board a vessel;*
>
> (b) *has been signed by the master of the vessel or by a person who was not the master but had the express, implied or apparent authority of the Carrier to sign Bills of Lading, shall, in favour of a person who has become the lawful holder of the bill, be conclusive evidence against the Carrier of the shipment of the goods or, as the case may be, of their receipt for shipment.*

This, however, does not do justice to a key feature of current law in the carriage of goods by sea, namely the Hague Rules 1924, as subsequently emended by the Hague-Visby Rules, and given the force of English statute law by the Carriage of Goods by Sea Act 1971. Article II of the Rules state:

> *Under every contract of carriage of goods by sea the Carrier, in relation to the loading, handling, stowage, carriage, custody, care and discharge of such goods, shall be subject to the responsibilities and liabilities, and entitled to the rights and immunities hereinafter set forth.*

The importance of evidence regarding the apparent order and condition of the goods, at the time they cross the ship's rail, is emphasised in Article III, which provides:

3 *After receiving the goods into his charge the Carrier or the master or agent of the Carrier shall, on demand of the shipper, issue to the shipper a Bill of Lading showing among other things –*

(a) *The leading marks necessary for identification of the goods as the same are furnished in writing by the shipper before the loading of such goods starts, provided such marks are stamped or otherwise shown clearly upon the goods if uncovered, or on the cases or coverings in which such goods are contained, in such a manner as should ordinarily remain legible until the end of the voyage;*

(b) *Either the number of packages or pieces, or the quantity, or weight, as the case may be, as furnished in writing by the shipper;*

(c) *The apparent order and condition of the goods.*

This rule concludes with an important condition for the Carrier, though:

> *Provided that no Carrier, master or agent of the Carrier shall be bound to state or show in the Bill of Lading any marks, number, quantity, or weight which he has reasonable ground for suspecting not accurately to represent the goods actually received, or which he has had no reasonable means of checking.*

By virtue of its provision in statute law, the Bill of Lading becomes a statutory document, meaning that it does not require any corroborative evidence but can stand alone in proceedings. It demands just two things:

- It must be in writing;
- Once signed, its terms cannot be altered and, so, any qualification defined in the proviso must be added in a clause which the Master will add to the end of the Bill.

The Carriage of Goods by Sea Act 1971 applies the provisions of the Hague-Visby Rules whether or not the Bill refers to the Rules, where the cargo is loaded in a UK port, or between ports in different States, even in those which have not implemented the Rules in their laws provided that the parties have agreed to their application in the Bill of Lading. This clarifies the point that the Act applies where the contract is governed by UK law and the parties agree that a Bill should be issued accordingly. Moreover, it applies to all cargoes except deck cargo and livestock.

The core of the matter of the Bill of Lading for the Master is that they sign it as the agent for the Carrier. It is worth reminding ourselves that Agency is the relationship in law that exists between two persons when one, called the agent, is considered in law to represent the other, called the principal, in such a way as to be able to affect the principal's legal position in respect of third parties by the making of contracts or the disposition of property. For the Owner or Carrier, the Agent logically must be the same one in whom they have contractually placed their trust to bring the ship safely home: the Master. For the Master, the law of agency gives them an escape clause from personal liability when they sign the Bill of Lading, for they are not then personally liable to the third party on the contract evidenced by the Bill. (Only if the Master had not identified or named the Owner as his principal could the third party bring a claim against him.)

The face of the Bill of Lading shows the key to this in plain sight. On the front of the Bill, the attestation clause contains words to the effect that the Master signs the Bill having received the cargo described in apparent good order and condition; but the Bill signed by the Master shall be deemed as signed on behalf of the Carrier. Section 4 Carriage of Goods by Sea Act 1992 provides that A Bill of Lading which *... has been signed by the master of the vessel ... shall, in favour of a person who has become the lawful holder of the bill, be conclusive evidence against the Carrier of the shipment of the goods or, as the case may be, of their receipt for shipment. In this way the Master will bind the owner in what they sign.*

A Word of Caution on Statutory Limitation Rules

It is important to note that the State of loading, not discharge, is what is crucial to the operation of the Rules. So shipment to the UK from non-Convention States will not involve the Hague-Visby Rules, so a State which has not ratified the Convention can apply something else, such as the United States which applies a version of the Hague Rules. As of 2021, 35 countries had ratified the Hamburg Rules, which patently omit the nautical fault defence, while the Rotterdam Rules were proposed for adoption in 1008; but only 4 States have ratified them, so they have not come into force. So what is the situation on limitation provisions to be incorporated into the Bill of Lading, if the State of loading has not ratified any rules at all? In this case, the terms contained in the Bill of Lading will have paramountcy, so what is contained about limitation will prevail, and the parties will be bound by that.

The Case of the *Tasman Discoverer*

In 1999, Tasman Orient Line agreed to carry a cargo of coils of electrolytic tin plate shipped Busan, Korea, to Tauranga in New Zealand. Korea was not a signatory to international conventions applicable to the Bill of Lading, but Tasman Orient Line incorporated a clause paramount, providing that:

> *Where no international convention or national law would apply [mandatorily], the liability of the Carrier for loss of or damage to the goods shall be determined by the Hague Rules contained in the International Convention for the Unification of Certain Rules relating to Bills of Lading dated 25 August 1924 (hereinafter called the Hague Rules), if the loss or damage is proved to have occurred at sea ... ; for the purpose of this sub-paragraph the limitation of liability under the Hague Rules shall be deemed to be £100 Sterling, lawful money of the United Kingdom per package or unit ... and the Hague Rules shall be construed accordingly.*

On arrival in Tauranga, the coils were found to be damaged by ingress of sea-water and the majority of them were sold as scrap to mitigate the loss. After deduction of salvage, the net claim of Dairy Containers amounted to $613,667. Tasman Orient accepted liability for the damage but maintained that they could limit their liability to the sum of £100 per package or unit, making a total amount due of £5,500.

The outraged cargo interests duly sued the Carrier for the full sum of their loss. The Court of first instance was sympathetic to them, and awarded Judgment in their favour. The Carrier appealed, however, and the Court of Appeal dismissed the Judgment of the lower Court, finding that, in the absence of statutory provision, the paramountcy of the bargain must prevail. The case ended up in the ultimate appeal court, the Judicial Committee of the Privy Council, who held that the Hague Rules were to apply, and that the monetary units contained in the Convention were to be taken to be gold value; in other words the value of gold which 100 pounds sterling would have bought in 1924.[1]

Much to the disgust of Dairy Containers, then, all they received was £5,500. Taking into account the burden of costs which they had to pay, it had been an expensive exercise, and an object lesson in reading the small print in the Bill of Lading.

The Functions of The Bill of Lading

Evidential Value of The Receipt

The Bill is prima facie evidence of the truth of the statements which it contains. For example, the Carrier who delivers to the cargo-owner a smaller number of packages than was acknowledged on the Bill, or goods torn and dirty when he had issued a Bill which had made no mention of such defect on receipt, will find great difficulty in resisting a claim for damages.

In *Compania Vascongada v Churchill*[2] a cargo of timber shipped under a Bill with the clause *shipped in good order and condition; quality unknown*, was in fact badly stained and saturated with petroleum when brought alongside for shipment. This condition was apparent and noticed by the Master, but he signed a clean bill. It was held, that the words *good order and condition* amounted to a representation as to the actual appearance of the goods when shipped. The endorsee of the Bill had taken delivery of the cargo in reliance upon the representation, and therefore the Carrier was estopped from denying that the damage was caused on board his vessel. This case had a lasting effect on the Bill of Lading, because, henceforth, the Carrier would insert the adjective *apparent* to qualify the assertion of *good order*.

This has been reinforced in the provisions of the Hague-Visby Rules, which states under Article III:

1 *Dairy Containers Ltd v Tasman Orient Line CV (The Tasman Discoverer)* [2004] 2 Ll R 647.

2 *Compania Vascongada v Churchill* [1906] 1 KB 237.

4 *Such a Bill of Lading shall be prima facie evidence of the receipt by the Carrier of the goods as therein described in accordance with paragraph 3 (a), (b) and (c). However, proof to the contrary shall not be admissible when the Bill of Lading has been transferred to a third party acting in good faith.*

In other words, the representations in the Bill concerning the cargo on receipt by the Carrier, shall be conclusive evidence of the condition, which would be very difficult to rebut in Court, if it is subsequently challenged by the Carrier.

The Clean Bill of Lading and its Effect on the Function of the Bill as a Receipt

We have seen that a clean Bill of Lading acts as prima facie evidence of the receipt of the cargo in apparent good order and condition. When the Bill is transferred to a third party acting in good faith, it is conclusive evidence of the apparent order and condition of the cargo, and the Carrier will be estopped from asserting as against that third party that, at the time of loading, the goods were not in apparent good order and condition. Wrongly issuing a clean Bill can therefore expose the shipowner to a high risk of liability. Clean Bills of Lading are also essential in order to trigger the right to receive payment under a documentary credit. A claused Bill will ordinarily be rejected by the buyer's bank, so, in the absence of special agreement with the buyer, a seller will be unable to obtain payment. A seller's inability to present clean Bills of Lading may operate as a repudiatory breach of the sale contract. As such, the purpose of the description clearly is to enable the shipper to transmit that information to subsequent holders of the Bill, so that they can use it as a document of title to the goods and as a mode of assignment of the contract of carriage. Subsequent holders can rely on the statement to reflect the reasonable judgment of a reasonably competent and observant Master in all the circumstances. This is an internationally recognised regime and there is no reason to add on to it any further obligation of a duty of care.

The Case of the *David Agmashenebeli*

The case of the *David Agmashenebeli*[3] illustrates dramatically how a claused Bill of Lading can affect maritime business dramatically. On 4 April 1995, a cargo of 35,000 tonnes of urea was sold by Transmarine Limited to Agrosin Pte Limited. The specification of the goods in the contract of sale was *white colour, free flowing, free from contamination, prilled form, treated against caking, free from harmful substances*. On 10 April, Agrosin sold the urea to Grand Prestige Enterprises of Hong Kong and arranged to sub-charter the *David Agmashenebeli* from Baff Shipping. Baff had entered into a voyage charter with Meezan Shipping

3 *Owners of the cargo lately laden on board the ship 'David Agmashenebeli' v Owners of the David Agmashenebeli* [2002] 2 All ER (Comm) 806; [2003] 1 Ll R92.

and Trading Inc, who, in turn, had time-chartered the vessel from her owners, Georgian Shipping Company. A number of clauses in the charterparty terms are relevant:

Clause 8 of the time charterparty provided that the charterers were *to load, stow and trim and discharge the cargo at their expense under the supervision and responsibility of the Captain, who is to sign, if required to do so by charterers, Bills of Lading for cargo as presented, in conformity with Mates' or Tally Clarks' receipts.*

Clause 45 in the voyage charterparty provided:

> *Under supervision of independent surveyor together with Master's/Officers' assistance no damaged cargo to be loaded into the hold. If such fact will take place Master has the right to stop loading but Charterers and Shippers to be immediately informed to arrange removing of any contaminations for Charterers' expenses/time. Quantity/quality of cargo as determined by an International Independent Surveyor ... together with Master and to be final and binding for both parties. Owners to be responsible for quantity of cargo taken on board.*

Clause 49 stated that Meezan was to authorise their Singapore agents to sign and release clean on board Bills of Lading upon confirmation that charter freight had been paid to Meezan. The Baff-Agrosin sub-charter included clauses similarly worded to clauses 45 and 49.

Three hours after loading began, the Master notified all parties that the cargo contained contaminants and was of a dirty colour. Despite protests by Agrosin's surveyor, the Mate's receipt was signed with the following wording: *Cargo discoloured also foreign materials, e.g., plastic, rust, rubber, stone, black particles found in cargo*. The Master refused to sign Bills of Lading without the same wording.

In the meantime, Grand Prestige, (the buyers of the cargo from Agrosin), had sold it to Guangxi Publications Import and Export Co Limited, payment to be by documentary credit. It was subsequently agreed that this documentary credit should be used to pay Agrosin direct. Documentary credit, of course, requires the presentation of clean Bills of Lading.

The Master's refusal to sign clean Bills of Lading resulted in deadlock: Agrosin declined to pay the freight due under the sub-voyage charter with Baff; Baff withheld voyage charter freight from Meezan; Meezan withheld time charter hire due to the shipowners; the shipowners threatened to lien the cargo to secure their hire; and Agrosin could not obtain payment under the documentary credit opened by Guangxi.

On 16 June 1995, the vessel arrived at Beihai in China and gave notice of readiness, but it could not enter port or deliver its cargo without Bills of Lading. A solution was reached to enable discharge of the cargo to begin. The terms included Agrosin agreeing to present the Mate's receipt and accepting (under protest) Bills of Lading claused with the same wording. But when Agrosin presented the claused bills to Guangxi's bank they were not accepted against the letter of credit. Eventually, Guangxi agreed to take delivery of the cargo for a reduced price (the market having fallen in the meantime).

Usually, disputes arise over allegations that the Master issued a clean Bill of Lading when the goods were not, in fact, in apparent good order when they were received. Here, however, the allegation was that the Master had claused Bills of Lading when he had no basis for doing so.

The Bills of Lading incorporated the Hague-Visby Rules. Article III rule 3 provides: *After receiving the goods into his charge, the Carrier, or the master or agent of the Carrier shall, on demand of the shipper issue to the shipper a Bill of Lading showing, amongst other things ... (c) The apparent order and condition of the goods*. A clean bill acts as prima facie evidence of the receipt by the Carrier of the goods in apparent good order and condition (Article III Rule 4).

Agrosin argued that this imposed a duty on the Carrier to ensure that the Bills of Lading are issued accurately and record the apparent order and condition of the goods. It was not sufficient that they showed what the Master honestly believed; they had to contain an objectively accurate description. In this, they relied on comments made the Judge in the *Arctic Trader*,[4] underlining the duty of the owners to the shipper to issue on demand a Bill which included the statement as to the apparent order and condition of the goods – as an *unqualified* or *absolute* contractual undertaking as to the apparent order and condition of the goods.

Agrosin argued in the alternative, that there was an implied term of carriage under which the shipowners were under a duty to the shippers that the Master would only sign bills that accurately stated the apparent order and condition of the goods. They also raised an argument that the shipowners (through the Master) owed a duty of care in tort not to misrepresent the apparent order and condition of the goods in the bills.

The shipowners argued that the Hague-Visby Rules did not require the statement to be objectively accurate. What mattered was what an ordinary and reasonably skilled Master reasonably and honestly believed to be the apparent order and condition of the goods. Numerous authorities showed that words in a Bill as to apparent condition are not contractual, in the sense of a promise or undertaking, but an affirmation of fact.[5] This is a core principle: the Bill is not in itself a binding agreement that the goods have been shipped as stated but merely prima facie evidence of that fact.[6] Indeed, many authorities on the Harter Act, the Hague Rules and the Hague-Visby Rules have confirmed that these codes stop short of imposing on the Carrier any contractual obligation as to the accuracy of statements in the bill about the order and condition of the goods, and the wording of Article III Rules 3 and 4 is consistent with this. In the light of the authorities, it is clear that the

4 [1996] 2 Lloyd's Rep 449.

5 See *Heskel v Continental Express* [1950] 83 Ll L Rep 438; *Rasnoimport v Guthrie & Co Ltd* [1966] 1 Ll R 1.

6 See *The River Gurara* [1998] QB 610.

Master should use their own discretion to decide whether, in all the circumstances, the cargo appears to satisfy the description of its apparent order and condition in the Bills of Lading tendered for signature. Equally, it would be somewhat disingenuous for the shipper to allege that the Master was negligent in signing a Bill that was wrong; the shipper, after all, should have actual knowledge of the order and condition of their own cargo. Similarly, the terms in which the Master thinks it appropriate to qualify the Bill of Lading are, again, a matter for their own judgment and they should use jargon that reflects reasonably closely the actual apparent order and condition of the cargo and the extent of any defect which he considers it to have.

The Master is unlikely to be criticised for failing to ask for expert advice, and the law does not require them to be an expert surveyor or have any greater knowledge or experience of the cargo in question than any other reasonably careful Master. If they honestly take the view that the goods are not in apparent good order and condition, and that is a view that could properly be held by a reasonably observant Master, they are entitled to clause the Bill of Lading. That being said, a great deal of soul-searching and potential litigation would be avoided by the expediency of getting a cargo survey.

The Judge found that there had been some contamination of the cargo, but that this was so slight that no reasonably observant Master would have seen fit to refer to it in the Mate's receipt. He also found that there had been some discolouration and that, given the extent to which the cargo was discoloured and the fact that shippers had described it as white, a reasonable Master might well have thought it appropriate to state such discolouration in the Mate's receipt; but the Master's description of the cargo as *discoloured* was misleading, as there was no indication that it referred to only about one per cent of the whole. A reasonable Master would have added some qualification to avoid creating a false impression that a substantial part of the cargo was discoloured. Consequently, the defendants, in breach of their contractual duty under Article III, rule 3, had failed to issue to the shippers a Bill that contained a statement as to the apparent order and condition of the cargo which a reasonably observant Master could properly have made.

In terms of Agrosin's claim in law, though, lawyers have expressed doubt that they had actually suffered a loss. The Master would have acted reasonably if he had claused the Bills of Lading (so long as he made the extent of the discolouration clear) for evidence of any defect, whether one per cent or more, and Agrosin would still not have got a clean Bill to present to Guangxi's bank. Moreover, since the market price had already fallen, they would have had to reach a similar settlement with Guangxi in any event. Accordingly, Agrosin had failed to show that the Master's failure to comply with Article III Rule 3 had caused them any loss.

The Authority of the Master's Signature Upheld

The solution from the point of view of the Master, remains that, if in any doubt, a cargo survey should be carried out before the Bill of Lading is signed. In the

2021 case of the *Tai Prize*[7] a cargo of soya beans was loaded in Santos, Brazil to Guangzhou, China, under a voyage charterparty in which a clean Bill of Lading was presented by the shipper to the Master for signature, but on discharge at Guangzhou, it was discovered that some of the cargo was subject to heat and mould damage. That damage was not visible on opening the hatches, but the Master signed it any way. The resultant case ended up in the English Court of Appeal, which held:

> *Presenting a draft Bill of Lading for signature to the Master, was merely an invitation for him to make representations of fact according to his own reasonable assessment of the apparent condition of the cargo on shipment. The shippers themselves made no representations, and hence did not misrepresent the apparent condition on shipment.*

In fact, the Bill signed by the Master was accurate; no damage was visible to the Master on loading, so in terms of the apparent good order and condition of the cargo, the representations on the face of the Bill were true.

It is well established that representations on the Bill must be based on the Master's own reasonable assessment of the apparent condition of the cargo on shipment.

Notwithstanding that, the charterparty incorporated the Hague Rules, Article III Rule 3 of which states the information that must be furnished by the shipper on a draft Bill of Lading. That does not extend to the apparent order and condition of the cargo, which the Master alone must assess.

In reality, although at first sight this case seems to be hard on the Carrier, it does not actually present anything new. The need for a cargo surveyor's report is underlined here; whether the particular issues in the voyage allow time and cost for a survey to be undertaken, must remain commercial considerations to be taken into account.

Beware the Letter of Indemnity

The *David Agmashenebeli* case briefly touches upon the process by which the shipper, or consignor, is paid for the cargo that they sell; namely, that the Master signs a clean Bill of Lading, which the consignee presents to their bank and the shipper is duly paid. Then, if the cargo does not correspond with the quality or quantity described in the Bill of Lading, the consignee will pursue the Carrier. In order to expedite the completion of the transaction, the shipper may offer a letter of indemnity to the Carrier, undertaking to indemnify them against such a claim. Another scenario is that in which the consignee simply cannot produce their counterpart Bill; until the cargo is released, of course, payment will not be authorised and, to

7 *Noble Chartering Inc v Priminds Shipping Hong Kong Co Ltd* [2021] EWCA Civ 87; [2021] 2 Ll R 36.

facilitate completion of the transaction, the Carrier releases the cargo any way, on the strength of a letter of indemnity.

In terms of its evidential value in litigation, there is a very real risk that a shipper may fail to honour the letter of indemnity, but the Court will not uphold it because, in reality, it is a dishonest document, created to practise a deceit on the consignee, by facilitating a clean Bill of Lading, which is patently fraudulent. Moreover, the Carrier's P & I insurer is likely to incorporate a condition into their policy that excludes cover for claims arising from the issue of a Bill known by the Master to contain an incorrect description of the cargo, its quantity or condition.

The Bill of Lading as a Document of Title

The Bill of Lading does not transfer ownership in the goods – that will be effected under the contract of sale. But the contract of sale cannot transfer constructive possession; that is, the right to immediate possession in the hands of a bailor, the Carrier. The Bill of Lading therefore has an important function as a document of title, transferring constructive possession to the consignee. No other document can do this, so the Carrier must be able to deliver the goods to the proper person; as such, the Bill of Lading evolved as *the keys to the warehouse*: it gives the right to demand of the Carrier the delivery of the goods on presentation of the Bill. So, at Port of Discharge the goods must be delivered by the Carrier:

- To the shipper;
- To the shipper's order, so that the shipper can, by endorsing on the document an order that the goods must be delivered to the buyer, empowering the buyer to collect the goods himself;
- To a named consignee or to his order, enabling the initial buyer to transfer, by endorsement of the Bill to successive buyers, the right to delivery of the goods by the Carrier.

But the Bill can only transfer constructive possession when it is the intention of the parties that the endorsee should acquire constructive possession, and negligently parting with the cargo in the absence of such intention can lead to misdelivery and litigation against the Carrier.

The Case of the *Taiko*

The case of *Barber v Trailer Marine*[8] involved a claim by the owner of the *Taiko* for indemnification against a cargo claim that had been lost due to the fault of the transhipper. At the time when the *Barber Hector* was built she was the largest roll on roll off Carrier in the world, and when the owner subsequently left the Barber Blue Sea Group the ship was acquired by another member of the group, and

8 *Barber Blue Sea v Trailer Marine Transport Corporation*, US District Court Florida 1989.

renamed *Taiko*. The cargo owner, China Rising Development Limited, sold a consignment of containerised merchandise to Trans-Caribbean Industries, of Antigua, who were named as the consignee in the Bill of Lading, evidencing the contract of carriage with Barber. As a result, Barber was the bailee in law of the cargo, and, in turn, engaged Trailer Marine Transport Corporation to act as contracting Carrier in the transhipment of the cargo to the port of discharge instructed by Barber, the Carrier. The contract between them contained an express provision that Trailer Marine would indemnify and hold Barber Blue Sea harmless *from all expenses and liabilities it may incur which in any way may be from or be connected with any loss, damage, delay or misdelivery of cargo while in the possession or custody of Trailer Marine Transport Corporation* ... The only thing missing was a clause for the recovery of attorney's fees.

Barber duly loaded the cargo on the *Taiko* in Hong Kong and delivered it to Trailer Marine at the Port of Miami, for transhipment to Antigua, the destination port, but as bailee Barber, not Trailer Marine, was liable to the cargo owners for the safe custody of the cargo according to the cargo owner's instructions, whatever those instructions may be.

However, China Rising did not receive payment for the merchandise from the consignee, Trans-Caribbean Industries, and so did not release the original Bills of Lading to them. However, Trailer Marine released the merchandise to Trans-Caribbean without the presentation of the original Bills of Lading, and thus the value of the cargo was lost to China Rising. Barber claimed loss and damage for Trailer Marine's negligence, alleging that despite repeated demands by Barber, Trailer Marine had failed, refused and or neglected to protect and defend Barber's interest or to indemnify Barber for expenses arising from the improper release of the merchandise. As such, Trailer Marine agreed to cover any liability for incorrectly released cargo at the destination by Trailer Marine, their agents or port authorities, including customs.

The parties settled the matter without litigation as to all issues, except attorney fees. Barber had retained an attorney to defend a claim made by China Rising, and argued that the responsibility for those fees belonged to Trailer Marine under the terms of the agreement; but China Rising did not eventually commence proceedings against Barber, hence the Defendants averred that the fees incurred by Barber could not be claimed as indemnity expenses.

The case proceeded according to the law attaching to the agreement, being New York law, which provided that the Plaintiff would not be permitted to recover attorney fees in seeking indemnification. In a previous case, the Court had held that where a promissory note did not provide for attorney fees in the guarantee but only for any and all expenses in collecting on the obligation, attorney fees were not recoverable, and thus created a precedent. In this case, the Court held that the language in the disputed contract, merely speaks of expenses and liabilities but does not directly address *defending a suit*. In all the circumstances, therefore, Barber's motion for the payment of their attorney's fees failed, and their case was dismissed.

The Bill of Lading as Evidence of the Contract with the Carrier

There are few contracts in maritime law that must be in writing, and a charterparty is not one of them. Hence, the Bill of Lading assumes greater importance because it must be in writing; therefore, as a statutory document it contains terms upon which the parties – and the Courts – may rely without other corroborating evidence. That being said, if the cargo is to travel under the Hague or Hague-Visby Rules, then they should be adopted verbatim into the Bill of Lading – but will still apply even if they are not there.

The normal rules of contract formation apply in the carriage of goods by sea. In practice therefore the fundamental requirements of a contract must be satisfied: offer, acceptance, consideration and intention to create legal relations, and the Bill is issued after that, indeed it will only be signed, and thus validated, after the cargo has crossed the ship's rail and the Mate's receipt delivered to the Master. Consequently, the Bill is merely evidence of the contract between the shipowner and the shipper. It is not the contract itself.

Of course, the charterparty may contain additional terms; it has no statutory content and, therefore, the parties may agree whatever they wish, and additional terms may be incorporated, by representations, even oral variations. In the case of the *Ardennes*[9] a deviation clause was negatived by an oral promise to follow a direct route; but such variations only apply as between the immediate parties to the contract. Third parties, such as consignees or their assignees, who acquire rights by way of endorsements of the Bill, are entitled and required[10] to assume that the Bill contains within its four corners either all the terms of the contract or at any rate references to other documents where such terms may be found.

The Case of *Pyrene v Scindia*

In practice, the contract of affreightment is closed long before the Bill is issued. Shipping space must be filled in advance of the scheduled sailing date. So as evidence of the contract, does it have retrospective effect? In *Pyrene Co v Scindia Navigation Co*[11] the Court held, that when parties enter into a contract of carriage in the expectation that a Bill of Lading will be issued to cover it they enter into it upon the terms which they know or expect the Bill of Lading to contain. Those terms must be in force from the inception of the contract; if it were otherwise the Bill of Lading would not evidence the contract but would be a variation of it. This case famously involved a fire tender which was sold and delivered alongside for loading. As it was being lifted onto the ship but before it crossed the rail, it was dropped and subsequently damaged. Under the contract of sale, possession had not passed by that stage; a Bill of Lading had been drawn up but was not issued, as the

9 Owners of Cargo ex SS Ardennes v Owners of SS Ardennes [1951] 1 KB 55.
10 See The El Amira and the El Minia [1982] 2 Ll R 28.
11 Pyrene Co v Scindia Navigation Co [1954] 2 QB 402.

cargo was never received into the Carrier's care, but it had been established that the Hague Rules would apply. The sellers sued the Carrier for the cost to repair the tender. The owners of the ship admitted liability but argued their liability would be limited by the Hague Rules, Article IV Rule 5. The sellers claimed that as the goods had not crossed the ship's rail, the incident had occurred off the ship and therefore outside the scope of the Hague Rules. Further to this, because the Bill had not been signed and conveyed, these terms had not been included in the contract between the parties. Lastly, the seller argued that even if the term had been included in the contract, they could not be applied to the agreement between the Carrier and themselves. The Court held that limited liability under the Hague Rules did extend to the loading of the cargo on to the ship. Moreover, it was found that the Bill of Lading was irrelevant because it was only evidence of the contract, not the contract itself, and the contract could be regarded as incorporating the terms in the draft Bill. As a result of this finding, the plaintiffs could only recover £200 in accordance with the Hague Rules which were considered to be included in the contract.

This function of the Bill of Lading as *evidence* of the contract of carriage can be blurred by confusion of the Carrier's own making, for many expressly state that the booking of cargo is subject to the terms and conditions in their Bill of Lading. It is essential that the Carrier states the terms (via a website or otherwise) so that the consignee can see and agree the terms before they place the order, because the commercial contract demands that the terms are agreed at the time that the contract is made.

Evidence Of The Transfer And Rights And Obligations under the Carriage of Goods by Sea Act 1992

Section 2 of the 1992 defines Rights under shipping documents.

(1) *Subject to the following provisions of this section, a person who becomes –*
the lawful holder of a Bill of Lading;
the person who (without being an original party to the contract of carriage) is the person to whom delivery of the goods to which a sea waybill relates is to be made by the Carrier in accordance with that contract;
the person to whom delivery of the goods to which a ship's delivery order relates is to be made in accordance with the undertaking contained in the order, shall (by virtue of becoming the holder of the bill or, as the case may be, the person to whom delivery is to be made) have transferred to and vested in him all rights of suit under the contract of carriage as if he had been a party to that contract.

The Case of the *Polar*

That being said, the rights under shipping documents carry obligations as well. In the case of *Herculito Maritime v Gunvor International*[12] the Court of Appeal held that the Bill of Lading did not exclude liability on the part of the holder of the Bill for payment of the cargo stakeholder's contribution in General Average. In this case the owners of the *Polar* pursued a claim to recover cargo interests' proportion in general average after the vessel, laden with 69,500 tonnes of fuel oil, was seized by pirates when transiting the Gulf of Aden, and demanded a ransom totalling $ 7.7 million to secure the vessel's release. The vessel was chartered with a clause stating that all bills issued under the charter were deemed to contain war risks clauses, which included 'acts of piracy.' When the vessel was seized by pirates, the owners declared General Average resulting in cargo underwriters providing a general average guarantee and the receiver providing a general average bond. Following the issuing of the General Average adjustment, which concluded that some $4.8 million was due to owners from the cargo interests, the latter resisted, so the owners commenced proceedings.

The case ended up in the Court of Appeal, which reiterated the point, much exercised in recent years, that the construction of terms should be tested against business common sense in defining the contractual rights and obligations. In this case, the Court held that the owners were entitled to look to cargo owners for a contribution in general average. The Court highlighted the fact that both parties were insured against the risk of piracy and that allowing owners' claim meant that each set of insurers would bear its share of the risk it had agreed to cover. This was contrasted against excluding owners' claim which would have had the downstream consequence that the entire loss would have been met by the owners' insurer and would allow cargo owners' insurers to escape liability for a risk which they had agreed to cover.

12 *Herculito Maritime Limited & others v Gunvor International BV & others* [2021] EWCA Civ 1828.

30 Liability in Negligence

Introduction

The Master's Duty of Care

The Master has a duty to take the standard of care, reasonably expected of such a professional in their position, to guard against acts or omissions which might cause loss or damage to persons and the breach of such duty of care which results in damage will give rise to a claim in negligence.

The Court's task is to determine from the evidence whether the facts reveal a case of negligence or a mere error of judgment. In *Grace v General Steam*,[1] Devlin J famously held,

> *The question of safety must be determined at the time when the Master has to make his decision to proceed ... The right to damages depends upon a wrong done and an injury actually sustained; not upon someone's estimate of whether a wrong is likely to be done or an injury likely to be sustained.*

But the Master had better have good evidence that they managed the risk to the expected standard, because an innocent party who suffers damage as a result of the Defendant's negligence will plead the right to compensation that would put them into the position they would have been in had the negligence not occurred.

The Case of the *Torepo*[2]

On 30 June 1997, the tanker *Torepo* departed La Plata, Argentina for Esmeraldas, Ecuador with a cargo of 23,700 tonnes of refined petroleum, gasoline. Three routes were considered: the Panama Canal, Cape Horn and the Magellan Straits. The decision was made to use the shortest route, through the Magellan Straits. At the time of her sailing, she did not have charts for the Magellan Straits, because it was custom and practice for the pilots to bring with them all the Chilean charts covering almost all the Magellan Straits.

1 *G W Grace & Company Ltd v General Steam Navigation Company Limited* [1950] 83 Ll.
2 *The Torepo* [2002] EWHC 1481 (Admlty), [2002] 2 Ll R 535.

DOI: 10.4324/9781003361916-30

On 7 July, two pilots boarded the *Torepo* at Possession Bay, the entrance to the Magellan Straits. The vessel then entered the straits as the pilots used the distance index and other items, including the passage plan, that they had brought with them. Consequently, no detailed passage plan was prepared for the vessel's voyage through the Magellan Straits. Two days later, while in the Patagonian Channels, the vessel failed to alter course at the point where this move was planned and instead remained on a straight course, as a result of which she ran aground at Wellington Island.

The Claimant cargo owner raised in Particulars of Negligence that the Master and her officers had been negligent in their navigation, and that the inadequacy of the passage plan had negligently rendered the ship unseaworthy, alleging:

- There was no passage plan in place to assist the officer of the watch or to encourage him to actively monitor the progress of the vessel.
- The ship's Master possessed a flawed attitude towards passage planning in general and passage planning whilst under pilotage.
- The passage plan was negligent as it omitted an important notation regarding Foot Island Light, a range line showing the closest permissible distance when off Wellington Island, and a parallel index for the track.

The Judge concluded, however:

> *Passage planning is not science. There was inevitably an element of judgment as to what annotations needed to be added to the charts. I certainly accept that the passage plan would have been improved by the addition of the three matters referred to. But it must be remembered that the passage was not prepared by the Master or officers of Torepo whose expertise in this field is criticised by the Claimants. It was prepared by pilots who had regularly taken vessels through the Patagonian Channels with no recorded difficulty.*

It was, of course, a fair conclusion for the Master, but the tort of negligence has not had an easy evolution into its present existence.

The Evolution of Negligence

In 1842, a mail coachman had been hired for his services by the Defendant, who had contracted with the Postmaster-General to supply a mail coach for the purpose of carrying the mail along the somewhat tortuous English highways of the day. The coachman, however, was injured as a result of several latent defects in the coach and commenced an action against the Defendant in negligence.

The Court had to consider whether the Defendant owed a duty to the coachman, who was an unnamed third party to his contract the Post office, in order to establish liability for the personal injuries suffered as a result of the negligent provision of the coach or, indeed, any other negligent actions in regard to the contract.

The Court held, that the Claimant's claim failed.[3] The reasons for the Judgment was found on the evidence of the Defendant's liability to him: although the Defendant contracted to maintain the mail coach in a safe condition and undoubtedly failed to do so, the duty was owed under the Defendant's contract with the Postmaster-General. The Defendant owed no duty to the Claimant because there was no evidence that the duty could extend beyond the contractual one. It was considered that to allow the Claimant's claim to succeed would cause a duty to be held in all circumstances where harm occurred, and that there would be no limit to the number of claims that might arise. It was recognised that leaving the claimant without remedy was harsh, but that this should not influence the court's decision.

In terms of practical justice, the problem was one of dragging the law of torts out of its medieval origins into the growingly litigious world of the Victorian industrial revolution; the Courts found it no simple task, for their function was to apply the law, but the law was lagging behind the society which had already been changed forever by the priorities of debit and credit.

Nowhere was this more bitterly contested than in litigation for the loss and damage to shipping in the crowded environment of the Thames, where sailing ships jostled for space with the new generation of steamships. There was a statutory obligation to observe the rules of navigation defined in Admiralty regulations and London River By-Laws, which created an evidential link to underpin a claim for breach of the duty, which would enable the Courts form a decision according to statutory liability; but that was not enough to establish the apportionment of fault and, consequently, the quantum of damages, because of inconsistencies in judicial approaches, in that, according to Admiralty Court rules, if both vessels were at fault the loss was equally divided: but in a Court of Common Law the Plaintiff had no remedy if his negligence in any degree contributed to the accident.

Thus, in the case of *Dowell v The General Steam Navigation Company*, which was heard in the Court of Queen's Bench in June 1855,[4] the Court felt compelled to express *great compassion when we think of the fate* of the Plaintiff's vessel and her crew but the Court's tortuous task was to unravel a Gordian knot of legislation which had grown into a fearful tangle in recent years, resulting in confusion and the decision necessarily had to be removed from concepts of compassion for those who had lost their lives. The Plaintiff, owner of a sailing collier, alleged that General Steam's ship collided with theirs *with great force and violence, ran foul of, and struck and came upon and against, the ship: whereby the ship was run down and wholly lost to Plaintiffs*. But it was not as easy as that. An Admiralty Regulation of the day provided that:

> *We hereby require that all sailing vessels when under sail, or being towed, approaching, or being approached by any other vessel, shall be bound to shew, between sunset and sunrise, a bright light, in such a position as can be best seen by such vessel or vessels, and in such time to avoid a collision.*

3 *Winterbottom v Wright* (1842) 10 M& W 109; 152 All ER 402.
4 *Dowell and Others v General Steam Navigation Company* (1855) 5 El & Bl 195.

The Jury heard evidence that the collier had exhibited a light but had withdrawn it two or three minutes before the collision, and was not visible to the steamship, until she was within two or three of the collier's lengths off; but the Plaintiff contended that, if the steamship had been managed with ordinary care and skill, the accident would not have happened.

The Learned Judge directed the Jury that, if there were any negligence on the part of the Plaintiff as well as on the part of the Defendant which led to the collision, the Plaintiff could not recover. He then put three questions to the Jury:

1 *Was there negligence on the part of the Plaintiffs with respect to the light, which led to the collision?*

The Jury concluded *We find there was fault on the part of the collier in not continuing the light till the danger was past.*

2 *Could the Defendants have avoided the collision by ordinary care and skill?*

The Jury found *It is the opinion of the Jury that the steamer was going at too great a speed on so dark a night, in which respect there was want of caution: but that it was impossible to have avoided the accident when the steamer was within two or three of the collier's lengths.*

3 *Was the damage occasioned by the accident the result of circumstances for which more blame attaches to the one side than the other?*

The Jury answered *We are much inclined to think the preponderance of blame to be with the steamer.*

The preponderance of blame clearly indicated their view that the blame was not one-sided, and the Judge concluded:

> *The Jury do not think that the accident was inevitable: they think that there was blame on both sides, by which the accident was occasioned: and, this being so, it is immaterial, with regard to the verdict, whether the preponderance of blame was with the steamer or the collier. For these reasons we think that the rule to enter the verdict for the Defendants should be made absolute. It is impossible not to feel great compassion when we think of the fate of the collier and her crew: but this appears to have arisen from the breach of Admiralty Regulations; and it is the duty both of jurors and Judges, in obedience to the Legislature, for the safety of navigation, and in furtherance of the cause of humanity, to take care that these regulations are duly enforced.*

It was clearly the evidence which had to be applied to the statutory regulation, that enabled the Court to make a decision, and in the evidence of such regulation, no evidential link could be established between cause and effect. It took a bottle of ginger beer to change things.

The case of *Donoghue v Stevenson*[5] was heard in 1932 and still defines the principles in the current law. In this case the appellant sought to recover damages from the respondent, who was a manufacturer of aerated waters, for injuries she suffered as a result of consuming part of the contents of a bottle of ginger beer which had been manufactured by the respondent, and which contained the decomposed remains of a snail. The ginger beer had been purchased for the appellant by a friend in a café and arrived at the table in its customary bottle of dark opaque glass, when the appellant had no reason to suspect that it contained anything but pure ginger beer; having had some of the contents poured into a tumbler, which she drank quite uneventfully, her friend was then proceeding to pour the remainder of the ginger beer into the tumbler when a decomposed snail accompanied the rest of the contents out of the bottle. The appellant claimed damages for alleged shock and severe gastro-enteritis. The appellant further averred that the respondent manufactured the ginger beer to be sold as a drink to the public (including the appellant); that it was bottled by the respondent and labelled by him with a label bearing his name; and that the bottles were thereafter sealed with a metal cap by the respondent. She further averred that it was the duty of the respondent to provide a system of working his business which would not allow snails to get into his ginger beer bottles, and that it was also his duty to provide an efficient system of inspection of the bottles before the ginger beer was filled into them, and that he had failed in both these duties and had so caused the event.

It was Lord Atkin's speech which defined the modern principle, introducing the concept of the *neighbour* as the party to whom the Defendant owed a duty of care:

> *You must take reasonable care to avoid acts or omissions which you can reasonably foresee would be likely to injure your neighbour. Who, then, in law is my neighbour? The answer seems to be – persons who are so closely and directly affected by my act that I ought reasonably to have them in contemplation as being so affected when I am directing my mind to the acts or omissions which are called in question.*[6]

Lord Atkin's colleagues illuminated his observation with their own analysis of this redefined principle of duty. It is apparent that *Donoghue v Stevenson* brought evolution, not revolution, to the law of negligence; nevertheless, it was this humble bottle of ginger beer which provided the hard case that led to the illumination of the principles underpinning the tort of negligence, although the principles themselves had not changed. This is well-evidenced by the nineteenth century collision cases in the River Thames, when the underpinning evidence was not contractual but statutory, in the form of the London River By-laws, Admiralty Regulations

5 *Donoghue (or McAlister) v Stevenson,* [1932] All ER Rep 1; [1932] AC 562.
6 *Donoghue (or McAlister) v Stevenson* [1932] All ER Rep 1; [1932] AC 562, p. 580.

and Common Law rules on liability – as *Dowell v General Steam* revealed (albeit demonstrating the inconsistency between the bodies of law).[7] That being said, *Donoghue v Stevenson* clarified the principle so that the Claimant must establish on the balance of probabilities:

a) That the Defendant, the party alleged to be negligent had a duty to the injured party to avoid acts or omissions which might cause him loss or damage – for example, the Master, who is responsible for safety on board their ship, clearly owes a duty of care as a result as regards lawful visitors to the ship, whether or not they are contracting parties;[8]
b) That the Defendant was in breach of that duty of care, generally by showing that his conduct fell below the reasonably expected standard to be owed by such persons in those circumstances;
c) The Claimant must have suffered damage as a reasonably foreseeable consequence of the Defendant's breach of duty.

Damages are awarded in compensation with the purpose of putting the Claimant in the position he would have been in, had the negligence not taken place – so long as that is all that the measure of damages does; they certainly cannot put the Claimant in a better position than he would have been.[9]

This gallop through the general principles of negligence starkly demonstrates the foundation principle characterising the tort that the Defendant's state of mind – their mens rea, essentially – is not the determining factor in their culpability. For the Master, it is how they manage the business of risk.

The Master and the Management of Risk

The parameters of negligence lie in the evidence about how the Master managed the risk in discharging their duty to take the standard of care, reasonably expected of such a professional in their position, to guard against acts or omissions which might cause loss or damage to persons and the breach of such duty of care which results in damage will give rise to a claim in negligence.

The decision in the risk management process is a fine one, and subject to the Master's absolute discretion set out in SOLAS Chapter V Regulation 34-1, for safe

7 *Dowell v. General Steam Navigation Co* (1855) 5 El & Bl 195.

8 Mention must be made of *Caparo Industries plc v Dickman* [1990] 2 AC 605, where the House of Lords held that in novel factual situations, for a duty of care to exist, there must be (a) proximity between the parties, (b) foreseeability of harm / loss and (c) it must be fair, just and reasonable for the law to impose the duty; subsequently applied in *Marc Rich & Co AG and Others -v- Bishop Rock Marine Co Ltd and Others* [1995] 3 All ER 307; [1995] UKHL 4; [1996] 1 AC 211; [1995] CLC 934; [1995] 2 LLR 299; [1996] ECC 120; [1995] 3 WLR 227; [1995] 2 Lloyd's Rep 299, in which Lord Steyn said that the common law of negligence *develops incrementally on the basis of a consideration of analogous cases where a duty has been recognised or desired.*

9 *The Argonaftis* [1989] 2 Ll R 487.

navigation and avoidance of dangerous situations, as we have seen, and now reinforced by reason of the Merchant Shipping (Safety of Navigation) Regulations 2020, which creates a criminal offence of disobedience of SOLAS Chapter V Regulation 34:

1. *Prior to proceeding to sea, the master shall ensure that the intended voyage has been planned using the appropriate nautical charts and nautical publications for the area concerned, taking into account the guidelines and recommendations developed by the Organization;*
2. *The voyage plan shall identify a route which:*
   2.1 *takes into account any relevant ships' routeing systems;*
   2.2 *ensures sufficient sea room for the safe passage of the ship throughout the voyage;*
   2.3 *anticipates all known navigational hazards and adverse weather conditions;*
   2.4 *takes into account the marine environmental protection measures that apply, and avoids, as far as possible, actions and activities which could cause damage to the environment.*

The downstream consequence of such an offence is that a conviction can be used as evidence of the Master's liability in civil proceedings for negligence.

In civil proceedings, the cargo owner has the additional assistance of the Hague-Visby Rules, which applies to the carriage of goods by sea:

To carriage between any ports in different states, provided that the bill of lading is issued in a state that has ratified the Protocol.

Where the contract is governed by UK law and the parties agree that a bill of lading or a non-negotiable receipt subject to the Rules shall be issued.

The Rules impose strict rules on the carrier under Article III:

1) *Art III(1)*
   The carrier shall be bound before and at the beginning of the voyage to exercise due diligence to:
   (a) *make the ship seaworthy;*
   (b) *properly man, equip and supply the ship;*
   (c) *make the holds, refrigerating and cool chambers, and all other parts of the ship in which goods are carried, fit and safe for their reception, carriage and preservation.*
2) *Art III(2)*
   Subject to the provisions of Art IV (below), the carrier shall properly and carefully load, handle, stow, carry, keep, care for and discharge the goods carried.

In a demonstration of fairness, they also impose certain defences under Article IV:

1) *Neither the carrier nor the ship shall be liable for loss or damage arising or resulting from unseaworthiness unless caused by want of due diligence on the*

part of the carrier to make the ship seaworthy, and to secure that the ship is properly manned, equipped and supplied, and to make the holds, refrigerating and cool chambers and all other parts of the ship in which goods are carried fit and safe for their reception, carriage and preservation in accordance with the provisions of paragraph 1 of Article III. Whenever loss or damage has resulted from unseaworthiness the burden of proving the exercise of due diligence shall be on the carrier or other person claiming exemption under this article.

2) *Neither the carrier nor the ship shall be responsible for loss or damage arising or resulting from:*
   - (a) *Act, neglect, or default of the master, mariner, pilot, or the servants of the carrier in the navigation or in the management of the ship;*
   - (b) *Fire, unless caused by the actual fault or privity of the carrier;*
   - (c) *Perils, dangers and accidents of the sea or other navigable waters;*
   - (d) *Act of God;*
   - (e) *Act of war;*
   - (f) *Act of public enemies;*
   - (g) *Arrest or restraint of princes, rulers or people, or seizure under legal process;*
   - (h) *Quarantine restrictions;*
   - (i) *Act or omission of the shipper or owner of the goods, his agent or representative;*
   - (j) *Strikes or lockouts or stoppage or restraint of labour from whatever cause, whether partial or general;*
   - (k) *Riots and civil commotions;*
   - (l) *Saving or attempting to save life or property at sea;*
   - (m) *Wastage in bulk of weight or any other loss or damage arising from inherent defect, quality or vice of the goods;*
   - (n) *Insufficiency of packing;*
   - (o) *Insufficiency or inadequacy of marks;*
   - (p) *Latent defects not discoverable by due diligence.*

Of these defences, the provisions in paragraph 2(a) are the most important in terms of the management of the ship, and are known as the Nautical Fault Defence. It was the Nautical Fault Defence that was central to the Claimant cargo owner's action in the case of the *Tasman Pioneer*,[10] which we examined in Chapter 6. Given that the Claimants pleaded all the criteria required to establish negligence by the Master, the Defendant Carrier argued their case for the Nautical Fault Defence under the statutory limitation rules, on the basis that Carriers are responsible for loss or damage caused by matters within their direct control, such as the seaworthiness and manning of the ship at the commencement of the voyage; but they are not responsible for loss or damage due to other causes, including acts or omissions of the

10 *Tasman Orient Line CV v New Zealand China Clays Ltd and Others* [2010] 2 Ll R 13.

master or crew during the voyage, which are outside their direct control; indeed, they could not override the Master's professional judgment in the navigation of the ship under SOLAS Chapter V Regulation 34-1.

Negligence or an Error of Judgment?

We have seen that, for the tort of negligence to be established, the Claimant has to establish on the balance of probabilities that the Defendant owed them a duty of care, that the Defendant broke that duty of care, and that the damage complained of was suffered as a reasonably foreseeable consequence. Thus, the Claimant must succeed in presenting the Court with the burden of proof, but that proof must then be applied to the law. In navigation, this can be achieved by expert witnesses whose opinion will persuade the Judge that the Defendant violated the International Regulations for Preventing Collisions at Sea, 1972, abbreviated to the COLREGS. So, for example, Rule 5 provides that:

> *Every vessel shall at all times maintain a proper look-out by sight and hearing as well as by all available means appropriate in the prevailing circumstances and conditions so as to make a full appraisal of the situation and of the risk of collision.*

Rule 7 deals with risk of collision:

(a) *Every vessel shall use all available means appropriate to the prevailing circumstances and conditions to determine if risk of collision exists. If there is any doubt such risk shall be deemed to exist.*

Rule 8 follows with action to avoid such risks:

(a) *Any action taken to avoid collision shall be taken in accordance with the Rules of this Part and shall, if the circumstances of the case admit, be positive, made in ample time and with due regard to the observance of good seamanship.*

Such matters are highly relevant in the task of assessing negligent navigation; but it may not necessarily be easy to determine.

The Case of the *Ever Smart*

This case involved much legal argument over the meaning and application of the Collision Regulations, to determine whether the crossing rules were inapplicable, or whether they should be disapplied where an outbound vessel is navigating within a narrow channel and has a vessel on her port (or starboard) bow on a crossing course approaching a narrow channel with the intention of, and in preparation for, entering it. If they were applicable, the Court had to consider whether there is a requirement for the putative give-way vessel to be on a steady course before the crossing rules can be engaged.

On 11 February 2015, the *Ever Smart*, a container ship owned by Evergreen (UK) collided with the *Alexandra 1*, a very large crude carrier owned by Nautical Challenge, at sea, at night, just outside the entrance/exit channel to the port of Jebel Ali in the United Arab Emirates.

Ever Smart was outbound from Jebel Ali and had been navigating along the channel at a speed of 12.4 knots at the time of the collision. *Alexandra 1* was inbound to Jebel Ali but had not entered the channel as she was waiting in the pilot boarding area to pick up a pilot, and was moving very slowly, approaching the channel at a speed over the ground of 2.4 knots, but with a varying course. Visibility was good enough for the vessels to have seen each other from about 23 minutes before the collision. For the whole of that period, the two vessels were approaching each other on a steady bearing. Given the application of the COLREGs, and upon the advice of a brother of Trinity House, the High Court held, that *Ever Smart* was 80 per cent liable for the damage caused by the collision and *Alexandra 1* was 20 per cent liable. The decision was appealed, and ended up in the Supreme Court.[11]

It is, perhaps, questionable that a Master managing the risk in navigation should be held accountable for making a decision on the bridge which was subsequently argued all the way to the Supreme Court, but two questions arise, namely whether in fact it was the right decision and, if not, whether the Master's decision was negligent or a mere error of judgment.

The Supreme Court tackled the question as to whether the crossing rules only engaged if the putative give-way vessel is on a steady course. *Alexandra 1* had been approaching *Ever Smart* on a steady bearing for over 20 minutes before the collision, on a crossing course, enough to engage the crossing rules even though she was not on a steady course. But the Court held that there was no 'steady course' requirement; for the same reason the stand-on vessel need not be on a steady course to engage the crossing rules either. Precedent cases concerned a vessel intending to enter the channel and, on her final approach to the entrance, shaping her course to arrive at the starboard side of it; they did not apply where the approaching vessel was waiting to enter rather than entering. *Alexandra 1* was the approaching vessel, intending and preparing to enter the channel but, crucially, waiting for her pilot rather than shaping her course for the starboard side of the channel, on her final approach. It is well established that the crossing rules should not be overridden in the absence of express stipulation, unless there was a compelling necessity to do so, and in this case there was no necessity for the crossing rules to be overridden, as the narrow channel had not yet dictated the navigation of the approaching vessel.

The Court held, that a vessel could comply with its obligations under the crossing rules, whether it was the give-way vessel or the stand-on vessel, and the rules were only displaced when the approaching vessel was shaping to enter the channel,

11 *Evergreen Marine (UK) Limited (Appellant) v Nautical Challenge Ltd (Respondent)* [2021] UKSC 6.

adjusting her course so as to reach the entrance on her starboard side of it, on her final approach. Here, the crossing rules applied and *Alexandra 1*, as the give-way vessel, was obliged to take early and substantial action to keep well clear of *Ever Smart*.

The Supreme Court unanimously allowed the appeal for Evergreen, and redirected the apportionment of liability to the High Court.

Liability must be fault-based, but just because fault was found with a Master (or with both), does not mean that either was actually negligent. The apportionment of liability was more a matter to determine the financial consequences on the respective insurers.

In many cases, however, fault may lead to a finding of negligence by the Master.

Passage planning involves compliance with SOLAS Chapter V Regulation 34 – Safe navigation and avoidance of dangerous situations:

1 Prior to proceeding to sea, the master shall ensure that the intended voyage has been planned using the appropriate nautical charts and nautical publications for the area concerned …

2 The voyage plan shall identify a route which:
   1. Takes into account any relevant ships' routeing systems;
   2. Ensures sufficient sea room for the safe passage of the ship throughout the voyage;
   3. Anticipates all known navigational hazards and adverse weather conditions;
   4. Takes into account the marine environmental protection measures that apply, and avoids, as far as possible, actions and activities which could cause damage to the environment.

In 2020 the Court of Appeal had to determine whether defective passage planning led to a finding of negligence, that would violate the shipowner's obligation to exercise due diligence to make a ship seaworthy. The claim focused on the shipowner's liability under the statutory limitation rules for damage to cargo, but the core issue was whether the Master was negligent in the navigation and management of the vessel.

The Case of the *CMA CGM Libra*

On 18 May 2011, whilst leaving Xiamen, the vessel grounded on a shoal outside of the buoyed fairway. According to the passage plan, the vessel was not meant to leave the buoyed fairway; nevertheless, while underway the Master decided to leave the fairway to pass west of buoy 14.1. The Trial Judge found:

> *It is more likely than not that the defect in the passage plan was causative of the Master's decision to leave buoy 14-1 to port. He explained that had there been a warning on the chart about charted depths being unreliable* [but] *the Master would have been, as it seems to me, most unlikely to have decided*

> *to navigate beyond the buoyed fairway to the west of buoy 14-1 and concluded that the defective passage plan and the Master's resulting negligence in deciding to navigate outside the buoyed fairway was a real and effective cause of the grounding.*

The Supreme Court concluded that the Trial Judge had directed himself properly in law *and the findings he made amply support the conclusion he reached that the defective passage plan involved a want of due diligence to make the vessel seaworthy.*[12]

Such want of due diligence necessarily defeated the shipowner's defence to liability under the statutory limitation rules.

Vicarious Liability

Aside from the provisions of the Hague-Visby Rules, the owner will generally be liable to an innocent party who suffers loss and damage as a result of a person who is employed or otherwise controlled by the owner. This was argued tenaciously by endless individuals who claimed that they had suffered loss and damage as a result of the negligence of the owner's employee; individuals such as Alfred Worrow.

Mr Worrow was a lorry driver from Stepney. On 12 July 1949, he had parked his lorry on Butler's Wharf, London, where he was going to collect some cases belonging to the Second Engineer of the *Starling*, who was leaving the ship. Mr Trubshaw's property was going to be unloaded by one of the deck cranes, but it was not going to be operated by a hand who had been trained in the crane's operation, but by Mr Trubshaw's colleague, Mr Proctor, the Third Engineer – presumably as a favour. Indeed, not only did Mr Proctor not have any training, but he did not have any permission or, indeed, any authority at all to use the crane.

As Mr Worrow was standing steadying a set of crates about to be lowered on to his lorry, he was struck by a case suspended from the jib of the crane. Worrow duly sued for damages. There would not have been much use in suing Mr Proctor, who would probably not have had sufficient assets against which Judgment could be enforced and, so, Worrow had to identify whom he could sue. The solution, of course, was to recover from General steam, Mr Proctor's employer.[13]

The Claimant had to plead with careful particularity to establish a compelling case in negligence against the employer, and it was not just the fact that the tortfeasor was the employee which would make them accountable. Accordingly, Worrow alleged that the Defendant company was negligent in that they operated the crane in such a manner as to cause it to strike him; that they failed to keep a proper lookout for persons who were or might be obstructed by or in the way of the case; that they operated the crane in such a way or at such a time as was unsafe by reason

12 *Alize 1954 and another (Appellants) v Allianz Elementar Versicherungs AG and others (Respondents)* [2021] UKSC 51.

13 *Worrow v General Steam Navigation Company Ltd* [1950] 84 Ll R 576.

of the presence of the Plaintiff; and that they failed to warn him that the case of crane was about to be moved or unloaded. Further or in the alternative, the Plaintiff alleged that the Defendants failed to prevent the crane being operated at the time when the Plaintiff was present; that they failed to issue or make any or any proper instruction or regulations concerning the use of the crane at a time when he was in danger of being struck; that they failed to issue or make or to have properly carried out any proper instructions or regulations to ensure that the crane was operated by persons competent and/or authorised to do so; that they failed to exercise any or any proper supervision so as to ensure that the crane was operated only by persons competent and/or authorised so to do or at a time when it was safe so to do, whereby he suffered personal injury, loss and damage.

The company could afford to be somewhat more laconic in their Defence; they denied the main allegations and pleaded that at all material times the crane was being operated by Mr Proctor, with no authority, express or implied, to operate the crane for that purpose or at all. Accordingly, if (which was denied) he was negligent as alleged or at all, such negligence did not occur in circumstances rendering the defendant vicariously liable. Moreover, they alleged, the accident must have been caused solely, or alternatively contributed to by the Plaintiff's failure to take sufficient care for himself. After all, he had remained in or near the vicinity of the jib of the crane as the case was being lowered and had failed to look out for his own safety.

The case was heard in the Mayor's and City of London Court, where His Honour Judge A Ralph Thomas tackled the thorny issue of the Master-Servant relationship in vicarious liability:

> *With regard to the question of law, the principles upon which a master is liable for the acts of his servant have been dealt with in a good many cases. He, of course, is liable for any act which the servant commits, which causes damage if the act is authorized by the master. Furthermore, he is liable if the act is within the scope of the servant's employment; and that is so even if the servant does the act in an unauthorized way – in fact, even if he does it in a way which has been prohibited.*
>
> *Proctor took upon himself to use the crane, and I am satisfied from the evidence that he was not good at it. I think he had some trouble in getting the gears in, and certainly when he swung the case ashore he swung the jib too far and hit the Plaintiff with the case ... I have to find in this case with regard to Proctor's negligence, which was undoubted, is that he was doing an act which was not in any way authorized or within the scope of his employment – either by implied authority or by practice or in any other way. He was not employed to put ashore the kit of other members of the crew or other officers ... And although, as I have said, one sympathises very strongly with the Plaintiff, I must in this case find that there must be Judgment for the Defendants.*

A succession of cases in intervening years widened the scope of vicarious liability, defining legal responsibility imposed on an employer, although he is himself free from blame, for a tort committed by his employee in the course of his employment to the point held in the decision in *Lister v Hesley Hall*.[14] This was a distressing case, in which a warden was employed at an annex of a boarding school for boys and responsible for the day-to-day running of the school, and the care and supervision over the boys. Between 1979 and 1982, the warden had sexually abused a number of the boys, although his employer had been unaware and were themselves blameless. The question arose as to whether the warden's employer might be held vicariously liable for his intentional sexual abuse of the boys placed under his care.

The House of Lords held that vicarious liability could apply to unauthorised, intentional wrongdoings committed by an employee acting for his own benefit, in so far as there exists a connection between the wrongdoings and the work for which he was employed to render it within the scope of employment. As such, the Court rejected the submission that vicarious liability could only arise when the employee is acting for his employer's benefit. On the facts of the case, the Court held that there was a sufficient connection between the work that the warden was employed to do and the abuse that he committed to render it within the scope of employment, and the employers were held liable.

This precedent was duly observed in successive cases of vicarious liability, until the case of *Morrisons v Various Claimants*[15] qualified it somewhat.

In this case, the Supreme Court held that the Court of Appeal and lower courts had misunderstood the correct test for determining whether an employer was vicariously liable for the actions of a disgruntled employee who posted the payroll details of some 100,000 employees online. The employee had received the data in the course of his employment as a senior IT internal auditor and had been asked to send it to the company's external auditor. However, he had copied it and disclosed it in an unauthorised way.

To this extent, the Court of Appeal held that, as this was closely connected to what he had been asked to do, there was a sufficient connection between the employee's actions and his employment to make Morrisons vicariously liable. The Supreme Court begged to differ, however and held that a sufficient causal connection between the employment and the actions of the employee does not in itself satisfy the close connection test. The correct analysis of the close connection test is whether 'the wrongful conduct was so closely connected with acts the employee was authorised to do that it may fairly and properly be regarded as done by the employee while acting in the ordinary course of his employment.'

The Supreme Court reasoned that the field of activities that Morrisons had entrusted to the employee excluded the illegal online disclosure of data; he had been authorised to transmit payroll data to the external auditor, but was not authorised to publish the payroll data online, as a result of which the offending act was

14 *Lister v Hesley Hall Ltd* [2001] UKHL 22.
15 *WM Morrison Supermarkets Plc v Various Claimants* [2018] EWCA Civ 2339.

not sufficiently closely connected with what he had been given authority to do in the ordinary course of his employment.

The consequence of the Court's decision in *Lister v Hesley Hall* so that the mere fact that an individual's employment gives them the opportunity to commit a wrongful act is not sufficient to impose vicarious liability on their employer. The Court proceeded to find that, on the correct analysis of the close connection test, the connection was not made out and Morrisons were not vicariously liable as the employee was pursuing a personal vendetta outside the authority given to him.

31 Marine Insurance

Fundamental Principles of Marine Insurance

We can identify three fundamental principles which are common to all marine insurance contracts:

- Insurable interest;
- Indemnity;
- The utmost good faith.

Insurable Interest

An insured can only recover under the policy if he has an insurable interest, or right of property, in the subject-matter of the insurance.

So, a contract of insurance is binding on the underwriter only if it is made to cover an interest which the law declares to be capable of being insured.

The Meaning of Insurable Interest

The definition of insurable interest was perfected by statute which still regulates the business of marine insurance. Section 5 Marine Insurance Act 1906 states that *every person has an insurable interest who is interested in a marine adventure. Notably: where he stands in any legal or equitable relation to the adventure or to any insurable property at risk therein, in consequence of which he may benefit by the safety or due arrival of the insurable property, or may be prejudiced by its loss, or by damage thereto, or by the detention thereof or may incur liability in respect thereof.*

It is not always easy to apply this definition. The question of when a person can actually have an insurable interest was discussed in a Commercial Court case in 2022 regarding a fraud on the loss of a cargo of Ukrainian grain,[1] which affected the Ukrainian agribusiness, and came to light in early 2019. The Court highlighted the key issues for an insurable interest in that:

1 Quadra Commodities S.A. v XL Insurance Company SE and Others [2022] EWHC 431 (Comm).

DOI: 10.4324/9781003361916-31

1. The assured [in the 1906 jargon] may benefit by the safety or due arrival of the insured property or be prejudiced by its loss, damage, or detention, or in respect of which he may incur a liability;
2. The assured stands in a legal or equitable relation to the adventure or to any insurable interest in such adventure;
3. The benefit, prejudice or incurring of liability must arise in consequence of the legal or equitable relation of the assured to the property or adventure.

Interests Which May Be Insured

- Ownership of the vessel.

As a preliminary, it must be remembered that, in the case of a shipping company, the company itself owns the ship, not the shareholders. Even the owner of practically all the shares in the company does not thereby acquire an insurable interest in the company's vessels, for the company is a legal person apart from its shareholders.[2]

Section 5 further states that a person must stand in a legal or equitable relationship to the property insured, and this direct relationship must cause him profit or loss according to whether or not the thing survives.

- Charterers.

Charterers may have a stake in the use and operation of ships, depending on the nature of the charterparty.

The bareboat (sometime called the demise) charterer has at least a possessory interest in the ship which would give him the right to insure. Indeed, standard demise charter agreements can require charterers to keep the vessel insured to protect the interests of both owners and charterers.

In time and voyage charters, the charterer's interest in the hull extends only to the potential liability which may arise if the ship is damaged through obeying the charterer's orders. But it is sufficient to have a right in the thing insured, or to have a right or be under a liability arising out of some contract relating to the thing insured.

- Lien holders.

While creditors in general cannot show an insurable interest, a creditor who holds a lien on maritime property has an interest to the extent of their lien. Maritime liens can arise to give rights to the holder in cases including:

2 *Salomon v A Salomon & Co Ltd* [1897] AC 22: Saloman sold his unincorporated business to the company when it was formed. Part of the price was treated as a loan to the company which gave him security over the company's assets. On winding-up, the company was insolvent but the loan to Saloman had to be repaid before ordinary unsecured creditors. Although Saloman owned nearly all the shares and was the Managing Director, the company was separate from him.

- Salvage;
- Master and seamen's wages;
- Disbursements and liabilities;
- Damage arising out of a collision or an allision.

The interest of the holder of a maritime lien will arise with the incident which brings the lien into being in such cases.

Although not directly relevant to seafarers, the following also have an insurable interest:

- Mortgagees.

It is clear from section 14(1) Marine Insurance Act 1906 that a mortgagee of the subject-matter has an insurable interest and may insure up to the full value of the ship but can only recover under the policy to the extent of the mortgage debt.

- Trustees.

If a ship is held in trust, the trustee alone is regarded as having a legal interest and as such may insure the full value of the property which is the subject of the trust.

- The Marine Adventure itself.

A person who has no insurable interest in the ship as such may nevertheless be able to insure the adventure on which she is engaged, if the risk forms the basis of an agreement in which both parties have closed, as a matter of contract, and the laws of contract will prevail.

- Creditors

A creditor of the shipowner, as opposed to the ship, has no such interest even though they may know that the only chance of the loan being repaid is the successful completion of a certain voyage. Nevertheless, a creditor may take some form of security over the assets of the company as a term of their agreement.

- The buyer of goods.

It is important to point out that cargo owners can buy a marine cargo insurance policy up to the value of the cargo at the time of its loss or damage. Naturally, during the course of the voyage the cargo may be sold to subsequent buyers repeatedly, when the insurance policy will duly follow the ownership, and the Master will be accountable for the condition of the cargo on discharge if it does not meet the specification in a clean Bill of Lading which they had signed.

The Term of the Insurable Interest

Section 6(1) Marine Insurance Act 1906 provides:

> *The insured must be interested in the subject-matter insured at the time of the loss though he need not be interested when the insurance is effected:*
>
> *Provided that where the subject-matter is insured 'lost or not lost,' the insured may recover although he may not have acquired his interest until after the loss, unless at the time of effecting the contract of insurance the insured was aware of the loss, and the insurer was not.*

The Value of the Insurable Interest

Subject to the key issue of Indemnity, any person may insure the whole of their interest, as long as they do not seek to profit from the loss in any claim. Thus, the owner may insure the whole value, and the mortgagee the value of the sum advanced (see section 14(1)). Indeed, section 14(2) of the Act provides that that the mortgagee may insure for the full value of the property at risk, but then becomes a trustee of the balance over and above his own interest for the other parties interested.

Indemnity

The principle: the insured is entitled to be compensated precisely to the extent of the loss he has suffered as a result of the occurrence of an event against which the insurer has agreed to protect him. But the insured is not permitted to make a profit on the insurance, hence the importance of ensuring the parity of the insured value with the value of the vessel as an asset in the owner's accounts.

The Doctrine of Subrogation

From the doctrine of indemnity two rules are derived:

- Where the insurer settles for a total loss the insured must abandon what is left of the thing insured to the underwriter;
- The doctrine of subrogation: if the loss or damage is occasioned through the negligence or other unlawful act of a third party, so that the insured can claim damages, or if the insured has a contractual right to compensation, then the insurer is entitled to take over such rights on settling the loss, though not until he has done so.

The Case of the *Titanic*

Shortly before noon on 10 April 1912, the White Star Line's new flagship left her moorings in Southampton's Ocean Dock, bound for New York via Cherbourg and Queenstown (now Cobh, port of Cork). She left land with 2,207 people aboard; 4 days later, at 23.40, as the liner steamed through at 21 ½ knots, the look-out in the crow's nest reported saw a faint, dark shadow. Focusing on it intently, he watched it emerge as a *Small black mass, dead in the Titanic's track.* The rest, of course, is history. She finally sank at 02.20, settling on the ocean bed some two and a half miles down, impossibly beyond the reach of any salvage operation at the time.

The wreck was originally discovered in 1985 and, in 1987, a joint American-French expedition began salvage operations and, during 32 dives, recovered approximately 1,800 artefacts. In 1993, a French administrator in the Ministry of Equipment, Transportation, and Tourism awarded the finder title to the artefacts. However, the Court failed to understand the key principle that an insurer who settles claims on a maritime loss assumes ownership of the goods, unless the wreck was actually lost and abandoned. In January 2006, an Appeal from the United States District Court for the Eastern District of Virginia, United States, heard a Motion from Claimants for Salvage and/or Finds Award, to gain title to all the artefacts (including portions of the hull) or alternatively a salvage award.[3] The Appeal Court, however, pointed out that a finder does not have the right to exclusive possession; while a salvor has rights in possession but has no right to sell the articles. They could not possibly have any title to sell the articles, because the doctrine of subrogation had already vested title in the original insurers who had settled the claims. They had not actually abandoned the wreck, they simply could not find her, and no doubt were very grateful to the finders who had saved them the trouble.

Good Faith

The principle of good faith is common to the entire law of contract, but the law of insurance requires an even higher standard of honesty than usual. This is necessary because of the special circumstances prevailing in this trade which put the insurer peculiarly at the mercy of the insured.

Insurance contracts demand something higher, though, requiring the contract be *Uberrimae Fidei*, of the utmost good faith.

Disclosure – The Heart of Good Faith

Section 18 the Marine Insurance Act 1906 requires that a person who is about to effect a policy must not only make no active misrepresentations, but must also disclose to the insurer every material circumstance, that is, everything which would influence the judgment of a prudent insurer in fixing the premium, or determining whether he will take the risk. If material misrepresentations are made or material facts not disclosed when the contract was made, then under the 1906 Act the insurer may avoid the policy by resisting an action for the sum insured or by claiming back money paid in error before the misrepresentation or nondisclosure had become known to him.

Whether a fact is material is always a question of fact. Section 18(3) only provides that in the absence of inquiry the following circumstances need not be disclosed:

3 *R.M.S. Titanic, Incorporated, (Appellant) v The Wrecked And Abandoned Vessel ... believed to be the RMS Titanic, in rem*, Appeal from the United States District Court for the Eastern District of Virginia, at Norfolk (2006).

- Circumstances diminishing the risk;
- Circumstances actually known to the insurer;
- Circumstances of common notoriety or knowledge;
- Matters which the insurer ought to know in the ordinary course of business, such as trade usages and political events;
- Circumstances in respect of which information has been waived by the insurer;
- Circumstances which it is superfluous to disclose by reason of any express or implied warranty.

Where the scope of proposed insurance cover is broad, the insured need not disclose that he plans to operate in a way that exposes the insurer to greater risk than necessary, provided that what he intends to do does not fall outside the range of possibilities that the insurer ought to have in mind. Such was the case in *Glencore International v Alpina Insurance*.[4]

In the same case, it was made clear that underwriters claiming an entitlement to avoid the insurance contract must be able to provide a cogent explanation as to why the matter complained of would have led them to act differently, given the nature of the underlying business, the terms of the coverage and the manner in which they underwrote the risk. That being said, particular or unexpected terms in a charterparty may be construed as amounting to material circumstances, so if the insurance contains a wide description in the voyage clause, the fact that the charterparty permits the vessel to call at a little known and particularly dangerous port must be disclosed. At the very least, there may be a breach of the obligation of good faith.[5]

This is important to the Master, who will manage the risk assessment process in an event involving deviation, meaning the voluntary and unjustified departure of a ship from her agreed route. In the carriage of goods by sea, deviation is treated as a breach of contract which has fundamental consequences which can terminate the contract if the deviation is unjustified, because the voyage has changed, thus the risks underwritten by the insurer have changed, and the carrier will only have a defence with very few exceptions:

- Where the Master must respond to save human lives or communicating with a ship in distress where lives may be in danger;
- Where the Master must avoid danger to the ship or its cargo such as bad weather conditions, war outbreaks, or for example danger from piracy or terrorism;
- Where the deviation is caused by default on the part of the charterer, in breach of the charterparty.

The point is that the cargo is likely to be insured not only by the cargo owner in the contract of sale and delivery but also by the carrier, who will have cover for third-party liability under their P&I insurance. If the carrier is responsible for causing

4 *Glencore International v Alpina Insurance Co. Ltd* [2003] EWHC 2792.
5 See *Laing v Union Marine Insurance Co (1895)* 1 Com Cas 11.

loss or damage, the P&I Club will pay; but the carrier may have a defence, which has been reinforced in international law through the Hague-Visby Rules, which provide under Article IV rule 4:

> *Any deviation in saving or attempting to save life or property at sea or any reasonable deviation shall not be deemed to be an infringement or breach of these Rules or of the contract of carriage, and the carrier shall not be liable for any loss or damage resulting therefrom.*

The crucial element, clearly, is for the Master to notify the owners so that all the material facts can be disclosed to the insurer.

The Insurance Act 2015

This is a general insurance Act which, nevertheless, changed the law on marine insurance in certain ways. The main provisions of the Act give broad effect to the recommendations set out in a report by the Law Commission specifically covering:

- Disclosure and misrepresentation in business and other non-consumer insurance contracts;
- Insurance warranties and other terms;
- Insurers' remedies for fraudulent claims.

It is plain that the effect of the 2015 goes beyond the limits of marine insurance, but the 1906 Act has not been repealed, merely its terms and effect have been amended.

The Duty of Fair Presentation

The 2015 Act updates and replaces the existing duty the insured in a marine insurance policy to disclose risk information to insurers before entering into an insurance contract. It redefines the duty under a new title of the Duty of Fair Presentation. This obliges the insured to undertake a reasonable search of information available to them, and clarifies what the insured knows or ought to know. The Act also requires insurers to play a more active role, asking questions in some circumstances. Importantly, the Act introduces a new system of proportionate remedies where the duty has been breached. This replaces the existing single remedy of avoidance of the contract, except where the policyholder has breached the duty deliberately or recklessly. Section 3 sets out three key elements of a fair presentation of the risk:

> *The first element of a fair presentation is a duty of disclosure ... which provides two ways to satisfy the duty of disclosure. This section effectively replicates the disclosure duty in section 18(1) of the 1906 Act. Its key features are that the insured must disclose every material circumstance which the insured knows or ought to know.*

The element of a fair presentation relates to the form of presentation rather than the substance. It is intended to target, at one end of the scale, data dumps, where the insurer is presented with an overwhelming amount of undigested information. At the other end, it is not expected that this requirement would be satisfied by an overly brief or cryptic presentation.

The third element of the duty of fair presentation is the duty not to make misrepresentations. It is contained in section 3(3)(c) and is based on section 20 of the 1906 Act.

The 2015 Act does provide exceptions: some of the provisions replicate section 18(3) of the 1906 Act, defining exceptions to the insured's duty of disclosure. The exceptions do not apply to the requirement to make the disclosure in a clear and accessible manner, nor to the duty not to make misrepresentations. Anything which is the subject of an exception does not have to be disclosed by the insured to the insurer unless the insurer makes enquiries about that matter.

Reform on Warranties

The reader should refer back to the chapter on the essentials of contract law: in general terms a warranty is not fundamental to the contract, but only collateral to it; hence, the aggrieved party has no specific right to repudiate – so they must perform their part of the contract. Under section 33 of the 1906 Act, however, a warranty is given by which the assured undertakes that some particular thing shall or shall not be done, or that some condition shall be fulfilled, or whereby he affirms or negatives the existence of a particular state of facts. It categorically is defined as a condition however, which must be exactly complied with, whether it be material to the risk or not.

The reform makes substantial changes, modifying the former strict compliance principle in marine insurance warranties, by which non-compliance with a term in the contract of insurance would automatically suspend the liability of the insurer under the contract from that point when the breach took place. It therefore follows, that if the insured makes some representation before the contract is closed, but it is not expressed in the contract terms, then this will not be considered as a warranty in law.

Under the 2015 Act, the suspension of liability remains until the breach has been remedied. As a result, the insurer is not obliged to pay for a loss which occurred at a moment while the suspension was active, but if the breach has been remedied, and a loss occurs after that.

The Insurer's Remedies for Fraudulent Claims

Section 12 of the 2015 Act sets out these issues, but does not define the distinction between a fraudulent claim and a fraudulent act. The fraudulent act addresses the behaviour that makes a claim fraudulent, which may be after the initial submission of the claim. The timing of the fraudulent act, of course, is relevant in determining when the liability of the insurer ceases for the purposes of section 12. It is the date of the insured's particular knowledge which triggers the term by which the contract may be treated as having been breached, and from which the insurer's liability is suspended.

The remedies will apply once fraud has been determined in accordance with the common law principle of forfeiture: where the insured commits a fraud against the insurer, the insurer is not liable to pay the insurance claim to which the fraud relates. Where the insurer has already paid out insurance monies on the claim and later discovers the fraud, the insurer may recover those monies from the insured.

Section 12(1)(c) provides the insurer with a further remedy, giving them the option to treat the contract as if it had been terminated at the time of the fraudulent act. This is dependent on the insurer giving notice of their election to do so to the insured, and once they have made their choice, they cannot then change it. If the insurer elects to treat the contract as terminated, they may refuse to pay claims relating to Relevant Events occurring after the time of the fraudulent act. It does not have to return any premiums already paid by the insured.

A Relevant Event refers to any event that would trigger the insurer's liability under the particular insurance contract. Usually, this will be the occurrence of loss or damage which is insured under the contract, although this may be subject to the wording of the contract.

The length and breadth of fraud spans the 1906 and the 2015 Acts, and reflects the dishonesty that can be illustrated in the cases of the *Salem* and the *Brilliante Virtuoso*.

In the case of the *Salem*, a partnership of crooks conspired to exploit the embargo of crude oil to South Africa by dressing up a purchase of crude as a legitimate transaction with an innocent trader, then, secretly delivering it to South African buyers at the inflated prices resulting from the embargo, then sinking the ship and claiming the insurance, leaving the innocent trader to claim on their insurance. Accordingly, they approached the South African Strategic Fuel Fund Association that they had access to supplies of Saudi Arabian light crude oil, and a deal was closed to supply them with the oil. A crude tanker, the *South Sun*, was duly purchased and renamed the *Salem*, registered in Liberia. They engaged a Greek Master (who subsequently produced a forged Liberian Certificate of Competency) and Chief Mate, and a Tunisian crew of 22, all of whom were involved in the conspiracy.

In December 1979, the *Salem* loaded 195,000 tonnes of crude oil in the Arabian Gulf for carriage from Kuwait to Italy, to the order of the innocent charterers. On the voyage south of the east African coast, she ostensibly changed her name from *Salem* to *Lema* by painting out *Sa* and adding *a*. Then instead of steam around the Cape she turned off to Durban, where she made fast to a single buoy mooring 1 ½ miles offshore. She pumped 180,000 tonnes of the oil through hoses into the tank farms ashore, but a failure in the pumps left 15,000 tonnes in the ship. The South African importers paid over $50 million for the oil through their banks by telex in a few minutes. The ship then took in sea-water to take the place of the oil, and proceeded on her voyage around the Cape. She sailed northward until she was off Dakar and Senegal, then in a calm sea there was a series of explosions on board and a distress signal was sent. The nearest vessel was the UK tanker *British Trident*, which diverted and put out her lifeboats, recovering the crew. She witnessed the sinking of the ship.

For all the complicated planning by the owners, the crew let them down, appearing from the lifeboats; they had a well-rehearsed story, claiming that they had spent hours fighting an engine room fire – yet they were clean and smartly dressed, carrying passports and suitcases, but not the ship's log. The chief innocent loser was Shell, which had innocently purchased the cargo; they were not concerned with criminal proceedings, but wanted their money back. Accordingly, proceedings were issued in London which ended up in the Court of Appeal,[6] seeking to recover the balance of monies through the insurance policy, when the construction and interpretation of the key terms were disputed bitterly, but in the end the only recovery possible under the insurance was the value of the oil that could not be pumped out and was lost innocently when the ship sank.

The case of the *Brilliante Virtuoso* involved the owner's claim following an alleged piracy attack in the Gulf of Aden on 5 July 2011, reporting that the vessel was sailing from Ukraine to China with a cargo of fuel oil when she was allegedly boarded by pirates. The owners maintained that the pirates directed the vessel to Somalia but when the engine failed and could not be re-started, they allegedly placed a detonator in the engine room causing a fire and huge damage to the vessel. Accordingly, a claim was made on the vessel's war risks policy by Suez Fortune Investments Limited, the vessel's owner and by Piraeus Bank AE, the vessel's mortgagee. The vessel's insured value was $55 million plus $22 million for disbursements and increased value, assessed on the basis that the vessel was a constructive total loss by reason of the damage caused by the fire.

In the first stage of the trial, Flaux J. determined that the vessel was, as claimed by the Owner and the Bank but denied by the underwriters, a constructive total loss under section 60(2)(i) of the Marine Insurance Act 1906, as she was damaged by an insured peril and the cost of repairs would exceed the insured value of the ship when repaired. But in 2016 the Owner's claim was struck out after Flaux J. had found that Mr Iliopoulos, the sole or principal beneficial owner of Suez Fortune, had refused, in breach of a court order, to provide his solicitors with an electronic archive of documents and had lied to the court in an attempt to prevent the claim from being struck out. Subsequently, in a Judgment handed down on 7 October 2019, Mr Justice Teare determined the facts:

> *The armed men who boarded the Vessel were pretending to be pirates and had no intention of hijacking the Vessel for ransom. Their intention was to start a fire with an explosive device they brought on board at the behest of the Owner. The master, the chief engineer and the local salvage company*

6 *Shell International Petroleum Company Ltd v Gibbs (The Salem)* [1982] EWCA Civ J0212-3.

which assisted the Vessel were complicit in the fraud. Mr. Iliopoulos was the instigator of the conspiracy. His motive was to make a fraudulent claim for the total loss of the Vessel in the sum of approximately US$77 million.

He therefore ruled that the constructive total loss of the *Brillante Virtuoso* was caused by the wilful misconduct of the Owner.

The second stage of the trial examined the issue of the liability of insurers after the claim had been continued by the Bank, which had an insurable interest as mortgagee, and the underwriters of that policy had paid out, which then enabled them to pursue the Bank under the doctrine of subrogation. In order to secure their claim to the insurance payment, the Bank had to show that the loss was caused by an insured peril. In these circumstances, the burden of proof, on the balance of probabilities, lay with the Bank to establish a loss by a named peril, while the underwriters had to prove wilful misconduct or scuttling, in order to recover the money paid. Given the finding on facts, the High Court dismissed the Bank's claim under the terms of the Vessel's war risks policy on the basis that the constructive total loss of the vessel was caused by the wilful misconduct of the Owner and not by an insured peril.

The Forms of Insurance

Shipowners will generally avail themselves of two forms of non-compulsory insurance:

Hull and Machinery insurance.

This is a form of ocean marine insurance which is specifically designed to cover the loss or damage to a vessel and her equipment caused by a peril of the sea or other defined perils within the policy. The purpose is to indemnify the shipowner to the value of the ship standing to credit in the Balance Sheet at the date of her loss.

Protection and Indemnity insurance.

In the nineteenth century, shipowners formed themselves into mutual associations in order to manage the risk liabilities in other claims, affording them some group protection and indemnity; hence they became known as Protection and Indemnity Associations, or P&I Clubs. These associations are not managed to make a profit, while each member shipowner has rights and obligations according to their size and commitment. The vast majority of shipowners now insure their liabilities by becoming a member of a P&I Club, which covers them specifically for liabilities arising out of the management or navigation of their vessels, in particular third party risks of cargo and environmental damage. The scope of cover available from P&I Clubs is detailed in their individual rulebooks, and inevitably evolves as the risks of twenty-first century shipping faces new challenges.

Standard risk cover commonly includes:

- Personal injury to or illness or loss of life of crew members;
- Personal injury to or loss of life of stevedores;
- Personal injury to or illness or loss of life of passengers and others;
- Loss of personal effects;
- Deviation (also known as Diversion) expenses;
- Life salvage;
- Collision Liabilities, such as when the ship is in collision with another vessel, or when she strikes a fixed or floating object, such as a dock or a buoy;
- Loss or damage to property other than cargo;
- Pollution;
- Towage contract liabilities;
- Liabilities under contracts and indemnities;
- Wreck liabilities;
- Cargo liabilities;
- Cargo's proportion of general average or salvage;
- Certain expenses of salvors, when a claim is made for special compensation under Article 14 Salvage Convention or under the SCOPIC clause in LOF;
- War risks, covering physical loss and damage to ships as well as seizure and internment by a Port State;
- Kidnap and ransom, covering the ransom cost and other expenses incurred following a kidnap of seafarers or others on board ship, in addition to liability for death or injury as a result of kidnap;
- Legal and other costs incurred in relation to disputes that are uninsured.

The P&I Clubs also provide a wide range of services to their members including claims handling, advice on legal issues and loss prevention, and they regularly play a leading role in coordinating the response to, and management of, maritime casualties. As a result, the Master has a key management function in liaising and co-operating with the relevant correspondent in the Club as soon as a risk emerges. In many cases, the owner's P&I Club will have direct communication with the Master, who will contact their correspondent to discuss some issue that arises.

Insurance and Conflict of Interest

The P&I Club necessarily covers the risk on behalf of their member, the shipowner and it is important to bear in mind that the Master's best interests may not map onto the owner's. In this situation, the P&I Club would potentially have a conflict of interest if they represented the interests of both and, so, they will inevitably represent the interests of the owner, however much that creates difficulties for the Master, as a result of which the Master must have their own professional indemnity insurance, which will cover the cost of instructing lawyers and expert witnesses, damages and interest in civil cases; they will also cover the cost of defence lawyers in a criminal prosecution, but not criminal penalties such as fines, for such contracts are void on the grounds of public policy.

The Application of Compulsory Insurance

Hull and Machinery, and P&I insurance, is not required as a matter of law, although P&I cover will include the shipowner's compliance with certain insurances that are compulsory. These are all defined by maritime conventions.

Athens Convention 1974

The Athens Convention 1974 was amended by the Protocol of 2002 on the carriage of passengers, and IMO Guidelines for Implementation of the Athens Convention were adopted in 2006. The carrier's liability is defined under Article 3:

> *The carrier shall be liable for the damage suffered as a result of the death of or personal injury to a passenger and the loss of or damage to luggage if the incident which caused the damage so suffered occurred in the course of the carriage and was due to the fault or neglect of the carrier or of his servants or agents acting within the scope of their employment.*

The Convention is implemented under English law by the Merchant Shipping (Carriage of Passengers by Sea) Regulations 2012:

> *A ship may not enter or leave a port in the United Kingdom, nor if the ship is a United Kingdom ship a port in any other country, unless there is insurance in force, in respect of that ship and a certificate complying with the provisions.*

The requirement applies only to vessels requiring a passenger ship safety certificate however, for subsection 2 states that the requirement for the ship to have insurance does not apply to any ship which is not licensed to carry more than 12 passengers.

Civil Liability Convention 1992

In the wake of marine environmental casualties, the International Convention on Civil Liability for Oil Pollution Damage 1992 (CLC) applies exclusively to pollution damage caused in the territory, including the territorial sea, of a Contracting State and to preventive measures, wherever taken, to prevent or minimise such damage, specifically applying to bulk cargoes. Article 2 provides that:

> *any sea-going vessel and seaborne craft of any type whatsoever constructed or adapted for the carriage of oil in bulk as cargo, provided that a ship capable of carrying oil and other cargoes shall be regarded as a ship only when it is actually carrying oil in bulk as cargo and during any voyage following*

> *such carriage unless it is proved that it has no residues of such carriage of oil in bulk aboard.*

The owner of a ship registered in a contracting state and carrying more than 2,000 tonnes of persistent oil in bulk as cargo must maintain insurance or other financial security to cover their liability for pollution damage under the convention. Insurance must also be in place in respect of any ship, wherever registered, entering or leaving a port or terminal in the territory of a contracting State. Insurance must be certified by a contracting State and ships must carry a State-issued certificate confirming that the ship is so insured. Evidence is produced on production of the certificate of insurance, issued by the insurer of the oil pollution liability of the registered owner, confirming that the owner has in place insurance to cover its liabilities under the CLC.

Bunker Convention 2001

The International Convention on Civil Liability for Bunker Oil Pollution Damage 2001 is designed to ensure the payment of adequate, prompt and effective compensation for damage caused by pollution resulting from the escape or discharge of bunker oil from ships.

The owner of a ship over 1,000 gross tonnes registered in a State party and owners of such ships trading into a State party must maintain insurance or other financial security in respect of the owner's liability arising under the convention. Insurance must also be in place in respect of any ship, wherever registered, entering or leaving a port or terminal in the territory of a State party. The insurance must be verified by a certificate issued by a State party and ships must carry on board such a certificate confirming that the ship is so insured.

Documentary evidence is provided by production of a certificate of insurance or other financial security in respect of civil liability for oil pollution damage.

Maritime Labour Convention 2006

This cornerstone Convention in maritime law requires compulsory indemnity insurance to cover the following:

- Compensation for seafarers' injury, loss or unemployment in the case of the loss or foundering of the ship;
- Liability for burial/cremation costs;
- Wages in case of the seafarer's incapacity due to sickness or injury. Financial security to assure compensation in the event of death or long-term disability of a seafarer due to occupational injury.

In addition, UK employers are obliged to comply with compulsory insurance against employee risk under the Employers' Liability (Compulsory Insurance) Act 1969, section 1(1) providing that:

> *Except as otherwise provided by this Act, every employer carrying on any business in Great Britain shall insure, and maintain insurance, under one or more approved policies with an authorised insurer or insurers against liability for bodily injury or disease sustained by his employees, and arising out of and in the course of their employment in Great Britain in that business, but except in so far as regulations otherwise provide not including injury or disease suffered or contracted outside Great Britain.*

It should be noted that an injury on a UK-registered ship is classified as an injury within the UK.

Wreck Removal Convention

The Nairobi International Convention on the Removal of Wrecks, 2007 provides a strict liability, compensation and compulsory insurance regime for States affected by a marine casualty. It makes the registered owner of a ship liable for locating, marking and removing a wreck deemed to be a hazard in a State's convention area. Registered owners of ships of 300 gross tonnes and over registered in a State party or entering or leaving a port in the territory of a State party must have in place insurance cover arrangements that meet the requirements of the convention and a certificate from a State party attesting that such insurance is in force. This certificate must be carried on board at all times.

A document, known as a blue card, is issued by the insurer of the wreck removal liability of the owner to the ship's Flag State, confirming that the owner has in place insurance to cover its liabilities under the Nairobi Convention. It enables the Flag State to issue a certificate of insurance or other financial responsibility to the ship.

The Convention is implemented under English law by the Merchant Shipping Act 1995; section 225M requires the Master of the ship to ensure the wreck removal insurance certificate is carried on board and to produce it when requested.

32 Salvage

Introduction

Under UK law, all wrecked vessels are presumed to have an owner. This may be an individual, an insurance company or underwriters.

Hence, after the wreck of the *Titanic* was found in 1987, litigation ensued in order to obtain exclusive legal title to the artefacts recovered, with a view to their sale. A United States Court awarded the Claimant, who found the wreck, the status of salvor-in-possession, but it did not do them much good because that did not give them the right to sell them, for ownership had passed to the Liverpool and London P&I Club, which had paid out following the vessel's loss in 1912. The American salvors had claimed that the wreck had been abandoned; the insurers had not abandoned it, though – they just did not know how to reach it, and no doubt were grateful to the salvor for finding it.

The Definition of Loss

Loss and abandonment are defined in the Marine Insurance Act 1906. Under section 56, a loss may be either total or partial; any loss other than a total loss, as defined, is a partial loss, while a total loss may be either an actual total loss, or a constructive total loss.

Section 57 defines actual total loss:

> *Where the subject-matter insured is destroyed, or so damaged as to cease to be a thing of the kind insured, or where the assured is irretrievably deprived thereof, there is an actual total loss. In the case of an actual total loss no notice of abandonment need be given.*

Section 58 addresses a missing ship:

> *Where the ship concerned in the adventure is missing, and after the lapse of a reasonable time no news of her has been received, an actual total loss may be presumed.*

Section 60 defines constructive total loss:

> *Subject to any express provision in the policy, there is a constructive total loss where the subject-matter insured is reasonably abandoned on account*

DOI: 10.4324/9781003361916-32

of its actual total loss appearing to be unavoidable, or because it could not be preserved from actual total loss without an expenditure which would exceed its value when the expenditure had been incurred.

The Definition of Salvage

Salvage was defined colourfully in the American case of the *Henry Ewbank* as offering *a premium, by way of honorary award, for prompt and ready assistance to human sufferings; for a bold and fearless intrepidity; and for that affecting chivalry, which forgets itself in an anxiety to save property, as well as life.*[1]

That being said, salvage can take a number of forms:

- Offshore salvage describes an operation which takes place beyond a state's territorial waters (defined by UNCLOS), in unsheltered waters, sometimes known as deep sea, where the weather and sea state can make operating conditions very difficult, demanding especially high skills (and risks) from the salvor;
- A ship may be damaged or wrecked close to a harbour, blocking port access or interrupting the flow of commercial traffic such as the *Ever Given* presented in the Suez Canal in 2021. The salvage contract necessarily will make time of the essence, to limit as rapidly as possible the economic loss arising out of the hazard. The removal is generally easier than offshore salvage, however, with facilities closer to hand and milder weather conditions;
- Towage of a stricken vessel to safety. If a vessel is seriously disabled, the nearest vessels will be called to her assistance, and a suitable ship will tow her into port, giving rise to a salvage situation. In this way, the Greek-flagged *Blue Sea* (ex-*Alice Bowater*) caught fire after an engine room explosion off North Africa in 1982, when she was successfully towed into port. It is irrelevant that she was then declared a constructive total loss;
- The perceived danger to the vessel does not have to be absolute or imminent, but must be of a kind that a prudent Master would not hesitate to accept assistance. If a vessel loses power in mid-ocean in fine weather, she is not in immediate danger, and the need for a tow into port in fine weather does not necessarily amount to distress; but the onset of foul weather would leave her in danger of sinking, and a Master would not take a risk, but would accept a salvage contract. The Royal National Lifeboat Institution would have the right in law to claim salvage on all the private yachts they tow into port; in practice they refrain from doing so;
- Salvage can also consist of a wreck or artefacts from a wreck that may have been lost and abandoned many years ago. Any person who recovers a wreck, or

1 The *Henry Ewbank*, 11 F. Cas. 1166, 1170 (D. Mass. 1833) (No. 6376) - quoted in the Judicial Opinion *in R.M.S. Titanic, Incorporated, (Appellant) v The Wrecked And Abandoned Vessel ... believed to be the RMS Titanic, in rem*, Appeal from the United States District Court for the Eastern District of Virginia, at Norfolk (2006).

any property from a wreck, becomes a salvor and, under section 236 Merchant Shipping Act 1995 must duly give notice to the Government authority known as the Receiver of Wrecks.

It is noteworthy that saving life does not feature in the contract. Salvage is a voluntary operation, whereas the safety of life at sea is a duty which must be observed as a priority by all vessels. Article 98 of the United Nations Convention on the Law of the Sea (UNCLOS) states:

1. *Every State shall require the master of a ship flying its flag, in so far as he can do so without serious danger to the ship, the crew or the passengers:*
   (a) *to render assistance to any person found at sea in danger of being lost;*
   (b) *to proceed with all possible speed to the rescue of persons in distress, if informed of their need of assistance, in so far as such action may reasonably be expected of him;*
   (c) *after a collision, to render assistance to the other ship, its crew and its passengers and, where possible, to inform the other ship of the name of his own ship, its port of registry and the nearest port at which it will call.*

Furthermore, every Master will be aware of their duty under the International Convention for the Safety of Life at Sea (SOLAS), 1974, Chapter V Regulation 33:

> *The master of a ship at sea which is in a position to be able to provide assistance on receiving information from any source that persons are in distress at sea, is bound to proceed with all speed to their assistance, if possible informing them or the search and rescue service that the ship is doing so.*

The Definition of the Salvor

A salvor is a volunteer with no pre-existing contract or official duty to undertake the salvage operation in question, which includes any act or activity undertaken to assist a ship in danger at sea, although the danger does not have to be actual or immediate, or imminent and absolute. The professional salvor will have the experienced know-how and specialist equipment, backed up by financial security and suitable vessels to respond promptly to the casualty, and failure to meet part of this complete requirement can result in substantial claims against the salvor who had held themselves out as capable of managing the risk. That being said, a passing ship that tows a stricken ship into port may equally claim salvage. Individual crew members of a lifeboat from the Royal National Lifeboat Institution (RNLI) that toes a stricken vessel safely into harbour may claim salvage; it is just that, by convention, they do not, as the institution discourages it.

The Definition of the Owner

The owner is the party in whose name the vessel is registered. In practical terms, the ship will be listed as an asset in their accounts, and so, until they notify the insurers of their abandonment, they will remain the party of interest and, of course, the party at risk. Once the insurer has received notice of abandonment under section 62 Marine Insurance Act 1906, or has completed payment in settlement of the risk, the wreck and any claims attached to it become theirs, under section 63 Marine Insurance Act 1906.

UK Statutory Provision

Part IX of the Merchant Shipping Act 1995 Act deals with Salvage and Wreck, in Chapter 1, *Salvage*.

Section 224 implements the International Salvage Convention 1989 in English law. This Convention replaced a convention on the law of salvage adopted in Brussels in 1910 which incorporated the *No cure, no pay* principle under which a salvor is only rewarded for services if the operation is successful.

Although this basic philosophy worked well in most cases, it did not take pollution into account, as environmental concerns were not prioritised by society then. A salvor who prevented a major pollution incident (for example, by towing a damaged tanker away from an environmentally sensitive area) but did not manage to save the ship or the cargo received no reward. There was therefore little incentive to a salvor to undertake an operation which has only a slim chance of success.

The 1989 Convention seeks to remedy this deficiency by making provision for an enhanced salvage award taking into account the skill and efforts of the salvors in preventing or minimising damage to the environment.

The Master, the Salvor and the SOSREP

Notwithstanding the Master's discretion, in a salvage case the Master will repose their confidence in the salvor unless the salvor does or intends to do something which puts the ship or others in greater peril; if the Master were to be proved wrong and the salvor right, the contract consequences can be serious in terms of liability.

In UK Port or Coastal State waters, the Secretary of State's Representative (SOSREP) will likely become involved in the operation. They are appointed by the MCA to oversee the UK's casualty response in order to reduce the risk of the environmental impact and financial cost of maritime casualties. Although appointed by the Government, they are independent and impartial; but they are not infallible. The SOSREP has wide ranging powers which include:

- Overall responsibility for monitoring response in offshore incidents (including vessel casualties) where there is a risk of pollution;
- The right to take management control if deemed to be in the UK interest;

- Intervention powers, giving them the power to intervene if a clean-up or incident response proposal is not deemed to be in the public interest;
- Overriding local administrations to offer ports of refuge to vessels in distress.

The Master, the Owner and the Salvor must be given clear instructions by the SOSREP what degree of responsibility remains with them and what limitations are being placed on their freedom of action. Failure to comply with their instructions may lead to very serious criminal charges, which will have downstream consequences on claims for compensation.

The SOSREP's good intentions may not always serve the purposes of the shipowners and other stakeholders, however. Salvage operations are highly skilled and often very dangerous, and the engineering risks and complexities are unlikely to be fully understood by civil servants such as the SOSREP unless they have some industrial background. Expert witnesses have expressed the opinion that the quickest solution to taking a wreck out of the marine environment may not always be the most beneficial for the owners but civil servants are employed by the Government and must respond to government pressure to get the whole casualty out of harm's way. Memories of the incompetent handling of the *Sea Empress* in 1996 still touch a nerve following the decisions of the Coast Guard Agency (as it then was), which led to the creation of the post of SOSREP, who has the authority in UK waters to make all decisions relating to intervention and/or salvage operations, in order to protect the marine environment. Unfortunately, however, an oil spill response plan cannot salvage a vessel.

The Case of the *MSC Napoli*

The vessel had been built in the 1990s by Daewoo, a highly competent South Korean shipyard, with dimensions of some 905 feet in length with a beam of 122 feet and a draft of about 45 feet. With a deadweight capacity of 60,000 tonnes, she could reach speeds of about 24 knots. Her life was not without incident, however. In 2001, she became a casualty when she stranded in waters near the Strait of Singapore. At the time, surveyors paid scant attention to her long-term structural stability, but the inherent weakness that had been caused became clear while she was on a voyage from Belgium to Portugal in January 2007. She was 50 miles off the coast of Cornwall when Storm Kyrill brought severe gale-force winds into the English Channel, and huge waves caused serious damage to the *Napoli*'s hull, opening a crack in one side and a flooding engine room.

At approximately 10.30, the Master sent out a distress call and, shortly thereafter, ordered the crew to abandon ship into one of the lifeboats, which was the lesser of two evils in the heavy seas and gale-force winds. But the safety of life had been secured, which was the prime obligation in law. On the following day, the ship was taken under tow by the salvage tug *Abeille Bourbon*, later joined by *Abeille Liberté*. The vessel was to be towed to Portland Harbour in Dorset, 140 miles away. There were closer places of refuge, but Plymouth rejected the risk, as did others in France, although the Falmouth Harbour Master Captain Mark Sansom said he had confirmed that *Napoli* could have been accommodated in Falmouth Bay.

The cluster of tugs and tow proceeded up the English Channel, but the *Napoli* increased her list and with strong winds forecast, Robin Middleton, the UK Government's SOSREP, exercised his powers to direct the vessel to be beached in Lyme Bay on the English coast with minimal delay, in order to prevent her from sinking in deeper waters where salvage and pollution control would have been far more difficult.

It was a controversial decision, due to the environmental sensitivity of the marine area, supporting species such as seahorse, dolphin, lobster and a thriving fishing industry. The SOSREP insisted, however, that the risk assessment had been thorough, asserting:

> *The beaching location was selected based on minimising the impact of any spillage and enabling salvage work to remove the vessel and cargo to take place. The local authorities and environmental groups have been notified and all agencies are working together to ensure that pollution is minimised.*

This may not have been entirely sincere, as Julian Wardlaw, who spoke for the Environment Group, an umbrella organisation for local green agencies, said Mr Middleton had contacted them and asked where in Lyme Bay was the best place to beach the *Napoli*. Wardlaw allegedly replied: *Nowhere in Lyme Bay. It is too important an environment*. He later qualified his opinion, supporting the decision to deliberately ground the stricken container ship off the East Devon coastline describing it as the *least worst option*.

The beaching location was at Branscombe and over the following week, an attempt was made to remove the oil and other hazardous materials from the vessel – no easy task because the winter temperatures had rendered the oil very viscous and difficult to pump out. The subsequent salvage of the ship and her cargo famously attracted the attention of scavengers, eager to get their hands on property to sell, in the manner of eighteenth-century wreckers along the coast. Their argument that they were contributing to the clean-up of the beach may have been made tongue-in-cheek; nevertheless, the consequent lawlessness attracted national media attention, and Devon and Cornwall Police took steps to seal off the beach area.

Once the P&I Club had paid out the insurance on the cargo, it all became their property, as a result of which they had every right to seek its recovery. In real terms, of course, that would prove highly problematic, as their investigators and police teams would have to scour the length and breadth of the country to where the well-publicised motorcycles, among other things, had been taken. Wrecking activities had probably not featured in the risk models of actuaries for two hundred years.

Salvage and Lloyd's Open Form (LOF)

The salvage agreement, whether LOF or any other, is in every sense a contract, an agreement made by the exchange of commercial promises, managed by terms and recognised as a legal obligation. In fact, very few contracts must be in writing as a matter of law, and salvage is not one of them, but the value of a written contract is immense. The contract is a voluntary one on both sides, and so it is critical that the terms are clear and precise; hence the value of a well-tested contract such as Lloyd's Open Form. The owner may limit the operation to the salvage of certain parts of the ship and not the entire vessel, but the salvor's reward is only earned on the successful recovery of the property mentioned in the salvage contract: hence the golden rule printed on the front of Lloyd's Open Form: *No Cure, No Pay*.

Internationally, LOF remains the preferred contract. It is designed to encourage quick action to save ships and cargoes by avoiding delays that might otherwise arise from commercial haggling. The resolution of disputes is deferred, together with the assessment of the salvage award, until the salvage task is completed. Thereafter the dispute is referred to Arbitration which, unusually under English law, will result in an award that is published, although the hearing process is in private.

Special Compensation Under the Salvage Convention 1989

Article 14 of the 1989 Convention introduced the notion of Special compensation to be paid to salvors who have failed to earn a reward in the normal way defined in the phrase *No Cure, No Pay*, by physically saving the ship and cargo, but have mitigated the risk of damage to the environment. Such damage is defined as:

> *substantial physical damage to human health or to marine life or resources in coastal or inland waters or areas adjacent thereto, caused by pollution, contamination, fire, explosion or similar major incidents.*

The compensation consists of the salvor's expenses, which are defined as:

> *out-of-pocket expenses reasonably incurred by the salvor in the salvage operation and a fair rate for equipment and personnel actually and reasonably used.*

The salvor is entitled to receive an additional award of up to 30 per cent of these expenses if, thanks to the efforts of the salvor, environmental damage has been minimised or prevented. The tribunal or arbitrator assessing the award may increase the amount of compensation to a maximum of 100 per cent of the salvor's expenses, if it deems it fair and just to do so.

If, on the other hand, the salvor is negligent and has consequently failed to prevent or minimise environmental damage, special compensation may be reduced or denied altogether. Payment of the reward is to be made by the vessel and other property interests in proportion to their respective salved values.

The SCOPIC Clause

SCOPIC is an acronym for Special Compensation P&I Club Clause. It is strictly supplemental to LOF and its notion of *No Cure, No Pay*.

One of the reasons for the innovation of the SCOPIC clause was that Special Compensation under the 1989 Convention proved to suffer from a time-consuming process, involving difficulties in assessing the amount due to the salvor. As a result, SCOPIC was devised by salvors, P&I Clubs, underwriters and shipowners as an alternative system, and the scheme took effect in 1999.

The SCOPIC is as voluntary as everything else in LOF, to be incorporated at the time when LOF is agreed, and may be invoked by the salvor at any time. There is no requirement to demonstrate the existence of a pollution threat in a particular geographic area. Remuneration is based on pre-agreed tariff rates for matters including:

- Recovery of the total of the tariff rates of personnel;
- Tugs and other craft;
- Portable salvage equipment;
- Out of pocket expenses;
- Any bonus due.

The risk to the salvor in invoking the SCOPIC clause is that, if the regular salvage award is higher than the assessed SCOPIC remuneration, then not only is no SCOPIC award payable but the traditional property-based award is reduced by 25 per cent of the difference between that and the SCOPIC remuneration.

No doubt because of the financial risk arising, SCOPIC is invoked in about 30 per cent of LOF cases and, since its introduction, few cases have gone to arbitration as a result of dispute.

In general, once the election has been made, it cannot be revoked, but when a SCOPIC clause is provided in LOF, the shipowner is required to place initial security in the sum of $3 million within two working days of SCOPIC being invoked, in default of which the salvor has the option to withdraw from the provisions of SCOPIC and revert to the main agreement. But what about the scenario in which it has been necessary to increase security? If the shipowner fails to do so within the relevant period, the salvor has the option to terminate its services under both the SCOPIC clause and the LOF agreement itself.

The Salvage Award

LOF is administered in London by Lloyd's Salvage and Guarantees Department. In return for salvage services, the salvor receives a salvage award, being a proportion of the salved value, the value of the salvaged ship, her bunkers and cargo. Traditionally, the reward depended on the success of the operation and the recovery of property; so, if no property had been recovered, there was no payment, whatever the expense of the operation. It is embraced in the 1989 Convention and remains a fundamental concept of salvage, the rationale being that the salvor should be encouraged by the prospect of an appropriate salvage award to intervene in any casualty situation to save the ship, property and, in particular, to save life and prevent pollution. The salvor's right to a reward is based on natural equity or fairness – which allows the salvor to participate in the benefit conferred to ship-owner, the ship itself and the ship's cargo. Since 2011 Lloyd's have been entitled to make public the Award, Appeal Award and Reasons in Law.[2]

How Awards Are Determined

Most cases are resolved by negotiation, avoiding the risks and costs inherent in losing control over the result by the appointment of an arbitrator; particularly in the circumstances since 2011 in which Lloyd's can make their awards public, which is something that nobody wants in their commercial affairs. Nevertheless, it is inevitable that disputes arise in which the parties themselves cannot reach an agreement; communication breaks down, and a state of deadlock can only be broken by referral to arbitration.

Despite advances in marine technology and engineering, and the standards of training of seafarers, there are still some 120 cases a year in which LOF is agreed. The majority are settled by negotiation or mediation without formal dispute resolution, while the remainder are referred to arbitration under the Lloyd's procedure.

The salvage award is fixed by an arbitrator appointed from a panel of Lloyd's salvage arbitrators. The criteria that the arbitrator uses to fix the award include:

- The degree of danger involved;
- The value of the property salved;
- The skill and effort in preventing damage to the environment;
- The expenses incurred;
- The level of the service provided;
- The salvor's long-term investment in tugs and other vessels and equipment that may be required only infrequently.

How Does Salvage Differ From Towage?

The 1880 case of *Spaight v Tedcastle* defined a towage contract, and it has never really been improved: *A towage service may be described as the employment of one vessel to expedite the voyage of another, when nothing more is required than the accelerating of her progress.*[3]

It is important to emphasise that this is not a salvage contract, but has defined terms which are closed at the time when the contract is made, so the risk and reward have already been established. But the contract price in towage will inevitably be less than that awarded in a salvage case, so a towage contract becomes and important solution in risks covered by insurance, when the ship is not in imminent peril, but the vessel herself will be saved. In any event, loss and damage can be

2 Notice 3 of LOF 2011.

3 *Spaight v Tedcastle* (1880) 6 AC 217.

suffered even in a routine towage operation, when standard terms impose liabilities on the tow even though they may have been caused by the tug.

The question arises, as to when does a towage contract become a salvage contract in the natural course of events in a given case. The transformation from towage to salvage obviously has a fundamental effect on the relationship between the parties and the reward that will arise. The key question addresses whether there have been supervening circumstances which would be justifying the tug to abandon the contract to tow and convert the contract to salvage. It must be ascertained as to whether the services that were to be rendered eventually by the tug changed beyond recovery, and were beyond the reasonable contemplation of the parties when they originally negotiated the towage contract, thus avoiding an implied term. If, therefore, the line parted in the towage operation, that itself would not automatically convert it into a salvage contract; rather, it would have to be not reasonably foreseeable that the operation would then have to be abandoned. The tug would have to establish:

- That the services they performed were of such an extraordinary nature that they could not have been with in the reasonable contemplation of the parties when closing the terms of the original towage contract;
- That the services in fact performed and the risks inherent in that performance would not have been reasonably remunerated if the towage remuneration only was paid.

In practice most towage contracts contain detailed terms, which if not expressed, will be implied by the Courts; for example, under section 13 Supply of Goods & Services Act 1982, the tug owner must carry out the towage with reasonable skill and care and, under section 14, within a reasonable time.

Both are governed by rules of contract but, in towage, the terms are negotiated and settled, and the outcome determined at the time the contract is closed. It is known as a closed contract, but Salvage is agreed under an open contract, in which certain critical terms cannot be agreed at the time it is made, because of the uncertainty of the outcome in the operation. The practical effect of the difference is that the contractual payment due to the tug is substantially lower than that to a salvor, as a result of which Masters are reluctant to request a salvage contract – and sometimes the delay can be disastrous. At the source of the issue is the Master's absolute discretion, for the ultimate decision must be theirs. The ancient rule has been embraced by SOLAS in Chapter V Regulation 34-1:

> *The owner, the charterer, the company operating the ship ... or any other person shall not prevent or restrict the master of the ship from taking or executing any decision which, in the master's professional judgement, is necessary for safety of life at sea and protection of the marine environment.*

Consequences: The Case of the *Union Star*

The *Union Star* was a diminutive bulk carrier grossing 935 tonnes. Registered in Dublin, on 17 December 1981 she sailed from the Netherlands to Arklow, Ireland, with a cargo of fertiliser, under the command of Captain Henry Moreton, a mate, engineer and two crewmen. Also on board were Morton's wife and two teenage stepdaughters.

During the course of the voyage westwards through the English Channel, Moreton discovered via Channel 16 that his previous vessel, the *Union Jupiter*, was taking shelter from heavy weather in St Ives Bay, and the two Masters discussed the respective qualities of their vessels in coping with the storm.

Near the south coast of Cornwall, eight miles east of the Wolf Rock, the ship's engine failed, most as a result of water flooding into the fuel tank. The crew was unable to restart the engine but continued to work on it and Moreton remained confident in the performance of the vessel, so did not make a distress call, knowing that, to do so, would inevitably raise a case for LOF. Monitoring the traffic on Chane 16, Captain Buurman in command of a powerful deep sea tug, the *Noord Holland*, offered Moreton assistance under LOF. Moreton was aware of his standing orders:

1. Not to hesitate to call for help if he thought it reasonably necessary for the safety of the ship and her cargo;
2. Not to refuse an offer of aid made with a claim for salvage unless he was reasonably certain that no other assistance for example by towage could be obtained in good time;
3. In the last resort to act upon his absolute discretion to engage salvage assistance.

Moreton assessed the risk with less gravity, however, balancing the situation against the expectation of restarting the engine. As a result, he declined the offer of salvage. By early evening the storm was worsening, however, and the engine had not been restarted. Winds were gusting at up to 90 knots – hurricane force 12 on the Beaufort scale – with waves up to 60 feet high. The powerless ship was blown across Mount's Bay towards the rocks of Boscawen Cove, near Lamorna. Moreton subsequently consulted the owners, and it was agreed to accept a salvage offer; but by then it was too late.

The Royal National Lifeboat Institution (RNLI) lifeboat *Solomon Browne*, based at the Penlee Lifeboat Station near Mousehole, received the alarm and Coxswain Trevelyan Richards took her out in pitch darkness at the height of the storm, with Second Cox Stephen Madron, Second Mechanic Nigel Brockman and five crewmen. They made the most heroic efforts to rescue the personnel on board the Union Star, and the little lifeboat found herself being washed up onto the vessel's main deck, and then washed back on the next wave. At 21.21 the lifeboat radioed Falmouth Coastguard:

> *We got four men off – look er hang on – we got four off at the moment er male – male and female. There's two left on board ...*

Then the radio went silent. On board the *Noord Holland* standing off, Captain Buurman saw the lifeboat high in the air on a crest, silhouetted by the lights of the Union Star. Then she disappeared.

The next morning, dawn broke somewhat less than twelve hours after the last contact with *Solomon Brown*. The wrecks of both vessels were identified, lost with all hands; 16 people died, including the 8 volunteer lifeboatmen. In a letter to the coroner, Lt Cdr Smith, pilot of the Royal Navy rescue helicopter, wrote:

> *Throughout the entire rescue evolution the Penlee crew never appeared to hesitate. After each time they were washed, blown, or bumped away from the casualty, the Penlee immediately commenced another run in ... They were truly the eight bravest men I've ever seen who were also totally dedicated to upholding the highest standards of the RNLI.*

Captain Moreton had exercised his absolute discretion, and hesitated in his fear that a salvage call would be more expensive than a towage contract.

General Average in Salvage

General Average will arise when one of the interests involved in the Common Maritime Adventure of a voyage is sacrificed for the common good of the rest of the interests. The aim of General Average is to distribute in an equitable way financial and material losses sustained in successfully bringing to safety a ship and cargo that find themselves in peril.

When the shipowner declares a General Average, the costs or loss arising out of this event – including the salvage costs if the operation is successful – are then shared collectively by all those interested in the voyage, in proportion to the value of their cargo on board, for example.

The key elements were concisely addressed in the American case of *Barnard v. Adams*,[4] which was the source of the modern law defined under section 66 Marine Insurance Act 1906:

> *A general average loss is a loss caused by or directly consequential on a general average act. It includes a general average expenditure as well as a general average sacrifice.*
>
> *There is a general average act where any extraordinary sacrifice or expenditure is voluntarily and reasonably made or incurred in time of peril for the purpose of preserving the property imperilled in the common adventure.*

The York-Antwerp Rules form one of the few Conventions which are applied without the necessity of enabling domestic legislation. As a result, it has been said that the Rules never had the force of law; but the Courts have consistently upheld them and bills of lading incorporate them verbatim.

4 *Barnard v Adams* (1850) 51 U.S. 270.

It will be apparent that the Master will have direct control of voluntary actions which, in their professional judgment, are necessary for the common good. So, for instance, in heavy weather, the stability of the vessel may be compromised and, having exhausted relieving procedures such as shifting ballast, the Master may decide that deck cargo will have to be jettisoned, or, indeed, other steps that may cause loss or damage. In that case, there will be little time to consult the owners, and the Master will have to take action.

The Rule Paramount of the York-Antwerp Rules states that in no case shall there be any allowance for sacrifice or expenditure unless reasonably made or incurred; as a consequence of which it is vital that the Master can present evidence supporting the reasonableness of their decision.

There is a general average act when, and only when, any extraordinary sacrifice or expenditure is intentionally and reasonably made or incurred for the common safety for the purpose of preserving from peril the property involved in a common maritime adventure.

A situation calling for General Average arises in salvage when the Master must incur the cost of some voluntary sacrifice that incurs extraordinary expenditure in order to save the ship. The general principles remain as applied to marine insurance generally, in that all parties involved in the marine adventure must share the resulting costs in proportion to the value of their stake, such as the cargo on board.

Importantly, expenditure involves financial outlay in engaging a salvor, the salvage award and fees in the port of refuge. It is the fact of incurring the cost which is important to general average, so even if the imminent peril is abated and the salvor is not needed, once the contract has been agreed and the parties committed, salvage must be paid.

The Case of the *Olivebank*[5]

In this admiralty and maritime appeal, Folger Coffee Co. and its insurer, Gulf Insurance Company, sought to reverse the US District Court's judgment that (1) the owners of the *Olivebank* were entitled to use general average on a salvage lien and (2) that Folger Coffee and Gulf Insurance owed their proportional share to the general average fund.

The general cargo ship *Olivebank* left the Port of Durban, South Africa on 12 June 1996, with a heavy break bulk cargo that included granite blocks, steel wire and earth moving equipment. On the morning of 15 June, the vessel encountered severe weather and extremely rough seas which caused seawater to wash over the aft deck. At about 08.00, seawater entered her alternator room, and short-circuited the two active alternators, causing complete loss of electrical power to the ship, disabling the engine and the steering. On subsequent investigation it was concluded that an engine room skylight had been opened during the voyage; the floor of the

5 *Folger Coffee v Olivebank 201 F.3d 632* (5th Cir. 2000).

room below the skylight was the ceiling of the alternator room, in which several small holes had been cut to enable equipment to operate properly while resting on the floor. Water coming through the skylight most likely found its way through these holes into the alternator room.

Without power or steering, the vessel was tossed at extreme angles as she could not position herself to best withstand the high waves. The Master sent out a distress call, and subsequently entered into a salvage agreement under LOF with Pentow Marine Limited, a salvage tug, which arrived in the late afternoon.

In the meantime, the ship's electrical engineer managed to engage the emergency system, which enabled them to restore lighting so that the engineers could examine and start the stand-by alternator. The main engines were ultimately started prior to the arrival of the salvors, and, after waiting out the storm, the *Olivebank* sailed to a port of refuge under her own power.

The salvors exercised their salvage lien by threatening arrest of the ship and her cargo. The owners of the *Olivebank* declared general average, forcing the cargo interests to provide general average bonds and guarantees. These remained outstanding, though, because Folger Coffee and their cargo insurers refused to submit to general average, arguing, *inter alia*, that the ship had been unseaworthy and that the skylight had been open due to a negligent management decision. In October 1998, the District Court found that the loss of power was caused by a fortuitous combination of events and that the vessel was seaworthy when she left port. Folger Coffee and Gulf Insurance duly appealed.

If Folger Coffee could establish that the ship had been unseaworthy and that the seawater had entered the ship due to negligent management decision, then the general average call would be defeated. The case was determined under United States law, but the principles mapped onto the English Carriage of Goods by Sea Act 1971, implementing in domestic law the Hague-Visby Rules, the key provisions of which state:

Article III: *The carrier shall be bound before and at the beginning of the voyage to exercise due diligence to ... make the ship seaworthy.*

Article IV, however, adds: *Neither the carrier nor the ship shall be liable for loss or damage arising or resulting from unseaworthiness unless caused by want of due diligence on the part of the carrier to make the ship seaworthy ... Whenever loss or damage has resulted from unseaworthiness the burden of proving the exercise of due diligence shall be on the carrier or other person claiming exemption under this article.*

Article IV also includes the Nautical Fault Defence, which provides that *Neither the carrier nor the ship shall be responsible for loss or damage arising or resulting from ... Act, neglect, or default of the master, mariner, pilot, or the servants of the carrier in the navigation or in the management of the ship.*

Folger Coffee and Gulf Insurance maintained that the *Olivebank* was not entitled to general average because the vessel was unseaworthy under the Carriage of Goods by Sea Act. The burden was on them to establish on evidence that the vessel was unseaworthy at the start of the voyage and that the unseaworthiness was the 'proximate'[6] cause of the general average event. If, however, they could prove this, then *Olivebank* may still prevail by proving that the owners had exercised due diligence to make the vessel seaworthy prior to the voyage.

The Appeal Court upheld the District Court's conclusion that the evidence did not support the proposed finding that the vessel was unseaworthy due to a defective emergency electrical system. The District Court found that the failure of the batteries and emergency system was due to entry of seawater and corresponding power surge, the same intervening event that caused the primary alternators to fail. The Appeal Court upheld the District Court's conclusion that the *Olivebank* was seaworthy when she left port and that the open skylight and the vent covers were not an issue of seaworthiness but a management decision.

The Appellants' case was not exhausted, as Folger Coffee and Gulf Insurance argued that the conditions of the skylight and vent covers were defective and the fact that they were not customarily closed made the vessel unseaworthy. The District Court found that the most likely explanation for the entry of water into the alternator room was through the skylight and the exhaust vents and that the vessel was relieved of liability because the decision not to close the skylight or the vent covers was a management decision. The District Court further found that these items, though not in ideal condition, functioned properly since, once closed and fastened, they did not let any more water inside.

The Appeal Court found no grounds to uphold any successful challenge of the District Court's decision and, so the case against the *Olivebank* failed, and the Appellants had to pay their fair proportion of the general average call.

A more recent case involving general average made global headlines. On 23 March 2021, the containership *Ever Given* ran aground while transiting the Suez Canal, lodging herself against both banks of the waterway, rapidly causing vessels to be backed up in the Mediterranean to the north and the Red Sea to the south. The quantum of damage claimed by ship- and cargo-owners, was outstripped by a claim and counterclaim with the Canal authority, while the recovery operation was the subject of a general average claim, as damage to the canal had been essential in excavating room for the vessel's escape.

The vessel was in a compulsory pilotage area, under the management of two Port State pilots. While pilotage liabilities would be addressed in the standard terms of the pilotage agreement, any damage caused to the vessel during the incident, such as to the bottom of the hull or her propeller, would be covered in first instance by hull and machinery insurance. H&M insurers are also responsible for the costs of the salvage operation, including the freeing, refloating and towing of the vessel. In addition, significant third-party liabilities may arise, not only from interests who had their cargo deliberately damaged in the recovery process, but also the repair of infrastructure costs such as that of the can authority. Of course, such matters may be addressed by insurance but it is also important to consider liability and the culpability of the pilots, subject to contractual limitations.

6 The adjective employed in the American Carriage of Goods by Sea Act.

Bibliography

Anon. *Corporate Manslaughter & Health and Safety Offences Causing Death – Definitive Guideline*. London: Sentencing Guidelines Council, 2010.

Behar, R. "Joe Hazelwood's Bad Trip on the *Exxon Valdez*." *Time Magazine*. New York, 1989.

Bingham, T. *The Rule of Law, CLJ 67*, 2007.

Central Maritime Safety Tribunal, Decision Junghaeshim No. 2008–26, Marine Pollution Caused by the Collision of "Samsung No. 1" (barge), Towed by Tugboats "Samsung T-5" and "Samho T-3," and M/V "Hebei Spirit" (oil tanker), Notice of Decision on December 4, 2008.

Chief Inspector of Marine Accidents, Report the Grounding and Subsequent Salvage of the Tanker SEA Empress at Milford Haven Between 15 and 21 February 1996, HMSO.

Cho, Hong Sik. Environmental Law,*Environmental Law* (Vol. 29)3, 1929, Lewis & Clark Law School.

Committee of Experts on the Application of Conventions and Recommendations. *General Survey of the Reports on the Merchant Shipping (Minimum Standards) Convention (No. 147) and the Merchant Shipping (Improvement of Standards) Recommendation (No. 155), 1976*. International Labour Office, 1990.

Crowhurst, P. *The Defence of British Trade, 1689–1815*. Folkestone: Dawson & Sons, 1977.

Daniels, S. *Responsibility & Accountability in Maritime Law*. Abingdon: Informa Law from Routledge, 2022.

De Morgan, A. *A Budget of Paradoxes*, 1872, Dover Publications Inc, New York.

Earle, S. p47; HCA 13/56, 30 May 1640; 13/88. 19 Sept 1728; 3 Feb 1728/9, fo 93, 7 Nov 1729.

Esler, D. et al. "Cytochrome P4501A Biomarker Indication of Oil Exposure in Harlequin Ducks up to 20 Years After the *Exxon Valdez* Oil Spill." *Environmental Toxicology and Chemistry*. Houston: Rice University, 2010.

Foster, W. *English Factories in India 1646–50*. Oxford: The Clarendon Press, 1908.

Geller, E. "Psychological Science and Safety: Large-Scale Success at Preventing Occupational Injuries and Fatalities. Association of Psychological Science." *Current Directions in Psychological Science*, 2011, 20,109- 114.

Herald of Free Enterprise, mv. Report of court No. 8074. Formal Investigation, July 1987.

Howard, R. *The Arctic Gold Rush*. New York: Continuum, 2009.

Kolstad, J. *Report Ref M-90-26 Through 31*. Washington, DC: National Transportation Safety Board, 1990.

Law Commission. *Statute law repeals [Twentieth report]*. London: Draft Statute Law (Repeals) Bill, 2015.

Linington, A. *Nautilus Telegraph*. London: Nautilus International, 2010.

Mauer, M. "Criminal Charges Were Levied After *Exxon Valdez* Spill." *Anchorage Daily News*. Sacramento, CA: a subsidiary of the McClatchy Company, 2010.

Middlemiss, N. *The Navvies*. Tyne & Wear: Shield Publications Ltd, 1999.

Posner, R. *The Problems of Jurisprudence*. Cambridge, MA: Harvard University Press, 1993.

Quick, G. *The Role of the Pilot in Risk Management*. International Organisation of Masters, Mates & Pilots of Maryland, n.d.

Report on the Investigation of the Collision Between Diamant/Northern Merchant, MAIB, April 2003.

Sale, R., and E. Potatov. *The Scramble for the Arctic*. London: Frances Lincoln, 2010.

United States Coast Pilot. *The Office of Coast Survey (OCS), an Office of the National Ocean Service (NOS)*. Narragansett, RI: National Oceanic and Atmospheric Administration (NOAA), 2008.

Index

For Product Safety Concerns and Information please contact our EU representative GPSR@taylorandfrancis.com
Taylor & Francis Verlag GmbH, Kaufingerstraße 24, 80331 München, Germany

www.ingramcontent.com/pod-product-compliance
Ingram Content Group UK Ltd.
Pitfield, Milton Keynes, MK11 3LW, UK
UKHW020155200926
475702UK00016B/2726
* 9 7 8 1 0 3 2 4 2 2 4 3 5 *